Communications
in Computer and Information Science 419

For further volumes:
http://www.springer.com/series/7899

Cyrille Artho · Peter Csaba Ölveczky (Eds.)

Formal Techniques for Safety-Critical Systems

Second International Workshop, FTSCS 2013
Queenstown, New Zealand, October 29–30, 2013
Revised Selected Papers

Springer

Editors
Cyrille Artho
Research Institute for Secure Systems
AIST
Amagasaki
Japan

Peter Csaba Ölveczky
Department of Informatics
University of Oslo
Oslo
Norway

ISSN 1865-0929   ISSN 1865-0937 (electronic)
ISBN 978-3-319-05415-5   ISBN 978-3-319-05416-2 (eBook)
DOI 10.1007/978-3-319-05416-2
Springer Cham Heidelberg New York Dordrecht London

Library of Congress Control Number: 2014935153

Printed on acid-free paper

Springer is part of Springer Science+Business Media (www.springer.com)

Preface

This volume contains the proceedings of the Second International Workshop of Formal Techniques for Safety-Critical Systems (FTSCS 2013), held in scenic Queenstown, New Zealand, during October 29–30, 2013, as a satellite event of the ICFEM conference.

The aim of FTSCS is to bring together researchers and engineers who are interested in the application of formal and semi-formal methods to improve the quality of safety-critical computer systems. FTSCS strives to promote research and development of formal methods and tools for industrial applications, and is particularly interested in industrial applications of formal methods. Specific topics of the workshop include, but are not limited to:

- Case studies and experience reports on the use of formal methods for analyzing safety-critical systems, including avionics, automotive, medical, and other kinds of safety-critical and QoS-critical systems;
- Methods, techniques, and tools to support automated analysis, certification, debugging, etc., of complex safety/QoS-critical systems;
- Analysis methods that address the limitations of formal methods in industry (usability, scalability, etc.);
- Formal analysis support for modeling languages used in industry, such as AADL, Ptolemy, SysML, SCADE, Modelica, etc.;
- Code generation from validated models.

The first FTSCS was held in Kyoto in 2012, also as a satellite event of ICFEM that year. The proceedings of FTSCS 2012 appeared as volume 105 of *Electronic Proceedings in Theoretical Computer Science*, and a special issue of the *Science of Computer Programming* journal devoted to selected papers from that workshop is in preparation.

FTSCS 2013 received 32 regular paper submissions and one position/work-in-progress paper submission. Each submission was reviewed by three reviewers; based on the reviews and extensive discussions, the Program Committee selected 17 of these regular papers and the position/work-in-progress paper for presentation at the workshop. This volume contains revised versions of these 17 regular papers, as well as an extended abstract of the invited talk by Ian Hayes. Extended versions of selected papers from the workshop will also appear in a special issue of *Science of Computer Programming*.

Many colleagues and friends have contributed to FTSCS 2013. First, we would like to thank Kokichi Futatsugi and Hitoshi Ohsaki for encouraging us to start this series of workshops in 2012. We thank Ian Hayes for accepting our invitation to give an invited talk and the authors who submitted their work to FTSCS 2013 and who, through their contributions, made this workshop an interesting event attracting more than 30 participants. We are particularly grateful that so many well-known researchers agreed to serve on the Program Committee, and that they all provided timely, insightful, and detailed reviews.

We also thank the editors of Springer's *Communications in Computer and Information Science (CCIS)* for agreeing to publish the proceedings of FTSCS 2013, Bas van Vlijmen for accepting our proposal to devote a special issue of *Science of Computer Programming* to extended versions of selected papers from FTSCS 2013, Jing Sun for his invaluable help with local arrangements, and Andrei Voronkov for the excellent EasyChair conference systems.

January 2014   Cyrille Artho
                                                    Peter Csaba Ölveczky

Organization

Workshop Chair

Hitoshi Ohsaki   AIST, Japan

Program Committee

Erika Ábrahám	RWTH Aachen University, Germany
Musab AlTurki	King Fahd University of Petroleum and Minerals, Saudi Arabia
Toshiaki Aoki	JAIST, Japan
Farhad Arbab	Leiden University and CWI, The Netherlands
Cyrille Artho (Chair)	AIST, Japan
Saddek Bensalem	Verimag, France
Armin Biere	Johannes Kepler University, Austria
Santiago Escobar	Universidad Politécnica de Valencia, Spain
Ansgar Fehnker	University of the South Pacific, Fiji
Mamoun Filali	IRIT, France
Bernd Fischer	Stellenbosch University, South Africa
Kokichi Futatsugi	JAIST, Japan
Klaus Havelund	NASA JPL/California Institute of Technology, USA
Marieke Huisman	University of Twente, The Netherlands
Ralf Huuck	NICTA/UNSW, Australia
Fuyuki Ishikawa	National Institute of Informatics, Japan
Takashi Kitamura	AIST, Japan
Alexander Knapp	Augsburg University, Germany
Paddy Krishnan	Oracle Labs Brisbane, Australia
Yang Liu	Nanyang Technological University, Singapore
Robi Malik	University of Waikato, New Zealand
César Muñoz	NASA Langley, USA
Tang Nguyen	Hanoi University of Industry, Vietnam
Thomas Noll	RWTH Aachen University, Germany
Peter Ölveczky (Chair)	University of Oslo, Norway
Paul Pettersson	Mälardalen University, Sweden
Camilo Rocha	Escuela Colombiana de Ingeniería, Colombia
Grigore Roşu	University of Illinois at Urbana-Champaign, USA
Neha Rungta	NASA Ames, USA
Ralf Sasse	ETH Zürich, Switzerland
Oleg Sokolsky	University of Pennsylvania, USA
Sofiène Tahar	Concordia University, Canada

Carolyn Talcott   SRI International, USA
Tatsuhiro Tsuchiya   Osaka University, Japan
Michael Whalen   University of Minnesota, USA
Peng Wu   Chinese Academy of Sciences, China

Additional Reviewers

Daghar, Alaeddine   Kong, Weiqiang
Elleuch, Maissa   Meredith, Patrick
Enoiu, Eduard Paul   Rongjie, Yan
Helali, Ghassen   Santiago, Sonia
Jansen, Nils

Contents

Towards Structuring System Specifications with Time Bands Using Layers of Rely-Guarantee Conditions

Ian J. Hayes[✉]

School of ITEE, The University of Queensland, Brisbane, Australia
Ian.Hayes@itee.uq.edu.au

Abstract. The overall specification of a cyber-physical system can be given in terms of the desired behaviour of its physical components operating within the real world. The specification of its control software can then be derived from the overall specification and the properties of the real-world phenomena, including their relationship to the computer system's sensors and actuators. The control software specification then becomes a combination of the *guarantee* it makes about the system behaviour and the real-world assumptions it *relies* upon.

Such specifications can easily become complicated because the complete system description deals with properties of phenomena at widely different time granularities, as well as handling faults. To help manage this complexity, we consider layering the specification within multiple time bands, with the specification of each time band consisting of both the rely and guarantee conditions for that band, both given in terms of the phenomena of that band. The overall specification is then the combination of the multiple rely-guarantee pairs. Multiple rely-guarantee pairs can also be used to handle faults.

Rely-Guarantee Specifications. Earlier research with Michael Jackson and Cliff Jones [3,4] looked at specifying a real-time control system in terms of assumptions about the behaviour of the system's environment – a *rely* condition – and the behaviour to be ensured by the system – a *guarantee* condition – provided its environment continues to satisfy the rely condition. Often the specification of the system's desired behaviour is best described in terms of the behaviour of physical objects in the real-world that are to be controlled by the computer system, in which case rely conditions are needed to link the real-world phenomena (which may not be directly accessible to the computer) to the computer's view of the world, i.e. the computer's sensors and actuators.

Multiple Rely-Guarantee Pairs. Our earlier work [4] allowed a specification to be structured into multiple rely-guarantee pairs, where each guarantee is paired with a rely condition expressing the assumptions about the behaviour of the environment needed to be able to achieve that guarantee. This allows one to give separate specifications of different aspects of the behaviour of a system. It also allows one to separate the specification of "normal" behaviour of the system

C. Artho and P.C. Ölveczky (Eds.): FTSCS 2013, CCIS 419, pp. 1–2, 2014.
DOI: 10.1007/978-3-319-05416-2_1, © Springer International Publishing Switzerland 2014

when the environment is behaving correctly according to the normal rely, and a fall-back or degraded mode of behaviour when the normal rely condition does not hold but a weaker rely does hold.

The Time Bands Framework. Too often when describing a system's specification (or requirements), the basic operation of the system gets lost in a plethora of low-level detail. For real-time systems it has been observed that it helps to view the system at multiple time bands or scales [1,2]. The phenomena relevant at one time band may be different to those at a finer-grained (lower) time band. The behaviour of a system may be specified by describing aspects of the behaviour separately for each time band in terms of the phenomena of that band. For example, an "instantaneous" event at one time band may correspond to an activity consisting of a set of events (occurring close together) at the next lower time band. Events at the lower time band may be defined in terms of phenomena only "visible" at that time band.

Rely-Guarantee for Each Time Band. The specification of the behaviour for each time band can be given in terms of a rely condition giving the assumed properties of the environment and a guarantee of the behaviour of the system, both in terms of the phenomena of the time band. In this way the behaviour of the overall system is described in terms of multiple rely-guarantee pairs (as described above) with at least one rely-guarantee pair for each time band used in structuring the description of the system behaviour.

Acknowledgements. The ideas presented here are based on joint research with Alan Burns, Brijesh Dongol, Michael Jackson and Cliff Jones. The author's research was supported by Australian Research Council Grants DP0987452 and DP130102901.

References

1. Burns, A., Baxter, G.: Time bands in systems structure. In: Besnard, D., Gacek, C., Jones, C.B. (eds.) Structure for Dependability: Computer-Based Systems from an Interdisciplinary Perspective, pp. 74–90. Springer, Heidelberg (2006)
2. Burns, A., Hayes, I.J.: A timeband framework for modelling real-time systems. Real-Time Syst. **45**(1–2), 106–142 (2010)
3. Hayes, I.J., Jackson, M.A., Jones, C.B.: Determining the specification of a control system from that of its environment. In: Araki, K., Gnesi, S., Mandrioli, D. (eds.) FME 2003. LNCS, vol. 2805, pp. 154–169. Springer, Heidelberg (2003)
4. Jones, C.B., Hayes, I.J., Jackson, M.A.: Deriving specifications for systems that are connected to the physical world. In: Jones, C.B., Liu, Z., Woodcock, J. (eds.) Formal Methods and Hybrid Real-Time Systems. LNCS, vol. 4700, pp. 364–390. Springer, Heidelberg (2007)

With an Open Mind: How to Write Good Models

Cyrille Artho[1]([✉]), Koji Hayamizu[1], Rudolf Ramler[2], and Yoriyuki Yamagata[1]

[1] RISEC, AIST, Amagasaki, Japan
c.artho@aist.go.jp
[2] Software Competence Center Hagenberg, Hagenberg, Austria

Abstract. Writing effective models for systems and their environment is a challenge. The task involves both mastering the modeling tool and its notation, and faithfully translating all requirements and specifications into a complete model. The former ability can be learned, while the latter one is a continuous challenge requiring experience and tools supporting the visualization and understanding of models. This paper describes our experience with incomplete models, the types of changes that were made later, and the defects that were found with the improved models.

Keywords: Model-based analysis · Model design · Model checking · Model-based testing

1   Introduction

Model-based techniques use abstract models to define many possible system behaviors. In *model-based testing,* a test model gives rise to many concrete test cases. In *model checking,* all possible behaviors of a given model are explored to check if given properties hold. Both types of analysis have in common that a model of the environment is needed, which represents possible stimuli to the system under test (SUT). Analysis of the SUT involves exploring interactions between the SUT (model) and the environment, and verifying if a set of stated properties holds for all possible interactions (see Fig. 1).

When using testing (run-time verification), tests can be executed against the implementation of the system. In model checking, a model of the SUT is needed; that model may be written by an engineer, or a tool may derive the system model from its implementation. In either case, the environment needs to be modeled from requirements, which is a largely manual task.

The resulting model should reflect the requirements and capture all relevant system behaviors. Creation of a good model is a challenge, both for modeling the system and maybe even more so for modeling its environment.

If a property is violated by a given execution trace, then the trace is analyzed to determine whether the model is incorrect or the SUT contains a defect. As long as such counterexample traces are found, there is an inconsistency between the stated properties and the possible state space, as determined by the model.

C. Artho and P.C. Ölveczky (Eds.): FTSCS 2013, CCIS 419, pp. 3–18, 2014.
DOI: 10.1007/978-3-319-05416-2_2, © Springer International Publishing Switzerland 2014

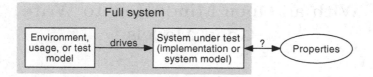

Fig. 1. Verification of a system in its environment.

Defect resolution may involve relaxing a property that is too strict, restricting an environment model that is too general, or fixing a defect in the SUT. No matter which artifact in the verification process is at fault, property violations always show that development is not complete yet.

Unfortunately, it is a common fallacy to believe that if a model is analyzed exhaustively, a system has been "proven correct" if no defects are found by the analysis. There are many subtle ways in which a model may be too restrictive, or a stated property too weak, to cover possible defects. This paper describes our experience with this problem, and suggests steps to be taken to improve the situation.

To highlight this issue, we label the right arrow in Fig. 1 with a question mark. We think that the common notion of "system *models* properties" as a verification goal is a good one. However, the notation is often thought of in the reverse direction as "properties hold for the system" once verification is complete. The danger in that notation lies in the fact that without *validation* of the model, property verification guarantees little in terms of system correctness.

Good models are those that help to exhibit defects in the system under test. What are the problems that restrict a model's defect detection capability?

In this paper, we first describe various projects in which initial models were insufficient to find certain defects. However, even small changes or additions to these models uncovered many additional features. We identify factors that negatively influenced the design of the original models, and propose both procedural as well as technical remedies.

This paper is organized as follows: Section 2 describes related work. Our experience with software test models is described in Sects. 3 and 4, while Sect. 5 shows a discrepancy between models and reality in hardware. Section 6 discusses our findings, and Sect. 7 concludes and outlines future work.

2   Related Work

In hardware and software analysis, properties may be trivially fulfilled, because not all relevant parts of a system have been analyzed, due to an incomplete system or environment model.

In hardware analysis, the problem of properties being trivially true has been well-known for two decades [4,5]. So-called *vacuous* properties include implications of type $a \rightarrow b$, where the antecedent a is never true. Regardless of the value of b, such a property holds. However, because the second part of the formula becomes irrelevant, this case of an "antecedent failure" is likely not what the modeler intended [4].

For temporal logics, so-called *zeno-timelocks* describe cases where parts of a model would have to execute infinitely fast (being subject to an infinite number of transitions in a finite amount of time) for a property to hold [8]. Such timelocks often relate to a problem in the way parts of a system are modeled [9].

More recently, a different case, parts of a property that are unsatisfiable per se, has been investigated [20]. This property can be used to "debug" a specification, i.e., to analyze why a specification does not hold. There is emerging work in the field of diagnosing model checker specifications using scenarios to analyze the model [17].

In software testing, modified condition/decision coverage (MC/DC) and similar test coverage criteria try to ensure that each part of a complex conditional statement is actually relevant for the outcome of a test suite [1, 26]. For each location in the software code where compound conditionals exist, MC/DC demands that, among other criteria, each condition in a decision is shown to independently affect the outcome of the decision [26]. If a condition has no effect on the outcome of a decision, it is likely incorrect (too weak) or redundant. The application of coverage criteria on the model level is emerging work, with only a few relatively simple coverage criteria such as state, transition, and path coverage, being commonly used so far [1].

Work investigating how human developers write test sequences has found that there is a bias towards designing a test case up to a "critical" operation that is expected to possibly fail, but not beyond [10, 18]. In particular, test cases are often designed to cover possible exceptions, but tend to stop at the first exception. This bias was confirmed in our case studies for designing models for network libraries [2, 3] and is described in more depth below.

Finally, the problem of model validation is also well known in model-driven engineering [6]. In that case, the model cannot be verified but only validated; recent work suggests generating questions about model properties as a form of sanity check [6].

3   Modeling the Java Network Library with Modbat

Even in widely used commercial software such as the Java platform [15], the official specification and documentation is written in English and not available as a fully rigorous formal document. This may give rise to ambiguities. In our experience, the biggest challenge in using the given specification was that many details are implicit, making it difficult to create a faithful model that also covers all relevant behaviors.

3.1   Setting

This section concerns the use of Modbat, a model-based test tool [2], for verifying a custom implementation of the `java.nio` network application programming interface (API) [15]. This network library allows the use of non-blocking input/output (I/O) operations. Unlike blocking operations, which suspend the current thread until the full result is obtained, non-blocking variants return a result immediately; however, the result may be incomplete, requiring that the operation be retried for completion.

The goal of this project was to test conformance of a custom version of the java.nio library [3] w.r.t. the official documentation [15]. The custom implementation of the java.nio library is designed to run on Java PathFinder [25], which requires a model implementation of code that interacts with the environment [3]. When using Modbat on this library, the model replaces the environment and generates calls to the API of the SUT.

Modbat uses an extended finite state machine [23] as its underlying model. State transitions are labeled with *actions* that are defined as program code (functions implemented in Scala [14]). This program code can directly execute the system under test (in our case, parts of the Java API). In addition to that, Modbat also supports exception handling, by allowing a declaration of possible exceptions that may result by (failed) actions. Finally, Modbat supports non-blocking I/O by allowing the specification of *alternative target states* to cover both the successful and the failed (incomplete) outcome of non-blocking I/O.

We have modeled the usage of the key classes ServerSocketChannel and SocketChannel with Modbat (see Fig. 2 for the server case). Both APIs have in common that a channel object first needs to be created by calling open. Our models take the resulting state as the initial state. In the server case, the created object represents the ability to accept incoming connections; the object therefore also needs to be bound to a port and IP address before a connection can be accepted. In the client case, the connection can be established directly by

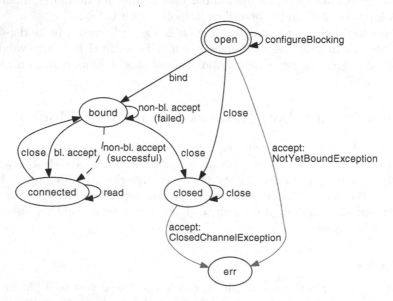

Fig. 2. Initial model for java.nio server API (Color figure online).

supplying the IP address and port of the server as a function argument. However, the client API is slightly more complex in general in the sense that finishing a pending connection (after an unsuccessful non-blocking `connect` call) attempt requires a different function than the initial attempt, viz., `finishConnect`. There are also more possible exceptions [15].

In the figure, dashed transitions correspond to the successful (completed) case of a non-blocking operation that would otherwise have to be repeated (non-blocking `accept`). Red, accordingly labeled edges correspond to exceptions resulting from actions that are not allowed in a given state. In these cases, the edge label denotes the exception type. Some nodes have a self-transition that denotes a possible switch from blocking to non-blocking mode using `configureBlocking`. A self-loop may also denote a retry of a previously failed non-blocking action; in the successful case, the dashed alternative transition is taken to the *connected* state. Finally, there is a self-transition in the connected state that reads from the newly connected channel before the connection is closed again.

3.2   Weaknesses of the Initial Model

We first executed the test cases generated from the models against the standard Java implementation, using it as a reference implementation. This ensures that no false positives are reported by the test model when it is used as an oracle against the reference implementation. We then used the given test model in a second test run, against our network model for JPF. Using this approach, we found a complex defect that was not covered with manually written tests [3]. However, several defects were not discovered by this initial model.

First, the initial model did not cover all possibilities of disallowed operations in the closed state. In that state, only `close` is allowed, as its semantics is defined to be idempotent in Java [15]. All other operations are expected to throw a ClosedChannelException. This part of the semantics is trivial to model, because most operations behave identically. However, the initial model missed several possible alternatives, because they have to be enumerated by the modeler. As it turned out, the implementation did not track its internal state correctly in all cases, and the wrong type of exception was thrown for a particular sequence of commands that included `close` and another operation after `close`. The challenge is that the model has to cover a large number of possible transitions, and it is easy to overlook some.

Second, it was difficult to express a property related to an end-of-file return code correctly [2]. An older version of the model was using a precondition to avoid reading from a stream where an end-of-file has been received. This meant that sequences that attempt to read beyond the end of a file were never generated, missing a defect in that case. A newer model included such sequences but its property to be checked was a bit too lenient. The reason for this was that it is not trivial to account for all possibilities of reading data in non-blocking mode. Even for an input of very limited length (2), the state space of all possibly incomplete read operations that eventually lead to the end-of-file is quite large (see Fig. 3).

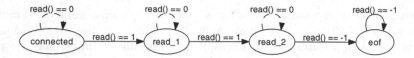

Fig. 3. Model of end-of-file semantics; dashed transitions are incomplete reads.

```
SocketChannel sc = connect();
sc.configureBlocking(false);
int n = 0;
boolean eof = false;
while (n < 4) {
  int read = readByte(sc);
  if (eof) assert (read == -1); // ensure no 0 non-bl. read after EOF
  if (read == -1) eof = true;
  if (read != 0) { // ignore non-bl. zero-reads
    if (n++ < 2) { // read data twice
      assert (read == 1);
    } else { // always read EOF after that
      assert (read == -1);
  } } }
sc.close();
```

Fig. 4. Unit test including the end-of-file property.

The property was initially written programmatically, and the code did not track the internal state strictly enough under all possible circumstances; Fig. 4 shows how a unit test that includes repeated calls to **readByte** and checks the result in a case where the input has length 2. Most of the code, including a counter and a flag, is devoted to expressing the property. As Fig. 3 shows, a finite-state machine can express the property much more succinctly [2].

Third, the initial model was also limited in that it included an error state for all cases where an exception has occurred [2]. This limits test cases to execute only up to a possible exception, but not beyond it. The reasoning behind this is that a well-behaved user of a library *never* triggers an exception due to incorrect use, of the types specified in the model. However, a component (an object provided by the SUT) can usually survive an incorrect command by refusing to execute it and throwing an exception instead. Because of this, it is possible to continue a test beyond such a step, issuing more correct or incorrect commands. This situation tends to be overlooked when modeling the environment of a system. Earlier case studies have shown that this is a common human bias in testing [10,18], and this has also carried over to modeling. While there indeed exist common cases where an object cannot be used after an exception has been thrown, this is not the case for incorrect operations used on communication channels.[1] In the updated server model (see Fig. 5), a trace can

---

[1] On the other hand, a communication channel is usually in an unrecoverable state after an exception thrown due to an I/O failure.

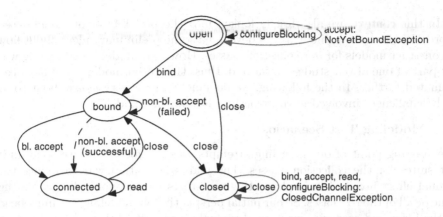

Fig. 5. Improved model for `java.nio` server API.

include other operations (or the same one) after a given operation resulted in an exception.

3.3 Summary

We found three problems with an initial model for a complex API in Java. The first problem was caused by the model not including all possible alternatives. The second problem was caused by a property that cannot be easily expressed in code, but where a finite-state machine may capture its semantics succinctly. Finally, the third problem stemmed from a human bias that tends to focus on operations up to a "critical" operation throwing an exception, which lead to the model being restricted by using an error state as a global target state for all exceptions. Instead, a self-loop should have been used to allow traces to continue beyond an exception.

4 Experiences with Models for Testing Collection Classes

4.1 Setting

In a series of experiments we studied the effectiveness of tool-supported test case generation in comparison to humans developing unit tests [18,19]. The experiment was based on a library of collection classes (i.e., containers such as list, array, set, stack, and map) with manually seeded defects. The library we used resembles the common Java collection classes. Thus, the study material had the benefit of being well known by the study participants and did not require additional background information or familiarization. The size of the library was about 2,800 lines of Java code distributed to 34 classes and interfaces and a total of 164 methods. Most classes showed high algorithmic complexity and used object-oriented concepts such as interfaces, abstract classes, inheritance, polymorphism and dynamic binding.

In this context, we also briefly looked into the possibilities of model-based approaches for unit testing [23] and developed some preliminary ideas about how to construct models for our collection classes. However, model-based testing was not part of one of our studies so far and, thus, the initial models have not been evaluated further. In the following, we document our observations about some of the challenges involved in constructing these initial models.

4.2 Modeling Test Scenarios

The starting point of our modeling attempts was the focus on developing unit test suites for the collection classes. The main motivation was to reduce the manual effort involved in implementing unit tests by automatically generating some or all of the test cases. So our initial perspective on modeling was influenced by the ideas and scenarios we wanted to explore in unit testing.

One of the first models was, thus, a generalization of a specific scenario that can be implemented as simple unit test. The objective of this test was to add and remove elements to/from a collection and to check the corresponding size of the collection as well as that the removed elements were those that had previously been added (Fig. 6).

This test implements one specific, representative case out of the many possible sequences in which elements may be added and removed. The model we initially developed still focused on the particular scenario of adding and removing elements (see Fig. 7).

Yet with the help of this model, we were able to generate a huge set of test cases that covered a wide range of combinations in which elements were added and removed, eventually including also all the combinations implemented in the manually developed test cases. Several other scenarios (e.g., using iterators or sorting) were modeled in the same way, again with the intention to explore them more extensively with huge sets of generated tests.

```
@Test public void testAddRemove() {
    LinkedList l = new LinkedList(); assertEquals(0, l.size());
    assertTrue(l.add("1"));          assertEquals(1, l.size());
    assertTrue(l.add("2"));          assertEquals(2, l.size());
    assertTrue(l.remove("1"));       assertEquals(1, l.size());
    assertTrue(l.remove("2"));       assertEquals(0, l.size());
}
```

Fig. 6. Exemplary unit test capturing a specific sequence of add/remove operations.

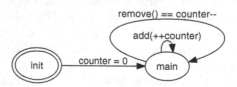

Fig. 7. Simple model for generating arbitrary sequences of add/remove operations.

A weakness all these initial models had in common was that no further defects were revealed, other than those that already had been found by the manually written unit tests. By simply transferring the unit test scenarios into test models, the resulting models were inherently limited to the underlying scenarios. Since in our case these scenarios were already sufficiently covered by a (small) set of manually implemented unit test cases, the model-based testing approach was not able to reveal new errors.

4.3   Modeling Actions on the System Under Test

To improve the initially generated test cases and to better unleash the potential of the model-based testing approach, we tried to advance the models towards more realistic usage patterns. For example, we added further actions to include all methods exposed in the public interface of a collection class and we removed the guards preventing invalid method calls to cover a broad range of interactions in addition and in combination to adding and removing elements. We also integrated the different small models into one large model. For example, we integrated the model testing iterators to make sure several iterators were used as part of a larger scenario where collections are modified concurrently. The advanced models actually generated new fault-revealing test cases we were not thinking about when manually writing tests. Eventually, thus, we reached the conclusion that the most realistic results will be achieved by developing a model that resembles the complete system under test as closely as possible in favor of developing several more specific models that reflect only individual test scenarios.

So far we have not completed the development of a full model for the collection classes. Nevertheless, we found that partial models or models at a higher level of abstraction are already capable of detecting some of the faults, although they are not rigorous enough to detect all the faults. Incrementally developing and refining the models provides the benefit of early defect detection and allows to balance the invested modeling effort to the achieved test results.

When proceeding towards a more complete model, we encountered another challenge that still remains an open issue. With the exponentially increasing number of possible scenarios described by a large model, the probability to sufficiently cover all the known interesting scenarios and critical corner cases tends to decrease. For example, since **add** and **remove** are equally probable, the number of elements in a collection usually stays low and collections rarely grow to the point where new memory is allocated. Another example is related to the special cases when inserting and removing list elements; the first and the last position of a filled list have to be treated differently and should to be covered by dedicated test cases. Yet this knowledge is not part of the model. However, since this knowledge is already available when creating the model, it would be useful to include it at this point as an aid to guide test case generation in direction of the relevant scenarios.

4.4 Modeling Test Data

Models of collection classes usually exhibit only a small number of relevant states. We found that an important aspect of the model relates to the test data, i.e., the data elements to be stored in the collections.

Our initial model concerning the add and remove operations used a counter *nrOfElements* to keep track of the size of the collection and to compute its state, i.e., empty or filled. When adding an element to the collection, we used the counter as new integer object to be added. When removing an element, we compared the obtained element with the counter to make sure the expected element had been returned. Thus, this simple mechanism dynamically generated reproducible test data. To avoid that the sequential order of the elements derived from the counter created unbalanced sequences, e.g., new elements are always added to the end of the collection, we used the counter as seed for a random number generator.

A weakness of this first model was that it missed errors caused by mixing data elements of different type. The containers *TreeSet* and *TreeMap* are sensitive to such errors as are the operations for sorting and searching in collections. Thus, the initial model did not find the related seeded defects since only comparable data objects of type Integer were used.

We extended the initial model by creating numerous test data elements of different types when setting up the model. The data elements were stored in an array in arbitrary order. The counter we previously used in the model now served as array index, which still allowed to determine the expected element to be returned by a remove operation.

Only later we found a new fault that indicated that there is still room for further improvement. The implementation of the collection classes was not able to handle the case of a collection being added to itself. Some operations such as `toString` would then lead to an unbounded recursion (see Fig. 8). We further extended the model to dynamically add new data elements to the test data set not only at startup but also while the model is executed. In future we plan to extended the model to incorporate the idea of feedback-directed test generation [16].

A related issue is involved in using `null` values, since the implementation of some container classes accept `null` as valid data elements whereas others do not. This issue was found when we tried to reuse generic models for different container classes. This observation led us to the (ongoing) discussion to what extent a model should reflect the behavior of the system under test versus its environment, i.e., the allowable inputs from the anticipated usage. While Utting et al. [24] classify this scope as a binary decision (input-only versus input-output models), we found that our models always combined both sides

```
Stack s = new Stack();  s.push(s);  s.toString();
```

Fig. 8. Sequence revealing an unbound recursion in the implementation of `Stack`.

since modeling the input side also required some knowledge about the expected output.

4.5 Summary

We reported on work on modeling the behavior of Java container classes. Initial models that were created from generalizations of existing unit tests ended up not being effective at finding defects that were not already covered by unit tests. When extending these models, we found that models that are convenient to define (for example, using only numbers) end up not covering important cases such as different data types or null values. Finally, creating modular and reusable models is difficult, because small differences in components result in pervasive differences in the allowable inputs requiring extra effort to adjust.

5 Industrial Project: Electric Circuit

5.1 Adapted Work Flow

As described in Sect. 2, various subtleties regarding the aspects of timed models and the reachability of model and system states in hardware are known. To avoid incorrect models, verification engineers validate their model with domain experts, who design the circuit. In this project, we employed the following work flow to eliminate false positives (spurious warnings) and false negatives (missed defects):

1. For a set of given desired states, reachability of these states is checked. For example, any terminal state in the system should be reachable.
2. The specification is negated and model checked. This means that the model checker analyzes whether there exist paths in the model that fulfill the desired property. In a correct model, correct execution paths should be generated. These execution paths are generated as counterexamples by the model checker, as the real property has been negated. Different counterexample paths are subsequently reviewed together with domain experts to determine whether they are correct and reflect the expected behavior of the system.
3. Properties that are trivially expected to hold are checked as well, as a form of sanity check.

5.2 Problem Found

The work flow described above prevents many defects in the model. However, despite this, a modeling problem was found in an industrial project on an electric circuit. The problem is related to how time is modeled in a real system. The system model uses discrete time, where the state of each component is updated on the next model clock tick. However, in real hardware, components can change their state almost immediately; the "slowness" introduced by discrete time gave rise to a counter-example in this model (see Fig. 9). The problem in this model is

```
next(gSet_PT_Voltage_A01) := case
  Gen_to_Load_A = 0 & Brk_A = 0 & GL_V_A = 0 & LG_V_A = 0 : V_Emp;
  Gen_to_Load_A = 0 & Brk_A = 0 & GL_V_A = 0 & LG_V_A = 1 : V_Lrd;
  Gen_to_Load_A = 0 & Brk_A = 0 & GL_V_A = 1 & LG_V_A = 0 : V_Gen;
  ...
esac;
```

Fig. 9. Part of a model transition describing an industrial circuit.

that gSet_PT_Voltage_A01 is updated in the next state even though the voltage change is immediate in real hardware.

After the counterexample was investigated together with domain experts, it was considered to be spurious (a false positive). To fix the model, the first line in the model was amended to gSet_PT_Voltage_A01 := case (i.e., next was removed). This eliminated the false positive.

6   Discussion

We have reported our experience from several modeling projects. In each project, there were unexpected problems with creating a correct and sufficiently good model to fulfill the purpose of model-based verification. In our opinion, it is interesting that the problems were not caused by ambiguities of the requirements or documentation. Where ambiguities caused problems, we were able to identify them and clarify the open points by checking the reference implementation.

6.1   Model Design

In our projects, problems arose when requirements were transformed into a model. We often failed to create a model that matches a wide range of all possible behaviors stated in the requirements. All of the models were "correct" but failed to cover certain behaviors of the system, some of which were even implemented incorrectly. In the software projects, the uncovered behaviors resulted in missed defects (false negatives); in the hardware project, it resulted in a spurious error (false positive), which gives an indication of a mismatch between the model and reality.

The lack of expressiveness in the models did not originate from unintended errors or oversights, but from intentional abstractions or decisions that led to elegant models. The resulting lack of coverage was therefore a side-effect of conscious design decisions. From this observation, we identify the right level of abstraction and human bias [10] as the key problems.

Abstraction. A major problem of creating a good model is to choose the right level of abstraction. This is a very difficult problem that takes years of experience to solve well. Some people even claim that this skill may not be teachable but an innate ability [12]. In the future, we expect (modeling/abstraction) teaching methods, and design tools, to improve to make the task a bit less daunting.

Human Bias. When choosing an abstraction, human bias also often exists in that the model is designed for a narrower purpose than necessary. This leads to the omission of certain behaviors in the model. Like abstraction, this is a fundamentally difficult problem to overcome; it requires to attack the problem from various angles to obtain a comprehensive solution. We think that involving a team of people in modeling, and making an effort to avoid any preconception, can at least mitigate this problem. Ideally, models are created with an open, fresh mind, and no possibilities, regardless of being difficult or trivial to handle, should be disregarded. In practice, this may require careful engineering of the model w.r.t. code reuse, if one takes into account that many small subtle differences in system components result in a large increase of different possible behaviors (and thus models or parameterizations thereof).

6.2 Model Validation

Our experience shows that model-based verification has to be grounded in an extensive validation of the model. Even though validation is in itself not a fully mechanized activity, there exists tool support for tasks such as coverage analysis and visualization, which contribute to validation. Furthermore, computer support can also be used in the modeling stage itself if certain artifacts such as a reference implementation are available.

Machine Learning. Machine learning of models has the obvious advantage of not missing system states due to a simple oversight. If a correct (reference) implementation of a system exists, then a model can be derived from the existing system using machine learning [13, 21]. The resulting model may not be human-readable but its verification verdict may confirm or refute the result obtained from a model designed by a human.

This approach can even be used if it is not known if a given system is correct; in that case, the model reflects its current (possibly not fully correct) behavior and can be used in regression testing to see if the behavior of the system changes in unexpected ways. Changes that violate a given property then would likely be found by a model that reflects the semantics of an older ("known good") version of the system.

Diagnosis and Visualization. Some of the weaknesses observed in models arose from the fact that they were generalizations of existing test scenarios. Therefore, just lifting a set of execution traces to a grammar-based model is not guaranteed to add much value. It is also necessary to check whether the existing test scenarios, and the derived model, are comprehensive enough.

We therefore advocate that model-based verification be combined with model diagnosis and visualization, so possible flaws in a model learned from an incomplete set of tests, or a defective system, may be found. In our hardware project, we already had adapted such a workflow by checking a sample of all possible execution traces generated by the model checker.

Model Coverage and Mutation Analysis. It is important to analyze the *coverage* of the model in the real system; this can be done for software testing in a straightforward way [1, 26]. However, coverage analysis on the final product gives us limited information on the expressiveness of the model itself (in addition to not being able to tell us whether all requirements are actually met). Hence, we also advocate mutation operators for models to find mutants that still pass the properties.

Mutating model properties is well-known [7] (and very similar to program code [11]). However, work needs to be done on mutating the structure of the model: a model could also be mutated by duplicating or deleting a transition, or changing its source or target state. This reflects what we have learned from our software model, where the model structure itself (and not just a given predicate or property) restricted its behavior.

Combination of Model-Based and Model-Free Techniques. When analyzing the implementation of a system, fully automated analysis techniques can complement human efforts. Unlike in the case where a model is designed by a human, automated techniques have no test oracle that evaluates the output of the analyzed behaviors; instead, they serve as a "sanity check" for a wide range of generic properties (accessed memory must be initialized, no deadlocks, etc.).

When using such "model-free" techniques, randomized testing [16] often finds defects that humans miss [18]. Defects found by such tools may in turn spur an improvement in a manually written model. A comparison of the states covered by model-free techniques with the coverage of a manually written model, may unveil weaknesses in the latter as well.

7   Conclusions and Future Work

Writing good models is a challenge. Models should not only be correct but sufficiently expressive and inclusive to fulfill the purpose of finding defects or ensuring their absence. Finding the right level of abstraction, and trying to avoid human bias, or two of the key challenges in this process. A high level of abstraction that allows an efficient encoding of a model (or reuse of existing model code) may not cover enough details of all possible behaviors. Modeling languages and tools should strive to improve this trade-off. Teaching engineers about commonly encountered problems or human bias is also essential.

We have listed several non-trivial flaws that we found in existing model development projects, and we have given suggestions how these may be avoided in the future. Tool-supported analysis of the model itself will help to explore the system behavior in its full breadth and may uncover missing model aspects that human inspection misses. In this context, we advocate using model-free, automated approaches where possible, so that their coverage can be compared with the coverage yielded by a model derived from the specification.

We believe that more case studies can also shed more light into why certain properties tend to be forgotten, and what types of modeling challenges engineers typically encounter. This may eventually lead to the creation of a body of knowledge for modeling and its effective use in practice. Existing work tends to focus on surveying approaches and tools, such as MCBOK, a body of knowledge on model checking for software development [22]; we hope that more fundamental cognitive and process-level issues will also be covered in the future.

Acknowledgments. We would like to thank Takashi Kitamura and Kenji Taguchi for their suggestions on this paper.

References

1. Ammann, P., Offutt, J.: Introduction to Software Testing, 1st edn. Cambridge University Press, New York (2008)
2. Artho, C., Biere, A., Hagiya, M., Platon, E., Seidl, M., Tanabe, Y., Yamamoto, M.: Modbat: a model-based API tester for event-driven systems. In: Bertacco, V., Legay, A. (eds.) HVC 2013. LNCS, vol. 8244, pp. 112–128. Springer, Heidelberg (2013)
3. Artho, C., Hagiya, M., Potter, R., Tanabe, Y., Weitl, F., Yamamoto, M.: Software model checking for distributed systems with selector-based, non-blocking communication. In: Proceedings of 28th International Conference on Automated Software Engineering (ASE 2013), Palo Alto, USA (2013)
4. Beatty, D., Bryant, R.: Formally verifying a microprocessor using a simulation methodology. In: Proceedings of 31st Conference on Design Automation (DAC 1994), San Diego, USA, pp. 596–602 (1994)
5. Beer, I., Ben-David, S., Eisner, C., Landver, A.: Rulebase: an industry-oriented formal verification tool. In: Proceedings of 33rd Conference on Design Automation (DAC 1996), Las Vegas, USA, pp. 655–660 (1996)
6. Bertolino, A., De Angelis, G., Di Sandro, A., Sabetta, A.: Is my model right? let me ask the expert. J. Syst. Softw. 84(7), 1089–1099 (2011)
7. Black, P., Okun, V., Yesha, Y.: Mutation of model checker specifications for test generation and evaluation. In: Wong, E. (ed.) Mutation Testing for the New Century Ages, pp. 14–20. Kluwer Academic Publishers, Norwell (2001)
8. Bowman, H.: How to stop time stopping. Form. Asp. Comput. 18(4), 459–493 (2006)
9. Bowman, H., Faconti, G., Katoen, J-P., Latella, D., Massink, M.: Automatic verification of a lip synchronisation algorithm using UPPAAL. In: Proceedings of 3rd International Workshop on Formal Methods for Industrial Critical Systems, CWI, pp. 97–124 (1998)
10. Calikli, G., Bener, A.: Empirical analyses of the factors affecting confirmation bias and the effects of confirmation bias on software developer/tester performance. In: Proceedings of 6th International Conference on Predictive Models in Software Engineering, PROMISE 2010, pp. 10:1–10:11. ACM, New York (2010)
11. Yue, J., Mark, H.: An analysis and survey of the development of mutation testing. IEEE Trans. Softw. Eng. 37(5), 649–678 (2011)
12. Kramer, J.: Is abstraction the key to computing? Commun. ACM 50(4), 36–42 (2007)
13. Memon, A., Nguyen, B.: Advances in automated model-based system testing of software applications with a GUI front-end. Adv. Comput. 80, 121–162 (2010)
14. Odersky, M., Spoon, L., Venners, B.: Programming in Scala: A Comprehensive Step-by-Step Guide, 2nd edn. Artima Inc., Sunnyvale (2010)
15. Oracle. Java Platform Standard Edition 7 API Specification. http://docs.oracle.com/javase/7/docs/api/ (2013)

16. Pacheco, C., Lahiri, S., Ernst, M., Ball, T.: Feedback-directed random test generation. In: Proceedings of 29th International Conference on Software Engineering, ICSE 2007, pp. 75–84. IEEE Computer Society, Washington, DC (2007)

17. Pill, I., Quaritsch, T.: Behavioral diagnosis of LTL specifications at operator level. In: Proceedings of 23rd International Joint Conference on Artificial Intelligence (IJCAI 2013), Beijing, China. IJCAI/AAAI (2013)

18. Ramler, R., Winkler, D., Schmidt, M.: Random test case generation and manual unit testing: substitute or complement in retrofitting tests for legacy code? In: 36th Conference on Software Engineering and Advanced Applications, pp. 286–293. IEEE Computer Society (2012)

19. Ramler, R., Wolfmaier, K., Kopetzky, T.: A replicated study on random test case generation and manual unit testing: How many bugs do professional developers find? In: Proceedings of 37th Annual International Computer Software and Applications Conference, COMPSAC 2013, pp. 484–491. IEEE Computer Society, Washington, DC (2013)

20. Schuppan, V.: Towards a notion of unsatisfiable and unrealizable cores for LTL. Sci. Comput. Program. **77**(7–8), 908–939 (2012)

21. Steffen, B., Howar, F., Isberner, M.: Active automata learning: from DFAs to interface programs and beyond. J. Mach. Learn. Res.-Proc. Track **21**, 195–209 (2012)

22. Taguchi, K., Nishihara, H., Aoki, T., Kumeno, F., Hayamizu, K., Shinozaki, K.: Building a body of knowledge on model checking for software development. In: Proceedings of 37th Annual International Computer Software and Applications Conference (COMPSAC 2013), Kyoto, Japan. IEEE (2013)

23. Utting, M., Legeard, B.: Practical Model-Based Testing: A Tools Approach. Morgan Kaufmann Publishers Inc., San Francisco (2006)

24. Utting, M., Pretschner, A., Legeard, B.: A taxonomy of model-based testing approaches. Softw. Test. Verif. Reliab. **22**(5), 297–312 (2012)

25. Visser, W., Havelund, K., Brat, G., Park, S., Lerda, F.: Model checking programs. Autom. Softw. Eng. J. **10**(2), 203–232 (2003)

26. Yu, Y., Lau, M.: A comparison of MC/DC, MUMCUT and several other coverage criteria for logical decisions. J. Syst. Softw. **79**(5), 577–590 (2006)

Model-Based Testing from Controlled Natural Language Requirements

Gustavo Carvalho[1]([✉]), Flávia Barros[1], Florian Lapschies[2], Uwe Schulze[2], and Jan Peleska[2]

[1] Universidade Federal de Pernambuco - Centro de Informática,
50740-560 Recife, Brazil
{ghpc,fab}@cin.ufpe.br
[2] Department of Mathematics and Computer Science, Universität Bremen,
28209 Bermen, Germany
{florian,uschulze,jp}@informatik.uni-bremen.de

Abstract. Model-Based Testing (MBT) techniques usually take as input models that are not available in the very beginning of a development. Therefore, its use is postponed. In this work we present an approach to MBT that takes as input requirements described in a Controlled Natural Language. Initially, the requirements are syntactically analyzed according to a domain specific language for describing system requirements, and their informal semantics is depicted based on the Case Grammar theory. Then, the requirements semantics is automatically represented as a Transition Relation, which provides formal basis for MBT, and test cases are generated with the support of a solver. Our approach was evaluated considering four examples from different domains. Within seconds, our approach generated 94 % of the test vectors manually written by specialists. Moreover, considering a mutant-based strength analysis, our approach yielded a mutation score between 54 % and 98 %.

Keywords: Natural language · Case grammar · Solver · Test case

1 Introduction

During the last fifty years, we have witnessed a significant increase of embedded HW-SW components in critical systems. Clearly, this trend goes along with increased software size and complexity, and strongly impacts critical systems' safety and reliability. Currently, many researchers are focusing on how to achieve the safety and reliability levels required for these systems. Some approaches to deal with such a problem rely on Model-Based Testing (MBT) techniques. However, these techniques usually take as input models (e. g., state diagrams) that are usually not yet available in the very beginning of the system development project. In the initial phases, only high-level and textual requirement descriptions are usually available. Therefore, the use of MBT is postponed.

To enable early MBT, we propose NAT2TEST$_{IMR}$—an approach to generate test cases from requirements described in Controlled Natural Language

C. Artho and P.C. Ölveczky (Eds.): FTSCS 2013, CCIS 419, pp. 19–35, 2014.
DOI: 10.1007/978-3-319-05416-2_3, © Springer International Publishing Switzerland 2014

(CNL) based on the RT-Tester[1] Internal Model Representation (IMR) [12]. The requirements can describe temporal properties besides functional behaviour. We opt for receiving textual requirements as input instead of a graphical notation because the former is usually available first and in some industries it is required to have textual descriptions for certification purposes.

Initially, our approach parses the textual system requirements to evaluate their conformance with the CNL structure. Our CNL (the *SysReq-CNL*) is a non-ambiguous and precise subset of the English language. After parsing, our approach provides a semantic interpretation for the requirements, using verb case frames as semantic representation [1]. This idea was first developed by the authors in a previous work [5], and this paper extends our original ideas. From the case frames, the requirements' semantics are mapped into an internal model representation whose formal semantics is given by means of a transition relation. Based on this model, our approach generates test vectors with the support of the RT-Tester and its SMT solver. This whole process is fully automated by supporting tools. The tests generated by NAT2TEST$_{IMR}$ provide means for early testing/simulation of models at design level.

To evaluate our proposal, we applied it to four examples from different domains: (i) a Vending Machine (a toy example); (ii) a control system for Safety Injection in a Nuclear Power Plant (publicly available [8]); (iii) one example provided by Embraer[2] (a Brazilian aircraft manufacturer); and (iv) part of the Turn Indicator System [11] of today's Mercedes vehicles (publicly available[3]).

The NAT2TEST$_{IMR}$ approach was evaluated from three perspective: (i) performance; (ii) automatically generated *versus* manually written test vectors (by Embraer); and (iii) mutant-based strength analysis. Within seconds, our approach generated 94 % of the test vectors manually written by Embraer specialists. Moreover, considering a mutant-based strength analysis, our approach yielded a mutation score between 54 % and 98 %.

Therefore, the main contributions of this work are: (1) an MBT approach for generating tests from textual requirements, (2) a formal representation of case frames by means of a transition relation, and (3) empirical evaluations of our approach considering four examples from different domains.

Section 2 describes how requirements are parsed and how verb case frames are inferred. Section 3 explains how case frames are represented by means of a transition relation, and how tests can be generated. Section 4 presents the tool support for our approach. Section 5 analyzes empirical evidence. Section 6 addresses related work, and Sect. 7 presents conclusions and future work.

2   Syntactic / Semantic Analyses

Here, we use Natural Language Processing (NLP) for parsing each system requirement according to our CNL (SysReq-CNL). For each valid requirement, the

---

parser returns the corresponding syntax tree (ST). As described later, case frames give semantic meaning for each obtained ST.

2.1 The SysReq-CNL

A Controlled Natural Language is a subset of an existing natural language that uses a restricted set of grammar rules and a predefined lexicon containing the application domain vocabulary. In general, CNLs are specially designed to avoid textual complexity and ambiguity. The SysReq-CNL was created for editing unambiguous requirements for critical systems. It is defined by a CFG, and a lexicon containing the application domain vocabulary.

The lexicon entries are classified into lexical classes (also known as *Parts Of Speech—POS* [1]). In this work, we consider the following commonly used lexical classes: determiners (*DET*), nouns (*NSING* for singular and *NPLUR* for plural), adjectives (*ADJ*), adverbs (*ADV*), verb inflections (for example, *VBASE*—base form, *VPRE3RD*—for 3rd person in present form), conjunctions (*CNJ*), prepositions (*PREP*) and numbers (*NUMBER*).

The SysReq-CNL grammar (see Fig. 1) conveys the syntactic rules used by the CNL-Parser to generate the requirements corresponding syntax trees. Words in uppercase denote terminal symbols, and a ";" delimits the end of each production. Here, terminal symbols correspond to lexical classes.

The grammar start symbol is *Requirement*, which is composed by a *ConditionalClause* and an *ActionClause*. Thus, the requirements have the form of action statements guarded by conditions. A *ConditionalClause* begins with a conjunction, and then its structure is similar to a *Conjunctive Normal Form* (CNF). The conjunctions are delimited by a *COMMA* and the *AND* keyword, whereas the disjunctions are delimited by the *OR* keyword. An *ActionClause* begins with

Requirement → *ConditionalClause COMMA ActionClause*;
ConditionalClause → *CONJ AndCondition*;
AndCondition → *AndCondition COMMA AND OrCondition* | *OrCondition*;
OrCondition → *OrCondition OR Condition*| *Condition*;
Condition → *NounPhrase VerbPhraseCondition*;
ActionClause → *NounPhrase VerbPhraseAction*;
NounPhrase → *DET? ADJ∗ Noun*+;
Noun → *NSING* | *NPLUR*;
VerbPhraseCondition → *VerbCondition NOT?ComparativeTerm? VerbComplement*;
VerbCondition → (*VPRE3RD* | *VTOBE_PRE3* | *VTOBE_PRE* |
    VTOBE_PAST3 | *VTOBE_PAST*);
ComparativeTerm → (*COMP (OR NOT? COMP)?*);
VerbPhraseAction → *SHALL* (*VerbActionVerbComplement* | *COLON VerbAction*
    VerbComplement (*COMMA VerbActionVerbComplement*)+);
VerbAction → *VBASE*;
VerbComplement → *VariableState? PrepositionalPhrase∗*;
VariableState → (*NounPhrase* | *ADV*| *ADJ* | *NUMBER*);
PrepositionalPhrase → *PREP VariableState*;

Fig. 1. Grammar for system requirements.

a *NounPhrase* (nouns eventually preceded by a determiner and adjectives) followed by a *VerbPhraseAction*, which describes action statements.

This concise grammar is able to represent requirements written using several different sentence formations, and it is not restricted to one specific application domain. We have successfully applied the SysReq-CNL in the different domains considered in this work. The requirement REQ-007 is a typical requirement from the Turn Indicator System adhering to the SysReq-CNL.

REQ-007: *When the voltage is greater than 80, and the flashing timer is greater than or equal to 220, and the left indication lights are off, and the right indication lights are off, and the flashing mode is left flashing or the flashing mode is left tip flashing, the lights controller component shall: assign 'on' to the left indication lights, assign 'off' to the right indication lights, reset the flashing timer.*

In the Embraer context, the requirements originally written by their Requirements Team are similar to the format imposed by the SysReq-CNL. In what follows, we present a typical requirement written by Embraer Team, and the corresponding form, rewritten to adhere to the SysReq-CNL.

Original: *The Priority Logic Function shall assign value 0 (zero) to Command In-Control output when: left Priority Button is not pressed AND right Priority Button is not pressed AND left Command is on neutral position AND right Command is on neutral position.*

Rewritten: *When the left priority button is not pressed, and the right priority button is not pressed, and the left command is on neutral position, and the right command is on neutral position, the Priority Logic Function shall assign 0 to the Command-In-Control output.*

2.2   The Case Frames Notation

We follow the Case Grammar linguistic theory [1] to represent Natural Language (NL) semantic meaning. In this theory, a sentence is not analysed in terms of the syntactic categories or grammatical functions, but in terms of the semantic (thematic) roles played by each word/group of words in the sentence.

The obtained semantic representation is then mapped into an internal model whose formal semantics is given by means of a transition relation. The thematic roles semantic representation frees the process of generating the internal model from depending upon the SysReq-CNL syntactic rules. Thus, if the CNL evolves to capture new syntactic structures without changing the underlying semantics, the process of generating the internal model will not change.

Within the Case Grammar theory, each verb is associated to specific thematic roles (TR), which form the verb's Case Frame (CF). Thus, a CF is a structure with slots (representing thematic roles) to be filled in by sentence elements. Roles may be obligatory or optional in a CF. In our work, each verb in the Lexicon is associated to a CF. We consider 9 TRs[4]: (1) *Action (ACT)*, the action that

---

[4] The adopted nomenclature was inspired by [1].

Table 1. Example of case frames.

Condition #1—Main Verb (**CAC**): is						
CPT: the voltage	**CFV**: -		**CMD**: greater than		**CTV**: 80	
Condition #2—Main Verb (**CAC**): is						
CPT: the flashing timer	**CFV**: -		**CMD**: greater than or equal to		**CTV**: 220	
Condition #3—Main Verb (**CAC**): is						
CPT: the flashing mode	**CFV**: -		**CMD**: -		**CTV**: left flashing	
OR—Main Verb (**CAC**): is						
CPT: the flashing mode	**CFV**: -		**CMD**:		**CTV**: left tip flashing	
Condition #4—Main Verb (**CAC**): are						
CPT: the left indication lights	**CFV**: -		**CMD**: -		**CTV**: off	
Condition #5—Main Verb (**CAC**): are						
CPT: the right indication lights	**CFV**: -		**CMD**: -		**CTV**: off	
Action #1—Main Verb (**ACT**): assign						
AGT: the lights controller component	**TOV**: on	**PAT**: the left indication lights				
Action #2—Main Verb (**ACT**): assign						
AGT: the lights controller component	**TOV**: off	**PAT**: the right indication lights				
Action #3—Main Verb (**ACT**): reset						
AGT: the lights controller component	**TOV**: -	**PAT**: the flashing timer				

shall be performed if the conditions are satisfied. (2) *Agent (AGT)*, entity who performs the action. (3) *Patient (PAT)*, entity who is affected by the action. (4) *To Value (TOV)*, the Patient value after action completion. (5) *Condition Action (CAC)*, the action that concerns each Condition Patient. (6) *Condition Patient (CPT)*, the element associated with each condition. (7) *Condition From Value (CFV)*, each Condition Patient previous value. (8) *Condition To Value (CTV)*, each Condition Patient value that satisfies the condition. (9) *Condition Modifier (CMD)*, some modifier related to the condition, e.g., a negation. The TR *Condition Modifier* was defined by us, whereas the others are defined in the related literature. Table 1 shows CFs corresponding to REQ-007.

The verb case frames are inferred from the syntax trees returned by the parser. This is done by visiting the syntax trees searching for particular patterns. For instance, the agent (AGT) always corresponds to the terminals of the *NounPhrase* that is a child of an *ActionClause*. Sometimes the ST structure is insufficient, and the patterns are dependent on the verb being used. For instance, consider the patient thematic role (PAT), and the verbs *change* and *assign*. For the verb *change*, we might have the following sentence structure: "... *shall change something from old value to new value*". However, when the verb *assign* is used, we have: "... *shall assign new value to something*". In both cases, the patient is *something*, but depending on the verb being used, this element appears in different parts of the sentence and of the corresponding ST. Thus, in this case, we need specific rules governed by each verb.

Currently, we consider the verbs: *to add, to assign, to be, to become, to change, to reset,* and *to subtract*. It is worth mentioning that they are sufficient to write all requirements (51 in total) of the examples considered in this work. These patterns were initially defined for the Embraer example, and then they were applied without changes to the other three examples.

3   Generation of Test Vectors

In our approach, system behavior is internally modeled by state machines, captured in the RT-Tester *Internal Model Representation* (IMR). For generating test cases with associated test data, the concurrent state machine semantics is represented by means of a transition relation Φ associating pre-states of locations, variables and current time with post-states. Below we describe the IMR, how state machines are inferred from the case frames, and how we use the transition relation for generating concrete test data.

3.1   Internal Model Representation

The system model is arranged in hierarchical components $c \in C$, so that a partial function $p_C : C \nrightarrow C$ mapping each component but the root c_r to its parent is defined [12]. Each component may declare variables, and hierarchic scope rules are applied in name resolution. Interfaces between Test Environment (TE) and System Under Test (SUT) as well as global model variables are declared on the level of c_r. All variables are typed. When parsing the model the scope rules are applied to all expressions and unique variable symbol names are used from then on. Therefore we can assume that all variable names are unique and taken from a symbol set V with pairwise disjoint subsets $I, O, T \subset V$ denoting TE $\to$ SUT inputs, SUT $\to$ TE outputs and timers, respectively.

Each leaf component is associated with a state machine $s \in SM$, where SM denotes the set of all state machines which are part of the model. State machines are composed of *locations* (also called *control states*) $\ell \in L(s)$ and *transitions* $(\tau = (\ell, g, \alpha, \ell') \in \Sigma(s) \subseteq L(s) \times G \times A \times L(s))$ connecting source and target locations ℓ and ℓ', respectively. Transition component $g \in \text{Bexpr}(V)$ denotes the guard condition of τ, which is a Boolean expression over symbols from V. For timer symbols $t \in T$ occurring in g we only allow Boolean conditions $\text{elapsed}(t, c)$ with constants c. Intuitively speaking, $\text{elapsed}(t, c)$ evaluates to `true` if at least c time units have passed since t's most recent reset. Transition component α denotes a set of value assignments to variables in V, according to expressions formed by variables of V. A transition without assignments is associated with an empty set $\alpha = \varnothing$. For more detailed definitions, refer to the RT-Tester technical report [12]. Code 1 presents the Turn Indicator System IMR (later described).

3.2   From Case Frames to State Machines

Concerning the internal model representation, we extract components and state machines from the case frames. Recall that the *Agent* (AGT) role represents who performs the action. Thus, for each different AGT we create a parallel

Code 1. IMR of the Turn Indicator System.

```
 1  SYSTEM { IMR { TOPLEVEL COMPONENT IMR {
 2    ATTRIBUTES {
 3      ATTRIBUTE _old_the_emergency_flashing {SYMBOLTYPE: GlobalVar TYPE: int}
 4      ...
 5      ATTRIBUTE the_emergency_flashing {SYMBOLTYPE: InputVar TYPE: int}
 6      ATTRIBUTE the_flashing_mode {SYMBOLTYPE: OutputVar TYPE: int}
 7      ATTRIBUTE the_flashing_timer {SYMBOLTYPE: GlobalVar TYPE: clock}
 8      ...
 9    }
10    SUT COMPONENT IMR.SUT.the_flashing_mode_component { SC-LOCATIONS {
11      LOCATION NAME: Initial { EMANATING TRANSITIONS {
12        [0] [ true ] / ... ----> the_flashing_mode_component_L0
13      }}
14      LOCATION NAME: the_flashing_mode_component_L0 { EMANATING TRANSITIONS {...}}
15    }}
16    SUT COMPONENT IMR.SUT.the_lights_controller_component { SC-LOCATIONS {
17      LOCATION NAME: Initial { EMANATING TRANSITIONS {
18        [33] [ true ] / ... ----> the_lights_controller_component_L0
19      }}
20      LOCATION NAME: the_lights_controller_component_L0 { EMANATING TRANSITIONS {
21        ...
22        [60] [ ((((((IMR.the_voltage > 80) &&
23                   ((_timeTick - IMR.the_flashing_timer) >= 220)) &&
24                   ((IMR.the_flashing_mode == 0) || (IMR.the_flashing_mode == 4))) &&
25                   (IMR.the_left_indication_lights == 0)) &&
26                   (IMR.the_right_indication_lights == 0)) &&
27                   ((IMR.the_left_indication_lights != 1)
28                   || (IMR.the_right_indication_lights != 0))) ]
29              / ... ----> the_lights_controller_component_L0
30        ...
31      }}
32    }}
33  }}}
```

component. Each system component comprises a state machine with a single location, and, based on the case frames, we infer self-transitions.

To illustrate this, consider the requirement REQ-007. We extract the transition: $\tau = (\ell_i, g_{i,j}, \alpha_{i,j}, \ell_i)$, where ℓ_i represents the location of the i_{th} state machine, which is the one corresponding to the *the lights controller component*. The guard of this transition is $[v > 80 \wedge elapsed(ft, 220) \wedge ll = 0 \wedge rl = 0 \wedge (fm = 0 \vee fm = 4)]$, where v represents the voltage, ft the flashing timer, ll the left indication lights, rl the right indication lights, and fm the flashing mode. Besides that, *off* is represented as 0, *on* as 1, *left flashing* as 0, and *left tip flashing* as 4. Moreover, the actions associated with this transition are $\{(ll, 1), (rl, 0), (ft, 0)\}$. See Code 1—this transition is presented in lines 22–29.

This code is not human-readable since it is a hidden artefact, which is automatically generated by our approach, whose purpose is to provide means for generation of tests. Despite that, using the RT-Tester infrastructure it would be possible to derive a readable UML model from it, but it is outside of the scope of this work.

To extract transitions like the one just presented, and to create the IMR from the case frames, we rely upon three main algorithms: (1) identify variables, (2) identify transitions, and (3) create the internal model representation.

In the IMR, variables are of three possible kinds: *input*, *output* and *global* variables (see Code 1, lines 2–9). Besides that, we support the following data types: *Integer*, *Floating* point numbers, *Boolean* and *Clock* (timers). We consider

Algorithm 1: Identify Variables

```
input    : caseFrameList
output   : varList

1  for cf ∈ caseFrameList do
2      for andCond ∈ cf do
3          for orCond ∈ andCond do
4              varName = orCond.CPT;
5              var = varList.find(varName);
6              if var == null then
7                  var = new Var(varName);
8                  if "timer" ∈ varName then
                       var.setKind(GLOBAL);
9                  else var.setKind(INPUT);
10                 varList.add(var);
11             value = orCond.CTV;
12             var.addPossibleValue(value);
13             action = orCond.CAC;
14             if isPastTense(action) then
                   var.hasOldVersion = true;

15         for action ∈ cf do
16             varName = action.PAT;
17             var = varList.find(varName);
18             if var == null then
19                 var = new Var(varName);
20                 if "timer" ∈ varName then
                       var.setKind(GLOBAL);
21                 else var.setKind(OUTPUT);
22                 varList.add(var);

23             else if var.kind == INPUT then
24                 var.setKind(OUTPUT);

25             value = action.TOV;
26             if "reset" ∈ action.ACT then value = 0;
27             var.addPossibleValue(value);

28 for var ∈ varList do
29     if var.hasOldVersion then
30         oldVarName = "_old" + var.name;
31         oldVar = new Var(oldVarName);
32         oldVar.setKind(GLOBAL);
33         oldVar.setType(var.type);
34         varList.add(oldVar);
```

Algorithm 2: Identify Transitions

```
input    : caseFrameList
output   : transMap

1  for cf ∈ caseFrameList do
2      guard = generateGuard(cf);
3      stmtMap = generateStatements(cf);
4      for stmtKey ∈ stmtMap.keys do
5          transList = transMap.find(stmtKey);
6          if transKey == null then
7              init trans;
8              trans.setGuard(guard);
9              trans.addStmts(
                   stmtMap[stmtKey]);
10             transList = new List();
11             transList.add(trans);
12             transMap.add(stmtKey,
                   transList);

13         else
14             hasSimilarTransition = false;
15             for trans ∈ transList do
16                 if guard == trans.guard then
17                     trans.addStmts(
                           stmtMap[stmtKey]);
18                     hasSimilarTransition
                           = true;
19                     break;

20             if !hasSimilarTransition then
21                 init trans;
22                 trans.setGuard(guard);
23                 trans.addStmts(
                       stmtMap[stmtKey]);
24                 transList.add(trans);
```

Algorithm 3: Create the IMR

```
input    : varList, transMap
output   : topCmp

1  init topCmp;
2  for var ∈ varList do topCmp.addVar(var);
3  init SUT;
4  topCmp.add(SUT);
5  init TE;
6  topCmp.add(TE);
7  for transKey ∈ transMap.keys do
8      init l0;
9      for trans ∈ transMap[transKey] do
10         specialGuard =
               avoidLivelock(trans.guard);
11         trans.setGuard(trans.guard ∧
               specialGuard);
12         l0.addTransition(l0, trans);

13     cmp = new Component(transKey);
14     cmp.addLocation(l0);
15     SUT.add(cmp);
```

inputs as variables provided to the SUT by the testing environment; their values cannot be modified by the system. Thus, a variable is classified as an input if and only if it appears only in conditions. All other variables, except the ones whose type is a clock, are classified as outputs. Clock variables (timers) are always classified as global variables. To distinguish between timers and others variables, we require the former to have the word "timer" as a suffix.

Our algorithm for identifying variables (Algorithm 1) iterates over the list of case frames (line 1) analyzing each condition (lines 2–3), which comprises a conjunction of disjunctions, and each action (line 15). When analyzing conditions, we extract variables from the *Condition Patient* (CPT) role. For example, Table 1 shows that *the voltage* is the CPT of the first condition. Thus, if the corresponding variable has not yet been identified (lines 5–6), we create a new variable considering the CPT content, besides replacing the white spaces by an underscore (line 7). So, in this case, we create the variable *the_voltage*, previously illustrated as *v*. If the variable is a timer, it is created as a global variable (line 8). Otherwise, the variable described by the CPT role is created as an input (line 9). Then we add the created variable to the list of identified variables (line 10).

To infer the type of the variable we analyze the value associated with it in the case frame, which is the content of the Condition To Value (CTV) role. For instance, the variable *the_voltage* is associated with the value *80* in the first condition of REQ-007 (see Table 1). Thus, the algorithm extracts the CTV content (line 11), and adds it to a list of values already identified (line 12).

The *addPossibleValue* is responsible for invoking the algorithm *updateType* (omitted here due to space restrictions), which is responsible for inferring and updating the variable type. Briefly speaking, variables associated with values are classified as integers or floating point numbers. Variables whose possible value is *true* or *false* are classified as Booleans. Variables related to other words are classified as integers, considering the enumeration of possible values. For example, the variable *the_left_indication_lights* is associated with the values *off*, *on* (see Table 1). In this case, this variable is classified as an integer where *off* is mapped to 0, and *on* is mapped to 1.

Lines 13–14 inspect the Condition Action (CAC) role to identify conditions referring to the old (previous) state of the variable. This occurs when a verb in the past tense is used (e. g., *the voltage was 80* describes the situation where the voltage was 80 in the previous system state). To deal with this situation, we create a special variable, named by adding the prefix *_old* to the variable name, which is responsible for storing the variable value in the previous system state (lines 28–34). As "old variables" are neither inputs nor outputs, they are always classified as global. For the previous example, we create the variable *_old_the_voltage*. Lines 15–27 behave analogously to the previous explanations. The differences are: (1) the variables are identified from the Patient (PAT) role; (2) if a variable was already identified as an input its kind is updated to output due to the reason presented in the beginning of this subsection; and (3) the variable value is the content of the To Value (TOV) role, excluding the case when the *reset* verb is used (the TOV is empty and we shall consider the value 0 as the possible value—see the last action of Table 1).

From the case frames we also extract transitions (see Code 1, lines 11–14, lines 17–31). They are associated with the respective Agent (AGT) roles representing system components (one component per agent—see Code 1, lines 10, 16). The algorithm for identifying transitions (Algorithm 2) iterates over each case frame (line 1) and returns a mapping of components to their self-transitions (output *transMap*). For each case frame, the algorithm extracts a guard expression (line 2) and statements (line 3). The *generateGuard* algorithm (not presented here) transverses recursively the conjunction of disjunctions of each case frame and returns the transition guard according to the IMR format. Besides identifying statements according to the IMR format, the algorithm *generateStatements* groups the identified statements by their respective agents. For example, all actions of the requirement REQ-007 are performed by the same agent—*the lights controller component* (see Table 1). Thus, in this case all statements of REQ-007 are grouped by the same agent.

For each different agent (line 4) we analyze if some transition has already been identified with respect to this system component (lines 5–6). If it has not, we create a new transition (line 7) considering the guard (line 8) and the respective statements (line 9), we create a list of transitions for this component (line 10), we add the created transition to this list (10), and we finally group this list by the component being considered (line 12). If transitions have already been identified to the component (line 13), we merge the actions of transitions whenever they have the same guard (lines 14–19). Otherwise, we create a new transition, and we add it to the list of transitions of this component (lines 20–24).

The third algorithm (Algorithm 3) is responsible for assembling the variables and transitions into one IMR top component (output *topCmp*), which comprises all parallel system components. First of all we initialize this top component (line 1), and add all variables to it (line 2). Then, we define that this top component has two main subcomponents: the *System Under Test* (SUT) model (lines 3–4), and the *Testing Environment* (TE) model (lines 5–6). In this work, as we focus on the SUT specification, the TE model is an empty component.

For each different agent (line 7), we create the single location $l0$ of the respective state machine (line 8). Then, we add the transitions associated to this agent as self-transitions of this location (lines 9–12). Considering the semantics of the IMR, which is detailed in Sect. 3.3, to avoid a livelock in the SUT specification (the indefinite execution of transitions without time passing), we augment each transition guard stating that it shall be performed if and only if the transition has some side effect (it changes the value of some SUT variable—lines 10–11). Finally, we create a system component (line 13), we add this single location to the component state machine (line 14), and we define this component as a SUT subcomponent (line 15). After performing these three algorithms we obtain a model of our system requirements according to the IMR notation.

3.3   Transition Relation

For generating test cases with associated test data, the model behavior is formally encoded by means of a transition relation Φ. We describe transition relations relating pre- and post-states by means of first order predicates over unprimed and primed symbols from $BCS \cup V \cup \{\hat{t}\}$, where $BCS =_{def} \bigcup_{s \in SM} L(s)$ ("BCS" stands for "basic control states"). The unprimed symbols refer to the symbol value in the pre-state, and the primed symbols to post-state values. The variables with prefix "_old" are interpreted as unprimed symbols.

The transition relation distinguishes between *discrete transitions* Φ_D and *timed transitions* (also called *delay transitions*) Φ_T, allowing the model execution time $\hat{t}$ to advance and inputs to change, while the basic configuration, internal (excluding the special "old" variables) and output variables remain frozen. The delay transition is also responsible for updating the variables with prefix "_old". Thus, before changing the value of inputs, it copies the current value of each variable, which has an old version, to its old version. Discrete transitions take place whenever at least one state machine has an enabled transition.

If a discrete transition is enabled its effects may be described as follows. (1) The current model execution time $\hat{t}$ remains unchanged. (2) All input variable values remain unchanged. (3) For every state machine possessing an enabled transition τ, the transition's effect becomes visible in the post-state. (5) All variables that are not modified by any executed transition retain their old values.

Delay transitions are characterized as follows. (1) The model execution time is advanced. (2) Inputs may change for the post-state of the delay transition, and the old version (pre-state) of variables are accordingly updated, but all other variables and basic control states remain unchanged. (3) The admissible time shift is limited by the point in time when the next timer will elapse. Due to space restrictions, we do not present here the formal definition of this transition relation. The reader can find it in the RT-Tester technical report [12].

3.4 Symbolic Test Cases, Concrete Test Data

In MBT test cases may be expressed as logical constraints identifying model computations that are suitable to investigate a given test objective. We use the term *symbolic test cases* for these constraints to emphasize that at this stage no concrete test data to stimulate a model computation satisfying them exists. As external representation of these constraints we use LTL formulas of the type $\mathbf{F}\phi$, where the free variables in ϕ are model variables, basic control states (interpreted as Booleans, true indicating that the machines currently resides in this location), and model execution time. The utilization of the finally operator $\mathbf{F}$ is motivated by the fact that to test a given objective ϕ, a computation prefix may have to be executed in order to reach a model state from where ϕ can be fulfilled. Since test cases need to be realized by finite model computation fragments, symbolic test cases are internally represented as so-called *bounded model checking instances*

$$tc(c, G) \equiv_{\text{def}} \bigwedge_{i=0}^{c-1} \Phi(\sigma_i, \sigma_{i+1}) \wedge G(\sigma_0, \ldots, \sigma_c) \tag{1}$$

In this formula σ_0 represents the current model state and Φ the transition relation, so any solution of 1 is a valid model computation fragment of length c. The test objective ϕ is encoded in $G(\sigma_0, \ldots, \sigma_c)$. For example 1, $G(\sigma_0, \ldots, \sigma_c) = G(\sigma_c) = ((\bigvee_i (\ell_i(\sigma_c) \wedge \psi_i(\sigma_c))) \wedge \phi_1(\sigma_c))$. Intuitively speaking, $tc(c, G)$ tries to solve $\mathbf{F}\phi$ within c computation steps, starting in model pre-state σ_0. To solve constraints of type 1 we use an SMT solver. Thus, the solver result can be seen as a test case (sequence of test vectors) where each test vector comprises the value of inputs and the system state with respect to a particular time moment.

Table 2 shows an example of a test case generated for the Turn Indicator System. The first line tests that no lights shall be turned on, even if, for instance, the turn indicator is on the right position, if the car voltage is too low (below 81 volts). However, when the voltage is greater than 80 (line 2), the lights shall be

Table 2. Example of test case.

TIME (ms)	Voltage	Emergency button	Turn indicator	Left lights	Right lights
0	80	Off	Right	Off	Off
7918	81	Off	Left	On	Off
8258	81	Off	Left	Off	Off
8478	81	Off	Left	On	Off

turned on based on the turn indicator position (in this case, left position), and the light shall remain on for 340 ms, and off for 220 ms, periodically.

Note that symbolic test cases are not necessarily satisfiable, since some goals $G(\sigma_0, \ldots, \sigma_c)$ in the bounded model checking instance (1) may not admit a solution, if they are generated by a purely syntactic evaluation of the IMR structure.

4   Tool Platform

The NAT2TEST$_{IMR}$ approach is fully supported by tools. The CNLParser is the tool that receives the system requirements and, for each valid requirement with respect to the SysReq-CNL, returns the corresponding ST. Next, the CF-Generator tool provides a semantic interpretation for each ST, using verb case frames (CF) as semantic representation. After that, the tool IMR-Generator translates the case frames into the IMR.

Then, we use RT-Tester, a tool developed by Verified Systems International GmbH in cooperation with the last author's team at the University of Bremen, which operates on the IMR and outputs test cases with concrete test data. Optionally, the tool also generates the test procedures executing these test cases in software or system testing (hardware-in-the-loop) environments. To check the SUT responses against the test model (IMR), RT-Tester generates test oracles from the given model. These run concurrently with the SUT, permanently checking SUT outputs against expected value changes and associated points in time.

5   Empirical Analyses

The NAT2TEST$_{IMR}$ approach was evaluated in four different examples. *The Vending Machine* (VM) example is an adaptation of the Coffee Machine presented in [7]. The machine outputs weak coffee (within 10 and 30 s after the user request) if the user selects coffee too quickly (i. e., within 30 s after inserting a coin), otherwise it outputs strong coffee. This example is an interesting one since its behavior is highly dependent on time constraints. *The Nuclear Power Plant Control* (NPP) is a simplified version of a control system for safety injection in a nuclear power plant (NPP) as described in [8]. *The Priority Command Function* (PC) was provided by Embraer. It comprises a system that decides whether the pilot or copilot will have priority in controlling the airplane side sticks based on their position and on a priority button. *The Turn Indicator System*(TIS) is a simplification of the specification that is currently used by Daimler for automatically deriving test cases, concrete test data and test procedures. In 2011, Daimler allowed the publication of this specification to serve as a "real-world" benchmark supporting research of MBT techniques. Our simplification results in a size reduction of the original model presented in [11], but serves well as a proof of concept, because it still represents a safety-critical system portion with real-time and concurrent aspects. Considering these examples, we evaluated the NAT2TEST$_{IMR}$ approach from three perspectives: (i) performance; (ii) automatically generated *versus* manually written tests (only for the Embraer example); and (iii) mutant-based strength analysis. All files related to the empirical analyses (textual specification, case frames, IMR, test cases, and Java code) are publicly available[5], except for the files related to the Embraer example due to disclosure restrictions.

5.1   Results and Analyses

Table 3 summarizes the data collected. As it can be seen, the TIS is the largest example: 1,124 words and 21 requirements, which comprises 600 thematic roles, whereas the other examples (VM, NPP, and PC) have an average of 320 words, 10 requirements, and 182 thematic roles. As a consequence of its complexity, more symbolic test cases are identified to the TIS example (193) when compared to the VM, NPP, and PC examples (62, 64, and 54 symbolic test cases, respectively).

The time measurements were done on an average configuration computer. The figures indicate that the time required to process (parse) the requirements and identify the thematic roles is linear with respect to the specification size. Furthermore, these two tasks are performed in order of seconds. Differently, the time required to generate the test cases from the obtained IMR had a sharper increase with respect to the specification size. The most complex and larger specification (TIS) required about 92 s, whereas the three other examples needed no more than a few seconds. Despite that, the total time required to apply the NAT2TEST$_{IMR}$ strategy is within 2 min in the worst case (TIS). As the RT-Tester infrastructure has already proven to scale up for the full TIS [11], we believe our strategy might scale as well since it reuses the RT-Tester infrastructure and only adds a small overhead to process the requirements.

To evaluate the meaningfulness of the generated test vectors we compared the vectors generated by our approach with the ones manually written by Embraer specialists. This analysis was not done for the other examples since we did not have access to test vectors manually written for them. Our strategy generated 16 of the 17 test vectors considered by the specialists (94.12 %). The single missing vector exercises a system behavior that is already tested by other test vectors, and the strategies of the RT-Tester solver did not consider it. To evaluate the test cases (sequence of test vectors) strength (ability to detect errors) we use mutation operators since it yields statistically trustworthy comparison of test cases strength in a controlled and systematic way [2]. Therefore, we created a

---

[5] http://www.mbt-benchmarks.org

Table 3. Empirical results of NAT2TEST$_{IMR}$.

	VM	NPP	PC	TIS
General information				
Words:	353	331	276	1,124
Requirements:	11	11	8	21
Thematic roles:	191	184	172	600
Symbolic test cases:	62	64	54	193
Covered symbolic test cases:	20 (32.26%)	48 (75.00%)	44 (81.48%)	121 (62.69%)
Time performance				
Time to parse the requirements	0.59 s	0.41 s	0.03 s	0.92 s
Time to identify thematic roles:	0.02 s	0.03 s	0.02 s	0.05 s
Time to generate IMR and test cases:	1.07 s	2.66 s	0.95 s	92.90 s
Total time:	1.68 s	3.10 s	1.00 s	93.87 s
Vector generation precision analysis				
Generated × manual vectors	-	-	16 (94.12%)	-
Mutant-based strength analysis				
Java (LOC):	57	46	34	226
Mutants generated:	364	317	144	1,126
Mutation score:	54.67%	69.04%	87.50%	98.05%

"correct" (at least with respect to our tests) Java implementation (224 non-blank lines of code (LOC) in the largest case—TIS, and 34 LOC in the smallest case—PC) for each example.

This implementation was created solely from the natural language requirements, and we avoided any design decision that could not be inferred from the requirements. In other words, the abstract level of the Java specification is similar to the requirements one. Furthermore, it is important to note that the Java code was created with the purpose of assessing our strategy, and in a real environment they would not be available yet, since we are generating test from initial and high-level requirements. We used the μJava tool [9] considering 12 method-level mutation operators for generating mutants. This tool created between 144, and 1,126 compiled mutants. Afterwards, we manually instrumented the Java code, and ran the test cases generated by the NAT2TEST$_{IMR}$ approach. From these mutants, 54.67% killed in the worst case (VM), whereas 98.05% were killed in the best case (TIS). It is worthy mentioning that the score obtained for the test cases manually written by Embraer is 91.67%—near the NAT2TEST$_{IMR}$ score (87.50%). We assumed a conservative approach [2] for analysis of large numbers of mutants: we consider that all mutants are non-equivalent mutants. Therefore, these figures might be higher if equivalent mutants are identified and discarded.

The mutation score variation is justified by the number and percentage of symbolic test cases covered by the RT-Tester standard MC/DC coverage strategy, which was considered in all examples. As described in Sect. 3.4, sometimes only a small number of the automatically generated symbolic test cases are satisfiable, and thus a small number of test vectors are generated[6]. When it happens, in this case it is necessary to write user-defined test objectives to guide the test generation process, and thus generate more test vectors. As this approach is dependent upon each example and user expertise, we did not consider it. As shown in Table 3, the lowest mutation score is related to the lowest number/coverage of symbolic test cases, and the symbolic test cases not covered are indeed not satisfiable. Considering these results, the NAT2TEST$_{IMR}$ approach seems to be a reasonable alternative for generating test cases from CNL requirements. Despite the promising results, some threats to validity might apply to our analyses. The main one concerns external validity: we considered few examples (small to medium size), and thus we cannot generalize our results to other examples.

6   Related Work

Previous works [3,13,16] have already addressed the generation of tests from NL specifications. Differently from this work, they do not impose a standardized way of writing as our SysReq-CNL does. Moreover, these works require user interaction during the process, whereas we do not. However, the strategy proposed in [13] is capable of generating tests for more concrete specifications (embedded with design decisions). We consider only high-level specifications. The works [4,10,15] provide a standardize way of writing requirements, but they do not deal with timed specifications and they generate non-executable test cases. However, the test generation of [10] is proved sound, whereas ours is not. The work [14] considers time but within more limited requirement structures. In [5] (NAT2TEST$_{SCR}$) we use a transformation from CNL to the SCR notation in [5] and apply the T-VEC tool for generating tests. Differently, this paper uses a novel semantic encoding of the CNL behavior in the form of a timed transition relation. This new approach can handle time in a natural way, whereas in [5] auxiliary construction based on counters had to be applied.

7   Conclusion

This paper presented NAT2TEST$_{IMR}$: an MBT technique based on natural language requirements. The requirements are syntactically analyzed according to our CNL, and their informal semantics is captured based on the Case Grammar theory. Then, the requirements semantics is automatically mapped into a Transition Relation, which provides the formal basis for MBT. Concrete test cases with associated data are generated with the support of an SMT solver.

---

[6] In the tests described by Table 3, test data for all *feasible* symbolic test cases could be generated in an automated way.

Our approach was evaluated considering four examples from different domains. Within seconds, it generated 94 % of the test vectors manually written by specialists. Moreover, considering a mutant-based strength analysis, our approach yielded a mutation score between 54 % (worst case) and 98 % (best case). Despite the promising results, our approach is tailored for generating tests for high-level requirements of the form of action statements guarded by conditions, and thus other MBT techniques should be considered when testing more concrete specifications. Therefore, the tests generated by NAT2TEST$_{IMR}$ provide means for early testing/simulation of models at design level. As future work we plan to (1) create a hierarchical IMR instead of our current flat structure, in order to enhance the performance of our approach (we plan to consider the results of [6] for this purpose), and (2) extend of our approach for textual specification of testing environments.

Acknowledgments. We thank Augusto Sampaio for his valuable advice. This work has been partially funded by the EU FP7 COMPASS project (no.287829).

References

1. Allen, J.: Natural Language Understanding. Benjamin/Cummings, San Francisco (1995)
2. Andrews, J.H., Briand, L.C., Labiche, Y.: Is mutation an appropriate tool for testing experiments? In: International Conference on Software Engineering, pp. 402–411. ACM, New York (2005)
3. Boddu, R., Guo, L., Mukhopadhyay, S., Cukic, B.: RETNA: from requirements to testing in a natural way. In: International Requirements Engineering (2004)
4. Brottier, E., Baudry, B., Traon, Y.L., Touzet, D., Nicolas, B.: Producing a global requirement model from multiple requirement specifications. In: International Enterprise Distributed Object Computing Conference, pp. 390–404. USA (2007)
5. Carvalho, G., Falcão, D., Barros, F., Sampaio, A., Mota, A., Motta, L., Blackburn, M.: Test case generation from natural language requirements based on SCR specifications. In: ACM Symposium on Applied Computing (2013)
6. Grieskamp, W., Gurevich, Y., Schulte, W., Veanes, M.: Generating finite state machines from abstract state machines. Softw. Eng. Notes **27**(4), 112–122 (2002)
7. Larsen, K., Mikucionis, M., Nielsen, B.: Online testing of real-time systems using UPPAAL: status and future work. In: Dagstuhl Seminar Proceedings volume 04371: Perspectives of Model-Based Testing (2004)
8. Leonard, E.I., Heitmeyer, C.L.: Program synthesis from formal requirements specifications using APTS. High. Order Symbol. Comput. **16**, 63–92 (2003)
9. Ma, Y.S., Offutt, J., Kwon, Y.R.: MuJava: an automated class mutation system: research articles. Softw. Test. Verif. Reliab. **15**(2), 97–133 (2005)
10. Nogueira, S., Sampaio, A., Mota, A.: Test generation from state based use case models. Formal Aspects Comput. **1**, 1–50 (2012)
11. Peleska, J., Honisch, A., Lapschies, F., Löding, H., Schmid, H., Smuda, P., Vorobev, E., Zahlten, C.: A real-world Benchmark model for testing concurrent real-time systems in the automotive domain. In: Wolff, B., Zaïdi, F. (eds.) ICTSS 2011. LNCS, vol. 7019, pp. 146–161. Springer, Heidelberg (2011)

12. Peleska, J., Vorobev, E., Lapschies, F., Zahlten, C.: Automated model-based testing with RT-Tester. Universität Bremen, Technical report (2011)
13. Jr Santiago, V., Vijaykumar, N.L.: Generating model-based test cases from natural language requirements for space application software. Softw. Qual. J. **20**, 77–143 (2012)
14. Schnelte, M.: Generating test cases for timed systems from controlled natural language specifications. In: International Conference on System Integration and Reliability Improvements, pp. 348–353 (2009)
15. Sinha, A., Suttan Jr., S.M., Paradkar, A.: Text2Test: automated inspection of natural language use cases. International Conference on Software Testing, Verification and Validation, pp. 155–164. IEEE Computer Society, Washington (2010)
16. Sneed, H.: Testing against natural language requirements. In: International Conference on Quality Software, pp. 380–387 (2007)

An UPPAAL Framework for Model Checking Automotive Systems with FlexRay Protocol

Xiaoyun Guo[1], Hsin-Hung Lin[2($\boxtimes$)], Kenro Yatake[1], and Toshiaki Aoki[1]

[1] School of Information Science,
Japan Advanced Institute of Science and Technology, Ishikawa, Japan
{xiaoyunguo,k-yatake,toshiaki}@jaist.ac.jp
[2] School of Information Science and Electrical Engineering, Kyushu University,
Fukuoka, Japan
h-lin@ait.kyushu-u.ac.jp

Abstract. This paper introduces a method and a framework for verifying automotive system designs using model checking. The framework is based on UPPAAL, a timed model checker, and focuses on checking automotive system designs with FlexRay communication protocol, a de facto standard of automotive communication protocols. The framework is composed of FlexRay model and application model where the former is built by abstractions to the specifications of FlexRay protocol. In the framework, FlexRay model is reusable for different application models with appropriate parameter settings. To the best of our knowledge, the framework is the first attempt on model checking automotive system designs considering communication protocols. Checking of core properties including timing properties are conducted to evaluate the framework.

1 Introduction

Automotive systems mainly adopt electronic control units (ECUs) to realize X-by-wire technology [10]. With the X-by-wire technology, requirements or functionalities which were not mechanically realizable are possible. Generally, ECUs in an automotive system follow communication protocols to communicate with each other through one or multiple buses. Since communication protocols greatly affect the performance of an automotive system, protocols which can support high transmission rate while still having reliability are demanded. Recently, FlexRay communication protocol is considered the de facto standard of automotive communication protocols [1,13]. FlexRay supports high transmission rate up to 10 Mbs while still having fault-tolerance abilities. These characteristics make FlexRay especially suitable for safety critical systems.

Increasing requirements for safety, driving assistance, etc., result in more complexity in the development of automotive systems. More ECUs are required in automotive systems and hence the need for handling heavy communications. Therefore, validation and verification of automotive systems became much harder. In industry, integration platform based solutions are proposed to support

C. Artho and P.C. Ölveczky (Eds.): FTSCS 2013, CCIS 419, pp. 36–53, 2014.
DOI: 10.1007/978-3-319-05416-2_4, © Springer International Publishing Switzerland 2014

automotive system design processes [7,14,15]. Integration platforms provide virtual simulation and testing for automotive system designs and implementations and thus save the cost of testing on devices. Although integration platforms can perform early phase analysis, behavioral analysis as well as verification of design models is hard to conduct because simulation and testing only focus on specific signals or nodes in a system. On the other hand, timed model checking techniques are proven effective on verification of real time systems [2,9]. Therefore, introducing timed model checking on verifying automotive system designs is considered appropriate and necessary.

This paper proposes a method for verifying design models of automotive systems using timed model checking technique. The method considers automotive systems with FlexRay protocol and focuses on communications between ECUs. Based on the method, a framework is implemented on UPPAAL, a timed model checker [3]. UPPAAL has a nice graphical user interface for precisely describing time constrained behaviors and is widely used in verifying time critical systems. However, when considering automotive systems with FlexRay protocol, it is recognized that the behaviors of FlexRay and tasks affect each other all the time. This phenomena is difficult to be precisely modeled using primitive channel synchronizations provided by UPPAAL. Therefore, we model an automotive system as the combination of FlexRay model and application model, where the former is reusable with different parameter settings of systems. Developers can build an automotive system design on application model and verify it with FlexRay model plus proper parameter settings.

The proposed model will focus on verification of design models, especially behavior and timing related to message transmissions. Three steps of abstractions are applied on the FlexRay communication protocol to remove parts and behaviors not in focus, and then build FlexRay model. To evaluate the framework, experiments on simple systems are demonstrated to examine if the framework precisely models the behavior of normal transmissions in FlexRay protocol and its ability of timing analysis for automotive system designs.

2   Related Work

Practically, automotive systems are tested and validated using integration platform solutions in the industry [7,14,15]. Integration platforms provide virtual environments for simulation and analysis of automotive systems. However, testing or simulation can only focus on specific signals or nodes in a system so that high level analyses such as behavioral analysis are difficult. Compared to integrated platforms, our framework focuses on behavior analysis and verification with time, which makes up the above deficiency. Also, to the best of our knowledge, the framework is the first attempt for verification support of automotive system designs considering communication protocol.

Another important issue of automotive systems is scheduling or performance analysis which analyzes expected execution time of applications and sees whether deadlines can be met or not. For FlexRay protocol, dealing with dynamic

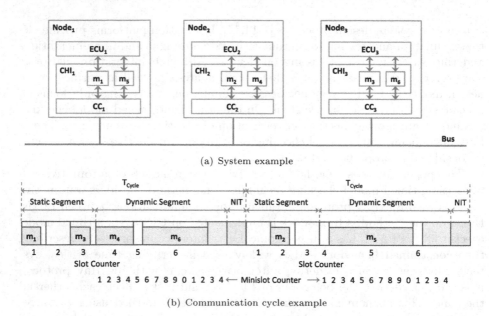

(a) System example

(b) Communication cycle example

Fig. 1. An example automotive system with FlexRay

segments in FlexRay protocol is the most important as well as difficult issue in approaches of scheduling analysis [8,11,16,17]. Though our work does not explicitly consider scheduling analysis due to simplification on ECUs, the framework is similar to model-based scheduling analysis which has been proved useful on other platforms [4,5]. Therefore, we argue that scheduling analysis is also possible using our framework with some improvements.

For FlexRay protocol itself, correctness of FlexRay protocol is verified in a few aspects. M. Gerke et al. verified the physical layer of FlexRay and proved the fault-tolerance guarantees in FlexRay [6]. J. Malinský and J. Novák verified the start-up mechanism of FlexRay [12]. Based on the results of the above work, our framework assumes the correctness of the physical layer, i.e. encoding and decoding of frames, and the start-up of FlexRay. As a result, we did not implement physical layer and start up mechanism in FlexRay model and focus only on the behavior of abstracted frame transmissions.

3   Automotive Systems with FlexRay Protocol

In the specification of FlexRay, the controller-host interface (CHI) is implementation dependent. For verification purpose, since different implementations need different models, it is necessary to declare which implementation is considered in this paper. In this section, an example of automotive system with FlexRay shown in Fig. 1 is introduced for demonstration.

As Fig. 1(a) shows, an automotive system consists of numbers of nodes connected to a bus for communications with each other. Each node consists of three parts: an ECU, a controller-host interface (CHI), and a communication controller (CC). In each node, tasks of applications are running on the ECU and send/receive data to/from buffers of the CHI. A CHI contains several buffers designated for specific data streams called frames in FlexRay. For every frame, a sending and a receiving buffer are specified. The sending buffer of a frame is implemented in the CHI where the ECU of same node has tasks designated to send data by the frame. The receiving buffer of a frame is implemented in the CHI where the ECU of same node has tasks designated to receive data by the frame. When an automotive system is executing, the CC of a node counts the time in each cycle and sends a frame from the corresponding buffer to the bus at the designated time. The CC also receives a frame and writes to the corresponding buffer if the frame is designated to be received by the node. Note that only one frame is allowed to be sent and received at the same time. It should also be noted that in a node, the status of the CC, i.e. current number of cycles, current number of slots, etc., is accessible to tasks in the ECU through the CHI and thus makes more complicated behaviors possible. In Fig. 1(a), The system has three nodes, $Node_1$, $Node_2$, and $Node_3$. Six frames are defined and sending buffers are specified in the corresponding CHIs: m_1 and m_5 in CHI_1, m_2 and m_4 in CHI_2, m_3 and m_6 in CHI_3[1].

Figure 1(b) demonstrates a two cycle instance of communications of the system shown in Fig. 1(a). Communications in FlexRay are performed based on periodic cycles. A cycle contains two time intervals with different policies for accessing the bus: static segment and dynamic segment[2]. The lengths of the two segments are fixed in every cycle and the time in a cycle is counted using slots: static slots and dynamic slots. A static slot has fixed length defined by global configuration parameter *gdStaticSlot* as a common time unit called macrotick (MT) for all nodes in a system and the length of a static segment of is defined by global configuration parameter *gNumberOfStaticSlots*. On the other hand, dynamic slots are flexible and composed of several minislots. A minislot is the basic unit of a dynamic segment and its length is defined by global configuration parameter *gdMinislot* as macroticks. The length of a dynamic segment is then defined by global configuration parameter *gNumberOfMinislots*. The index of a frame should be defined to map with a slot number therefore a frame will be sent at designated time interval, i.e. slot, in a cycle.

In Fig. 1(b), the index of a frame is set to the same slot number for convenience. Frame m_1, m_2, and m_3 are set to static slots, slot 1, 2, and 3. Frame m_4, m_5, and m_6 are set to dynamic slots, slot 4, 5, and 6. In the static segment of the first cycle, frame m_1 and m_3 are sent in slot 1 and slot 3. Though frame m_2 is not sent, the time interval of slot 2 is still elapsed with no transmission.

---

[1] Receiving buffers are not shown in the figure.

[2] Here we ignore symbol window (SW) and network idle time (NIT). The former is optional and the latter is for adjustment of cycle length. Both SW and NIT do not affect communications in automotive system designs.

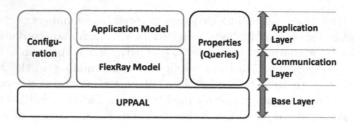

Fig. 2. The framework

In the dynamic segment of the first cycle, m_4 and m_6 are sent in slot 4 and slot 6. Frame m_4 has the length of four minislots and m_6 has the length of seven minislots. Slot 5 is not sent in first cycle but still occupies the time interval of one minislot. When the maximum slot number is reached but the maximum minislot number is not, the time proceeds with no transmission till the end of the dynamic segment. The second cycle is similar where only m_2 and m_5 are sent.

4 The Framework

Figure 2 shows the structure of the UPPAAL framework for verification of automotive systems with FlexRay demonstrated in Sect. 3. The framework consists of several parts: *UPPAAL engine, FlexRay model, Application model, Configuration,* and *Properties*. The parts of the framework are associated with three layers: base, communication, and application layers. The foundation of the framework is the UPPAAL model checker. *FlexRay model* which models the FlexRay protocol is the main component of the communication layer. *Application model* which represents the design model of an automotive system belongs to the application layer. *Configuration* and *Properties* are associated to both communication and application layers: *Configuration* contains parameters relating to both FlexRay and application models; *Properties* specify queries for verification of both FlexRay and application models in UPPAAL. FlexRay model and application model, which are the main components of the framework, will be described in Sects. 4.1 and 4.2 separately. *Configuration* and *Properties* will be mentioned within examples in Sects. 4.3 and 5.

4.1 FlexRay Model

The specifications of the FlexRay communication protocol include details of implementations on hardwares irrelevant to verification of design models of automotive systems. Therefore, to build FlexRay model in our framework, abstractions are needed to trim off irrelevant parts and behaviors. Generally, the abstractions are processes of modeling the specifications of the FlexRay protocol based on our understanding of the FlexRay protocol and our knowledge/experiences of using UPPAAL. We divide the processes of the abstractions

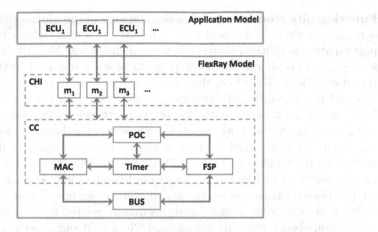

Fig. 3. The structure of FlexRay model

into three steps: (1) essential component selection, (2) functionality reduction, and (3) state space reduction. Figure 3 shows the structure of the FlexRay model after the abstraction. The details of the three steps abstraction are described as follows.

Essential Component Selection. For the purpose of verifying the design model of an automotive system, we only focus on functionalities relating to sending and receiving frames when building FlexRay model. The first step is then to select essential and necessary components providing frame transmission functionalities. Since we only focus on design level verification, specifications regarding low level behaviors such as clock synchronization and frame encoding/decoding are out of focus. We also assume that there is no noise interference in transmissions[3]. Therefore, we only need three components in FlexRay protocol: *protocol operation control (POC)*, *media access control (MAC)*, and *frame and symbol processing (FSP)*. POC monitors overall status of CC and manages other components. MAC is responsible for sending frames in corresponding sending buffers of CHI at specific times in each cycle. FSP is responsible for receiving frames and storing data to receiving buffers in CHI for tasks in ECUs to read. Besides POC, MAC, and FSP, we also need Timer which helps monitoring of timing in each cycle and slot. Timer is not treated as a component in the specifications of the FlexRay protocol but we have to build it since timer is used everywhere in almost all components of a CC. The bus is implemented as a variable accessible to MAC and FSP. The sending/receiving of frames is then represented by writing/reading data to/from the bus variable.

---

[3] Generally, FlexRay only captures and throws errors. An application has the responsibility to handle errors thrown by FlexRay. Though not in the scope of this paper, if transmission errors are of interest, they can be modeled by adding error situations/states explicitly in FlexRay model.

Functionality Reduction. After the first step of the abstractions, the selected components *POC*, *MAC*, and *FSP* still have irrelevant behaviors which do not participate in activities related to frame transmissions. Also, the irrelevant behaviors may still cooperate with components already removed in the first step of the abstractions. Therefore, the second step is to remove the irrelevant behaviors and functionalities of the selected components. In the framework, we only focus on regular transmissions of frames and therefore only the normal state of *POC* is meaningful and other states are ignored. Furthermore, we consider that the clock is synchronized between nodes and there is no external interference in normal transmissions. This results that some functionalities of CC become unnecessary for FlexRay model. For example, functionalities such as adjustments for reactions on transmission errors, e.g. fault tolerance feature of the bus, can be ignored. Also, similar functionalities mainly related to error managements in other components and CHI are ignored. Note that our most priority of modeling the FlexRay protocol is to fulfill the need of timing analysis, which is not required to consider situations with errors in the first place. Therefore, the modeling process is more like picking up the traces of successful frame transmissions but trimming off error processing behaviors.

State Space Reduction. After the above two steps of the abstractions, FlexRay model looks simple considering the number of explicit states and transitions. However, the complexity is still high and hardly acceptable since there are many variables especially clocks in FlexRay model. In some cases even the size of an application is not considered large, UPPAAL suffers from state explosion when checking properties. Therefore, further abstraction is necessary to reduce the state space while the behaviors of frame transmissions in the FlexRay protocol is still precisely modeled. By reviewing the above two steps of abstractions, recall that there are two assumptions of FlexRay model in the framework: (1) all nodes are synchronized all the time; (2) there is no error during frame transmissions. With (1), all nodes start a cycle at the same time; with (2) all nodes finish a cycle at the same time. That is, no node is going to be late because of transmission errors. Therefore, it is reasonable to conclude that we do not need a CC for every node, i.e. one CC is enough. This helps us to remove the complicated behaviors which only synchronize the clocks of nodes of a system. Furthermore, we also cancel the process of counting minislots in dynamic segment and instead calculating the number of minislots directly using lengths of dynamic frames and related parameters. This helps avoiding small time zones not meaningful in checking properties. Most properties concern the timing of the start and the end of a frame transmission but not in the middle of a frame transmission.

FlexRay model constructed after three steps of abstraction is shown in Figs. 4 and 5, where *MAC* is separated into *MAC_static* and *MAC_dynamic*. An example will be given in Sect. 4.3 for demonstrating how FlexRay model works in cooperation with *Application model* explained in Sect. 4.2.

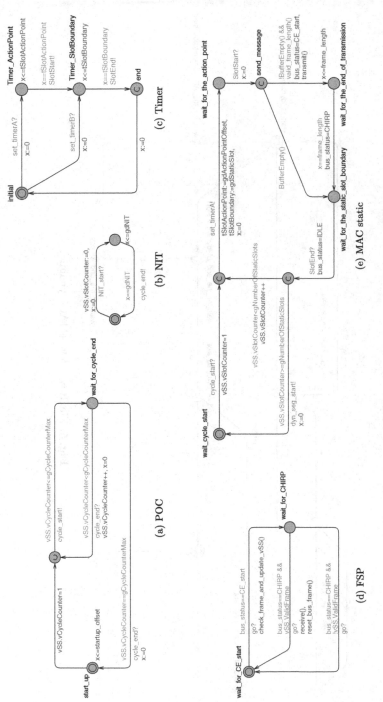

Fig. 4. FlexRay model (POC, NIT, Timer, FSP, MAC static)

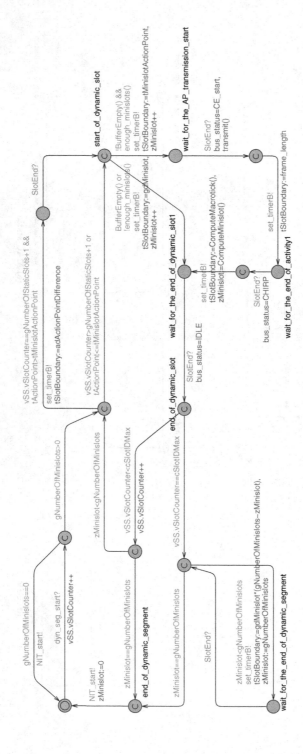

Fig. 5. FlexRay model (MAC dynamic)

4.2   Application Model

Application model represents ECUs in an application and thus consists of multiple tasks. As shown in the upper part of Fig. 3, application model accesses the buffers in CHIs to communicate with CCs for sending/receiving frames. Since *Application model* tightly depends on actual automotive systems to be designed by developers, we leave most of the jobs to developers in building *Application model* and give only simple directions on how to use *FlexRay model* of the framework.

Only One Task in an ECU. For simplicity, in this paper we build one module in UPPAAL to represent one task and an ECU only has one task. Therefore we can omit modeling of schedulers in ECUs. Developers have to build a scheduler module when scheduling in an ECU is considered necessary.

Use of Functions to Access Buffers in CHIs. In an automotive system with FlexRay protocol, tasks in different nodes cannot communicate directly but through FlexRay protocol, i.e. *FlexRay model* of the framework. Therefore, when sending data, a task has to write data to the corresponding sending buffer in the CHI of the same node, and let the CC do the transmissions. When receiving data, the process is similar but in the reverse order. To make things simple, we prepare functions for reading and writing data from and to specified buffer. Developers only need to put these functions as actions on transitions of tasks and insert proper parameters. The functions are defined as follows:

```
void write_msg_to_CHI(t_msg_slot msg, int value, int len);
int read_msg_from_CHI(t_msg_slot msg);
void clean_send_buffer_CHI(t_msg_slot msg);
void clean_receive_buffer_CHI(t_msg_slot msg);
```

Since we do not focus on the contents of the data in a frame, the data is represented simply by integer type and may be ignored. Note that msg of type integer is the index of a frame as well as the index of the corresponding buffer; len is the length of the frame in macroticks. Note that reading the data from a buffer does not clean up the buffer so there are also functions for cleaning buffers. Developers have to clean a buffer by themselves using buffer cleaning functions.

4.3   Example

In this section, a simple sender/receiver example [18] will be demonstrated to show how the design model of an automotive system built as *Application model* looks like and how frames are transmitted by *FlexRay model*. This example consists of tasks having simple behaviors so that we can focus on reading/writing buffers, frame transmissions, and parameter settings of the system. Figure 6 shows the plan of assigning indexes of frames. There are ten messages/frames

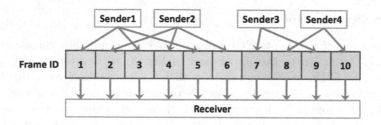

Fig. 6. Frame setting of the sender/receiver example (SR1)

indexed from 1 to 10. The frames are used in five ECUs/tasks, Sender1, Sender2, Sender3, Sender4, and Receiver. Which task sends/receives which frame can be easily recognized by directions of the arrows. For example, Sender1 is designed to send frames 1, 3, and 5, and Receiver is designated to receive all frames. Frames 1 to 6 are static frames and frames 7 to 10 are dynamic frames.

```
typedef int[1,cSlotIDMax] t_msg_slot;
const t_msg_slot msg1= 1;
...
const t_msg_slot msg10= 10;
```

As mentioned in Sect. 4.2, the indexes of frames are the same as the indexes of buffers. Also, the indexes of frames indicate the slot numbers of the communication cycles in *FlexRay model*. Below shows the major parameters of the example. The unit of parameters is macrotick except the first four parameters.

```
int gCycleCounterMax=6; //max. number of cycle
int gNumberOfStaticSlots=6; //number of static segment slots
int gNumberOfMinislots=32; //number of dynamic segment minislots
int cSlotIDMax=10; //max. number of slot ID
int gdNIT=4; //period of NIT (in macrotick)
int gdActionPointOffset=2; //static offset
int gdStaticSlot=5; //number of macroticks in a static slot
int gdMinislotActionPointOffset=1; //offset of minislot
int gdMinislot=3; //number of macroticks in a minislot
```

Figure 7 shows modules of Sender1, Sender3, and Receiver in *Application model*, where Sender2 and Sender4 are similar and skipped. Note that go? is the reception of the urgent channel go. Urgent channel always sends a signal immediately without delay when a transition with go? is fired. For example, by using go?, Sender1 watches the status of related buffers and writes data to a buffer immediately when the buffer is detected empty. On the other hand, Sender3 sends dynamic frames whose length vary from 18 to 20 macroticks. In the framework we define global variables to represent buffers (i.e. status of CHIs) and slot status (i.e. status of CCs). *Application model* can access the status of CHIs and CCs through global variables CHI_Buffer_send, CHI_Buffer_receive, and vSS.

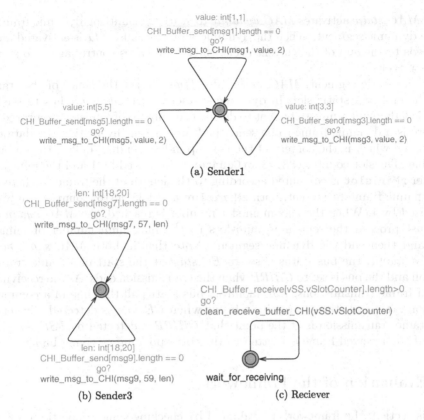

(a) Sender1

(b) Sender3

(c) Reciever

Fig. 7. Selected tasks of the sender/receiver example (*SR1*)

```
typedef struct {
    int[0,MaxDataValue] data;
    int[0,pPayloadLengthDynMax] length;
} Buffer;
Buffer CHI_Buffer_send[cSlotIDMax+1]; //sending buffers
Buffer CHI_Buffer_receive[cSlotIDMax+1]; //receiving buffers

typedef struct{
    int[0,gCycleCounterMax] vCycleCounter; //current cycle
    int[0,cSlotIDMax] vSlotCounter; //current slot
} T_SlotStatus;
T_SlotStatus vSS; //slot status of CC
```

In this system, sending buffers can be considered always filled for convenience. Therefore we may focus on the flow of a static or dynamic frame transmission in FlexRay model shown in Figs. 4 and 5. When the system starts, FlexRay model starts from *POC*. Like the ordering of segments in a communication cycle shown in Fig. 1(b), *POC* counts the number of cycles and activates *MAC_static* for transmitting static frames in the static segment. When the static segment ends, *MAC_static* activates *MAC_dynamic* to start transmitting dynamic frames in the dynamic segment. When the dynamic segment ends, *NIT* is activated and proceeds to the end of the current cycle, then *POC* takes control again to start another cycle.

In the static segment, *MAC_static* calls *Timer* to set the times of the start and the end of a static slot. In dynamic segment, *MAC_dynamic* has to see if there is a dynamic frame to be sent to decide the number of minislots to proceed. If there is a dynamic frame to be sent, the frame is sent by writing the data of the frame, which is the content of the corresponding sending buffer, to the bus variable. The slot counter `vSS.vSlotCounter` is increased by 1 and the minislot counter `zMinislot` is computed according to the length of the frame. If there is no dynamic frame to be sent, both `zMinislot` and `vSS.vSlotCounter` are just increased by 1. When the maximum slot number is reached, the *MAC_dynamic* will just proceed the remaining minislots to the maximum number of minislots, and then end the dynamic segment. Note that in both *MAC_static* and *MAC_dynamic*, the bus status is set to *EC_start* at the start of a frame transmission and the bus is set to *CHIRP* when the transmission ends. As the receiving side of frame transmissions, *FSP* monitors bus status all the time in a communication cycle and starts to receive a frame when *CE_start* is detected. The end of a frame transmission is at the point that *CHIRP* is detected by *FSP* and the data of the received frame is written to the corresponding receiving buffer.

5   Evaluation of the Framework

In this section, the framework is evaluated by checking some properties on two example applications [18]. Firstly, the sender/receiver example (*SR1*) demonstrated in Sect. 4.3 is used to verify core properties related to frame transmissions of FlexRay protocol to see whether the framework is built right on the scope of frame transmissions. Then we introduce another sender/receiver example (*SR2*) to illustrate possible usage of the framework for timing analysis. Both examples are checked by using UPPAAL 4.1.14 on a machine of following specifications: Windows 8 with Intel i5 2.3GHz and 8GM RAM. Memory usage and CPU times in checking *SR1* are listed in Table 1[4].

Table 1. CPU time/state space/memory usage in checking *SR1*

Query	CPU time (s)	States explored	Memory usage (MB)
q1	1.8	343,821	27.5
q2	14.2	1,121,950	107.3
q3	14.5	1,118,872	112.1
q4	4.8	470,860	106.0
q5	7.2	470,860	106.7

---

[4] We used `verifyta` in command-line with -u option.

Is the Framework Built Right? For *SR1*, we give and check some properties/queries based on the specifications of the FlexRay protocol relating to frame transmissions. The results give the hints for evaluating whether *FlexRay model* of the framework is built right, i.e. follows the specifications of the FlexRay protocol in the scope of normal frame transmissions. Recall that the designs of the tasks in SR1 make it reasonable for us to keep the focus on only frame transmissions in FlexRay model. The checked queries are listed as follows:

```
q1. A<> forall (i:int[1,10]) (CHI_Buffer_send[i].length>0);
q2. (CHI_Buffer_send[1].length>0) --> (CHI_Buffer_send[1].length==0);
q3. (CHI_Buffer_send[1].length>0) --> (CHI_Buffer_receive[1].length>0);
q4. A[] forall (i:int[1,10]) ((CHI_Buffer_receive[i].length>0)
      imply (vSS.vSlotCounter==i ));
q5. A[] forall (i:int[1,10]) forall (j:int[1,10])
      (CHI_Buffer_receive[i].length>0 && CHI_Buffer_receive[j].length>0)
      imply (j==i);
```

Queries q1, q2, q3 check basic functionalities considering the buffers in the CHI. q1 says all buffers in the system can be filled with data, which means the tasks can successfully write messages to sending buffers. q2 says the data in a sending buffer will be erased/sent eventually. q3 says for a sending buffer with data, the corresponding receiving buffer will be filled, which means frames can be correctly delivered by the CC. Since q1, q2, and q3 are all satisfied[5], we can confirm that the tasks do communicate through FlexRay model. That is, frame transmissions are performed by *FlexRay model* as expected in the task designs in *Application model*. Then we check queries q4 and q5 considering the time of frame transmissions (slots). q4 says if a receiving buffer has data, the communication cycle is in the interval of the corresponding slot, which means frame transmissions are occurring in the right slot (time interval)[6]. q5 says there is only one frame being sent in any slot. From the result that q4 and q5 are both satisfied, we can confirm that *FlexRay model* does follow the specifications of the FlexRay protocol regarding normal frame transmissions. Therefore, we conclude that we built the framework right under the scope of normal frame transmissions of the FlexRay protocol.

How to Check Timing Properties? One of the major characteristics of the framework is the ability to describe behaviors with time constraints. Here we introduce another sender/receiver example (*SR2*) shown in Fig. 8 [18]. In this system, *Sender* sends a message periodically while *Receiver* receives a message immediately when the receiving buffer is detected having data. Note that *Sender* checks periodically if the sending buffer is filled and only writes data to the buffer when the buffer is empty. The major parameter settings are as follows:

```
int gCycleCounterMax=6; //max. number of cycle
int gNumberOfStaticSlots=3; //number of static segment slots
int gNumberOfMinislots=30; //number of dynamic segment minislots
```

---

[5] For q2 and q3, all ten messages of indexes 1 to 10 are checked.

[6] Note that *Receiver* receives the data as soon as a receiving buffer is filled.

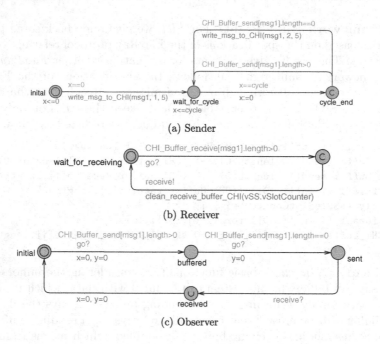

(a) Sender

(b) Receiver

(c) Observer

Fig. 8. Another sender/receiver example (SR2)

```
int cSlotIDMax=6;  //maximum number of slot ID
int gdNIT=2; //period of NIT (in macrotick)
int gdActionPointOffset=2; //static offset
int gdStaticSlot=10; // number of macroticks in a static slot
int gdMinislotActionPointOffset=2; //offset of minislot
int gdMinislot=5; // number of macroticks in a minislot
```

Though there is only one frame to be sent/received, the system is defined to have six slots including three static slots. Also, the only frame is set to slot 1, i.e. the first static slot, and the length of the cycle of *Sender* is set to 100 macroticks.

To write property of response time of msg1, we built *Observer* to monitor changes in the sending buffer of msg1. *Observer* moves from the initial state to state **buffered** once the sending buffer is written by *Sender*. Once the sending buffer is cleaned by FlexRay model when the transmission starts, *Observer* immediately moves to state **sent** and waits *Receiver* to send signal **receive**. The signal **receive** indicates that the transmission is finished and the receiving buffer is written with the data of the received frame. Note that *Observer* has two clocks x and y where x starts counting at the time the sending buffer is written, and y starts counting at the time the sending buffer is cleaned. Therefore, by examining the value of clock x at state **received** of *Observer*, we can know the response time (macrotick, MT) of msg1; by examining the value of clock y at state **received** of *Observer*, we can know the frame transmission time of msg1. Now we can write some queries about the response times of msg1.

```
q1[Y].  A[] (observer.received imply observer.y == 5)
q2[Y].  E<> (observer.received && observer.x == 6)
q3[N].  E<> (observer.received && observer.x < 6)
q4[Y].  E<> (observer.received && observer.x == 182)
q5[N].  E<> (observer.received && observer.x > 182)
```

Note that in each query, [Y] or [N] indicates the checking result of the query as satisfied or not satisfied. The result of q1 shows that the frame transmission time of msg1 is 5MT, which exactly matches the setting of the length of *msg1*. The results of q2 and q3 show that the best case response time (BCRT) of msg1 is 6MT, which is the sum of the frame length (5MT) and the static slot offset (1MT). The results of q4 and q5 show that the best case response time (WCRT) of msg1 is 182MT, which is the sum of the lengths of the static segment (30MT), the dynamic segment (150MT) and the NIT (2MT).

Discussions. In SR1, we focus on frame transmissions in *FlexRay model* and checked some related properties. With the results, we conclude that the framework is built right in the scope of normal frame transmissions of the FlexRay protocol. With only a few properties checked, one may doubt that it is not sufficient to confirm that *FlexRay model* of the framework conform to the specifications of the FlexRay protocol. For this issue, we argue that since we only focus on normal frame transmissions of the FlexRay protocol, the checking results are satisfiable at current status of the framework. Furthermore, since the structure of the framework follows the structure of the specifications of the FlexRay protocol, when we want to extend the functionalities of *FlexRay model*, current status of *FlexRay model* can be a base to implement the extensions.

In SR2, the checking of the response times shows that the framework is able to check timing properties with the help of *Observer*. This is a common technique for checking complex properties since UPPAAL only support simple timed computational tree logic (TCTL) formulas. Also, to decide the value of BCET and WCET to be filled in a query, currently we have to guess according to the parameters of a system. This may result some trial and error, or we may utilize some traditional timing analysis techniques.

For the feasibility of applying the framework in the industry, since in this paper we only focus on building *FlexRay model*, the modeling of the tasks in a system is left to developers. Therefore, developers have to be familiar with the usage of UPPAAL. Also, it is necessary to have a methodology of modeling tasks, which may be adopted from the experiences of the modeling on integrated platforms. Another issue is the performance of the framework. From the results shown in Table 1, the state space is quite large considering that the system of SR1 is very simple. The performance issue would be a major problem when applying the framework to industrial automotive system designs.

6   Conclusion and Future Work

In this paper, an UPPAAL framework for model checking automotive system designs with FlexRay protocol is introduced and evaluated. The framework consists of FlexRay model and application model: the former is built by abstractions to the FlexRay protocol and can be reused for different applications with proper parameter settings represented by global variables in UPPAAL. To the best of our knowledge, the framework is the first attempt for model checking automotive system designs considering communication protocols. To evaluate the framework, we demonstrated two simple systems and checked some queries/properties. From the results, we conclude that the framework is built right in accordance with normal frame transmissions of the FlexRay protocol and is able to check timing properties.

In this paper, we showed that a reusable module on top of UPPAAL, i.e. FlexRay model, could be realized for verification of applications with FlexRay protocol. We argue that only providing a general purpose model checker is not sufficient for verifying practical systems. Additional descriptions and mechanisms such as scheduling of tasks and emulation of hardware devices are usually needed to precisely model and verify the behavior of practical systems. Furthermore, these additional mechanisms are usually common for systems belonging to a specific application domain and are possible to be provided as reusable frameworks and libraries. Therefore, integrating such frameworks and libraries is crucial for promoting practical applications of model checkers in the industry.

Currently, the framework can only support scheduling analysis in systems that an ECU has only one task, or developers have to build scheduler modules, which is not easy. Therefore, we plan to add scheduler modules to support general scheduling analysis. We also plan to conduct more experiments on practical automotive systems to discover more usages and possible improvements of the framework.

References

1. Altran Technologies: FlexRay Specifications Version 3.0.1 (2010)
2. Bel Mokadem, H., Berard, B., Gourcuff, V., De Smet, O., Roussel, J.-M.: Verification of a timed multitask system with UPPAAL. IEEE Trans. Autom. Sci. Eng. **7**(4), 921–932 (2010)
3. Bengtsson, J., Larsen, K., Larsson, F., Pettersson, P., Yi, W.: UPPAAL - a tool suite for automatic verification of real-time systems. Hybrid Systems III. LNCS, vol. 1066, pp. 232–243. Springer, Heidelberg (1996)
4. Bøgholm, T., Kragh-Hansen, H., Olsen, P., Thomsen, B., Larsen, K.G.: Model-based schedulability analysis of safety critical hard real-time java programs. In: Proceedings of the 6th International Workshop on Java Technologies for Real-Time and Embedded Systems (JTRES'08), pp. 106–114 (2008)
5. David, A., Rasmussen, J.I., Larsen, K.G., Skou, A.: Model-based framework for schedulability analysis using Uppaal 4.1. Model-Based Design for Embedded Systems. Computational Analysis, Synthesis, and Design of Dynamic Systems, pp. 93–119. CRC Press, Boca Raton (2009)
6. Gerke, M., Ehlers, R., Finkbeiner, B., Peter, H.-J.: Model checking the FlexRay physical layer protocol. In: Kowalewski, S., Roveri, M. (eds.) FMICS 2010. LNCS, vol. 6371, pp. 132–147. Springer, Heidelberg (2010)

7. Giusto, P., Ferrari, A., Lavagno, L., Brunel, J.Y., Fourgeau, E., Sangiovanni-Vincentelli, A.: Automotive virtual integration platforms: why's, what's, and how's. In: IEEE International Conference on Computer Design: VLSI in Computers and Processors, pp. 370–378 (2002)
8. Hagiescu, A., Bordoloi, U.D., Chakraborty, S., Sampath, P., Ganesan, P.V.V., Ramesh, S.: Performance analysis of FlexRay-based ECU networks. In: DAC'07, pp. 284–289 (2007)
9. Hessel, A., Larsen, K.G., Mikucionis, M., Nielsen, B., Pettersson, P., Skou, A.: Testing real-time systems using UPPAAL. In: Hierons, R.M., Bowen, J.P., Harman, M. (eds.) FORTEST. LNCS, vol. 4949, pp. 77–117. Springer, Heidelberg (2008)
10. Hiraoka, T., Eto, S., Nishihara, O., Kumamoto, H.: Fault tolerant design for X-by-wire vehicle. In: SICE'04 Annual Conference, vol. 3, pp. 1940–1945 (2004)
11. Jung, K.H., Song, M.G., Lee, D.I., Jin, S.H.: Priority-based scheduling of dynamic segment in FlexRay network. In: International Conference on Control, Automation and Systems (ICCAS'08), pp. 1036–1041 (2008)
12. Malinský, J., Novák, J.: Verification of FlexRay start-up mechanism by timed automata. Metrol. Measur. Syst. **17**(3), 461–480 (2010)
13. Navet, N., Song, Y., Simonot-Lion, F., Wilwert, C.: Trends in automotive communication systems. Proc. IEEE **93**(6), 1204–1223 (2005)
14. Qtronic GmbH, Germany: Virtual integration and test of automotive ECUs. In: Automotive Testing Expo North America, ASAM Open Technology Forum (2011)
15. Sangiovanni-Vincentelli, A.: Electronic-system design in the automobile industry. IEEE Micro **23**(3), 8–18 (2003)
16. Tanasa, B., Bordoloi, U., Kosuch, S., Eles, P., Peng, Z.: Schedulability analysis for the dynamic segment of FlexRay: a generalization to slot multiplexing. In: IEEE 18th Real-Time and Embedded Technology and Applications Symposium (RTAS'12), pp. 185–194 (2012)
17. Zeng, H., Ghosal, A., Di Natale, M.: Timing analysis and optimization of FlexRay dynamic segment. In: IEEE 10th International Conference on Computer and Information Technology (CIT'10), pp. 1932–1939 (2010)
18. UPPAAL models used in this paper: https://github.com/h-lin/FTSCS2013

Early Analysis of Soft Error Effects
for Aerospace Applications
Using Probabilistic Model Checking

Khaza Anuarul Hoque[1][(✉)], Otmane Ait Mohamed[1], Yvon Savaria[2],
and Claude Thibeault[3]

[1] Concordia University, Montreal, Canada
{k_hoque,ait}@ece.concordia.ca
[2] Polytechnique Montréal, Montreal, Canada
yvon.savaria@polymtl.ca
[3] École de Technologie Supérieure, Montreal, Canada
claude.thibeault@etsmtl.ca

Abstract. SRAM-based FPGAs are increasingly popular in the
aerospace industry for their field programmability and low cost. However, they suffer from cosmic radiation induced Single Event Upsets
(SEUs), commonly known as soft errors. In safety-critical applications,
the dependability of the design is a prime concern since failures may have
catastrophic consequences. An early analysis of dependability and performance of such safety-critical applications can reduce the design effort
and increases the confidence. This paper introduces a novel methodology
based on probabilistic model checking, to analyze the dependability and
performability properties of safety-critical systems for early design decisions. Starting from a high-level description of a model, a Markov reward
model is constructed from the Control Data Flow Graph (CDFG) of the
system and a component characterization library targeting FPGAs. Such
an exhaustive model captures all the failures and repairs possible in the
system within the radiation environment. We present a case study based
on a benchmark circuit to illustrate the applicability of the proposed
approach and to demonstrate that a wide range of useful dependability and performability properties can be analyzed using our proposed
methodology.

1   Introduction

Dependability and performability are major concerns in safety-critical and
mission-critical applications common in the aerospace industry. Electronic components are exposed to more intense cosmic rays when flying at high altitude. It
has been reported that long-haul aircrafts flying at airplane altitudes experience
a neutron-flux roughly 500 times higher than that at ground level in the worst
case [13]. For space missions, the rate of single event effects can be much worse.
Due to field programmability, absence of non-recurring engineering costs, low

C. Artho and P.C. Ölveczky (Eds.): FTSCS 2013, CCIS 419, pp. 54–70, 2014.
DOI: 10.1007/978-3-319-05416-2_5, © Springer International Publishing Switzerland 2014

manufacturing costs and other advantages, SRAM-based FPGAs are increasingly attractive. Unfortunately, a great disadvantage of these devices is their sensitivity to radiation effects that can cause bit flips in memory elements and ionisation induced transient faults in semiconductors, commonly known as soft errors and soft faults [1,21]. Therefore, in aerospace industry, the possibility of cosmic radiation induced soft error grows dramatically at higher altitudes. However, an early analysis of dependability and performance impacts of such errors and faults on the design provides opportunities for the designer to develop more reliable and efficient designs and may reduce the overall cost associated with the design effort. Our work aims at achieving these goals.

This paper proposes a means by which formal verification methods can be applied at early design stages to analyze the dependability and performability of reconfigurable systems. In particular, the focus is on probabilistic model checking [8]. *Probabilistic model checking* is used to verify the systems whose behavior is stochastic in nature. It is mainly based on the construction and analysis of a probabilistic model, typically a Markov chain or a Markov process. These models are constructed in an exhaustive fashion. Indeed, the models explore all possible states that might occur in a system. Probabilistic model checking can be used to analyze a wide range of dependability and performability properties. In contrast, in discrete-event simulations, approximate results are generated by averaging results from large number of random samples. Probabilistic model checking applies numerical computations to provide exact and accurate results.

To analyze a design at high level, we start from its Control Data Flow Graph (CDFG) [17] representation, obtained from a high-level description of the design expressed using a language such as C++. The possible implementation options of the CDFG, with different sets of available components and their possible failures, fault recovery and repairs in the radiation environment are then modeled with the PRISM modeling language [24]. The failure rate of the components are obtained from a worst-case component characterization library. Since the FPGA repair mechanism known as scrubbing [5] can be used in conjunction with other forms of mitigation techniques such as TMR [6] to increase the reliability, we demonstrate in this paper that *rescheduling* [4,16] could be a good alternative candidate in some cases compared to a redundancy-based solution. In the proposed methodology, we show how to use the PRISM model checker tool to model and evaluate dependability, performability and area trade-offs between available design options. Current work in this area either separates the dependability analysis from performance/area analysis, or do not analyze such safety-critical applications at early design stage. Commercial tools for reliability analysis, such as Isograph [15], cannot be used for performance evaluation of such systems as they do not support Markov reward models [27]. Since the probabilistic model checker PRISM allows reward modeling, our work overcomes this limitation. The motivation of the work, the application area, the fault model, considered fault tolerance techniques and the use of probabilistic model checking for system analysis, makes our work unique.

The remainder of the paper is organized as follows. Section 2 reviews motivations and related works. Section 3 describes the background about soft error effects, soft error mitigation techniques and probabilistic model checking. The proposed methodology and modeling details are discussed in Sect. 4, and in Sect. 5, we present a case study using our proposed methodology. Section 6 concludes the paper with future research directions.

2 Motivation and Related Work

Consider the CDFG of a synchronous dataflow DSP application shown in Fig. 1. Based on data dependencies, this application can be carried out in a minimum of three control steps using the CDFG-1 shown in Fig. 2, with two adders and two multipliers. Such implementation provides a throughput of $1/3 = 0.33$. Another alternative consists of implementing the application with only one multiplier and two adders but in four control steps, as shown by CDFG-2 in Fig. 2. In that case the throughput is 0.25. Based on the priority of throughput or area metric, the appropriate CDFG is selected.

However, inclusion of a reliability metric based on a fault recovery mechanism can make the case more complex and difficult to evaluate. When a resource fails (due to a configuration bit flip), an alternative schedule can be derived to continue the system operation using the remaining resources, most likely at a lower throughput. For example, to maximize the throughput, CDFG-1 is implemented. For a single component failure, e.g. a multiplier, the application can be rescheduled to implement CDFG-2 with lower throughput. Such fault tolerance approach was introduced in [4,12,16] for fault-secure microarchitectures and multiprocessors. For FPGA-based designs, such a fault recovery technique can be adopted as well and we explore the dependability, area and performance trade-offs for such systems. We must mention that the controller for rescheduling the operations is assumed to be fault-free. This controller can be implemented in a separate chip with proper fault-tolerance mechanisms. Considering the example again, we observe that, if another multiplier fails, the CDFG cannot be rescheduled and the system fails to continue its operation. For FPGA-based safety-critical applications, systematic system failure at first occurrence of a soft-error is not acceptable. *Scrubbing* with partial reconfiguration capability [5] can repair bit-flips in the configuration memory without disrupting system operations. Scrubbing can be done at a specified rate meaning that there might be

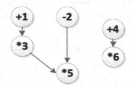

Fig. 1. Sample CDFG

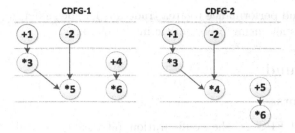

Fig. 2. CDFGs scheduled over available resources

a period of time between the moment the upset occurs and the moment when it is repaired. That is why another form of mitigation is required, such as a redundancy-based solution [6]. In this work, we use probabilistic model checking to evaluate the dependability and performability vs area trade-offs and demonstrate that in some cases, a redundancy-based solution might not be the best choice as one may expect. Alternatively, for those cases, *rescheduling* in conjunction with *scrubbing* can be a good option.

High-level synthesis algorithms such as forced-directed list scheduling [23] can generate different CDFGs depending on components availability. Switching to another CDFG allows recovering from a failure while a system can continue its operation, possibly with a lower throughput. For many years, fault tolerance techniques and reliability analysis of complex systems have been active research area both in academia and industry. In [29], the authors proposed a reliability-centric high-level synthesis approach to address soft errors. Their framework uses reliability characterization to select the most reliable implementation for each operation fulfilling latency and area constraints. In addition, researchers dedicated lots of efforts in modeling the behavior of gracefully degradable large-scale systems using continuous-time Markov reward models [3,14]. In [26], a case study is presented to measure the performance of a multiprocessor system using a continuous-time Markov reward model. An approach for analyzing performance, area and reliability using a Markov reward model is presented in [19]. The authors used transistor lifetimes to model the reliability and performance, hence the model is composed of non-repairable modules. Use of a non-formal commercial tool makes their approach quite rigid in terms of analysis. Moreover, in their proposed approach, the reward calculation is manual, as the traditional commercial tools for reliability analysis do not support reward modeling.

Even though our model has similarities to performance analysis, our approach is more flexible because we use probabilistic model checking. Our work focuses on a different fault model: cosmic radiation induced configuration bit-flips in FPGAs. Since scrubbing is possible in FPGA designs, we also add repair to our Markov reward model. In consideration of the failure type, repair capability, use of a characterization library to model the system, the application of our work and our methodology is different from and novel when compared to all the related works described above. To our knowledge, this is the first attempt to analyze the dependability and performance to area trade-offs for such safety-critical systems at early design stage using probabilistic model checking.

3   Background

3.1   Soft Errors

In SRAM-based FPGAs, the configuration bitstream determines the routing and functionality of the design. However, a change in the value of one of the SRAM cells can potentially modify the functionality of the design and can lead to catastrophic consequences. The major reason for such inadvertent bit flips in high-altitude is soft errors caused by cosmic radiation. When these particles impact a silicon substrate, they result in the generation of excess carriers, which when deposited on the internal capacitances of a circuit node can result in an upset to the data value stored. The lowering of supply voltages and nodal capacitances with recent technologies have increased the possibility of observing bit flips. Due to this increasing concern, there are several mitigation techniques proposed for tackling the soft error problem.

A mainstream SEU repair technique in SRAM-based FPGAs is configuration scrubbing [11]. Scrubbing refers to the periodic readback of the FPGA's configuration memory, comparing it to a known good copy, and writing back any corrections required. By periodically scrubbing a device, maximum limits may be placed on the period of time that a configuration error can be present in a device. A variation to improve scrubbing is known as *partial reconfiguration* [5]. This is beneficial as it allows a system to repair bit-flips in the configuration memory without disrupting its operations. Configuration scrubbing prevents the build-up of multiple configuration faults. Although scrubbing ensures that the configuration bitstream can remain relatively free of errors, over the long run, there is a period of time between the moment an upset occurs and the moment when it is repaired in which the FPGA configuration is incorrect. Thus the design may not function correctly during that time. To completely mitigate the errors caused by SEUs, scrubbing is used in conjunction with another form of mitigation that masks the faults in the bitstream.

A scrub rate describes how often a scrub cycle should occur. It is denoted by either a unit of time between scrubs, or a percentage (scrub cycle time divided by the time between scrubs). There are direct relationships between scrubbing rate, device size, device reliability and device safety, hence the scrub rate should be determined by the expected upset rate of the device for the given application.

3.2   Probabilistic Model Checking

Model checking [8] is a well established formal verification technique to verify the correctness of finite-state systems. Given a formal model of the system to be verified in terms of labelled state transitions and the properties to be verified in terms of temporal logic, the model checking algorithm exhaustively and automatically explores all the possible states in a system to verify if the property is satisfiable or not. If not, a counterexample is generated. *Probabilistic model checking* deals with systems that exhibit stochastic behaviour, such as fault-tolerant systems. Probabilistic model checking is based on the construction and analysis of a probabilistic model of the system, typically a Markov chain. In this paper, we focus on the continuous-time Markov chains (CTMCs) and Markov reward models [27], widely used for reliability and performance analysis.

A CTMC comprises a set of states S and a transition rate matrix $\mathbf{R} : S \times S \to \mathbb{R}_{\geq 0}$. The rate $\mathbf{R}(s, s')$ defines the delay before which a transition between states s and s' takes place. If $\mathbf{R}(s, s') \neq 0$ then the probability that a transition between the states s and s' might take place within time t can be defined as $1 - e^{-\mathbf{R}(s,s') \times t}$. No transitions will take place if $\mathbf{R}(s, s') = 0$. Exponentially distributed delays are suitable for modelling component lifetimes and inter-arrival times.

In the model-checking approach to performance and dependability analysis, a model of the system under consideration is required together with a desired property or performance/dependability measure. In case of stochastic modelling, such models are typically CTMCs, while properties are usually expressed in some form of extended temporal logic such as Continuous Stochastic Logic (CSL) [2], a stochastic variant of the well-known Computational Tree Logic (CTL) [8]. Below are a number of illustrative examples with their natural language translation:

1. $P_{\geq 0.98}[\Diamond \ complete]$ - "The probability of the system eventually completing its execution successfully is at least 0.98".
2. $shutdown \Rightarrow P_{\geq 0.95}[\neg \ fail \ U^{\leq 200} \ up]$ - "Once a shutdown has occurred, with probability 0.95 or greater, the system will successfully recover within 200 h and without any further failures occurring".

Additional properties can be specified by adding the notion of rewards. Each state (and/or transition) of the model is assigned a real-valued reward, allowing queries such as:

1. $R = [\Diamond \ success]$ - "What is the expected reward accumulated before the system successfully terminates?"

Rewards can be used to specify a wide range of measures of interest, for example, the number of correctly delivered packets or the time that the system is operational. Of course, conversely, the rewards can be considered as costs, such as power consumption, expected number of failures, etc.

4   Proposed Methodology

In Fig. 3, we present the proposed methodology, which reuses some elements from a methodology proposed in [28], namely the CDFG extraction and the concept of using a characterization library (which was created with a different set of tools). We start from the dataflow graph of the application. Different tools such as GAUT [9], SUIF [10] etc. could be used to extract the dataflow graph from a

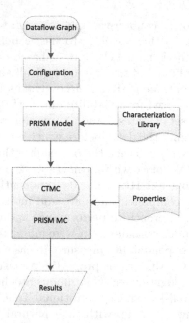

Fig. 3. Proposed methodology

high-level design description expressed using a language such as C++. As mentioned earlier, a CDFG can be implemented with different component allocations (design options). We will refer to the term *design options* as *configurations* in the rest of the paper. Upon a failure, if possible with available resources, the CDFG is rescheduled for fault recovery and the system continues its operation -that is reflected in the CTMC as the next states. For rescheduling the CDFG with available components, a high-level synthesis algorithm, such as *forced-directed list scheduling* [23] can be used. To analyze each configuration, we model them with the PRISM modeling language. Such a model is described as a number of modules, each of which corresponds to a component of the system. Each module has a set of finite-ranged variables representing different types of resources. The domain of the variables represent the number of available components of a specific resource. The whole model is constructed as the parallel composition of these modules. The behaviour of an individual module is specified by a set of guarded commands. For a CTMC, as is the case here, it can be represented in the following form:

$$[] \ \texttt{<guard>} \ \rightarrow \ \texttt{<rate>} \ : \ \texttt{<action>} \ ;$$

The **guard** is a predicate over the variables of all the modules in the model. The update comprises of **rate** and **action**. A **rate** is an expression which evaluates to a positive real number. The term **action** describes a transition of the module in terms of how its variables should be updated. The interpretation of the command is that if the **guard** is satisfied, then the module can make the corresponding transition with that associated `rate`. A very simple command for a module with only one variable z might be:

$$[] <z = 0> \rightarrow 7.5 : <z' = z + 1> ;$$

which states that, if z is equal to 0, then it will be incremented by one and this action occurs with rate 7.5. For another example, consider an application that requires 2 adders and 2 multipliers and such a configuration in the PRISM modeling language can be described as follows:

```
module adder
  a : [0..num_A] init num_A;
  [] (a > 0) -> a*lambda_A : (a' = a - 1);
  [] (a < num_A) -> miu : (a' = num_A);
endmodule

module mult
  m : [0..num_M] init num_M;
  [] (m > 0) -> m*lambda_M : (m' = m - 1);
  [] (m < num_M) -> miu : (m' = num_M);
endmodule
```

In the PRISM code above, num_A and num_M represent the number of adders and multipliers available in the initial state of the configuration. The lambda_A and the lambda_M variable represents the associated failure rates of the adders and multipliers whereas miu represents the repair rate. Each repair transition (scrub) leads back to the initial state reflecting the scenario that the configuration bit flips have been repaired. The value of lambda_A and lambda_M is obtained from a component characterization library, that will be explained later in the paper. PRISM then constructs, from this, the corresponding probabilistic model, in this case a CTMC. The resulting CTMC for this configuration is shown in Fig. 4. PRISM also computes the set of all states which are reachable from the initial state and identifies any deadlock states (i.e. reachable states with no outgoing transitions). PRISM then parses one or more temporal logic properties (e.g. in CSL) and performs model checking, determining whether the model satisfies each property.

4.1 Markov Model for Dependability

CTMC models are very commonly used for reliability and dependability modeling. To analyze each configuration, a separate CTMC is built with the help of the PRISM tool and a wide range of dependability properties are verified. For the FIR application in Fig. 5, at a minimum, an adder and a multiplier pair is required for successful operation, hence any state that does not fulfill the minimum resource availability, is labeled as a *failed state*. At the end, the state labeled as *all fail* represents a state where all the components in the system have

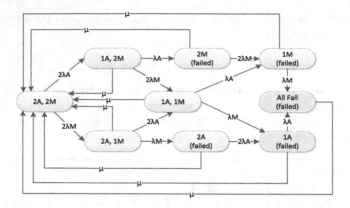

Fig. 4. Sample Markov model

failed due to soft errors one-by-one. The initial state of the configuration has the maximum throughput and all the components are functional. The edges between the states represent transition rates. The assumptions for our model are defined as follows:

Assumption 1: The time-to failure for a component due to a configuration bit flip is exponentially distributed. Exponential distribution is commonly used to model the reliability of systems where the failure rate is constant. The scrubbing behavior is assumed to follow Saleh's probabilistic model [25], e.g. *scrubbing* interval is distributed exponentially with a rate $1/\mu$, where μ represents the scrub rate.

Assumption 2: Only one component can fail at a time due to a soft error. This assumption is made to ensure the complexity in the Markov model is managable.

Assumption 3: *Cold spare* components are used to provide redundancy and are actived only when a same type of component fails. The *cold spare* components are only error prone to cosmic radiation when they are active.

Assumption 4: The reconfiguration and rescheduling times (i.e. the time taken for the system to reschedule when a component fails and the time taken for repair via partial reconfiguration) are extremely small compared to the times between failures and repairs. The time required for rescheduling is at most few clock cycles and the time required for scrubbing is only a few seconds, which is significantly smaller than the failure and repair rate.

Assumption 5: All the states in the CTMC model can be classified into three types: *operational*, -where all the component are functional and the system has the highest throughput; *degraded*, -where at least one of the components is faulty; and *failed*, -where the number of remaining non-faulty components is not sufficient to perform successful operation and hence has a throughput of 0. In PRISM, a *formula* can be used to classify such states as follows:

```
formula operational = (a = num_A) & (m = num_M)  ;
```

4.2 Markov Reward Modeling

Markov chains can be augmented with *rewards* to specify additional qualitative measures, known as a Markov Reward Model (MRM). In a Markov reward model, a reward rate function or reward structure $r(X_i)$ where $X \to \mathbb{R}$ ($\mathbb{R}$ is a set of real numbers) is associated with every state X_i such that r represents the performance of the system when in state X_i. The transient performability is defined as the *expected value* of a random variable defined in terms of a reward structure :

$$E[X(t)] = \sum_{X_i \in X} P_{X_i}(t) * r(X_i)$$

A steady-state accumulated mean reward is obtained by integrating this function from start to an convergent time beyond which rewards are invariant. For performance analysis, we use the throughput metric, hence each state in the MRM is augmented with associated throughput (in a non-pipelined design, throughput is the inverse of latency). The throughput reward at each state in the CTMC is obtained using the forced-directed list scheduling algorithm and all the *failed states* are augmented with a throughput reward of zero. In our MRM model, the area that is required, to implement the design on the FPGA, is assumed to be invariant between the states for a specific configuration. The reason is, once the system is implemented on FPGA, the area is fixed and if a fault occurs, then the system will be rescheduled. So only the control signals will change, not the components. For *overall reward* calculation e.g. to evaluate the throughput-area trade-offs for a configuration, we use the following equation:

$$Overall\ reward = (1/A) * E[X]$$

In the above equation, A represent the area of the design and $E[X]$ represents the expected throughput. This equation is similar to [20] , however instead of calculating the reward up to a specified time-step, we use the notion of steady-state throughput. Such modeling can be considered as a direct optimization of throughput, area and reliability. Rewards can be weighted based on designer's requirements. In the case study, the rewards are set to equal weight.

4.3 Characterization Library

The reliability of a particular device can be calculated by multiplying the estimated nominal SEU failure rate that is expressed in failure-in-time per megabyte (FIT/Mb) and the number of *critical bits*. A bit that is important for the functionality of a design can be categorized as a *critical bit*. For the analysis of *critical bit*, we follow the procedure from [7]. The components to be analyzed are implemented on Virtex-5 xc5vlx50t device. According to Rosetta experiment [21] and the recent device reliability report [30], a Virtex-5 device has a nominal SEU failure rate of 165 FIT/Mb.

The above failure rate estimation was done for atmospheric environment. At places with high elevation above the sea, the SEU rates can be three or four

Table 1. Characterization library

Component	No. of LUTs	No. of essential bits	MTBF (years)
Wallace tree multiplier	722	133503	9.22
Booth multiplier	650	130781	9.41
Brant-Kung adder	120	29675	41
Kogge-Stone adder	183	41499	30

times higher than at the sea-level. Long-haul aircrafts flying at altitudes near 40,000 ft along flight paths above 60 °C latitude experience the greatest neutron flux of all flights, roughly 500 times that of a ground-based observer in New York City [13]. However, results from the Rosetta experiment [21] for different altitude and latitude shows a worst-case derating factor of 561.70, and hence for commercial avionics applications the worst-case derating factor should be used.

In order to build a characterization library for the first-order estimate of soft error effects, we use the *bitgen* feature of Xilinx ISE tool to identify the *essential bits*, also known as *potentially critical bits*. It is well known that the number of *critical bits* is less than the number of *potentially critical bits*. More accurate SEU susceptibility analysis can be performed using the fault injection techniques [18,22], however, for first-order worst-case estimation, it is a valid assumption that all the *essential bits* are considered as *critical bits*. This is important to mention that we use the characterization library to obtain the failure rate of the components for the CTMC model and the methodology is generic enough to be used with a different characterization library with more precise and accurate data, without any major changes.

Table 1 presents the first-order worst-case estimate of component failures due to soft errors. We characterize different adder and multiplier components, namely 32-bit Brent-kung adder, 32-bit Kogge-stone adder, 32-bit Wallace-tree multiplier and 32-bit Booth multiplier. The Xilinx Synthesis Technology (XST) tool is used to synthesize the components from their HDL codes and the number of required LUTs to implement them is also obtained. We observe that a 32-bit Wallace-tree multiplier has about 0.134 million bits that are sensitive to SEUs. So this multiplier has a worst-case MTBF of 9.22 years for avionic applications.

5   Case Study

To illustrate the applicability of the proposed methodology for early design decision, this section presents a case study from a high-level synthesis benchmark. Figure 5 shows the CDFG for a 16-point FIR Filter [16]. For the experiments, we consider the 32-bit Kogge-stone adders and 32-bit Wallace tree multipliers as available components from the characterization library. To achieve a schedule with minimum number of control steps, the minimum allocation is two adders and two multipliers for the FIR filter application. At a minimum a pair of one adder and one multiplier is required for successful operation. The first part of the

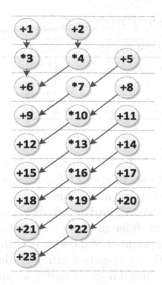

Fig. 5. FIR filter

case study presents the dependability analysis on different configurations. The later part of the case study focuses on the performance-area trade-off analysis using overall reward calculation.

Table 2 shows the statistics and model construction time in PRISM for four different configurations. The first configuration consists of two adders and two multipliers with no redundancy. The second and third configuration consists of one spare multiplier and one spare adder respectively used as redundant components (*coldspare*). Configuration 4 is equipped with full component-level redundancy, with a spare of each type of components. All the four configurations have approximately the same model generation time around 0.002 s. Configuration 4 has maximum number of states and and maximum number of transitions in the generated Markov model.

Probabilistic model checking allows us to reason about the probability of occurrence of an event or of reaching a state within a specific time period, or at any point of time in the lifetime of the system. Such measures can be formalized using CSL as P = ? (F[t_1, t_2] "operational"), which must be read as follows: *"the probability that the system is operational within the specified*

Table 2. Model construction statistics

Configuration	No. of states	No. of transitions	Time (s)
2A 2M	9	24	0.002
2A 3M	12	34	0.002
3A 2M	12	34	0.002
3A 3M	16	48	0.002

Table 3. Configurations vs classes of states

Configurations	Operational (days)	Degraded (days)	Failed (days)
2A 2M	3212.16	419.81	18.02
2A 3M	3212.16	434.64	3.20
3A 2M	3212.16	421.45	16.39
3A 3M	3212.16	436.28	1.55

time-bound where $[t_1, t_2] \in \mathbb{R}$". In Table 3, we analyze the number of days the design spends in different classes of states for a mission time of 10 years with a scrub rate of 6 months. The first column of the table shows the different configurations for evaluation. The second, third and fourth column presents the number of days the design spends in different classes of states. All the configurations spend approximately similar number of days in *operational state* (rounded to 2 decimal points). Configuration 1 spends around 18 days in *failed state*. Interestingly, we observe that adding an extra adder as spare does not help much whereas adding an extra multiplier as spare significantly reduces the number days spent in *failed state*. In configuration 4, the added spares for both adder and multiplier provide the best result in terms of dependability. This is obvious but will cost more area on the FPGA. Configuration 1 spends the least number of days in degraded state and configuration 4 spends the highest number of days in *degraded state*. For many safety-critical applications, low performance for a period of time is acceptable. For such systems the number of days spent in *failed state* is a major concern and hence, configuration 4 and configuration 2 are the two best candidates.

Choice of scrub rate affects the dependability of the system. Table 4 shows the effects of different scrub rates on configuration 2 for a mission time of 10 years. From the experimental results, we observe that the increase in the scrub rate increases the number of days spent in *failed* and *degraded* states. Thus, it decreases the number of days spent in *operational* state. For a scrub rate of 10 months, the system spends around 10 days in *failed state* whereas for a scrub rate of 4 months, the design spends only around 1 days in *failed* state. For a scrub rate of 1 month, the system spend only around 1.5 h in *failed state*. Such an analysis can help designers to choose an effective scrub rate best suited for the application.

In Fig. 6 and Table 5, we compare the four available configurations with respect to different scrub rates to calculate their failure probability for the same mission time. The experimental results show that for configuration 1, the failure probability varies from 0.020 to 0.145. Configuration 2 has a lower failure probability than configuration 3 for all the scrub rates. The failure probability of configuration 4 for all different scrub rates shows the best result with associated extra area overhead.

Steady state analysis of a design is useful to evaluate its dependability in the long-run. The steady-state properties can be formalized using CSL as S = ? [fail], which must be read as follows: *"the long-run non-availability*

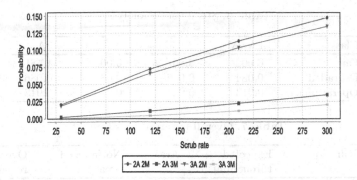

Fig. 6. Failure probability vs scrub rate (days)

Table 4. Scrub rate vs Classes of states

Scrub rate (months)	Operational (days)	Degraded (days)	Failed (days)
1	3567.06	82.87	0.06
4	3343.21	305.49	1.30
7	3151.41	494.09	4.49
10	2985.99	654.35	9.65

Table 5. Scrub rate vs configurations

Scrub rate (Months)	2A 2M	2A 3M	3A 2M	3A 3M
1	0.020	0.002	0.019	3.36E-4
4	0.071	0.011	0.066	0.004
7	0.111	0.022	0.104	0.011
10	0.145	0.035	0.135	0.020

of the system", i.e. the steady-state probability that the system is in *failed state*. The results of steady-state analysis is presented in Table 6 for a scrub rate of 4 months. From the results, we observe that configuration 2 is really an attractive alternative to configuration 4. On the other hand, configuration 1 and configuration 3 offer similar results (rounded to 2 decimal points) over the long-run.

For throughput-area trade-off analysis, Table 7 shows the long-run *overall reward* calculation for the configurations with a scrub rate of 4 months. The rewards are setup so that the area and expected throughput have equal weights. For every configuration, the maximum throughput is used to normalize the throughput for other states in the Markov reward model. Similarly, the maximum area is used to normalize the other area values among different configurations. The normalized long-run expected throughput for each configuration is shown in column 2. Column 3 shows the area of each configuration and their normalized value is shown in column 4. Column 5 shows the overall area-throughput reward for each configuration. The reward for each configuration is calculated

Table 6. Steady state analysis

Class	2A 2M	2A 3M	3A 2M	3A 3M
Fail	0.002	3.86E-4	0.002	1.58E-4
Degraded	0.084	0.086	0.084	0.086
Operational	0.913	0.913	0.913	0.913

Table 7. Overall reward calculation

Configurations	Expected throughput	Area	Normalized area	Overall reward
2A 2M	0.983	1710	0.667	1.46
2A 3M	0.991	2432	0.948	1.04
3A 2M	0.990	1834	0.715	1.39
3A 3M	0.999	2565	1.000	0.99

by multiplying the value of column 2 with the reciprocal of the normalized area. Based on the equal reward weighting, configuration 1, which has no redundancy (spare components), shows the best throughput-area reward. This indicates that the extra reliability provided by the redundancy is not always useful to suppress the extra area overhead. However, rescheduling with scrubbing is good enough to serve as a fault recovery and repair mechanism in such cases. Another important observation is that adding a spare adder significantly improves the throughput-area reward, much more than adding a spare multiplier. It clearly show, how the inclusion of throughput-area metrics can influence design decisions toward solutions that differs from those resulting from an analysis based on a dependability metric alone, as in Table 3. Such an analysis, using the proposed methodology, can be very useful at early design stages for designers of safety-critical applications concerned with dependability, performance and area constraints.

6   Conclusion

This paper illustrated how probabilistic model checking, a formal verification technique which has already been applied to a wide range of domains, can be used to analyze designs at early stage for avionic applications. The design options are modeled using a Markov reward model that captures the possible failures, recoveries and repairs possible in high-altitude radiation environments. Afterwards, a wide range of properties are verified to evaluate the design options, in terms of throughput, area and dependability. Such analysis is useful to reduce the overall design cost and effort. A FIR filter case study demonstrated how the proposed methodology can be applied to drive the design process. Future works include automation of the process to generate the PRISM code for a given configuration and to analyze designs in the presence of other kinds of faults such as Single-Event Functional Interrupts (SEFI).

Acknowledgments. This research was performed as part of the AVIO-403 project financially supported by the Consortium for Research and Innovation in Aerospace in Quebec (CRIAQ), Fonds de Recherche du Québec - Nature et Technologies (FRQNT) and the Natural Sciences and Engineering Research Council of Canada (NSERC). The authors would also like to thank Bombardier Aerospace, MDA Space Missions and the Canadian Space Agency (CSA) for their technical guidance and financial support.

References

1. Adell, P., Allen, G., Swift, G., McClure S.: Assessing and mitigating radiation effects in Xilinx SRAM FPGAs. In: 2008 European Conference on Radiation and its Effects on Components and Systems (RADECS), pp. 418–424 (2008)
2. Baier, C., Katoen, J.-P., Hermanns, H.: Approximate symbolic model checking of continuous-time Markov chains (extended abstract). In: Baeten, J.C.M., Mauw, S. (eds.) CONCUR 1999. LNCS, vol. 1664, p. 146. Springer, Heidelberg (1999)
3. Beaudry, M.D.: Performance-related reliability measures for computing systems. IEEE Trans. Comput. C−27(6), 540–547 (1978)
4. Borgerson, B.R., Freitas, R.F.: A reliability model for gracefully degrading and standby-sparing systems. IEEE Trans. Comput. 24(5), 517–525 (1975)
5. Salazar, A., Carmichael, C., Caffrey, M.: Correcting single-event upsets through virtex partial configuration (XAPP216 v1.0), Xilinx corporation (2010)
6. Carmichael, C.: Triple module redundancy design techniques for virtex FPGAs (XAPP197 v1.0.1), Xilinx corporation (2006)
7. Chapman, K.: Virtex-5 SEU critical bit information: extending the capability of the virtex-5 SEU controller, Xilinx corporation (2010)
8. Clarke, E.M., Emerson, E.A., Sistla, A.P.: Automatic verification of finite-state concurrent systems using temporal logic specifications. ACM Trans. Program. Lang. Syst. 8, 244–263 (1986)
9. Coussy, P., Chavet, C., Bomel, P., Heller, D., Senn, E., Martin, E.: GAUT: a high-level synthesis tool for dsp applications. In: Coussy, P., Morawiec, A. (eds.) High-Level Synthesis, pp. 147–169. Springer, Netherlands (2008)
10. Aigner, G., et al.: The SUIF program representation. http://suif.stanford.edu/suif/suif2/index.html, January 2010
11. Heiner, J., Sellers, B., Wirthlin, M., Kalb, J.: FPGA partial reconfiguration via configuration scrubbing. In: International Conference on Field Programmable Logic and Applications 2009, FPL 2009, pp. 99–104 (2009)
12. Hong, I., Potkonjak, M., Karri, R.: Heterogeneous BISR-approach using system level synthesis flexibility. In: Proceedings of the Asia and South Pacific Design Automation Conference 1998, ASP-DAC '98, pp. 289–294 (1998)
13. Hu, C., Zain, S.: NSEU mitigation in avionics applications (XAPP1073 (v1.0) 17 May 2010), October 2011
14. Huslende, R.: A combined evaluation of performance and reliability for degradable systems. In: Proceedings of the 1981 ACM SIGMETRICS Conference on Measurement and Modeling of Computer Systems, pp. 157–164. ACM (1981)
15. ISOGraph. http://www.isograph-software.com
16. Karri, R., Orailoglu, A.: High-level synthesis of fault-secure microarchitectures. In: 30th Conference on Design Automation 1993, pp. 429–433 (1993)
17. Kavi, K.M., Buckles, B.P., Narayan Bhat, U.: A formal definition of data flow graph models. IEEE Trans. Comput. C−35(11), 940–948 (1986)

18. Kenterlis, P., Kranitis, N., Paschalis, A.M., Gizopoulos, D., Psarakis, M.: A low-cost SEU fault emulation platform for SRAM-based FPGAs. In: IOLTS, pp. 235–241 (2006)
19. Kumar, V.V., Verma, R., Lach, J., Bechta Dugan, J.: A markov reward model for reliable synchronous dataflow system design. In: 2004 International Conference on Dependable Systems and Networks, pp. 817–825 (2004)
20. Kumar, V.V., Lach, J.: IC modeling for yield-aware design with variable defect rates. In: Proceedings of the Annual Reliability and Maintainability Symposium, 2005, pp. 489–495 (2005)
21. Lesea, A.: Continuing experiments of atmospheric neutron effects on deep submicron integrated circuits (WP286 v1.1), October 2011
22. Mansour, W., Velazco, R.: SEU fault-injection in VHDL-based processors: a case study. J. Electron. Test. 29(1), 87–94 (2013)
23. Paulin, P.G., Knight, J.P.: Force-directed scheduling for the behavioral synthesis of asics. IEEE Trans. Comput. Aided Des. Integr. Circuits Syst. 8(6), 661–679 (1989)
24. PRISM. http://www.prismmodelchecker.org
25. Saleh, A.M., Serrano, J.J., Patel, J.H.: Reliability of scrubbing recovery-techniques for memory systems. IEEE Trans. Reliab. 39(1), 114–122 (1990)
26. Smith, R.M., Trivedi, K.S., Ramesh, A.V.: Performability analysis: measures, an algorithm, and a case study. IEEE Trans. Comput. 37(4), 406–417 (1988)
27. Stewart, W.J.: Introduction to the Numerical Solution of Markov Chains. Princeton University Press, Princeton (1994)
28. Thibeault, C., Hariri, Y., Hasan, S.R., Hobeika, C., Savaria, Y., Audet, Y., Tazi, F.Z.: A library-based early soft error sensitivity analysis technique for SRAM-based FPGA design. J. Electron. Test. 29(4), 457–471 (2013)
29. Tosun, S., Mansouri, N., Arvas, E., Xie, Y.: Reliability-centric high-level synthesis. In: Proceedings of DATE (2005)
30. Device reliability report: Second quarter (UG116 v9.1), Xilinx corporation (2012)

A Strand Space Approach to Provable Anonymity

Yongjian Li[1,3][✉] and Jun Pang[2]

[1] State Key Laboratory of Computer Science, Institute of Software,
Chinese Academy of Sciences, Beijing, China
lyj238@ios.ac.cn
[2] Faculty of Science, Technology and Communication,
University of Luxembourg, Luxembourg, Luxembourg
[3] College of Information Engineering, Capital Normal University, Beijing, China

Abstract. We formalize in the strand space theory the notion of provable anonymity. Bundle in a strand space is used to formalize a session of a protocol. Behaviors of an observer can then be formalized as extensions of a bundle. Reinterpretation function can be naturally derived from the mapping from one message term of an edge of a bundle in a strand space to that in another strand space. We formally define observational equivalence on bundles and use it to formalise anonymity properties. The novelty of our theory lies in the observational model and the construction of reinterpretation functions in the strand space theory. We build our theory in Isabelle/HOL to achieve a mechanical framework for the analysis of anonymity protocols.

1 Introduction

Nowadays, people are getting used to carry out their daily activities through networked distributed systems, e.g., online social networks, location-based application, providing electronic services to users. In these systems, people become more and more concerned about their privacy and how their personal information have been used. Anonymity is one of the desired properties of such systems, referring to the ability of a user to own some data or take some actions without being tracked down. For example, a user wants to keep anonymous when visiting a particular website or posting a message on a public bulletin board.

Due to its subtle nature, anonymity has been the subject of many research paper. For instance, the proposed definitions aim to capture different aspects of anonymity (either possibilistic [1–5] or probabilistic [6–11]). Formal verification of anonymity has been applied to a number of application domains, including electronic voting [12,13], electronic cash protocols [14], file sharing [15,16] and electronic healthcare [17]. However, automatic approaches to the formal verification of anonymity have mostly focused on the model checking approach on systems with fixed configurations [1,4,6,9], while theorem proving seems to be a more suitable approach when dealing with systems of infinite state

C. Artho and P.C. Ölveczky (Eds.): FTSCS 2013, CCIS 419, pp. 71–87, 2014.
DOI: 10.1007/978-3-319-05416-2_6, © Springer International Publishing Switzerland 2014

spaces [18]. In this paper, we extend our previous effort on formalising provable anonymity in a powerful general-purpose theorem prover, Isabelle/HOL [19], to semi-automatically verify anonymity properties.

In the epistemic framework of provable anonymity [3], the notion of observational equivalence of traces plays an important role. Essentially, two traces are considered equivalent if an intruder cannot distinguish them. The distinguishing ability of the intruder is formalized as the ability to distinguish two messages, which is in turn based on message structures and relations between random looking messages. The notion of *reinterpretation function* is central in the provable anonymity framework – proving two traces equivalent essentially is boiled down to prove the existence of a reinterpretation function. Our formalization [20] of provable anonymity in Isabelle/HOL relies on inductive definitions of message distinguishability and observational equivalence on traces observed by the intruder. This makes our theory differ from its original proposal.

Our main contribution of this paper is twofold: a proposal of formalizing provable anonymity in the strand space theory [21–23] and its implementation in a theorem prover. We briefly discuss the novelties of our work below:

- We define an observational model of a passive intruder, meaning that the intruder does not actively modify the messages or inject new messages. The intruder only analyzes or synthesizes new messages to tell the difference between his observation on sessions. These analyzing and synthesizing actions are naturally represented by extensions of a bundle by adding separation and decryption (or concatenation and encryption) actions.
- We propose a notion of *reinterpretation mapping*, which can be naturally derived from the mapping from one message term of an edge of a bundle in a strand space to that in another strand space. Intuitively, a reinterpretation mapping requires that the relation, composed of the corresponding message pairs, should be *single_valued*. Furthermore, such a reinterpretation mapping should remain valid after applying the analyzing and synthesizing extension operations of a bundle. Combining the concepts of reinterpretation mapping with that of extensions of a bundle, we propose an (adapted) definition of observational equivalence between two sessions, which are represented by a bundle in two strand spaces. Thus in the framework, we naturally incorporate the concept of reinterpretation function which is extensively used in [3].
- We proceed to formalize anonymity properties, i.e., sender anonymity and unlinkability, in an epistemic framework as in [3]. We then define the semantics of an anonymity protocol, e.g., Onion Routing [24,25], in the strand space theory, and formally prove that the protocol realizes sender anonymity and unlinkability.
- We build our theory in Isabelle/HOL [19] to have a mechanical framework for the analysis of anonymity protocols. We illustrate the feasibility of the mechanical framework through the case study on Onion Routing.

In this paper, we assume readers have some knowledge with Isabelle/HOL syntax and present our formalization directly without elaborated explanation.

Notably, a function in Isabelle/HOL syntax is usually defined in a curried form instead of a tuple form, that is, we often use the notation $f \; x \; y$ to stand for $f(x, y)$. We also use the notation $[\![A_1; A_2; ...; A_n]\!] \implies B$ to mean that with assumptions $A_1, ..., A_n$, we can derive a conclusion B.

2 Preliminaries

The basic notations and terminologies are mainly taken from [23].

2.1 Messages

The set of messages is defined using the BNF notation:

$$h:: = \text{Agent } A \mid \text{Nonce } N \mid \text{Key } K \mid \text{MPair } h_1 \; h_2 \mid \text{Crypt } K \; h$$

where A is an element from a set of agents, N from a set of nonces, and K from a set of keys. Here we use K^{-1} to denote the inverse key of K. MPair $h_1 \; h_2$ is called a composed message. Crypt $K \; h$ represents the encryption of message h with K. We use the free encryption assumption, where Crypt $K \; h =$ Crypt $K' \; h'$ if and only if $K = K'$ and $h = h'$. The set of all messages is denoted by Messages. Terms of the form Agent A, Nonce N, or Key K are said to be atomic. The set of all atomic messages is denoted by Atoms. A message h is a text message if $h \neq$ Key K for any K. The set of all atomic text messages is denoted by T.

In an asymmetric-key protocol model, an agent A has a public key pubK A, which is known to all agents, and a private key priK A. pubK A is the inverse key of priK A ((priK $A)^{-1} =$ pubK A), and vice versa. In a symmetric-key model, each agent A has a symmetric key shrK A. The inverse key of shrK A is itself ((shrK $A)^{-1} =$ shrK A). We also assume that (1) asymmetric keys and symmetry keys are disjoint; (2) the functions shrK, pubK and priK are injective, e.g., if shrK $A =$ shrK A' then $A = A'$. The public key, private key, and shared key of an agent are long-term because the agent holds them forever. In contrast, some keys are created and used only in a session by some agents, and these keys are short-term. In the following, we abbreviate Crypt $K \; h$ as $\{\!| \; h \; |\!\}_K$, and MPair $h_1 ...$ MPair $h_{n-1} \; h_n$ as $\{\!| \; h_1, ..., h_{n-1}, h_n \; |\!\}$. Such abbreviations are supported in Isabelle by syntax translation [19]. In order to reduce the number of $\{\!|$ or $|\!\}$ for readability, we abbreviate Crypt K (MPair $h_1 ...$ MPair $h_{n-1} \; h_n$) as $\{\!| \; h_1, ..., h_{n-1}, h_n \; |\!\}_K$ in this paper.

2.2 Strands and Strand Space

Actions. The set of actions that agents can take during an execution of a protocol include send and receive actions. We denote send and receive actions by a set of two signs Sign $= \{+, -\}$, respectively.

Events. An event is a pair (σ, t), where $\sigma \in$ Sign and $t \in$ Messages.

Strands and Strand Spaces. A protocol defines a sequence of events for each agent's role. A strand represents a sequence of an agent's actions in a particular protocol run, and is an instance of a role. A strand space is a mapping from a strand set Σ to a trace SP $: \Sigma \Rightarrow$ (Sign $\times$ Messages) list.

- A node is a pair (s, i), with $s \in \Sigma$ and $0 \leq i <$ length (SP s). We use $n \in$ strand s to denote that a node $n = (s, i)$ belongs to the strand s. The set of all nodes in SP is denoted as Domain SP. Namely, Domain $SP = \{(s, i).s \in \Sigma \wedge i <$ length $(SP\ s)\}$.
- If $n = (s, i)$ and (SP s)$!i = (\sigma, g)$, where (SP s)$!i$ means the i-th element in the strand s. Then we define strand $SP\ n$, index $SP\ n$, term $SP\ n$ and sign n to be the strand, index, term and sign of the node n respectively, namely strand $SP\ n = s$, index $SP\ n = i$, term $n\ SP = g$ and sign $n = \sigma$. A node is positive if it has sign $+$, and negative if it has sign $-$.
- If $n, n' \in$ Domain SP, the relation $n \Rightarrow_{SP} n'$ holds between nodes n and n' if $n = (s, i)$ and $n' = (s, i+1)$. This represents event occurring on n followed by that occurring on n'.
- If $n, n' \in$ Domain SP, the relation $n \rightarrow_{SP} n'$ holds for nodes n and n' if strand $SP\ n \neq$ strand $SP\ n'$, term $SP\ n =$ term $SP\ n'$, sign $SP\ n = +$ and sign $SP\ n' = -$. This represents that n sends a message and n' receives the message. Note that we place an additional restriction on the relation $\rightarrow$ than that in [21,22], we require strand $SP\ n \neq$ strand $SP\ n'$, i.e., n and n' are in different strands, which means that actions of sending or receiving a message can only occur between different strands.
- A term g originates in a strand space from a node $n \in$ Domain SP iff sign $SP\ n = +$ and $g \sqsubset$ term $SP\ n$, and whenever n' precedes n on the same strand, $g \not\sqsubset$ term $SP\ n'$. We write it originate $SP\ g\ n$.
- A term g uniquely originates in a strand space from node n iff g originates on a unique node n. Nonces and other freshly generated terms are usually uniquely originated. We write it uniqOrig $SP\ g\ n$.

Bundles. A bundle $b = (N_b, E_b)$ in a strand space SP is a finite subgraph of the graph (Domain $SP, (\rightarrow_{SP} \cup \Rightarrow_{SP})$), representing a protocol execution under some configuration. N_b is the set of nodes, and E_b is the set of the edges incident with the nodes in N_b, and the following properties hold:

- b is an acyclic finite graph;
- If the sign of a node n is $-$, and $n \in N_b$, then there is a unique positive node n' such that $n' \in N_b$, $n' \rightarrow_{SP} n$ and $(n', n) \in E_b$;
- If $n' \Rightarrow_{SP} n$ and $n \in b$, then $n' \in N_b$ and $(n', n) \in E_b$.

The set of all the bundles in a strand space SP is denoted as bundles SP.
Causal Precedence. Let b be a graph, we define $m \prec_b n$ for $(m, n) \in E_b^+$, and $m \preceq_b n$ for $(m, n) \in E_b^*$. $\prec_b$ and $\preceq_b$ represent causal precedence between nodes.

From the definition of a bundle b in a strand space SP, we can derive that it is a casually well-founded graph [21,22].

Lemma 1. *For a bundle b in a strand space SP, b is casually well-founded graph, and every non-empty subset of the nodes in it has $\prec_b$-minimal members.*

2.3   Intruder Model

We discuss anonymity properties based on observations of the intruder. The Dolev-Yao intruder model [26] is considered standard in the field of formal symbolic analysis of security protocols – all messages sent on the network are read by the intruder; all received messages on the network are created or forwarded by the intruder; the intruder can also remove messages from the network. However, in the analysis of anonymity protocols, often a weaker attacker model is assumed – the intruder is *passive* in the sense that he observes all network traffic, but does not actively modify the messages or inject new messages – the intruder gets a message issued by an agent from the network, then stores it for traffic analysing, and forwards it directly to its intended destination. In the strand space model, the above behavior is typically modelled by a Tee strand. Furthermore, the copied messages are only used internally for checking observation equivalence between protocol sessions.

In the study of the anonymity, we are more interested in the observational equivalence between sessions. A session is modeled by a bundle in a strand space. Observational equivalence between two session bundles is modelled by comparing the similarity between bundles which are extended from the above two bundles by analyzing and synthesizing actions. The observational equivalence holds if a one-to-one mapping always holds between the corresponding extended bundles.

2.4   Protocol Modeling Using Strands

A protocol usually contains several roles, such as initiators, responders and servers. The sequence of actions of each regular agent acting some role in a protocol session is pre-defined by the protocol and represented as a parameterized strand. Parameters usually include agent names and nonces. Informally, we denote a parameter strand acting some role by role[*parameter list*]. The strands of the legitimate agents are referred to as regular strands.

A bundle can also contain penetrator strands. We explain them in more details in the next section. We now use the Onion Routing protocol [24,25] (see Fig. 1) as an example to illustrate the modelling strategy using strands. In this figure, we abbreviate Agent A as A, Nonce N as N, and pubK A as PK_A. This figure uses the case when the threshold k of the router is 2, i.e., when the router has received two messages, then it turns into the status of forwarding messages after peeling the received messages. There are four roles in this protocol: OnionInit1, OnionInit2, OnionRouter and OnionRecv. The strands of these roles are defined below:

- OnionInit1 SP s A M Y N' N, if the agent acting the role is A and the trace of s in the strand space SP is $[(+, \{\!\mid N', Y, \{\!\mid N \mid\!\}_{\mathsf{pubK}\ Y} \mid\!\}_{\mathsf{pubK}\ M})]$.
- OnionInit2 SP s A M N, if the agent acting the role is A and the trace of s in the strand space SP is $[(+, \{\!\mid N \mid\!\}_{\mathsf{pubK}\ M})]$.

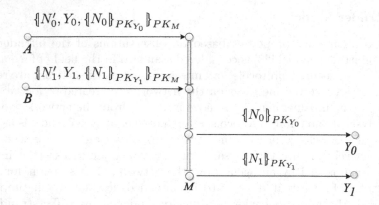

Fig. 1. Onion routing with $k = 2$.

- OnionRouter SP s M k, if the agent acting the role is M and the trace of s in the strand space SP satisfies:
  $(\forall\, i. 0 \leq i < k \longrightarrow ((\exists\, N'\; N\; Y.\text{term } SP\,(s, i) = \{\!| N', Y, \{\!| N \,|\!\}_{\mathsf{pubK}\; Y} |\!\}_{\mathsf{pubK}\; M})$
  $\vee\; (\exists\, N.\text{term } SP\,(s, i) = \{\!| N \,|\!\}_{\mathsf{pubK}\; M}))) \wedge$
  $(\forall i.k \leq i < \text{length }(SP\; s) \longrightarrow (\exists\, N\; N'\; Y\; j. (0 < j < k \wedge\; \text{term } SP\,(s, j) =$
  $\{\!| N', Y, \{\!| N \,|\!\}_{\mathsf{pubK}\; Y} |\!\}_{\mathsf{pubK}\; M} \wedge\text{term } SP\,(s, i) = \{\!| N \,|\!\}_{\mathsf{pubK}\; Y})))$.
- OnionRecv SP s Y N, if the trace of s in the strand space SP is
  $[(-, \{\!| N \,|\!\}_{\mathsf{pubK}\; Y})]$.

2.5   Penetrator

The symbol bad denotes the set of all penetrators. If an agent is not in the set bad, then it is regular. The strands of the penetrators are referred to as penetrator strands. If a strand is not a penetrator one, it is referred to as a regular strand. We say a node is regular if it is at a regular strand.

There is a set of messages known to all penetrators initially, denoted as initKP, containing agent names, public keys of all agents, private keys of all penetrators, and symmetric keys initially shared between the penetrators and the server.

In the classic strand space theory, a penetrator can intercept messages and generate messages that are computable from its initial knowledge and the messages it intercepts. These actions are modeled by a set of penetrator strands, and they represent atomic deductions. More complex deduction actions can be formed by connecting several penetrator strands together.

Definition 1. *A penetrator' trace relative to* initKP *is one of the following, where* initKP *is the initial knowledge of penetrator:*

- *text message* - M a: $[(+, a)]$, *where* $a \in$ T *and* $a \in$ initKP.
- *issuing known key* - K K' : $[(+, \text{Key } K')]$, *where Key* $K' \in$ initKP.
- *concatenation* - C $g\ h$: $[(-, g), (-, h), (+, \{\!| g, h |\!\})]$.
- *separation* - S $g\ h$: $[(-, \{\!| g, h |\!\}), (+, g), (+, h)]$.
- *encryption* - E $h\ K$: $[(-, \text{Key } K), (-, h), (+, \{\!| h |\!\}_K)]$.
- *decryption* - D $h\ K$: $[(-, \text{Key } K^{-1}), (-, \{\!| h |\!\}_K), (+, h)]$.
- *Flush* - F g: $[(-, g)]$.
- *Tee* - T g: $[(-, g), (+, g), (+, g)]$.

Roughly speaking, penetrator strands can represent two kinds of actions: analyzing messages (a combination of K and D strands, or just a separation strand); synthesizing messages (a combination of K and E strands, or just a concatenation strand). Tee strand is just for copying a message.

A bundle can be extended by adding more penetrator actions to a new bundle. The set of extended bundles of a bundle b in a strand space SP is inductively defined in Isabelle/HOL below. Intuitively, a bundle in a strand space is a formal representation of a protocol session. If a bundle $b' \in$ extendByAnalz $SP\ b$ (or $b' \in$ extendBySynth $SP\ b$), then b' contains the same behaviors of regular agents as those in session b. However, b' contains more information which is revealed by the penetrator's analyzing (or synthesizing) actions.

In our framework, in order to check the observational equivalence between two bundles, we not only need to compare the correspondence of messages in two sessions, but also need to check the correspondence of messages in two sessions which are extended from the original two sessions.

```
inductive_set extendByAnalz:: strand_space ⇒ graph ⇒ graph set
for SP::strand_space and b::graph where
itSelf: b ∈ bundles SP ⟹ b ∈ extendByAnalz SP b;
| Add_Decrypt: [ b' ∈ extendByAnalz SP b;
Is_K_strand SP ks; (ks,0) ∉ (nodes b');
Is_D_strand SP s; (s,0) ∉ (nodes b');
(s,1) ∉ (nodes b'); (s,2) ∉ (nodes b');
(ks,0) → SP (s,0); n ∈ nodes b'; n → SP (s,1) ]
⟹ extendGraphByAdd1 (extendGraphByAdd2 b' ks)
s (ks,0) n ∈ extendByAnalz SP b
| Add_SepOrTee: [ b' ∈ extendByAnalz SP b;
Is_Sep_strand SP s ∨ Is_Tee_strand SP s;
(node_sign SP n) = +; n ∈ (nodes b');
n → SP (s,0); (s,0) ∉ (nodes b');
(s,1) ∉ (nodes b'); (s,2) ∉ (nodes b') ]
⟹ extendGraphByAdd3 b' s n ∈ extendByAnalz SP b
```

```
inductive_set extendBySynth:: strand_space ⇒ graph ⇒ graph set
for SP::strand_space and b::graph where
itSelf: b ∈ bundles SP ⟹ b ∈ extendBySynth SP b
| Add_Encrypt: ⟦ b' ∈ extendBySynth SP b;
Is_K_strand SP ks; (ks,0) ∉ (nodes b');
Is_E_strand SP s; (s,0) ∉ (nodes b');
(s,1) ∉ (nodes b');(s,2) ∉ (nodes b');
(ks,0) → SP (s,0); n ∈ nodes b'; n → SP (s,1) ⟧
⟹ extendGraphByAdd1 (extendGraphByAdd2 b' ks)
s (ks,0) n ∈ extendBySynth SP b
| Add_Cat: ⟦ b' ∈ extendBySynth SP b;
Is_Cat_strand SP s; (s,0) ∉ (nodes b');
(s,1) ∉ (nodes b');(s,2) ∉ (nodes b');
n ∈ nodes b'; n → SP (s,0); n' ∈ nodes b';
n' → SP (s,1); n ≠ n'
⟧ ⟹ extendGraphByAdd1 b' s (ks,0) n ∈ extendBySynth SP b
| Add_Tee: ⟦ b' ∈ extendBySynth SP b;
Is_Tee_strand SP s; (node_sign SP n) = +;
n ∈ (nodes b'); n → SP (s,0);
(s,0) ∉ (nodes b'); (s,1) ∉ (nodes b');
(s,2) ∉ (nodes b') ⟧ ⟹ extendGraphByAdd3 b' s n ∈ extendBySynth SP b
```

3   Message Reinterpretation and Observational Equivalence on Bundles

We give a definition of message mapping from terms of a node set in a strand space to those of nodes in another strand space as follows:

```
mapping:: strand_space ⇒ strand_space ⇒ (node set) ⇒ ( msgPair set)
where mapping SP SP' NodeSet
≡ {p. ∃n. n∈ NodeSet ∧ p= (term SP n, term SP' n )}
```

Then we can naturally derive a definition from messages of a node set of a bundle in a strand space to those in another strand space. A session which is modeled by a bundle b in a strand space SP, is said to be reinterpreted to another which is modeled by b in another strand space SP', if the following conditions hold:

- Let $r =$ mapping SP SP' (nodes b), single_valued r guarantees that an agent cannot reinterpret any message differently.
- The casual relation of b in strand space SP is the same as that of b in SP'.
- For a message pair $(m, m') \in r$, if m is an atomic message, then $m = m'$. This means that an agent can uniquely identify a plain-text message he observes. An agent can only reinterpret the encrypted messages.

The corresponding formalization of Reinterp in Isabelle/HOL is given below.

```
Reinterp::graph ⇒ strand_space ⇒ strand_space ⇒ bool where
Reinterp b SP SP' ≡
let r= mapping SP SP' (nodes b) in
single_valued r ∧
( ∀ n1 n2. (n1 → SP n2) ⟶ (n1 → SP' n2 )) ∧
( ∀ n1 n2. ( n1 ⇒ SP n2) ⟶ ( n1 ⇒ SP' n2 )) ∧
( ∀ n. n ∈ nodes b
⟶ ofAgent SP (strand n)= ofAgent SP' (strand n)) ∧
( ∀ m m'. Is_atom m ⟶ (m,m') ∈ r ⟶ m = m')
```

Next lemma says that b is also a bundle in SP' if b is a bundle in SP and Reinterp b SP SP'.

Lemma 2. ⟦Reinterp b SP SP'; b ∈ bundles SP⟧⟹ b ∈ bundles SP'

With the concepts of reinterpretation and the extensions of bundles, we can formalize the definition of observational equivalence between sessions as follows:

```
obsEquiv::graph ⇒ strand_space ⇒ strand_space ⇒ bool where
obsEquiv b SP SP' ≡
∀ b' b''. b' ∈ (extendByAnalz SP b ) ⟶
b'' ∈ (extendBySynth SP b' )⟶
( b' ∈ extendByAnalz SP' b ∧
b'' ∈ extendBySynth SP' b' ∧ Reinterp b' SP SP')
```

This definition obsEquiv means that for any extension b' of the bundle b, the reinterpretation relation will be kept between the two sessions which are modelled by b' in strand space SP and SP' respectively.

Remark 1. The intuition behind the above definition is that messages in two sessions look the same to an agent if they are the same for the messages the agent understands and if a message in one sequence looks like a random bit-string to the agent, then the corresponding message in the other sequence also looks like a random bit-string. In detail,

1. For a plain-text, if the agent observes it in an action of a session, then he should observe the exact same message in the corresponding action of the other session.
2. A message looks like a random bit-string if the decryption key is not possessed by the agent. Then the corresponding message should also be like a random bit-string, which means that it is also a message encrypted by a key whose inverse key is not possessed by the observer.
3. The reinterpretation should be preserved by the synthesizing and analyzing operations on the observed messages. In the strand space theory, these operations are modelled by the penetrator strands, thus the preservation is checked by comparing the corresponding messages mapping from an extended session to another extended session which are extended by the same similar penetrator strand.

In the work of Garcia et al. [3], a reinterpretation function between two message sequences is used as a underlining concept. In our work, the single-valued requirement of the message mapping between two bundles gives a sufficient condition for the existence of a reinterpretation function. Moreover, the bundle extensions give a mechanical way to derive the reinterpretation function.

4   Anonymity Properties

Using the observational equivalence relations over a set of possible observation equivalent bundles, we can formally introduce epistemic operators [3] as follows:

```
diamond :: graph ⇒ strand_space set⇒ strand_space
⇒ assertONBundle ⇒ bool where
diamond b SPS SP Assert ≡ ∃ SP'. SP' ∈ SPS
∧ ((obsEquiv b SP SP') ∧ Assert b SP')


box :: graph ⇒ strand_space set ⇒ strand_space
⇒ assertONBundle ⇒ bool where
box b SPS SP Assert ≡
∀ SP' ∈ SPS. (obsEquiv b SP SP') ⟶ (Assert b SP')
```

Intuitively, $b \models \Box\ bs\ \varphi$ means that for any bundle b' in bs, if b' is observationally equivalent to b, then b' satisfies the assertion φ. On the other hand, $b \models \Diamond\ trs\ \varphi$ means that there is a bundle b' in trs, b' is observationally equivalent to b and b' satisfies the assertion φ. Now we can formulate some information hiding properties in our epistemic language. We use the standard notion of an anonymity set: it is a collection of agents among which a given agent is not identifiable. The larger this set is, the more anonymous an agent is.

Suppose that b is a bundle of a protocol in which a message m is originated by some agent. We say that b provides sender anonymity w.r.t. the anonymity set AS and a set of possible runs if it satisfies:

```
origInBundle::agent ⇒ msg ⇒ graph ⇒ strand_space ⇒ bool where
origInBundle A g b SP ≡
∃ n. n ∈ nodes b ∧ originate SP g n

senderAnonymity::agent set ⇒ msg ⇒ graph
⇒ strand_space set⇒ strand_space ⇒ bool where
senderAnonymity AS g b SPS SP ≡
( ∀ X. X:AS ⟶ diamond b SPS SP (origInBundle X g))
```

Here, AS is the set of agents who are under consideration, and SPS is the set of all the strand spaces where b represents a protocol session. Intuitively, this definition means that each agent in AS can originate g in a session which is represented by b in SP. Therefore, this means that B cannot be sure of anyone who originates this message in the session.

5 A Case Study: Onion Routing

Onion Routing [24,25] provides both sender and receiver anonymity for communication over the Internet and servers as the basis of the Tor network [27]. Its main idea is based on Chaum's mix cascades [28] that messages in Onion Routing have a layered encryption (thus called *onions*) and travel from source to destination via a sequence of proxies (called *onion routers*). Each onion router can decrypt (or peel) one layer of a received message and forward the remainder to the next onion router. To disguise the relations between incoming and outgoing messages, an onion router collect incoming messages until it has received k messages, permutes the messages and sends in batch to their intended receivers.

5.1 Modeling Onion Routing

We model a simplified version of Onion Routing with only one onion router as done in [3]. We assume a set of users AS and one router M, with $M \notin AS$. We also assume that each agent can send a message before the router M launches a batch of forwarding process, and the router does not accept any message when it is forwarding. We define its initiator and receiver and router strands. For instance, we define the two kinds of an initiator strands as follows:

```
is_initiator1::strand_space ⇒ sigma ⇒ agent ⇒ agent ⇒ nat
⇒ nat ⇒ bool where
is_initiator1 SP s M Y NO N ≡
(SP s)=[(+, (Crypt (pubEK M) {|(Nonce NO),(Agent Y),
    Crypt (pubEK Y) (Nonce N)|}))]
∧uniqOrig (Nonce N) (s,0)
∧uniqOrig (Nonce NO) (s,0)

is_initiator2::strand_space ⇒ sigma ⇒ agent ⇒ nat ⇒ bool where
is_initiator2 SP s M N ≡
(SP s)=[(+, Crypt (pubEK M) (Nonce N) )]
∧uniqOrig (Nonce N) (s,0)
```

Next we define the strands in a strand space of onion protocol to be the union of the above kinds strands and penetrator strands.

```
onionStrandSpec:: agent ⇒ strand_space ⇒ bool where
onionStrandSpec M SP≡
∀ s. (Is_penetrator_strand SP s ∨
(∃ Y NO N. is_initiator1 SP s M Y NO N) ∨
(∃ N. is_initiator2 SP s M N) ∨
( ∃ k. is_router SP s M k ∧ (ofAgent SP s=M)) ∨
( ∃ Y N. is_recv SP s Y N)
onionStrandSpaces::agent ⇒ strand_space set where
onionStrandSpaces M≡{SP. onionStrandSpec M SP}
```

5.2   An Overview of our Proof Strategy

In the following sections, we will formalize and prove the anonymity properties of Onion Routing. Due to the complexity of the epistemic operators in property definitions, the proof is rather envolved. We give an overview of our formalization and the main proof steps.

We will formalize the sender anonymity of Onion Routing in the view of a Spy for a session w.r.t. a set of honest agents and all possible equivalent bundles. Consider a session, which is modelled by a bundle b in a strand space SP, according to the definitions of epistemic operators, which are used in the definition of sender anonymity, we need to construct another strand space SP' which satisfies the following two conditions:

(1) SP' is still an Onion routing strand space.
(2) b in strand space SP is observationally equivalent to b in SP'. That is to say, obsEquiv b SP SP'. In order to show this, by the definition of obsEquiv, we need to prove that for any bundle $b' \in$ extendByAnalz SP b, $b'' \in$ extendBySynth SP' b' and Reinterp b'' SP SP'.

Whether two sessions are observationally equivalent for a protocol depends on the knowledge of the intruder after his observation of the two sessions. Therefore, we need to discuss some secrecy upon on the intruder's knowledge. We introduce a new predicate:

nonLeakMsg g M $\equiv$ $\forall$ B N_0 $N.(g =$ (Crypt (pubK M)
{| Nonce N_0, Agent B, Crypt (pubK B)(Nonce N) |})) $\longrightarrow$ ($B \notin$ bad $\vee$ $N_0 \neq N$)

Formally, nonLeakMsg m M specifies that if a message m has the form of Crypt (pubK M) {| Nonce N_0, Agent B, Crypt (pubK B)(Nonce N) |}, then either $B \notin$ bad or $N_0 \neq N$. This specifies a non-leakage condition of nonce part N_0 in a message of the aforementioned form which is sent to the router even if its nonce part N is forwarded to the intruder.

5.3   Message Swapping

In this section, we present a method for the construction of an observationally equivalent session.

The swap Function. We define a function swapMsg g h msg, which swaps g with h if either g or h occurs in msg. Then we extend the *swap* operation naturally to events (applying to the message field of an event) and to strand space (applying to the message field of every event in a strand).

```
primrec swapMsg::msg ⇒ msg ⇒ msg ⇒ msg where
swapMsg g h (Nonce na) =
(if (g=(Nonce na)) then h else if (h=(Nonce na))
then g else (Nonce na)) |
swapMsg g h (Agent A ) =
(if (g=(Agent A)) then h else if (h=(Agent A))
then g else (Agent A)) |
swapMsg g h (Crypt K m ) =
(if (g= (Crypt K m )) then h else if (h= (Crypt K m ))
then g else (Crypt K (swapMsg g h m)))

swapSignMsg::msg ⇒ msg ⇒ (Sign × msg) ⇒ (Sign × msg) where
swapSignMsg g h sMsg ≡ (fst sMsg, swapMsg g h (snd sMsg))

definition swapStrandSpace::msg ⇒ msg ⇒ strand_space ⇒ strand_space
where swapStrandSpace g h SP ≡(%s. if ((Is_D_strand SP s)
∧ (node_term SP (s,1)=g ∨ node_term SP (s,1)=h))
then [(-,node_term SP (s,0) ),
(-,swapMsg g h (node_term SP (s,1)) ),
(+,plainTxt (swapMsg g h (node_term SP (s,1)))) ]
else if ((Is_E_strand SP s)
∧ (node_term SP (s,2)=g ∨ node_term SP (s,2)=h))
then [(-,node_term SP (s,0) ),
(-,plainTxt (swapMsg g h (node_term SP (s,2)))),
(+,swapMsg g h (node_term SP (s,2)))]
else (map (swapSignMsg g h) (SP s)))
```

Here plainTxt g is a function which returns the plain text of g which is of an encrypted form. E.g., plainTxt $\{\!|$ Nonce N $|\!\}_{\text{pubK } Y}$ = Nonce N. We emphasize that g and h are two messages of encrypted form when we use the definition swapStrandSpace g h SP in this work.

In strand space SP, if message $g(h)$ is uniquely originated in node $n(n')$, $g(h)$ is not a subterm of $h(g)$, $n(n')$ is in Domain SP, then $g(h)$ is uniquely originated in node $n'(n)$. Here we also assume that $g(h)$ is an encrypted message.

Lemma 3. $[\![$uniqOrig SP g n; $\neg g \sqsubset h$; $\neg h \sqsubset g$; uniqOrig SP h n'; ofEncryptForm g; ofEncryptForm h; $n \in$ Domain SP; $n' \in$ Domain $SP]\!]$
$\Longrightarrow$ uniqOrig (swapStrandSpace g h SP) g n'

swap g h SP is an Onion Strand Space. This is stated as a lemma below.

Lemma 4. $[\![SP \in$ onionStrandSpaces M; term SP $(s,0) = g$; term SP $(s',0) = h$; is_initiator M SP s g; is_initiator M SP s' $h]\!]$
$\Longrightarrow$ (swapStrandSpace g h SP) $\in$ onionStrandSpaces,
where is_initiator M SP s g $\equiv$ ($\exists Y$ N_0 N. is_initiator1 M SP s Y N_0 $N \wedge g =$ Crypt (pubK M)$\{\!|$ Nonce N_0, Agent B, Crypt (pubK B) (Nonce N) $|\!\}$)$\vee$
($\exists N$. is_initiator2 SP s M $N \wedge g =$ Crypt (pubEK M) (Nonce N).

Alignment Properties. Now we first define a predicate, initBundle SP b $\equiv$ $b \in$ bundles $SP \wedge (\forall s.(\exists i.(s,i) \in$ nodes $b) \longrightarrow$ is_regular_strand SP $s \vee$ Tee SP $s)$. We can show that the relation, $r =$ mapping SP SP' nodes b, which is composed of the corresponding message pairs of two sessions, which are modelled by b in SP and b in swapStrandSpace g h SP respectively, is single_valued. Here we also assume that initBundle SP b.

Lemma 5. $\llbracket b \in$ bundles SP; $SP \in$ onionStrandSpaces M; term SP $(s,0) = g$; term SP $(s',0) = h$; is_initiator M SP s g; is_initiator M SP s' h; initBundle SP b; $SP' =$ swapStrandSpace g h SP; $r =$ mapping SP SP' (nodes b)$\rrbracket$ $\Longrightarrow$ Reinterp b SP SP'

After applying analyzing operations pairwise on b, we can extend b to b', let $SP' =$ (swapStrandSpace g h SP), then we also have $b'' \in$ extendsByAnalz $b'SP'$ and Reinterp b'' SP SP'. After applying synthesizing operations pairwise on the b' in Lemma 5, we obtain another bundle b'', let $r =$ mapping SP SP' nodes b', if M is not in bad, and both nonLeakMsg g M and nonLeakMsg h M, then we also have $b'' \in$ extendsBySynth b'(swapStrandSpace g h SP) and Reinterp b'' SP SP'.

Observational Equivalence Between b and swap g h b. Next we show that b in SP is observationally equivalent to b in swap g h SP if the following constraints are satisfied: $g = \{\!\!|$ Nonce n_0, Agent Y, $\{\!\!|$Nonce n $\}\!\!|_{\mathsf{pubK}\ Y} \}\!\!|_{\mathsf{pubK}\ M}$, g is sent to the router, and h is also sent to the router M, and both g and h satisfy the nonLeakMsg conditions.

Lemma 6. $\llbracket SP \in$ onionStrandSpaces M; $b \in$ bundles SP; initBundle SP b; $g =$ Crypt (pubEK M)$\{\!\!|$ (Nonce N_0), (Agent Y), (Crypt (pubEK Y) (Nonce N)) $\}\!\!|$; term SP $n = g$; $n \in$ nodes b; term SP $n' = h$; $n' \in$ nodes b; $M \notin$ bad; nonLeakMsg g M; nonLeakMsg h M; is_initiator M SP (strand n) g; is_initiator M SP (strand n') $h\rrbracket$ $\Longrightarrow$ obsEquiv b SP (swap g h SP).

5.4   Proving Anonymity Properties

Let us give two preliminary definitions: the senders in a bundle, and a predicate nonLeakBundle b M specifying that b is a bundle where each honest agent sends a message m which satisfies nonLeakMsg m b.

```
sendersInBundle::strand_space ⇒ graph ⇒ agent set
where sendersInBundle SP b ≡
{A.∃ s. ofAgent SP s= A ∧ (s,0) ∈ nodes b
((∃ Y n0 n. is_initiator1 SP s M Y n0 n ) ∨
(∃ n. is_initiator2 SP s M n ))}


nonLeakBundle::strand_space ⇒ graph⇒ agent⇒bool
where nonLeakBundle SP b M ≡
∀ g n n'. ((n → SP n') ∧ n' ∈ nodes b ∧
ofAgent SP (strand n) ∉ bad ) ⟶ nonLeakMsg g M
```

Message g is forwarded to B by the router M, and is originated by some honest agent, and the bundle in SP satisfies nonLeakBundle SP b M, then the honest agent who originates g cannot be observed. Namely, the sender anonymity holds for the intruder w.r.t. the honest agents who send messages to M in the session modeled by b. This is summarized by the following theorem.

Theorem 1. $[\![SP \in$ onionStrandSpaces $M; b \in$ bundles $SP; g =$ Crypt (pubEK B) (Nonce N); $n \in$ nodes b; sign SP $n = - $; regularOrig (Nonce N) b SP; term SP $n = g$; nonLeakBundle SP b M; $M \notin$ bad$]\!] \Longrightarrow$ senderAnonymity (sendersInBundle SP $b -$ bad) (Nonce N) b (onionStrandSpaces M) SP.

6 Conclusion and Future Work

We presented a strand space approach to provable anonymity and formally implemented it in the theorem prover Isabelle/HOL. In order to do this, we extended the classical strand space theory. We built the concept of a protocol session based on the notion of "bundle" in a strand space. In the classical strand space theory, secrecy and authentication are studied by focusing individual sessions. However, two protocol sessions are needed in order to decide observational equivalence according to the adversary's knowledge obtained in the two separate sessions – in our extended strand space theory, they are represented by a similar bundle in two different strand spaces. Moreover, an observer needs to compare corresponding messages to decide the equivalence of two sessions based on his knowledge. In the strand space theory, knowledge deduction actions are represented by penetrator strands. Therefore, we proposed two kinds of bundle extensions: analyzing and synthesizing extensions, which improve the deduction ability of an observer. In the end, we proposed a natural definition on reinterpretation relation between two sessions. Essentially, the two compared sessions should have the same topological relation, and the message mapping of the two sessions should be single-valued. Combining reinterpretation relation and bundle extensions, we arrived at the key concept of observational equivalence between sessions. Based on this, we defined the semantics of anonymity properties in an epistemic framework and formally proved sender anonymity for the Onion Routing protocol. In the future, we plan to extend the whole theory to active intruders in the style of Dolev-Yao [26], and perform more case studies.

Acknowledgments. The first author, Yongjian Li, was supported by a grant 61170073 from the National Natural Science Foundation of China.

References

1. Schneider, S., Sidiropoulos, A.: CSP and anonymity. In: Martella, G., Kurth, H., Montolivo, E., Bertino, E. (eds.) ESORICS 1996. LNCS, vol. 1146, pp. 198–218. Springer, Heidelberg (1996)

2. Hughes, D., Shmatikov, V.: Information hiding, anonymity and privacy: a modular approach. J. Comput. Secur. **12**(1), 3–36 (2004)
3. Garcia, F.D., Hasuo, I., Pieters, W., van Rossum, P.: Provable anonymity. In: Proceedings of the 3rd Workshop on Formal Methods in Security Engineering, pp. 63–72. ACM (2005)
4. Chothia, T., Orzan, S., Pang, J., Torabi Dashti, M.: A Framework for automatically checking anonymity with μ CRL. In: Montanari, U., Sannella, D., Bruni, R. (eds.) TGC 2006. LNCS, vol. 4661, pp. 301–318. Springer, Heidelberg (2007)
5. Arapinis, M., Chothia, T., Ritter, E., Ryan, M.D.: Analysing unlinkability and anonymity using the applied pi calculus. In: Proceedings of the 23rd IEEE Computer Security Foundations Symposium, pp. 107–121. IEEE CS (2010)
6. Shmatikov, V.: Probabilistic model checking of an anonymity system. J. Comput. Secur. **12**(3/4), 355–377 (2004)
7. Halpern, J.Y., O'Neill, K.R.: Anonymity and information hiding in multiagent systems. J. Comput. Secur. **13**(3), 483–514 (2005)
8. Bhargava, M., Palamidessi, C.: Probabilistic anonymity. In: Abadi, M., de Alfaro, L. (eds.) CONCUR 2005. LNCS, vol. 3653, pp. 171–185. Springer, Heidelberg (2005)
9. Deng, Y., Palamidessi, C., Pang, J.: Weak probabilistic anonymity. In: Proceedings of the 3rd Workshop on Security Issues in Concurrency, vol. 180 of ENTCS, pp. 55–76 (2007)
10. Chen, X., Pang, J.: Measuring query privacy in location-based services. In: Proceedings of the 2nd ACM Conference on Data and Application Security and Privacy, pp. 49–60. ACM Press (2012)
11. Chen, X., Pang, J.: Protecting query privacy in location-based services. GeoInformatica (2013, To appear)
12. Delaune, S., Kremer, S., Ryan, M.D.: Verifying privacy-type properties of electronic voting protocols. J. Comput. Secur. **17**(4), 435–487 (2009)
13. Jonker, H.L., Mauw, S., Pang, J.: A formal framework for quantifying voter-controlled privacy. J. Algorithm Cogn. Inf. Logic **64**(2–3), 89–105 (2009)
14. Luo, Z., Cai, X., Pang, J., Deng, Y.: Analyzing an electronic cash protocol using applied pi calculus. In: Katz, J., Yung, M. (eds.) ACNS 2007. LNCS, vol. 4521, pp. 87–103. Springer, Heidelberg (2007)
15. Yan, L., Sere, K., Zhou, X., Pang, J.: Towards an integrated architecture for peer-to-peer and ad hoc overlay network applications. In: Proceedings of the 10th Workshop on Future Trends in Distributed Computing Systems, pp. 312–318. IEEE CS (2004)
16. Chothia, T.: Analysing the MUTE anonymous file-sharing system using the pi-calculus. In: Najm, E., Pradat-Peyre, J.-F., Donzeau-Gouge, V.V. (eds.) FORTE 2006. LNCS, vol. 4229, pp. 115–130. Springer, Heidelberg (2006)
17. Dong, N., Jonker, H., Pang, J.: Formal analysis of privacy in an eHealth protocol. In: Foresti, S., Yung, M., Martinelli, F. (eds.) ESORICS 2012. LNCS, vol. 7459, pp. 325–342. Springer, Heidelberg (2012)
18. Kawabe, Y., Mano, K., Sakurada, H., Tsukada, Y.: Theorem-proving anonymity of infinite state systems. Inform. Process. Lett. **101**(1), 46–51 (2007)
19. Nipkow, T., Paulson, L.C., Wenzel, M.T. (eds.): Isabelle/HOL. LNCS, vol. 2283. Springer, Heidelberg (2002)
20. Li, Y., Pang, J.: An inductive approach to provable anonymity. In: Proceedings of the 6th Conference on Availability, Reliability and Security, pp. 454–459. IEEE CS (2011)

21. Javier Thayer, F., Herzog, J.C., Guttman, J.D.: Strand spaces: why is a security protocol correct? In: Proceedings of the 19th IEEE Symposium on Security and Privacy, pp. 96–109. IEEE CS (1998)
22. Thayer, J.F., Herzog, J.C., Guttman, J.D.: Strand spaces: proving security protocols correct. J. Comput. Secur. **7**(1), 191–230 (1999)
23. Li, Y., Pang, J.: An inductive approach to strand spaces. Formal Aspects Comput. **25**(4), 465–501 (2013)
24. Goldschlag, D.M., Reed, M.G., Syverson, P.F.: Hiding routing information. In: Anderson, R. (ed.) Information Hiding. LNCS, vol. 1774, pp. 137–150. Springer, Heidelberg (1996)
25. Syverson, P.F., Goldschlag, D.M., Reed, M.G.: Anonymous connections and onion routing. In: Proceedings of the 18th IEEE Symposium on Security and Privacy, pp. 44–54. IEEE (1997)
26. Dolev, D., Yao, A.: On the security of public key protocols. IEEE Trans. Inf. Theory **29**(12), 198–208 (1983)
27. Dingledine, R., Mathewson, N., Syverson, P.F.: Tor: the second-generation onion router. In: Proceedings of the 13th USENIX Security Symposium, pp. 303–320 (2004)
28. Chaum, D.L.: Untraceable electronic mail, return addresses, and digital pseudonyms. Commun. ACM **24**(2), 84–90 (1981)

Counterexample Generation
for Hybrid Automata

Johanna Nellen[1], Erika Ábrahám[1]([✉]), Xin Chen[1], and Pieter Collins[2]

[1] RWTH Aachen University, Aachen, Germany
{johanna.nellen,abraham}@cs.rwth-aachen.de,
pieter.collins@maastrichtuniversity.nl
[2] Maastricht University, Maastricht, The Netherlands

Abstract. The last decade brought us a whole range of over-approximative algorithms for the reachability analysis of *hybrid automata*, a widely used modeling language for systems with combined discrete-continuous behavior. Besides theoretical results, there are also some tools available for proving *safety* in the continuous time domain. However, if a given set of critical states is found to be reachable, these tools do not provide *counterexamples* for models beyond timed automata.

This paper investigates the question whether and how available tools can be used to generate counterexamples, even if this functionality is not directly supported. Using the tools SpaceEx and FLOW*, we discuss possibilities to solve our task with and without modifying the tools' source code, report on the effort and the efficiency of implementation, and propose a simulation-based approach for the validation of the resulting (possibly spurious) counterexamples.

1 Introduction

Hybrid systems are systems that exhibit both continuous and discrete behavior. Typical examples are physical systems regulated by discrete controllers, e.g., automotive control systems or controlled chemical plants. Hybrid systems are often modeled as *hybrid automata* [1], for which the reachability problem is undecidable. Despite undecidability and driven by the fact that most hybrid systems in industrial context are safety-critical, a lot of effort was put into the development of *reachability analysis* techniques for hybrid automata. State-of-the-art tools like SpaceEx [2] and FLOW* [3] try to compute an *over-approximation* of the reachable state space and can therefore be used to prove safety, i.e., that a given set of unsafe states cannot be reached from a set of initial states in a given model. However, if the over-approximation of the reachable states contains unsafe states then no conclusive answer can be given.

The original publication is available at http://www.springerlink.com.
This work is supported by the DFG research training group AlgoSyn and the DFG research project HyPro.

C. Artho and P.C. Ölveczky (Eds.): FTSCS 2013, CCIS 419, pp. 88–106, 2014.
DOI: 10.1007/978-3-319-05416-2_7, © Springer International Publishing Switzerland 2014

Counterexamples in form of system runs leading to unsafe states would be extremely valuable, even if they are *spurious*, i.e., if they were considered in the analysis but are not possible in the given model. For safe models they could help to reduce the approximation error in the analysis efficiently, whereas for unsafe models they could provide important information about the source of the critical system behavior. Counterexamples would enable the application of counterexample-guided abstraction refinement (CEGAR) techniques and could also play an important role in controller synthesis.

Unfortunately, none of the available tools for hybrid automata reachability analysis with continuous time domain computes counterexamples. It is surprising since *internally* they possess sufficient information to generate at least a coarse over-approximation of a counterexample in form of a sequence of jumps (i.e., changes in the discrete part of the system state), augmented with time intervals over-approximating the time durations between the jumps. In this paper we

1. examine whether it is possible to either use *augmented* system models or to extract information from the *output* of the SpaceEx tool such that we can *synthesize* over-approximations of counterexamples;
2. study how the *efficiency* can be improved by extending the functionality of the FLOW* tool *internally*, i.e., by making modifications to the source code;
3. develop a simulation-based approach to *validate* the counterexample over-approximations, i.e., to determine unsafe paths in the over-approximation.

We have chosen SpaceEx and FLOW* for our experiments because on the one hand SpaceEx is one of the most popular hybrid automata reachability analysis tools and on the other hand some of the authors belong to the implementation team of FLOW*, i.e., the modification of the source code of FLOW* could be done safely. Unfortunately, counterexample generation without tool extension is unsatisfactory: we need either expensive additional analysis runs for enlarged systems or parsing hidden information from debug output. The results demonstrate the need to extend the functionality of available analysis tools to generate counterexamples internally. However, even if that task is done, the results strongly over-approximate counterexamples, whose existence can be indicated but not proven. Thus we need novel methods to refine and validate the results, posing highly challenging problems in both theory and practice.

Related Work. In this paper we focus on reachability analysis techniques for continuous-time hybrid automata that apply a fixed-point-based forward-reachability iteration [1]. Such algorithms need two main ingredients: (a) A technique to *represent* state sets and to compute certain operations on them like union, intersection, Minkowski sum, etc. All the available tools work with *over-approximative* representations and computations. Popular approaches use either geometric objects like hyperrectangles [4], polyhedra [5–9], zonotopes [10,11], orthogonal polyhedra [12] or ellipsoids [13], or symbolic representations like support functions [14,15] or Taylor models [16,17]. The choice of the representation is crucial, as it strongly influences the *approximation error* and the *efficiency* of the computations. (b) A method to compute *one-step-successors* of state sets both for continuous flow and discrete jumps. A *flowpipe* is an over-approximation of the states that are reachable from a given initial set of states by letting time progress within a certain maximal time horizon. To compute a flowpipe, the maximal time horizon is often divided into smaller intervals and the flowpipe is represented as a (finite) union of state sets (flowpipe segments), each covering one of the smaller intervals [5].

The analysis tools HyTech [6], PHAVer [7] and the Multi-Parametric Toolbox [8] use convex polyhedra for the over-approximative representation of state sets, SpaceEx [2] additionally allows the usage of support functions. In [18], the state sets are over-approximated by level sets. The tool d/dt [19] uses grid paving as over-approximations. MATISSE [20] over-approximates state sets by zonotopes. The MATLAB Ellipsoidal Toolbox [21] supports the over-approximative representation of sets by ellipsoids, FLOW* by Taylor models. In ARIADNE [22], the state sets may be over-approximated by Taylor models or grid pavings. In contrast to the other tools, FLOW*, HyTech, PHAVer, ARIADNE and d/dt also support the analysis of non-linear hybrid automata (with non-linear differential equations).

None of these tools supports the generation of counterexamples. There are some works [23, 24] related to counterexample generation for hybrid systems, but they are mostly devoted to CEGAR approaches for restricted classes of hybrid automata like, e.g., (initialized) rectangular automata.

Outline. After some preliminaries in Sect. 2, we describe in the Sects. 3 and 4 how we can compute over-approximations of counterexamples for unsafe models, whose validation is discussed in Sect. 5. Section 6 concludes the paper.

2 Preliminaries

By $\mathbb{N}$, $\mathbb{Z}$ and $\mathbb{R}$ we denote the set of all natural (with 0), integer and real numbers, respectively, by $\mathbb{R}_{\geq 0}$ the non-negative reals, and use $\mathbb{N}_{>0} = \mathbb{N}\backslash\{0\}$. For some $n \in \mathbb{N}_{>0}$, let $Var = \{x_1, \ldots, x_n\}$ be an ordered set of variables over $\mathbb{R}$. We use the notation $x = (x_1, \ldots, x_n)$, and denote by Var' and $\dot{Var}$ the renamed variable sets $\{x_1', \ldots, x_n'\}$ and $\{\dot{x}_1, \ldots, \dot{x}_n\}$, respectively. Given a real-arithmetic formula ϕ over Var, its satisfaction set is $[\![\phi]\!] = \{v \in \mathbb{R}^n \mid \phi[v/x] = true\}$; we call ϕ *convex* if $[\![\phi]\!]$ is convex. Let $\Phi(Var)$ be the set of all quantifier-free convex real-arithmetic formulas (so-called *predicates*) over Var. A predicate is *linear* if it can be expressed in linear real arithmetic.

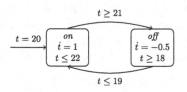

Fig. 1. The thermostat example

Definition 1 (Syntax of Hybrid Automata). *A* hybrid automaton (HA) *is a tuple* $\mathcal{H} = (Loc, Var, Edge, Dyn, Inv, Init)$ *with the following components:*

– *Loc is a finite set of* locations *or* modes.

- $Var = \{x_1, \ldots, x_n\}$ is a finite ordered set of variables over $\mathbb{R}$. A valuation $v = (v_1, \ldots, v_n) \in \mathbb{R}^n$ defines for each $i = 1, \ldots, n$ the value v_i for x_i. A state is a mode-valuation pair $\sigma = (l, v) \in Loc \times \mathbb{R}^n = \Sigma$.
- $Edge \subseteq Loc \times \Phi(Var \cup Var') \times Loc$ is a finite set of edges. For an edge $e = (l, \phi, l') \in Edge$ we call l (l') the source (target) mode of e and ϕ its transition relation.
- $Dyn : Loc \to \Phi(Var \cup \dot{Var})$ assigns a dynamics to each mode.
- $Inv : Loc \to \Phi(Var)$ assigns an invariant to each mode.
- $Init : Loc \to \Phi(Var)$ specifies the initial valuations for each mode.

Since we do not use the parallel composition of hybrid automata in this paper, for simplicity we skipped composition-relevant parts in the above definition.

A toy example of a *thermostat* is depicted graphically in Fig. 1. The rectangles represent modes; their names, dynamics and invariants are specified inside the rectangle. Initial valuations are specified on an incoming edge of a given mode without a source mode; a missing incoming edge stays for the initial condition *false*. Figure 2 shows the *navigation benchmark* [25], used later for experiments. It models an object moving in the $\mathbb{R}^2$ plane. The velocity (v_1, v_2) of the object depends on its position (x_1, x_2) in a grid. For some experiments we add a parameter ε to the navigation benchmark to enlarge the satisfaction sets of guards and invariants by replacing all upper bounds ub (lower bounds lb) by $ub + \varepsilon$ ($lb - \varepsilon$).

Definition 2 (Semantics of Hybrid Automata). *The* operational semantics *of a HA* $\mathcal{H} = (Loc, Var, Edge, Dyn, Inv, Init)$ *with* $Var = \{x_1, \ldots, x_n\}$ *is given by the rules of Fig. 3. The first rule specifies time evolution (time steps), the second one discrete mode changes (jumps).*

Let $\to := \bigcup_{t \in \mathbb{R}_{\geq 0}} \overset{t}{\to} \cup \bigcup_{e \in Edge} \overset{e}{\to}$. A path of $\mathcal{H}$ is a (finite or infinite) sequence $(l_0, v_0) \to (l_1, v_1) \to \ldots$. For an initial path we additionally require $v_0 \in [\![Init(l_0)]\!]$. A state $(l, v) \in \Sigma$ is called reachable in $\mathcal{H}$ if there is an initial path $(l_0, v_0) \to (l_1, v_1) \to \ldots$ of $\mathcal{H}$ and an index $i \geq 0$ such that $(l_i, v_i) = (l, v)$.

Please note that each reachable state (l, v) of $\mathcal{H}$ can be reached via an initial path of $\mathcal{H}$ of the form $(l_0, v_0) \overset{t_0}{\to} (l_0, v'_0) \overset{e_0}{\to} \ldots (l_{n-1}, v_{n-1}) \overset{t_{n-1}}{\to} (l_{n-1}, v'_{n-1}) \overset{e_{n-1}}{\to} (l_n, v_n) \overset{t_n}{\to} (l_n, v'_n) = (l, v)$ with alternating time steps and jumps for some $n \in \mathbb{N}$. In the following we consider only paths of this form.

A *trace* $e_0, e_1, \ldots$ describes a sequence of jumps with $e_i \in Edge$ such that the target mode of e_i equals the source mode of e_{i+1} for all $i \in \mathbb{N}$. If we can assume that there is at most one jump between each mode pair, we also identify traces by the sequence $l_0, l_1, \ldots$ of modes visited. Such a trace *represents* the set of all paths $(l_0, v_0) \overset{t''_0}{\to} (l_0, v'_0) \overset{e_0}{\to} (l_1, v_1) \overset{t''_1}{\to} (l_1, v'_1) \overset{e_1}{\to} \ldots$. We say that those paths are *contained* in the symbolic path.

A *timed trace* $e_0, [t_0, t'_0], e_1, [t_1, t'_1], \ldots$ annotates a trace $e_0, e_1, \ldots$ with time intervals and *represents* the set of all paths $(l_0, v_0) \overset{t''_0}{\to} (l_0, v'_0) \overset{e_0}{\to} (l_1, v_1) \overset{t''_1}{\to} (l_1, v'_1) \overset{e_1}{\to} \ldots$ with $t''_i \in [t_i, t'_i]$ for all $i \in \mathbb{N}$. We say that $e_0, [t_0, t'_0], e_1, [t_1, t'_1], \ldots$ is a timed trace of the represented paths, which are *contained* in the timed trace.

$$\begin{pmatrix}\dot{x}_1\\\dot{x}_2\end{pmatrix}=\begin{pmatrix}v_1\\v_2\end{pmatrix} \text{ and } \begin{pmatrix}\dot{v}_1\\\dot{v}_2\end{pmatrix}=\begin{pmatrix}-1.8&-0.2\\-0.2&-1.8\end{pmatrix}\begin{pmatrix}v_1\\v_2\end{pmatrix}+\begin{pmatrix}b_1\\b_2\end{pmatrix} \text{ in each location}$$

with b_1, b_2 as specified inside the location, $c = 0.7017$

$x_1 \in [3, 3.8]$,
$x_2 \in [3, 4]$,
$v_1 \in [-0.1, 0.1]$,
$v_2 \in [-0.8, -0.5]$

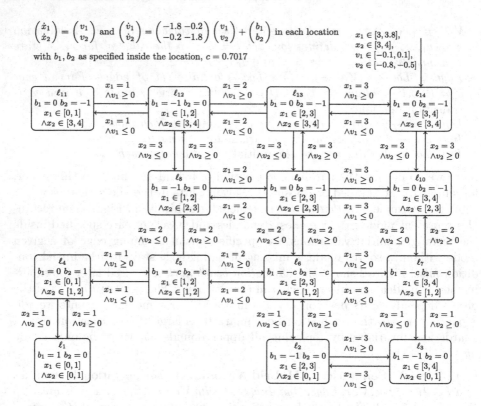

Fig. 2. The navigation benchmark

$$\frac{l \in Loc \quad v, v' \in \mathbb{R}^n \quad t \in \mathbb{R}_{\geq 0} \quad f:[0,t]\to\mathbb{R}^n \; differentiable \quad \dot{f}=\frac{df}{dt}}{f(0)=v \quad f(t)=v' \quad \forall t' \in [0,t].\; f(t')\in[\![Inv(l)]\!] \wedge (f(t'),\dot{f}(t'))\in[\![Dyn(l)]\!]}{(l,v)\xrightarrow{t}(l,v')} \text{ TIME}$$

$$\frac{l, l' \in Loc \quad v, v' \in \mathbb{R}^n \quad v\in[\![Inv(l)]\!] \quad v'\in[\![Inv(l')]\!] \quad e=(l,\phi,l')\in Edge \quad (v,v')\in[\![\phi]\!]}{(l,v)\xrightarrow{e}(l',v')} \text{ JUMP}$$

Fig. 3. Operational semantics rules for hybrid automata

Given a HA $\mathcal{H}$ and a set B of unsafe states of $\mathcal{H}$, the *reachability problem* poses the question whether the intersection of B with the reachable state set of $\mathcal{H}$ is empty, i.e., whether $\mathcal{H}$ is safe. If $\mathcal{H}$ is unsafe, a *counterexample* is an initial path of $\mathcal{H}$ leading to an unsafe state from B. For models with weaker expressivity, for example hybrid automata defined by linear predicates and constant derivatives (i.e., dynamics of the form $\bigwedge_{x\in Var}\dot{x}=c_x$ with $c_x\in\mathbb{Z}$ for all $x \in Var$), the *bounded* reachability problem is decidable and, for unsafe models, counterexamples can be generated (e.g., by bounded model checking using SMT solving with exact arithmetic). However, the computation of counterexamples for general hybrid automata is hard. Theoretically, it could be done by (incom-

plete) *under-approximative* reachability computations, but currently there are
no techniques available for this task.

We propose an approach to generate and refine *presumable counterexamples*, which are timed traces that *might* contain a counterexample; presumable
counterexamples that do *not* contain any counterexample are called *spurious*.

3   Generating Traces for Presumable Counterexamples

Existing hybrid automata analysis tools like SpaceEx offer as output options either
the computed over-approximation of the reachable state space, its intersection with
the unsafe states, or just the answer whether unsafe states are reachable or not (in
the over-approximation). However, in contrast to tools for discrete automata, none
of the tools for hybrid automata provides counterexamples.

In this section we show how a *trace* explaining the reachability of unsafe
states can be computed. We present three different approaches: The first approach augments hybrid automata with auxiliary variables to make observations
about the computation history of the analysis. The second approach can be
used if the analysis tool outputs sufficient information about the paths that
have been processed during the analysis. The third approach suggests to implement some new functionalities efficiently in existing tools. In our experiments we
used SpaceEx v0.9.7c, VMware server, and the latest FLOW* version but with
the proposed extensions.

3.1   Approach I: Model Augmentation

We extend the model with new variables to make book-keeping about traces
that lead to unsafe states in the reachability analysis. First we augment the
model and analyze the augmented system to observe the *number of jumps* until
an unsafe state is reached. Then we augment and analyze an unrolled model to
observe unsafe *traces*.

Determining the Counterexample Length. We augment the model and analyze
it to gain information about the length of paths leading to unsafe states. We
introduce a counter tr with initial value 0, define $\dot{tr}=0$ in each mode, and let
each jump increase the counter value by one.

However, the unboundedness of tr would render the fixed-point analysis to
be non-terminating. To bound tr from above, we define a constant max_{tr} and
either extend the invariants or the edge guards to forbid higher values.

The value of max_{tr} should be guessed, and in case the analysis of the augmented model reports safety, increased. A possible guess could be the number of
iterations during the fixed-point analysis of the original model, which is reported
by SpaceEx and specifies how many times the tool computed a (time+jump) successor of a state set. To get a smaller value (and thus shorter counterexamples
with less computational effort), the reachability analysis could be stopped when
an unsafe state is reached. Unfortunately, SpaceEx does not offer this option.

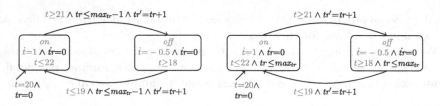

Fig. 4. The guard (left) and the invariant (right) augmentation of the thermostat model

Definition 3. (Guard and Invariant Augmentation). *Let* $\mathcal{H} = (Loc, Var,$ *Edge, Dyn, Inv, Init) be a HA and* $max_{tr} \in \mathbb{N}$. *The* guard augmentation *of* $\mathcal{H}$ *is the HA* $\mathcal{H}_{guard} = (Loc, Var \cup \{tr\}, Edge', Dyn', Inv, Init')$ *with*

- *Edge'* $= \{(l, (\phi \wedge tr \leq max_{tr} - 1 \wedge tr' = tr+1), l') \mid (l, \phi, l') \in Edge\};$
- *Dyn'(l)* $= (Dyn(l) \wedge \dot{tr}{=}0)$ *for each* $l \in Loc$;
- *Init'(l)* $= (Init(l) \wedge tr{=}0)$ *for each* $l \in Loc$.

The invariant augmentation *of* $\mathcal{H}$ *is the HA* $\mathcal{H}_{inv} = (Loc, Var \cup \{tr\}, Edge'',$ *Dyn', Inv'', Init') with Dyn' and Init' as above and*

- *Edge''* $= \{(l, (\phi \wedge tr' = tr+1), l') \mid (l, \phi, l') \in Edge\};$
- *Inv''(l)* $= (Inv(l) \wedge tr \leq max_{tr})$ *for each* $l \in Loc$.

Figure 4 illustrates the augmentation on the thermostat example. Note that, apart from restricting the number of jumps, the above augmentation does not modify the original system behavior. The size of the state space is increased by the factor $max_{tr}+1$, since the value domain of tr is $[0, max_{tr}] \subseteq \mathbb{N}$ for the constant max_{tr}.

When we analyze the augmented model, SpaceEx returns for each mode in the over-approximated set of reachable unsafe states an over-approximation $[l, u]$ for the values of tr.

Since tr takes integer values only, the lower and upper bounds are not approximated, i.e., during analysis both after l and after u (over-approximative) jump computations unsafe states were reached, but we do not have any information about the values in between. Therefore we fix the number k, describing the length of counterexamples we want to generate, to be either l or u.

We made some experiments for the thermostat example with unsafe states $t \leq 19$, and for the navigation benchmark with unsafe states $(x_1, x_2) \in [1, 2] \times [0, 1]$. Table 1 compares for different max_{tr} values the number of SpaceEx iterations, the running times, and the resulting tr values for the original models, the guard and the invariant augmentations. For the same number of iterations, the augmented models need in average some more (but still comparable) time for the analysis than the original models; the invariant and guard augmentations seem to be similar in terms of running time.

Trace Encoding. In order to observe the traces leading to unsafe states, we need to remember the jumps in the order of their occurrences. We achieve this by

Table 1. Evaluation of the guard and invariant augmentations with a sampling time of 0.1 and a time horizon of 30

Model	Augment.	max_{tr}	#iter.	Fixed point	Running time [s]	tr
Thermostat	none	-	5/11/31	no/no/no	0.11/0.24/0.69	-
example	guard	4/10/30	5/11/31	yes/yes/yes	0.25/0.65/2.15	$[1,4]/[1,10]/[1,30]$
	invar.	4/10/30	5/11/31	yes/yes/yes	0.30/0.78/2.53	$[1,4]/[1,10]/[1,30]$
Navigation	none	-	29/168/3645	no/no/no	1.54/8.63/1598.63	-
benchmark	guard	4/10/30	29/168/3645	yes/yes/yes	1.92/12.25/2088.88	$[4,4]/[4,10]/[4,30]$
	invar.	4/10/30	29/168/3160	yes/yes/yes	2.06/13.02/1466.08	$[4,4]/[4,10]/[4,30]$
Navigation2	none	-	32/524	no/no	7.55/254.91	-
benchmark,	guard	4/10	32/524	yes/yes	7.55/284.19	$[4,4]/[4,10]$
$\varepsilon = 0.1$	invar.	4/10	32/524	yes/yes	7.35/293.88	$[4,4]/[4,10]$

unrolling the transition relation of the original model k times, where k is the counterexample length determined in the previous step.

We could define the unrolling by copying each mode $k+1$ and each edge k times, and let the ith copy of an edge connect the ith-copy of the source mode with the $(i+1)$st copy of the target mode. To remember the jumps taken, we introduce k auxiliary variables $tr_1, \ldots, tr_k$ and store on the ith copy of an edge the edge's identity in tr_i. Such an unrolling would cause a polynomial increase in the size of the model.

However, in such an unrolling there might be different traces leading to the same mode. SpaceEx would *over-approximate* these trace sets by a mode-wise closure, such that we cannot extract them from the result. E.g., for two traces l_1, l_2, l_4, l_5, l_7 and l_1, l_3, l_4, l_6, l_7, resp., also the trace l_1, l_2, l_4, l_6, l_7 would be included in the over-approximation. Therefore, we copy each mode as many times as the number of different traces of length up to k leading to it. This yields an exponential growth in k for the number of locations and transitions.

We augment the unrolled model to observe the traces to unsafe states. In a naive encoding, we identify edges $e_1, \ldots, e_d$ by numbers $1, \ldots, d$, and introduce new variables tr_i for $i=1, \ldots, k$ to store the edges taken.

We also define an advanced encoding which needs less auxiliary variables. If the domain of a variable includes $[0, |Edge|^n]$ for some $n \in \mathbb{N}$ then we can use it to store a *sequence* of n edges: Each time an edge is taken, we multiply the current value by $|Edge|$ and add the identity of the taken edge. This way we need $\lceil \frac{k}{n} \rceil$ auxiliary variables to encode a path of length k.

Definition 4 (k-unrolling, Trace Encoding). *Assume a HA $\mathcal{H} = (Loc, Var, Edge, Dyn, Inv, Init)$ with an ordered set $\{e_1, \ldots, e_d\}$ of edges. The k-unrolling of $\mathcal{H}$ is the HA $\mathcal{H}_u = (Loc_u, Var_u, Edge_u, Dyn_u, Inv_u, Init_u)$ with*

- $Loc_u = \bigcup_{i=1,\ldots,k+1} Loc^i$;
- $Var_u = Var$;
- $Edge_u = \{((l_1,\ldots,l_i), \phi, (l_1,\ldots,l_i,l_{i+1})) \mid 1 \leq i \leq k \wedge (l_i, \phi, l_{i+1}) \in Edge\}$;
- $Dyn_u(l_1,\ldots,l_i) = Dyn(l_i)$ *for all* $(l_1,\ldots,l_i) \in Loc_u$;
- $Inv_u(l_1,\ldots,l_i) = Inv(l_i)$ *for all* $(l_1,\ldots,l_i) \in Loc_u$;
- $Init_u(l_1,\ldots,l_i) = Init(l_i)$ *for* $i = 1$ *and false otherwise, for all* $(l_1,\ldots,l_i) \in Loc_u$.

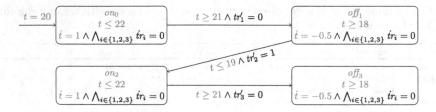

Fig. 5. Naive trace encoding of the thermostat example with depth 3

Table 2. Evaluation of the naive and advanced trace encodings for the thermostat example and the navigation benchmark ($k = 4$, time step 0.1, time horizon 30) using $\pi_1 = l_{14}, l_{13}, l_9, l_6, l_2$, $\pi_2 = l_{14}, l_{10}, l_7, l_6, l_2$, $\pi_3 = l_{14}, l_{10}, l_7, l_3, l_2$ and $\pi_4 = l_{14}, l_{10}, l_9, l_6, l_2$

Model	Trace	#locs	#trans	#vars	n	Time [s]	Solutions
Thermostat	none	2	2	1	-	0.136	-
example	naive	5	4	5	4	0.312	on, off, on, off, on
	adv.	5	4	2	4	0.147	on, off, on, off, on
Navigation	none	14	36	5	-	1.372	-
benchmark	naive	81	80	9	3	1.777	$\pi_1; \pi_2; \pi_3; \pi_4$
	adv.	81	80	7	3	1.503	$\pi_1; \pi_2; \pi_3; \pi_4$

The naive trace encoding of $\mathcal{H}$ *is the HA* $\mathcal{H}_1 = (Loc_u, Var_1, Edge_1, Dyn_1, Inv_u, Init_1)$ *with*

- $Var_1 = Var \cup \{tr_1, \ldots, tr_k\}$;
- $Edge_1 = \{((l_1, \ldots, l_i), \phi \wedge tr_i' = j, (l_1, \ldots, l_i, l_{i+1})) \mid 1 \leq i \leq k \wedge e_j = (l_i, \phi, l_{i+1}) \in Edge\}$;
- $Dyn_1(l_1, \ldots, l_i) = Dyn_u(l_1, \ldots, l_i) \wedge \bigwedge_{j=1}^{k} \dot{tr}_j = 0$ *for all* $(l_1, \ldots, l_i) \in Loc_u$;
- $Init_1(l_1, \ldots, l_i) = Init_u(l_1, \ldots, l_i) \wedge \bigwedge_{j=1}^{k} tr_j = 0$ *for all* $(l_1, \ldots, l_i) \in Loc_u$.

Let $n \in \mathbb{N}_{>0}$ *such that* $[0, d^n]$ *is included in the domain of each* tr_i *and let* $z = \lceil \frac{k}{n} \rceil$. *The advanced trace encoding of* $\mathcal{H}$ *with depth* k *is the HA* $\mathcal{H}_2 = (Loc_u, Var_2, Edge_2, Dyn_2, Inv_u, Init_2)$ *with*

- $Var_2 = Var \cup \{tr_1, \ldots, tr_z\}$;
- $Edge_2 = \{((l_1, \ldots, l_i), \phi \wedge tr_{\lceil i/n \rceil}' = tr_{\lceil i/n \rceil} \cdot d + j, (l_1, \ldots, l_i, l_{i+1})) \mid 1 \leq i \leq k \wedge e_j = (l_i, \phi, l_{i+1}) \in Edge$;
- $Dyn_2(l_1, \ldots, l_i) = Dyn_u(l_1, \ldots, l_i) \wedge \bigwedge_{j=1}^{z} \dot{tr}_j = 0$ *for all* $(l_1, \ldots, l_i) \in Loc_u$;
- $Init_2(l_1, \ldots, l_i) = Init_u(l_1, \ldots, l_i) \wedge \bigwedge_{j=1}^{z} tr_j = 0$ *for all* $(l_1, \ldots, l_i) \in Loc_u$.

An example unrolled model for the thermostat with naive trace encoding is shown in Fig. 5. Note that depending on the chosen trace encoding, up to k auxiliary variables are added to the system.

Using our implementation for the proposed trace encodings, in Table 2 we compare the model sizes and the analysis running times for the thermostat example and the navigation benchmark. Compared to the original model, the analysis running times for the trace encodings increase only slightly. The last column lists the computed traces, which are (as expected) the same for both encodings.

3.2   Approach II: Parsing the Output of SpaceEx

The approach introduced above does not scale for large systems, since the unrolling blow up the models too strongly. If the verification tool offers enough information about the analyzed system traces, it is perhaps also possible to extract from the tool's output the same information we gathered by system augmentation and additional analysis runs. We are interested in determining traces that lead to unsafe states during the analysis, since they are candidates for presumable counterexamples. Without loss of generality, we assume that unsafe states are restricted to a single mode.

SpaceEx stores in a FIFO list a sequence of *symbolic states*, each of them consisting of a mode and a state set, whose successors still have to be computed in the forward reachability analysis algorithm. This so-called *waiting list* contains initially each mode with its initial valuation set (if not empty). In each iteration, the next element from the list is taken. Its flowpipe for a user-defined time horizon and all possible (non-empty) jump successors of the flowpipe seg-

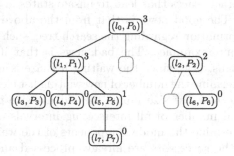

Fig. 6. SpaceEx search tree

ments are computed and those that were not yet processed are added to the list. As illustrated in Fig. 6, this computation hierarchy corresponds to a tree whose nodes are processed in a breadth-first manner. Each node corresponds to a mode and a set of valuations, which was found to be reachable. The upper indices on the nodes show the number of computed successor sets, whereas gray nodes in the figure represent successors that are contained in another already processed set in the same mode and are therefore not added to the tree.

SpaceEx does not output the structure of this tree. However, using *debug level 2*, we can make use of more verbose console outputs to get additional informations.

- When an iteration starts, SpaceEx outputs a text from which we can extract the iteration number i ("Iteration 5...").
- SpaceEx starts the flowpipe computation and outputs the mode of the current symbolic state ("applying time elapse in location loc()==114").
- The computation of jump successors follows, which is edge-wise. For each edge, whose source is the current mode, its label, source, target is printed ("applying discrete post of transition with label navigation.trans from location loc()==114 to location loc()==113").
- SpaceEx determines, which of the previously computed flowpipe segments intersect with the guard ("found 1 intervals intersecting with guard").
- The jump successors for the intersecting flowpipe segments are computed and, if not yet processed, put to the waiting list. Before switching to the next

outgoing edge, some information on the computation time is given ("`Discrete post done after 0.098s, cumul 0.098s`").

- When all outgoing edges are handled, the iteration is done, and the following output gives us the total number of processed symbolic states and the current size of the waiting list ("`1 sym states passed, 2 waiting`").
- After termination of the analysis some general analysis results are printed, e.g., the number of iterations, whether a fixed point was found or not, the analysis time, and whether unsafe states were reached.

If we would succeed to re-construct the search tree (or at least the involved mode components and their hierarchy) using the above information, we could extract traces that lead to unsafe states in the tree.

The good news is that from the above outputs we can extract quite some information regarding the search tree, such that in some cases we can construct counterexamples. The bad news is that it is not sufficient to reconstruct all details. E.g., since the waiting list size is reported after each iteration, we can determine the number of new waiting list elements added during the last iteration (the new list size minus the old list size minus 1). If this number equals the total number of all intersecting intervals over all analyzed edges then we can determine the mode components of the waiting list elements. However, if some of the successors are already processed and therefore not added to the queue then we cannot know for sure which sets were added. For example, if out of two sets having the same mode component only one was added to the queue, then we cannot know which of them. To avoid wrong guesses, those cases are skipped and not considered further in our implementation.

Without model augmentation, it is not possible to restrict the SpaceEx search to paths of a given length, therefore we cannot directly compare this method to the results of Table 2. We made experiments with the navigation benchmark using the debug output *D2* of SpaceEx. For 50 iterations, with a computation time of 32.28 s we found 11 traces leading to unsafe states in l_2. When considering only 25 iterations, the computation time is 12.69 s and only 4 traces are found. The increase of running time for using SpaceEx with debug level *D2* instead of the default value *medium* was negligible in our experiments.

A single analysis run suffices to extract traces of counterexamples thus this method seems to be superior to the augmentation approaches if the analysis tool communicates enough information about the system traces. However, if not all relevant details are accessible, not all traces can be rebuilt safely.

3.3   Approach III: Extending the Functionality of Flow*

Extracting information from the textual output of a tool is an overhead, since the information was already computed during analysis. Moreover, it might be imprecise if we do not have access to all needed information.

Instead, we could generate counterexample traces on-the-fly by attaching to each symbolic state in the waiting queue the trace that lead to it during the search. The waiting queue initially contains initial symbolic states, to which we

Table 3. Trace generation using FLOW* ($k = 4$, time step 0.1, time horizon 30, $\pi_1 = l_{14}, l_{13}, l_9, l_6, l_2$, $\pi_2 = l_{14}, l_{10}, l_7, l_6, l_2$ and $\pi_3 = l_{14}, l_{10}, l_7, l_3, l_2$)

Model	Running time [s]	Solutions
Thermostat example	0.23	on, off, on, off, on
Navigation benchmark	8.37	π_1, π_2, π_3

attach themselves. If we add a new symbolic state with location l as a successor of another symbolic state, then we attach to the new state the path of the predecessor state extended with the jump whose successor the new state is. The reachability computation will stop when the tree is complete till depth k (the maximal jump depth). Next, FLOW* intersects each tree node with the unsafe set. If a non-empty intersection is detected, the tool dumps the trace attached to the unsafe node.

To implement the above functionality, only minor changes had to be made in FLOW*, but it saves us the time of augmenting the system or parsing tool output. We made experiments in line with Table 2 for the thermostat example and the navigation benchmark. The results are shown in Table 3. Please note that FLOW* does not compute the trace $l_{14}, l_{10}, l_9, l_6, l_2$, which is spurious. We additionally analyzed the navigation benchmark with $k = 8$, where FLOW* generated 8 traces to unsafe states in l_2 with initial valuation $x_1 \in [3, 3.5]$, $x_2 \in [3, 4]$, $v_1 \in [-0.1, 0.1]$ and $v_2 \in [-0.8, -0.5]$.

4   Generating a Presumable Counterexample

In this section we show how we can generate presumable counterexamples by extending the previously computed traces to *timed* traces. Given a trace, we compute a reduced model that has the jumps of the trace only. This model is augmented with a clock *timer* and variables $tstamp_i$, $i = 1, \ldots, k$, one for each jump in the trace. The clock is initialized to 0 and has derivative 1. Whenever a jump is taken, the clock value is stored in the timestamp of the jump and the clock is reset to 0. Figure 7 illustrates the above transformation.

Definition 5 (Trace Model). *Given a hybrid automaton* $\mathcal{H} = (Loc, Var, Edge, Dyn, Inv, Init)$ *and a finite trace* $e_1, \ldots, e_k$ *of* $\mathcal{H}$ *with* $e_i = (l_i, \phi_i, l_{i+1})$*, the trace model of* $\mathcal{H}$ *for* $e_1, \ldots, e_k$ *is the HA* $\mathcal{H}' = (Loc', Var', Edge', Dyn', Inv', Init')$ *with*

- $Loc' = \{(l_1, 0), \ldots, (l_k, k), (l_{k+1}, k + 1)\}$;
- $Var' = Var \cup \{timer, tstamp_1, \ldots, tstamp_k\}$;
- $Edge' = \{((l_i, i),\ \phi_i \wedge tstamp'_i = timer \wedge timer' = 0,\ (l_{i+1}, i + 1)) \mid i \in \{1, \ldots, k\}\}$;
- $Dyn'(l, i) = Dyn(l) \wedge timer = 1 \wedge \bigwedge_{i=1,\ldots,k} tstamp_i = 0$ *for all* $(l, i) \in Loc'$;
- $Inv'(l, i) = Inv(l)$ *for all* $(l, i) \in Loc'$;
- $Init'(l, i) = Init(l) \wedge timer = 0$ *for all* $(l, i) \in Loc'$.

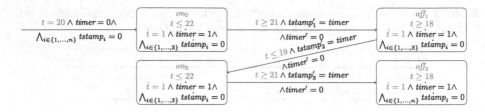

Fig. 7. Trace model of the thermostat example for $k = 3$

Table 4. Comparison of the timed traces for the navigation benchmark computed by SpaceEx and FLOW* ($k = 4$, time step 0.1, time horizon 30, traces from Table 2 and 3)

Initial states: l_{14}, $x_1 \in [3.0, 3.8]$, $x_2 \in [3.0, 4.0]$, $v_1 \in [-0.1, 0.1]$, $v_2 \in [-0.8, -0.5]$									
SpaceEx result in 6.46s:									
$\pi_1:$ l_{14},	$[0.0, 0.6]$,	l_{13},	$[0.0, \mathbf{1.4}]$,	l_9,	$[1.5, \mathbf{1.8}]$,	l_6,	$[2.3, 2.5]$,	l_2	
$\pi_2:$ l_{14},	$[0.0, 1.9]$,	l_{10},	$[1.5, 1.9]$,	l_7,	$[0.2, 2.5]$,	l_6,	$[0.0, 2.4]$,	l_2	
$\pi_3:$ l_{14},	$[0.0, 1.9]$,	l_{10},	$[1.5, 1.9]$,	l_7,	$[2.3, 2.5]$,	l_3,	$[0.0, 1.0]$,	l_2	
$\pi_4:$ l_{14},	$[0.0, 1.9]$,	l_{10},	$[0.0, 0.6]$,	l_9,	$[0.9, 1.4]$,	l_6,	$[0.0, 0.0]$,	l_2	
FLOW* result in 8.37s:									
$\pi_1:$ l_{14},	$[0.000, \mathbf{0.566}]$,	l_{13},	$[0.000, 1.420]$,	l_9,	$[\mathbf{1.531}, 1.880]$,	l_6,	$[\mathbf{2.421}, \mathbf{2.422}]$,	l_2	
$\pi_2:$ l_{14},	$[0.000, \mathbf{1.854}]$,	l_{10},	$[\mathbf{1.534}, 1.836]$,	l_7,	$[\mathbf{0.310}, \mathbf{2.371}]$,	l_6,	$[0.000, \mathbf{2.385}]$,	l_2	
$\pi_3:$ l_{14},	$[0.000, \mathbf{1.854}]$,	l_{10},	$[\mathbf{1.534}, 1.836]$,	l_7,	$[\mathbf{2.415}, 2.416]$,	l_3,	$[0.000, \mathbf{0.912}]$,	l_2	

Another method to get timing information is as follows. Both in SpaceEx and in FLOW*, the time horizon $[0, T]$ of a flowpipe is divided into smaller time intervals $[0, \delta], [\delta, 2\delta], \ldots, [(n-1)\delta, n\delta]$ with $n\delta = T$. The flowpipe is computed as a union of flowpipe segments, one for each smaller interval. Thus the tools have internal information about the timestamps of the symbolic states in the waiting list. We make use of this fact and label the symbolic states in FLOW* with the timed traces which lead to them. This way we get the timing information for free. Please note that this would also be possible for SpaceEx. In FLOW* an additional backward refinement of the time intervals of the timed trace would be also possible, which we cannot describe here due to space limitations.

Table 4 shows some experimental results for the navigation benchmark. We compute timed extensions of the previously computed counterexample traces to build presumable counterexamples. The running times include for FLOW* a complete reachability analysis up to jump depth 4, and for SpaceEx the generation of the traces with Approach II and extracting timing information by building and analyzing the trace models. Both tools have their advantages: SpaceEx computes the results faster, FLOW* gives sometimes better refinements.

5   Simulation

To gain counterexamples, we identifying some suitable *candidate initial states* (*CIS*) from the initial state set and *refine* the timed trace separately for each CIS by restricting the timing informations.

Then we apply simulation to each CIS to find concrete counterexamples starting in the given CIS and being contained in the corresponding refined timed trace. Based on the refined timed trace of a CIS, each jump can take place within a bounded but dense time interval. We let the simulation branch on a finite set of jump time points chosen from those intervals. The choice is guided by the invariant and guard satisfaction and uses a heuristics, which iteratively discretizes time intervals with dynamic step sizes to drive the selection towards hitting conditions, e.g., in the presence of strict equations. Furthermore, the heuristics tries to abort simulation paths that do not lead to a counterexample as early as possible.

Finding Candidate Initial States. The task of identifying CISs for simulation is non-trivial, since the timed traces over-approximate counterexamples, such that not all initial states lead to unsafe states within the given time bounds. W. l. o. g., we assume that the initial set is given as a hyperrectangle (otherwise we over-approximate the initial set by a hyperrectangle and use in the following the conjunction of the hyperrectangle with the initial set). We obtain CISs by applying a binary search on the initial set combined with a reachability analysis run to check whether the unsafe states are still reachable. As long as unsafe states are detected to be reachable from a hyperrectangle, the corner points of the hyperrectangle are added to the set of CISs. If in at least one dimension the width of the hyperrectangle is larger than a specified parameter ε, the interval is splitted (in this dimension) in the middle and both halves are analyzed again. The binary search stops if either the specified number of CISs are computed or if all hyperrectangles reach the minimal width in each dimension.

The user can choose between a depth- (DFS) and a breadth-first search (BFS) to generate CISs. DFS computes closely lying points fast, BFS searches for widely spread points at a higher computation time.

For the trace $l_{14}, l_{10}, l_7, l_6, l_2$ of the navigation benchmark, our implementation needs 19ms to create the trace model. For the DFS, SpaceEx has to be run 42 times until 10 CISs are computed from which the unsafe state l_2 is reachable in the SpaceEx over-approximation. The corresponding computation time is 7.14 s. The BFS finds the first 10 CISs within 29.90 s and with 133 SpaceEx calls.

For each selected CIS we determine a refined timed trace using the same method as before for computing presumable counterexamples, but now restricted to the given CIS as initial state.

Simulating the Dynamics. For linear differential equations the initial value problem is solvable, i.e., we can compute for each state the (unique) state reachable from it in time t. Thus, for linear differential equations we use the matrix exponential (e.g. in the homogeneous case, $\dot{x} = Ax$ is solved by $x(t) = x_0 e^{At}$, where t is the time and x_0 is the initial value of x), whereas for non-linear differential

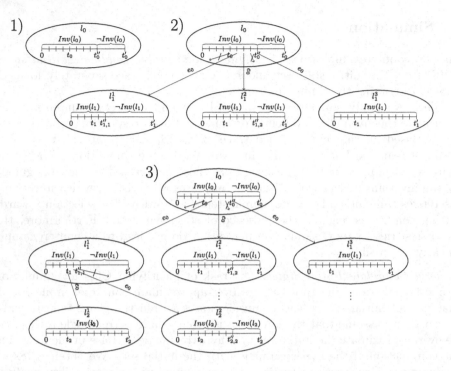

Fig. 8. Simulation: (1) Checking the invariant for $[0, t_0']$; (2) Taking the enabled edges within $[t_0, t_0'']$ to l_1; (3) Expanding the next level

equations numerical methods (e.g. Runge-Kutta) can be used. However, since either exponential function values must be determined or numerical methods are used, the computation is not exact.

Checking Invariants. Along a simulated timed trace, time can pass in a location only as long as the location's invariant is satisfied. The timed trace provides us for each location l_i a time interval $[t_i, t_i']$, within which a jump to a successor location should be taken. We have to assure that the invariant is constantly fulfilled from the time where a location was entered till the time point where the jump is taken. Therefore, we compute the time successors for a set of sample time points homogeneously distributed (with a user-defined distance δ) within the time interval $[0, t_i']$. We check the invariant for those sample time points in an increasing order. If the invariant is violated at a sample time point $t \in [0, t_i']$, no further time can elapse in the current location. Thus all simulation paths via time points from $[t, t_i']$ are cut off and the time interval for jumps is restricted to $[t_i, t_i'']$, where t_i'' is the time point before t.

Dynamic Search for Suitable Jump Time Points. Non-determinism (at which time point a jump is taken) is handled by branching the simulation for those previously selected sample time points that lie inside $[t_i, t_i']$. If the edge's guard is fulfilled at a given sample, the jump successor is computed and the corre-

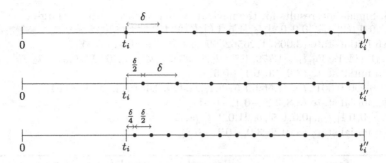

Fig. 9. Adaptive-step-size simulation

sponding simulation branch is explored in a depth-first search. The first steps of a simulation are shown in Fig. 8.

The naive discretization of the dense time intervals has sometimes problems to hit guard conditions. Especially hard for the simulation are guards containing equations. To allow simulation for guards defined by equations, we enlarge the model behavior be replacing the guard equations by inequations, allowing values from a small box around a point instead of hitting the point exactly.

However, even with such an enlarging it can happen that the guard is not fulfilled at any of the selected sample time points, or from the states after the jump no counterexamples can be simulated. In this case we dynamically determine new sample time points for the jump as follows. We use two parameters, an offset and a step size, specifying a set $\{t_i + \mathit{offset} + j \cdot \mathit{stepsize} \in [t_i, t'_i] \mid j \in \mathbb{N}\}$ of sample points. Initially (as described above), the offset is 0 and the step size has the value δ. If the simulation for these sample time points does not succeed, we set the offset to $\delta/2$ and let the step size unchanged. If those points are also not successful, we iteratively half both parameter values. This adaption terminates if either the target location of the timed trace is reached (i.e., a counterexample is found) or the step size reaches some predefined lower bound. The dynamic step-size-adaption is visualized in Fig. 9.

If a single counterexample suffices, the simulation can be stopped as soon as the unsafe location was reached. However, by heuristically searching for further counterexamples, it is also possible to provide additional information about a counterexample: Instead of the time points of the jumps along the simulation path, the biggest time intervals can be computed, such that the unsafe state is still reachable.

Table 5 shows the simulation results for some timed traces, each with a single initial state. Note that we find counterexamples (i.e., we reach the maximal jump depth) only in the two middle cases. We additionally run SpaceEx analyses with the given initial point for the first trace and could not reach the bad state with a time step of 0.001, i.e., the first timed trace is spurious. The last trace was not computed by FLOW* and is therefore also spurious.

Table 5. Simulation results for the navigation benchmark with ε-enlarging
$\pi_1 = l_{14}, [0.0, 0.2], l_{13}, [0.0, 0.4], l_9, [1.5, 1.6], l_6, [2.4, 2.5], l_2$
  with initial state $(3.0084472656250005, 3.21875, -0.1, -0.8)$
$\pi_2 = l_{14}, [1.834, 1.835], l_{10}, [1.779, 1.78], l_7, [1.934, 1.936], l_6, [0.511, 0.514], l_2$
  with initial state $(3.2, 4.0, 0.1, -0.5)$
$\pi_3 = l_{14}, [0.000, 0.001], l_{10}, [1.569, 1.570], l_7, [2.429, 2.431], l_3, [0.514, 0.517], l_2$
  with initial state $(3.8, 3.0, -0.1, -0.8)$
$\pi_4 = l_{14}, [0.0, 0.1], l_{10}, [0.0, 0.5], l_9, [1.0, 1.3], l_6, [2.3, 2.5], l_2$
  with initial state $(3.0125, 3.0, -0.1, -0.8)$

Timed trace	Step size	ε	Reached jump depth	Simulated paths	Unsafe	Time [s]
π_1	0.0005	0.0005	2	$128 \cdot 10^8$	0	20.91
	0.05	0.5	3	128	0	04.26
π_2	0.0005	0.5	4	964	>50	14.82
π_3	0.0005	0.05	4	96	>50	14.44
	0.0005	0.0005	4	96	50	10.51
π_4	0.0005	0.0005	2	$480 \cdot 10^8$	0	15.46
	0.05	0.05	3	480	0	07.88

6   Conclusion and Future Work

In this paper we described an approach to find presumable counterexamples for hybrid automata based on existing reachability tools. Next we plan to improve our method by (1) a backward refinement of the time intervals on timed paths, (2) a rigorous simulation technique for hybrid automata, (3) giving a better heuristics to select the initial points for simulation and (4) use several tools and take the best results to minimize the overestimation in a presumable counterexample. Preliminary results suggest that the function calculus of the tool ARIADNE can be used to validate counterexamples.

References

1. Alur, R., Courcoubetis, C., Halbwachs, N., Henzinger, T.A., Ho, P., Nicollin, X., Olivero, A., Sifakis, J., Yovine, S.: The algorithmic analysis of hybrid systems. Theor. Comput. Sci. **138**, 3–34 (1995)
2. Frehse, G., et al.: SpaceEx: scalable verification of hybrid systems. In: Gopalakrishnan, G., Qadeer, S. (eds.) CAV 2011. LNCS, vol. 6806, pp. 379–395. Springer, Heidelberg (2011)
3. Chen, X., Ábrahám, E., Sankaranarayanan, S.: Flow*: an analyzer for non-linear hybrid systems. In: Sharygina, N., Veith, H. (eds.) CAV 2013. LNCS, vol. 8044, pp. 258–263. Springer, Heidelberg (2013)
4. Stursberg, O., Krogh, B.H.: Efficient representation and computation of reachable sets for hybrid systems. In: Maler, O., Pnueli, A. (eds.) HSCC 2003. LNCS, vol. 2623, pp. 482–497. Springer, Heidelberg (2003)

5. Chutinan, A., Krogh, B.H.: Computing polyhedral approximations to flow pipes for dynamic systems. In: Proceedings of CDC'98, vol. 2, pp. 2089–2094. IEEE Press (1998)
6. Henzinger, T.A., Ho, P., Wong-Toi, H.: HyTech: a model checker for hybrid systems. Softw. Tools Technol. Transfer 1, 110–122 (1997)
7. Frehse, G.: PHAVer: algorithmic verification of hybrid systems past HyTech. In: Morari, M., Thiele, L. (eds.) HSCC 2005. LNCS, vol. 3414, pp. 258–273. Springer, Heidelberg (2005)
8. Kvasnica, M., Grieder, P., Baotić, M.: Multi-parametric toolbox (MPT). http://control.ee.ethz.ch/~mpt/ (2004)
9. Chen, X., Ábrahám, E.: Choice of directions for the approximation of reachable sets for hybrid systems. In: Moreno-Díaz, R., Pichler, F., Quesada-Arencibia, A. (eds.) EUROCAST 2011, Part I. LNCS, vol. 6927, pp. 535–542. Springer, Heidelberg (2012)
10. Kühn, W.: Zonotope dynamics in numerical quality control. In: Hege, H.-C., Polthier, K. (eds.) Mathematical Visualization: Algorithms, Applications and Numerics, pp. 125–134. Springer, Heidelberg (1998)
11. Girard, A.: Reachability of uncertain linear systems using zonotopes. In: Morari, M., Thiele, L. (eds.) HSCC 2005. LNCS, vol. 3414, pp. 291–305. Springer, Heidelberg (2005)
12. Bournez, O., Maler, O., Pnueli, A.: Orthogonal polyhedra: representation and computation. In: Vaandrager, F.W., van Schuppen, J.H. (eds.) HSCC 1999. LNCS, vol. 1569, pp. 46–60. Springer, Heidelberg (1999)
13. Kurzhanski, A.B., Varaiya, P.: On ellipsoidal techniques for reachability analysis. Optim. Meth. Softw. 17, 177–237 (2000)
14. Le Guernic, C.: Reachability analysis of hybrid systems with linear continuous dynamics. Ph.D. thesis, Université Joseph Fourier (2009)
15. Le Guernic, C., Girard, A.: Reachability analysis of hybrid systems using support functions. In: Bouajjani, A., Maler, O. (eds.) CAV 2009. LNCS, vol. 5643, pp. 540–554. Springer, Heidelberg (2009)
16. Chen, X., Ábrahám, E., Sankaranarayanan, S.: Taylor model flowpipe construction for non-linear hybrid systems. In: Proceedings of RTSS'12, pp. 183–192. IEEE Computer Society (2012)
17. Collins, P., Bresolin, D., Geretti, L., Villa, T.: Computing the evolution of hybrid systems using rigorous function calculus. In: Proceedings of ADHS'12, IFAC-PapersOnLine (2012)
18. Mitchell, I., Tomlin, C.J.: Level set methods for computation in hybrid systems. In: Lynch, N.A., Krogh, B.H. (eds.) HSCC 2000. LNCS, vol. 1790, pp. 310–323. Springer, Heidelberg (2000)
19. Asarin, E., Dang, T., Maler, O.: The d/dt tool for verification of hybrid systems. In: Brinksma, E., Larsen, K.G. (eds.) CAV 2002. LNCS, vol. 2404, pp. 365–370. Springer, Heidelberg (2002)
20. Girard, A., Pappas, G.J.: Approximation metrics for discrete and continuous systems. IEEE Trans. Autom. Control 52, 782–798 (2007)
21. Kurzhanskiy, A., Varaiya, P.: Ellipsoidal toolbox. Technical report, EECS, UC Berkeley (2006)
22. Balluchi, A., Casagrande, A., Collins, P., Ferrari, A., Villa, T., Sangiovanni-Vincentelli, A.L.: Ariadne: A framework for reachability analysis of hybrid automata. In: Proceedings of MTNS'06 (2006)

23. Prabhakar, P., Duggirala, P.S., Mitra, S., Viswanathan, M.: Hybrid automata-based CEGAR for rectangular hybrid systems. In: Giacobazzi, R., Berdine, J., Mastroeni, I. (eds.) VMCAI 2013. LNCS, vol. 7737, pp. 48–67. Springer, Heidelberg (2013)
24. Duggirala, P.S., Mitra, S.: Abstraction refinement for stability. In: Proceedings of ICCPS'11, pp. 22–31. IEEE (2011)
25. Fehnker, A., Ivančić, F.: Benchmarks for hybrid systems verification. In: Alur, R., Pappas, G.J. (eds.) HSCC 2004. LNCS, vol. 2993, pp. 326–341. Springer, Heidelberg (2004)

TTM/PAT: Specifying and Verifying Timed Transition Models

Jonathan S. Ostroff[1], Chen-Wei Wang[1]([✉]), Simon Hudon[1], Yang Liu[2], and Jun Sun[3]

[1] Department of Electrical Engineering and Computer Science, York University,
Toronto, Canada
jackie@cse.yorku.ca
[2] School of Computer Engineering, Nanyang Technological University,
Singapore, Singapore
[3] Singapore University of Technology and Design,
Singapore, Singapore

Abstract. Timed Transition Models (TTMs) are event-based descriptions for specifying real-time systems in a discrete setting. We propose a convenient and expressive event-based textual syntax for TTMs and a corresponding operational semantics using labelled transition systems. A system is specified as a composition of module instances. Each module has a clean interface for declaring input, output, and shared variables. Events in a module can be specified, individually, as spontaneous, fair or real-time. An event action specifies a before-after predicate by a set of (possibly non-deterministic) assignments and nested conditionals. The TTM assertion language, linear-time temporal logic (LTL), allows references to event occurrences, including clock ticks (thus allowing for a check that the behaviour is non-Zeno). We implemented a model checker for the TTM notation (using the PAT framework) that includes an editor with static type checking, a graphical simulator, and a LTL verifier. The tool automatically derives the tick transition and implicit event clocks, removing the burden of manual encoding them. The TTM tool performs significantly better on a nuclear shutdown system than the manually encoded versions analyzed in [6].

Keywords: Real-time systems · Specification · Verification · Timed transition models · Fairness · Model checking

1 Introduction

Checking the correctness of real-time systems is both challenging and important for industrial applications. In [6], the authors find it convenient to use a Timed Transition Model (TTM) to describe and verify a nuclear reactor shutdown system. A graphical statechart-based model checker for TTMs developed in [7] is no longer supported.

C. Artho and P.C. Ölveczky (Eds.): FTSCS 2013, CCIS 419, pp. 107–124, 2014.
DOI: 10.1007/978-3-319-05416-2_8, © Springer International Publishing Switzerland 2014

To verify the correctness of the shutdown system, authors of [6] manually translate TTMs into timed automata and discrete transition systems, and perform the real-time verification using, respectively, the Uppaal [5] and SAL [3] model checkers. Real-time models of substantial systems tend to be complex. The manual translation of a TTM to other formats (as in [6]) is time consuming and error prone, may introduce extra states or transitions in the process, and makes it hard to trace the generated counterexamples back to the original model.

In this paper, we develop a new and convenient event-based notation for TTMs consisting of a textual syntax and formal operational semantics. The one-step semantics allows us to use the PAT toolset [9,10] to develop an explicit state model checker for the new notation. The resulting model checker performs significantly better than the manually encoded model using other tools, at the same time bypassing the need to do manual translation. The new model checker has good support for type checking, visual simulation, and convenient counterexample traceability back to the model.

The event-based syntax also makes the language amenable to formal reasoning using theorem proving in the spirit of Event-B [1] and compositional reasoning. This provides a timed extension to the Event-B notation (although, in this paper, we do not consider refinement).

Outline and Contributions. This paper presents three main contributions. *First,* our new TTM notation allows for the description of a variety of discrete reactive systems (see Sect. 2 for a pacemaker example) by cooperating modules that contain variables and events. Events have implicit clocks for imposing lower and upper time bounds on their occurrences. Our notation also supports spontaneous, fair, and timed behaviours at both the event level and the system level. Timers are explicit clocks that may be used to constrain system behaviour. *Second,* we develop a formal operational semantics with digitization (see Sect. 3) that is amenable to automated tool support. *Third,* we implement the TTM/PAT tool for specifying and verifying TTMs (see Sect. 4 for its evaluation). System properties can be expressed in the linear-time temporal logic (LTL) and may refer to timers and event occurrences (see Sect. 3 for representing event occurrences as state predicates). The properties language directly supports healthiness checks such as non-Zeno behaviour[1] and the monotonicity of timers. More details on the tool and experimental data are discussed in an extended report [8], and the grammar of TTM textual syntax and the tool are available at https://wiki.eecs.yorku.ca/project/ttm/.

---

[1] In TTM/PAT we consider a discrete time domain, where there is an explicit transition for the tick of a global clock. Zeno behaviour then denotes executions in which the tick transition does not occur infinitely often (i.e., at some point, time stops).

2   A Small Pacemaker Example

We use a small pacemaker example (similar to the one in [4]) to illustrate the real-time features of TTMs. A cardiac pacemaker is an electronic device implanted into the body to regulate the heart beat by delivering electrical stimuli (called paces) over leads with electrodes that are in contact with the heart. The pacemaker may also detect (or sense) natural cardiac stimulations.

A pacemaker in the VVI mode operates in a timing cycle that begins with a ventricular pacing or sensing. The basis of the timing cycle is the lower rate interval (LRI = 1000 ms): the maximum amount of time between two consecutive ventricular sensing. If the LRI elapses and no sensing has occurred since the beginning of the cycle, a pace is delivered and the cycle is reset. On the other hand, if a heart beat is sensed, the cycle is reset without delivering a pace.

At the beginning of each cycle, there is a ventricular refractory period (VRP = 400 ms): chaotic electrical activity that immediately follows a heart beat, and may lead to spurious sensing that interferes with future pacing. Sensing is therefore disabled during the VRP period. Once the VRP period is over, a ventricular sensing inhibits the pacing and resets the LRI, starting a new timing cycle.

In the VVI mode, hysteresis pacing can be enabled to delay pacing beyond the LRI in order to give the heart a chance to resume the normal operation. In that case, the timing cycle is set to a larger value, namely the hysteresis rate interval (HRI = 1200 ms). It becomes enabled after a natural heart beat has been sensed. In [4], hysteresis pacing is enabled after a ventricular sense is received, and disabled after a pacing signal is sent.

Using the textual syntax of TTM, we define constants and a timer t for the cardiac cycle as follows:

#**define** *VRP* 400;
#**define** *LRI* 1000;
#**define** *HRI* 1200;
	timers
	    t: 0..(*HRI*+1)
	        enabledinit
	end
		share initialization
		    sense: **BOOL** = **false**
		    pace: **BOOL** = **false**
		end

Timer t has a range from zero to HRI + 1, and it is initially zero and enabled. When the value of t reaches one beyond HRI + 1, it stops counting up and its monotonicity predicate, $mono(t)$, becomes false. This predicate holds so long as that timer t is ticking in synch with a *tick* of a global clock, and that it is not stopped or restarted (see Sect. 3). The *tick* transition is an implicit transition (i.e., it is not given by the text of a TTM) representing the ticking of a global clock. The tick transition increments timers and implicit clocks associated with events. We also defined shared variables *sense* and *pace* to represent, respectively, a ventricular sensing or pacing.

We declare a module template for the heart as follows:

module *HEART*
interface
  pace: **share BOOL**
  sense: **share BOOL**
local
  ri : **INT** = *HRI*
  last_ri: **INT** = *HRI*
  pc: **INT** = 0
events
  hbn[*VRP*, ∗] // *natural heart beat*
  when !*pace* && *pc*==0
  do *sense* := **true**,
    ri := *HRI*,
    last_ri:=*ri*,
    pc := 1
end

hbp[0,0] // *paced heart beat*
when *pace* && *VRP* <= *t* && *pc*==0
do *pace* := **false**,
  ri := *LRI* ,
  last_ri := *ri*,
  pc := 1
end

new_cycle[0,0] // *restart a new cycle*
when *pc*==1
start *t*
do *pc* := 0
end

The interface of module template *HEART* declares the access to shared variables *sense* and *pace*. The local variable *ri* (rate interval) is either HRI or LRI depending on whether hysteresis pacing is enabled. Likewise *last_ri* records the last value of the rate interval. They are auxiliary variables: they annotate the system state without affecting[2] the behaviours and are used in LTL specifications. Variable *pc* (program counter) is used as a sequencing mechanism for events.

The heart module has a natural heartbeat (event *hbn*) and a paced heartbeat (event *hbp*). If there is a natural heart beat, then the *sense* flag is set, *ri* is set to HRI, and the last rate interval is also recorded in *last_ri*. After the VRP period, it is also possible for a paced heart beat to occur if the *pace* flag is set. Thus *pace* ∧ VRP ≤ *t* is part of the guard of the urgent event *hbp*[0,0]. After either a natural or paced heart beat, the timer *t* is restarted by the *new_cycle* event and the cardiac cycle begins again.

A natural heart beat might occur at any time after the ventricle refractory delay VRP, or it might never occur. Thus the lower time bound of *hbn* is VRP and the upper time bound is ∗ (i.e ∞). If the upper time bound is ∗ then we have a spontaneous event (i.e., an event that is not urgent or forced to occur). We can thus accommodate a variety of fairness assumptions (discussed further in Sect. 3), including spontaneous events, just or compassionate events, and real-time events that must occur between their lower and upper time bounds. An urgent event *e*[0, 0] is one that must occur before the next *tick* of the global clock (provided its guard continuously remains true).

We formulate the requirements using linear time temporal logic (LTL) solely in terms of the phenomena of the environment (i.e., the heart) as follows:

---

[2] Variables *ri* and *last_ri* are used in neither event guards nor the right hand side of assignments to non-auxiliary variables.

R1: $\Box\Diamond((H.hbn \lor H.hbp) \land (VRP \le t \le HRI))$.[3] Infinitely often, a natural or paced heart beat occurs between VRP and HRI time units from each other.

R2: $\Box(H.hbn \rightarrow (VRP \le t \le H.last\_ri))$. A natural heartbeat occurs only in the closed interval [VRP, $H.last\_ri$] in the cardiac cycle. $H.last\_ri$ records the required rate interval in the heart for the last complete cycle, either LRI or HRI, depending upon whether hysteresis pacing has been properly enabled. Thus, $\Box((H.last\_ri = LRI) \lor (H.last\_ri = HRI))$ also holds.

R3: $\Box(H.hbp \rightarrow (t = H.last\_ri))$. A paced heart beat occurs only if the timer t is at the relevant rate interval. The ventricle controller will have to estimate $H.ri$ (which, as opposed to $H.last\_ri$, relates to the current cycle) in order to ensure that the heart paces according to this requirement.

There is a concern that some event (either in the heart module or elsewhere) might illegally set the timer t to a value that makes the specification trivially true. Of course, in a small system, inspection of the TTMs (or timed automata in the case of Uppaal) might re-assure us that all is well. Nevertheless, it would be advantageous to check that timers tick monotonically and uninterruptedly. Thus each TTM timer t must be equipped with a corresponding monotonicity predicate $mono(t)$ that holds so long as timer t is not stopped or restarted (see Sect. 3). We may thus check ($\Box\Diamond H.new\_cycle) \land \Box(H.new\_cycle \rightarrow t = 0)$ and $\Box(H.new\_cycle \rightarrow mono(t)\mathcal{U}((H.hbn \lor H.hbp) \land (VRP \le t \le HRI)))$, which guarantee that there is an appropriate heart beat in each cardiac cycle.

When using events with upper time bound 0, we must provide a way of checking Zeno behaviour [7]. We can directly check that time always progresses with the LTL formula $\Box\Diamond tick$. The tick event is implicit. That is, it is automatically constructed by the tool with the precise semantics described in Sect. 3. The ability to refer to the occurrences of events in the TTM assertions makes it possible to specify the required behaviour more directly than in other tools, e.g. Uppaal. We now devise a ventricle controller whose cooperation with the heart will satisfy requirements **R1** to **R3**.

```
module VENTRICLE_CONTROLLER
interface
  pace : share BOOL
  sense: share BOOL
local
  ri : INT = HRI; pc: INT = 0
events
  vpace[0,0]
  when pc==0 && !sense && t==ri
  do ri := LRI, pace := true, pc:= 1
  end
```

```
vsense[0,0]
  when pc==0 && sense
  do ri := HRI, sense := false, pc :=1
  end

compute_delay[1,1]
  when pc==1
  do pc:= 0
  end
end
```

---

[3] $H.hbn$ designates the event hbn in module instance H. The same syntax works for *local* variables as well.

The controller maintains its own estimate VC.ri of the heart's rate interval $H.ri$, where VC and H are module instances that we construct below. We may now compose the heart together with the controller as follows:

instances	#**define** rt $(t{=}H.last\_ri)$;
$H = HEART$	#**define** $t0$ $(t{=}0)$;
(**share** *pace*, **share** *sense*)	#**define** wr $VRP <= t$ && $t <= HRI$;
$VC = VENTRICLE\_CONTROLLER$	#**assert** *System* $\models$ [] $(H.hbp \rightarrow rt)$;
(**share** *pace*, **share** *sense*)	#**assert** *System* $\models$ []$<>(H.new\_cycle$ && $t0)$;
end	#**assert** *System* $\models$
composition	[] $(H.new\_cycle$ && $t0 \rightarrow$
$System = H \parallel VC$	**mono**(t) **U** $((H.hbn \parallel H.hbp)$ && $wr))$;
end	#**assert** *System* $\models$ []$<>$**tick**;

The above syntax is accepted by the TTM/PAT tool, and all the requirements are verified in a few seconds. The syntax also allows us to compose an indexed set of instances. For example, in Fischer's mutual exclusion algorithm (Sect. 4.2), we write:

    composition *fischer* = $\parallel$ i: 1..n @ *PROCESS*(**share** x, **share** c, **in** i)   **end**

More details on this example is discussed in an extended report [8].

3   TTM Syntax and Semantics

Section 2 provides an example of the new concrete textual syntax for TTMs. In this section, we provide a one-step operational semantics for TTMs.

3.1   Abstract Syntax

Following [7] and using the mathematical conventions of Event-B [1], we define the abstract syntax of a TTM module instance $\mathcal{M}$ as a 5-tuple, i.e., $\mathcal{M} = (V, s_0, T, t_0, E)$ where (1) V is a set of variable identifiers, declared local or in a module interface; (2) T is a set of timer identifiers; (3) E is a set of events that may change the state; (4) $s_0 \in$ STATE is the initial variable assignment, with STATE $\triangleq V \rightarrow$ VALUE; and (5) $t_0 \in$ TIME is the initial timer assignment, with TIME $\triangleq T \rightarrow \mathbb{N}$.

We use an 8-tuple $(id, l, u, fair, grd, start, stop, action)$ to define the abstract syntax of an event e, and we use the dot notation "." to access the fields, as shown on the right of Fig. 1. The string identifier of an event e is written as $e.id$. The guard of event e, i.e., $e.grd$, is any Boolean expression in V and T. For example, on the left of Fig. 1, we have $V = \{v_1, v_2, v_3, \cdots\}$ and $T = \{t_1, t_2, t_3, t_4, \cdots\}$. Functions $boundt \in T \rightarrow \mathbb{N}$ and $type \in T \rightarrow \mathbb{P}(\mathbb{N})$ provide, respectively, the upper bound and the type of each timer. For example, if timer t_1 is declared in the TTM as $t_1 : 0..5$, then $boundt(t_1) = 5$ and $type(t_1) = \{0..6\}$. As will be detailed

Concrete syntax of event e:	Abstract syntax of the event e:
$event\_id$ $[l,u]$ **just**	$- e.id \in \text{ID};$
when grd	$- e.l \in \mathbb{N};$
start t_1, t_2	$- e.u \in \mathbb{N} \cup \{\infty\}$
stop t_3, t_4	$- e.fair \in \{\text{spontaneous, just, compassionate}\}$
do $v_1 := exp_1,$	$- e.grd \in \text{STATE} \times \text{TIME} \rightarrow \text{BOOL};$
if $condition$ **then** $v_2 := exp_2$	$- e.start \subseteq T;$
else skip fi,	$- e.stop \subseteq T;$
$v_3 :: 1..4$	$- e.action \in \text{STATE} \times \text{TIME} \leftrightarrow \text{STATE};$
end	

Fig. 1. Concrete and abstract syntax of TTM events

below, timers count up to one beyond the specified bound at which point they remain fixed until they are restarted.

An event e must be taken between its lower time bound $e.l$ and upper time bound $e.u$, provided that its guard $e.grd$ remains true. The event action involves simultaneous assignments to $v_1, v_2, \cdots$. The notation $v_3 :: 1..4$ is an example of a demonic assignment in which v_3 takes any value from 1 to 4. All the assignments in the event action are applied simultaneously in one step.

In an assignment $y := exp$, the expression on the right may use primed (e.g. x') and unprimed (e.g. x) state variables as well as the initial value of timers. A variable with a prime refers to the variable's value in the next state and a variable without prime refers to its value in the current state. The use of primed variables in expressions allows for simpler and more expressive descriptions of state changes. The state changes effected by an event e is described in the abstract syntax by a before-after predicate $e.action$. The concrete syntax also allows for assignments to be embedded in (possibly nested) conditional statements.[4]

3.2 Formal Semantics

We provide a one-step operational semantics of a TTM module instance $\mathcal{M}$ in LTS (Labelled Transition Systems).

Definition: LTS: Given a TTM module instance $\mathcal{M}$, an LTS (Labelled Transition System) is a 4-tuple $\mathcal{L} = (\Pi, \pi_0, \mathbf{T}, \rightarrow)$ where (1) Π is a set of system configurations; (2) $\pi_0 \in \Pi$ is an initial configuration; (3) $\mathbf{T}$ is a set of transitions names; and (4) $\rightarrow \subseteq \Pi \times \mathbf{T} \times \Pi$ is a transition relation.

We now describe the LTS semantics of TTMs. Let $E_{id} \triangleq \{e \in E \bullet e.id\}$ be the set of event names (identifiers). A configuration $\pi \in \Pi$ is defined by a 6-tuple (s, t, m, c, x, p). We explain each of the six components as follows:

---

[4] With all the complexity of structures allowed by the syntax of actions, sequential composition is not allowed. This is in an effort to make actions into specifications rather than implementations. This would allow us to generalize TTMs to allow an Event-B style of symbolic reasoning.

• $s \in$, is a value assignment for all the variables of the system. The state can be read and changed by any transition corresponding to an event in E.

• $t \in$ TIME is a value assignment for the timers of the system. Events (and hence their corresponding transitions) may only start, stop and read timers. As will be discussed below, we introduce a special transition, called *tick*, which also changes the timers. Timers t_i that are stopped have values $boundt(t_i) + 1$.

• $m \in T \rightarrow$ BOOL records the status of monotonicity of each timer. Suppose event e_1 in a TTM starts t_1. In LTL we might write $\Box(e_1 \wedge t_1 = 0 \rightarrow \Diamond(q \wedge t_1 \leq 4))$ (note that $t_1 = 0$ is redundant) to specify that q becomes true within 4 time units of event e_1 occurring. However, other events might stop or restart t_1 before q is satisfied hence breaking the synchronicity between t_1 and a global clock.[5] Instead, we express the intended property as $\Box(e_1 \wedge t_1 = 0 \rightarrow m(t_1) \, \mathcal{U} \, (q \wedge t_1 \leq 4))$. The expression $m(t_1)$ (standing for monotonicity of t_1) holds in any state where t_1 is not stopped or being reset. We explain monotonicity further below.

• $c \in E_{id} \rightarrow \mathbb{N} \cup \{-1\}$ is a value assignment for a clock implicitly associated with each event. These clocks are used to decide whether an event has been enabled for long enough and whether it is urgent. An event $e \in E$ is enabled when its clock's value is between the event's lower time bound (i.e., $e.l$) and its upper time bound (i.e., $e.u$). Furthermore, the type (or range) of $c(e.id)$ is $\{-1, 0, ...e.u\}$. When an event's clock is disabled, as opposed to the convention used with timers, the clock's value is -1.

• $x \in E_{id} \cup \{\bot\}$ is used as a sequencing mechanism to ensure that each transition e is immediately preceded by an $e\#$ transition whose only function is to update the monotonicity record m. For example, in the following execution $\cdots \xrightarrow{e_1} \pi_1 \underset{x=\bot}{\xrightarrow{e_2\#}} \pi_2 \underset{x=e_2}{\xrightarrow{e_2}} \pi_3 \xrightarrow[x=\bot]{} \cdots$, suppose in π_1 the value of timer t_2 is 3 and that e_2 restarts t_2. Then, in π_2, we have $x = e_2 \wedge t_2 = 3 \wedge m(t_2) = $ false. In π_3, we have $x = \bot \wedge t_2 = 0 \wedge m(t_2) = $ true. In order to record the breaking of monotonicity, the $e_2\#$ transition sets $m(t_2)$ to false, which gets set back to true in the next execution step. The precise effect of these transitions will be described below.

• $p \in E_{id} \cup \{tick, \bot\}$ holds the name of the last event to be taken at each configuration. It is $\bot$ in the initial configuration as no event has yet occurred. It allows us to refer to events in LTL formulas in order to state that they have just occurred. For instance, in the formula above, $(s, t, m, p) \models e_1 \wedge t_1 = 0$ (which reads: the configuration *satisfies* the formula) evaluates to $p = e_1 \wedge t(t_1) = 0$.

Given a flattened module instance $\mathcal{M}$, the transitions of its corresponding LTS are given as $\mathbf{T} = E_{id} \cup E\# \cup \{tick\}$. As explained above, for each event $e \in E$, we introduce a monotonicity breaking transition $e.id\#$. We thus define $E\# \triangleq \{e \in E \bullet e.id\#\}$. The *tick* transition represents one tick of a global clock. Explicit timers and event lower and upper time bounds are described with

---

[5] Suppose that event e_2 also starts t_1, that e_3 establishes q and events occur in the following order: $\pi_0 \xrightarrow{e_1} \pi_1 \underset{t_1=0}{\xrightarrow{tick^3}} \pi_4 \underset{t_1=3}{\xrightarrow{e_2}} \pi_5 \underset{t_1=0}{\xrightarrow{tick^2}} \pi_7 \underset{t_1=2}{\xrightarrow{e_3}} \pi_8 \underset{t_1=2 \wedge q}{\cdots}$. This execution satisfies the first LTL formula but does not satisfy the intended specification: when q becomes true, $t_1 = 2$ but it is 5 ticks away from the last occurrence of e_1.

respect to this tick transition. We define the enabling condition of event $e \in E$ as $e.en \triangleq e.grd \wedge e.l \le e.c \le e.u$, where $e.c$ evaluates to $c(e.id)$ in a configuration whose clock component is c. Thus an event is enabled in a configuration that satisfies its guard and where the event's implicit clock is between its lower and upper time bound.

The initial configuration is defined as $\pi_0 = (s_0, t_0, m_0, c_0, \perp, \perp)$, where s_0 and t_0 come from the abstract syntax of the TTM. m_0 and c_0 are given by:

$$m_0(t_i) \equiv t_0(t_i) = 0$$

$$c_0(e_i.id) = \begin{cases} 0 & (s_0, t_0) \vDash e_i.grd \\ -1 & (s_0, t_0) \nvDash e_i.grd \end{cases}$$

for each $t_i \in T$ and $e_i \in E$. It is implicit in the above formula that $m_0(t_i)$ depends only on whether or not t_i is initially enabled (specified using the keyword **enabledinit** or **disabledinit**). If the keyword **enabledinit** is specified, $t_0(t_i)=0$; otherwise, if the keyword **disabledinit** is specified, $t_0(t_i) = boundt(t_i) + 1$.

An execution σ of the LTS is an infinite sequence, alternating between configurations and transitions, written as $\pi_0 \xrightarrow{\tau_1} \pi_1 \xrightarrow{\tau_2} \pi_2 \to \cdots$ where $\tau_i \in \mathbf{T}$ and $\pi_i \in \Pi$. Below, we provide constraints on each one-step relation $(\pi \xrightarrow{e} \pi')$ in an execution. If an execution σ satisfies all these constraints then we call σ a *legal* execution. We let $\Sigma_{\mathcal{L}}$ denote the set of all legal executions of the labelled transition system $\mathcal{L}$. The set $\Sigma_{\mathcal{L}}$ provides a precise and complete definition of the behaviour of $\mathcal{L}$. If a state-formula q holds in a configuration π, then we write $\pi \vDash q$. In some formulas, such as guards, all the components of a configuration are not necessary. We express this by dropping some components of the configuration on the left of the double turnstile ($\vDash$), as in $(s_0, t_0) \vDash e.grd$. Given a temporal logic property φ and an LTS $\mathcal{L}$, we write $\mathcal{L} \vDash \varphi$ iff $\forall \sigma \in \Sigma_{\mathcal{L}} \bullet \sigma \vDash \varphi$. The three possible transition steps are:

$$(s, t, m, c, \perp, p) \xrightarrow{e\#} (s, t, m', c, e, p) \tag{3.1}$$

$$(s, t, m, c, e, p) \xrightarrow{e} (s', t', m', c', \perp, e) \tag{3.2}$$

$$(s, t, m, c, \perp, p) \xrightarrow{tick} (s, t', m', c', \perp, tick) \tag{3.3}$$

Each of the above transitions has side conditions which we now enumerate.

3.2.1 Taking $e\#$

The monotonicity breaking transition $e\#$, specified in Eq. 3.1 (p. 115), is taken only if $(s, t, c) \vDash e.en$ and the x-component of the configuration is $\perp$. For each $t \in T$, $m'(t) \equiv t \notin e.start \wedge m(t)$. This ensures that, for timer t, just before it is (re)started, $m(t) =$ false. It is set back to true by the immediately following event, e, and it remains true as long as t is not restarted and has not reached its upper bound. Transition $e\#$ modifies only m and x in the configuration, and thus maintains the truth of $(s, t, c) \vDash e.en$.

3.2.2 Taking e

The transition e, specified in Eq. 3.2 (p. 115), is taken only if $(s, t, c) \vDash e.en$ and the x-component of the configuration is e. The component s' of the next configuration in an execution is determined nondeterministically by $e.action$, which is a relation rather than a function. This means that any next configuration that satisfies the relation can be part of a valid execution, i.e., s' is only constrained by $(s, t, s') \in e.action$. The other components are constrained deterministically. The following function tables specify the updates to m, t and c upon occurrence of transition e.

For each timer $t_i \in T$		$m'(t_i)$	$t'(t_i)$
$t_i \in e.start$	$t_i \in e.stop$	*impossible*	
	$t_i \notin e.stop$	true	0
$t_i \notin e.start$	$t_i \in e.stop$	false	$boundt(t_i) + 1$
	$t_i \notin e.stop$	$m(t_i)$	$t(t_i)$

For each event $e_i \in E$		$c'(e_i.id)$
$(s', t') \not\vDash e_i.grd$		-1
$(s', t') \vDash e_i.grd$	$(s, t) \vDash e_i.grd \ \wedge \ \neg e_i = e$	$c(e_i.id)$
	$(s, t) \not\vDash e_i.grd \ \vee \ e_i = e$	0

In the above, we start and stop the implicit clock of e_i as a consequence of executing e, according to whether $e_i.grd$ becomes true, is false (i.e., becomes or remains false) or remains true. Since event e_i becomes enabled $e_i.l$ units after its guard becomes true, this allows us to know when to consider e_i as enabled, i.e., ready to be taken. As a special case, the implicit clock of event e (under consideration) is restarted when $e.grd$ remains true.

3.2.3 Taking $tick$

The tick transition, specified in Eq. 3.3 (p. 115), is taken only if $\forall e \in E \bullet c(e.id) < e.u$ and the x-component of the configuration is $\perp$ (thus preventing $tick$ from intervening between any $e\#$ and e pair). For any timer $t_i \in T$, the updates to t', m' and c' are:

$$t'(t_i) = (t(t_i) \downarrow boundt(t_i)) + 1$$
$$m'(t_i) \equiv \neg (t(t_i) = boundt(t_i) + 1)$$

For each event $e \in E$		$c'(e.id)$
$(s', t') \not\vDash e.grd$		-1
$(s', t') \vDash e.grd$	$(s, t) \not\vDash e.grd$	0
	$(s, t) \vDash e.grd$	$c(e.id) + 1$

Thus, $tick$ increments timers and implicit clocks to their upper bounds. Transition $tick$ also marks timers as non-monotonic when they reach their upper bound and reset clocks when the corresponding events are disabled.

3.2.4 Scheduling

So far, we have made no mention of scheduling: we constrained executions so that the state changes in controlled ways, but a given execution may still make no progress. To make progress, we need to assume fairness. In the current implementation of TTM/PAT, the possible scheduling assumptions[6] on TTM events are restricted to the following four:

1. Spontaneous event. Even when it is enabled, the event might never be taken. This is assumed when no fairness keyword is given and the upper time bound is * or unspecified.

2. Just event scheduling (also known as weak fairness [10]). For any execution $\sigma \in \Sigma_{\mathcal{L}}$, if an event e eventually becomes continuously enabled, it has to occur infinitely many times, that is $\sigma \models \Diamond\Box e.en \rightarrow \Box\Diamond e$. This is assumed when the keyword **just** is given next to the event and the upper time bound is * or unspecified. We use $e.en$ and not $e.grd$ in the fairness formula as the event can only be taken $e.l$ units after its guard became true.

3. Compassionate event scheduling (also known as strong fairness [10]). For any execution $\sigma \in \Sigma_{\mathcal{L}}$, if an event e becomes enabled infinitely many times, it has to occur infinitely many times, that is $\sigma \models \Box\Diamond e.en \rightarrow \Box\Diamond e$. This is assumed when the keyword **compassionate** is given next to the event and the upper time bound is * or unspecified.

4. Real-time event scheduling. The (finite) upper time bound (u) of the event e is taken as a deadline: if the event's guard is true for u units of time, it has to occur within u units of after the guard becomes true or after the last occurrence of e. To achieve this effect, the event e is treated as just. Since *tick* will not occur as long as e is urgent (i.e., $e.c = e.u$), transition e will be forced to occur (unless some other event occurs and disables it).

To accurately model time, the *tick* transition is treated as compassionate in the LTS. This ensures that time progresses except in cases of Zeno-behaviors (discussed below). Spontaneous events cannot be used to establish liveness properties. Justice and compassion are strong enough assumptions to establish liveness properties but not real-time properties. Finally, real-time events can establish both liveness and real-time properties.

The above semantics allows for Zeno behaviours which occur when there are loops involving events with zero upper time bound (i.e., $e[0,0]$). We could ban $e[0,0]$ events altogether, but that would eliminate behaviours that are feasible and useful, e.g., where we describe a finite sequence of immediately urgent events (not in a loop). We can check that the system is non-Zeno by checking that the system satisfies $\Box\Diamond tick$.

The abstract TTM semantics provided above can be (and has been) implemented efficiently. For example, in the abstract semantics every event e is preceded by a breaker of monotonicity $e\#$. Most of the $e\#$ events do not change the configuration monotonicity component m and can thus be safely omitted from the reachability graph thereby shrinking it.

---

[6] The scheduling assumptions are taken care of by the model-checking algorithms [10].

3.3 Semantics of Module Composition

We have specified so far the semantics of individual TTM machines. However, the TTM notation includes a composition operator which was not discussed so far. The semantics of systems comprising many machines is defined through flattening, i.e. by providing a single machine which, by definition, has the same semantics as the whole system.

Instantiation. When integrating modules in a system, they first have to be instantiated. This means that the interface variables of the module must be linked to variables of the system it will be a part of. For example if we had a *Phil* module with two shared variables, *left_fork* and *right_fork*, and two global fork variables $f1$ and $f2$, we could instantiate them as:

> **instances** $p1 = Phil(\textbf{share } f1, \textbf{share } f2)$; $p2 = Phil(\textbf{share } f2, \textbf{share } f1)$ **end**

This makes $f1$ the left fork of $p1$ and the right fork of $p1$, and makes $f2$ the left fork of $p2$ and the right fork of $p1$. Philosopher $p1$ is therefore equivalent to the module *Phil* with its references to *left_fork* substituted by $f1$ and its references to *right_fork* substituted by $f2$.

Composition. The composition $m1\|m2$ is an associative and commutative function of two module instances. Before flattening the composition, we rename the local variables and the events so that the name of each local variable will be unique across the whole system. The renaming is done in the variable declarations, in the expressions in events, and on the left-hand sides of assignments. This is strictly a syntactic change and does not affect the semantics of the instances.

We then proceed to creating the composite machine. Its local variables will be the (disjoint) union of the local variables of the two instances. Its interface variables will be the (possibly non-disjoint) union of the interface variables of both instances with their mode (in, out, share) adjusted. The set of the events of the composition is the union of the set of events of both machines.

Iterated Composition. Iterated composition is the mechanism that allows us to compose a number of similar instances without specifying each individually. For example, in the case of a network of processes, we may want to specify the processes once and instantiate them many times with a different process identifier.

> $system = \| \; pid : PID \; @ \; Process(\textbf{in } pid)$

where PID is the set of process identifiers. It allows us to change the number of processes by just changing that set. In this case, if $PID = 1..3$, the above is equivalent to:

> **instances** $p1 = Process(\textbf{in } 1)$; $p2 = Process(\textbf{in } 2)$; $p3 = Process(\textbf{in } 3)$ **end**
> **composition** $system = p1 \; \| \; p2 \; \| \; p3$ **end**

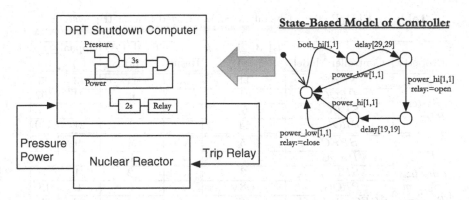

Fig. 2. DRT system: context diagram and transition diagram of controller

4   Evaluation

In Sect. 4.1, we report on the performance of our new TTM model checker in comparison with the manual encoding in Uppaal and SAL in [6]. If the system was implemented directly in Uppaal (as opposed to using the manual encoding from a TTM), the Uppaal results would likely have been much better. This section merely shows that if a designer finds the TTM notation more convenient to use, then our new tool (1) saves the designer from the effort of manual translation; and (2) performs better than the manually encoded version in other formats.

In Sect. 4.2, we address the current limitation of TTM/PAT, implemented using digitization, by reporting on its performance on the Fischers mutual exclusion algorithm, in comparison with the symbolic model checkers Uppaal and RTS. Experiments were conducted on a 64-bit Windows 7 PC with Intel(R) Core(TM) i7 CPU 860 @ 2.80 GHz (16.0 GB RAM).

4.1   Delayed Reactor Trip System

The DRT (delayed reactor trip) shutdown system, analyzed in [6], is illustrated in Fig. 2. The old implementation of the DRT used timers, comparators and logic gates as shown on the left of Fig. 2. The new DRT system is to be implemented on a microprocessor system with a cycle time of 100 ms. The system samples the inputs and passes through a block of control code every 0.1 s. A high-level state/event description (*SPEC*) of the code that replaces the analogue system is shown on the right of Fig. 2 ([6]). When the reactor pressure and power exceed acceptable safety limits in a specified way, we want the DRT control system to shut down the reactor. Otherwise, we want the control system to be reset to its initial monitoring state.

In [6], the *SPEC* level TTM description of the controller is refined into a lower level *PROG* description that is closer to implemented code (in a cyclic executive). Translations to PVS are used to show that *PROG* refines *SPEC*. The

Table 1. TTM/PAT vs. Uppaal vs. SAL: delayed reactor trip system

Property	Controller Model	TTM: $\Box\Diamond\,tick$ (s)	Result	TTM/PAT (s)	Uppaal (s)	SAL (s)
F_{res}: System Response	$SPEC$	11	×	11	13	25
	$PROG$	31	×	32	24	407
	$SPEC_r$	5	×	3	12	15
	$PROG_r$	14	×	9	21	330
F_{ires}: Initialized System Response	$SPEC$	.5	✓	.4	.9	11
	$PROG$	1	✓	1	1	20
	$SPEC_r$	.3	✓	.2	.4	7
	$PROG_r$	.8	✓	.6	1	13
	$SPEC_{r1}\|SPEC_{r2}$	16	✓	11	62	235
	$PROG_{r1}\|PROG_{r2}$	109	✓	70	76	>1h
F_{rec}: System Recovery	$SPEC$	.3	×	.08	.1	6
	$PROG$	.8	×	.2	.3	7
	$SPEC_r$	.1	✓	.07	.2	4
	$PROG_r$	.3	✓	.07	.6	5
	$SPEC_{r1}\|SPEC_{r2}$	22	×	.06	145	18
	$PROG_{r1}\|PROG_{r2}$	142	×	.1	11	>1h

reactor itself is represented by a TTM that can change the power and pressure levels arbitrarily every 0.1 s (1 tick of the clock), by using a demonic assignment setting them to either low or high. The system thus consists of the controller (either $SPEC$ or $PROG$) executing in parallel with plant (the reactor). The system must satisfy two essential properties:

Response Formula F_{res}. Henceforth, if Power and Pressure simultaneously exceed their threshold values for at least 2 clock ticks, and 30 ticks later Power exceeds its threshold for another 2 ticks, then within 30 to 32 ticks, open the reactor relay for at least 20 ticks.

Recovery Formula F_{rec}. Henceforth, if the relay is open for 20 ticks, and after the 20th tick the power is low for at least 2 ticks, then the relay is closed before the 22nd tick.

With an observer and timers, the response formula F_{res} is represented in LTL by a liveness property $\Box p \rightarrow \Diamond q$ where p and q use timers to capture the timed response (see [6] for the details). Likewise, the recovery formula F_{rec} can be reduced to a safety property $\Box\neg(T_w = 2 \wedge relay = open)$ where T_w is a timer describing a state in which the power has returned to normal for 2 ticks of the clock, but the relay is still open. Both $SPEC$ and $PROG$ did not satisfy F_{res} due to an error in the observer. Thus, verification of F_{res} should produce counterexamples in any model checker. Also, it was discovered that there was an error in the controller (in both $SPEC$ and $PROG$) as the recovery property was not satisfied. The revised and corrected descriptions of the controller are $SPEC_r$ and $PROG_r$, respectively, whose response property is referred to as F_{ires}.

To generate large reachability graphs, multiple controllers were run in parallel. For example, in checking the response property F_{ires} on $PROG_{r1}\|PROG_{r2}$,

Table 2. TTM/PAT vs. RTS/PAT vs. Uppaal: Fischer's algorithm

Property	Result	n	Uppaal (s)	PAT/RTS clock zone (s)	digitization (s)	TTM/PAT (s)
non-zenoness: $\Box\Diamond\ tick$	✓	4		not directly supported		.5
		5				4
		6				31
		7				230
		8				>1h
P1 mutual exclusion: $\Box\ (c \leq 1)$	✓	4	.04	.12	.08	.26
		5	.1	.2	.4	1.9
		6	.8	2	3	14
		7	14	21	28	104
		8	563	250	244	768
		9	>1h	2918	>1h	>1h
P2 liveness: $\Box(request \rightarrow \Diamond wait)$	✓	4	.06	.07	.1	.3
		5	.2	.3	.8	3
		6	4	3	6	24
		7	181	29	58	177
		8	>1h	307	>1h	>1h
P3 liveness: $\Box(request \rightarrow \Diamond cs)$	×	4	.2	.06	.09	.01
		5	.2	.3	.9	.01
		6	.3	3	19	.03
		7	.2	70	942	.04
		8	.2	2277	>1h	.03

the TTM tool explored 421,442 states and 821,121 transitions (in 70 s). These systems and their LTL specifications (some valid and some invalid) provide a rich set of examples to test the performance of the various model checkers. In [6], the TTMs were manually encoded into the Uppaal and SAL model checkers. The authors of [6] show that, in general, Uppaal performed better than SAL given its real-time features.

The manual encoding of TTMs into Uppaal and SAL is a time-consuming process. This is where the new TTM/PAT tool is useful as the encoding is automatic. What about performance? In Table 1, we compare TTM/PAT to the encodings in SAL and Uppaal for response and recovery, and for the various versions of the controller. The 4th column labelled "Result" has a checkmark where the LTL property is valid; otherwise, the model checker produces a counterexample. The 3rd column provides the time it takes to check for non-Zeno behaviour in the TTM tool (not supported in the other tools). In general, TTM/PAT significantly outperforms both encodings in SAL and in Uppaal. There is only one exception in the second row for F_{res}. TTM/PAT finds the formula invalid in 9 s versus 18 s for Uppaal (not shown in the table) where a counterexample is not requested. However, it takes TTM/PAT 32 s to find the counterexample versus 24 s for Uppaal.

Table 3. TTM vs. Uppaal: language of assertions

Assertion	TCTL of Uppaal	LTL of TTM/PAT
Henceforth p	$S \vDash A\Box\, p$	$S \vDash \Box\, p$
Eventually p	$S \vDash A\Diamond\, p$	$S \vDash \Diamond\, p$
Whenever p, eventually q	$S \vDash p \longrightarrow q$	$S \vDash \Box\, (p \to (\Diamond\, q))$
Infinitely often p	$S \vDash true \longrightarrow p$	$S \vDash \Box\Diamond\, p$
Referring to a state	$M.state$	$pc = state$
Non-Zenoness	$\times$	$S \vDash \Box\Diamond\, tick$
p until q	$\times$	$S \vDash p\,\mathcal{U}\,q$
q releases p	$\times$	$S \vDash q\,\mathcal{R}\,p$
Nesting of temporal operators	$\times$	e.g., $\Box\,(\Diamond\, p \to (p\mathcal{U}q))$
Referring to occurrences of event e	$\times$	e
Timer t has increased monotonically	$\times$	$mono\,(t)$
Eventually henceforth p	$\times$	$S \vDash \Diamond\Box\, p$
S possibly maintains p	$S \vDash E\Box\, p$	inverse of $S \vDash \Diamond\,(\neg p)$
S possibly reaches p	$S \vDash E\Diamond\, p$	S **reaches** p
Nesting of path quantifiers	$\times$	$\times$
$\forall\Diamond\;\forall\Box\, p$	$\times$	$\times$

4.2   Fischer's Mutual Exclusion Algorithm

TTM/PAT is an explicit state tool for discrete systems. The expectation was that it would perform well in the category of explicit state model checkers. Nevertheless, it was expected that symbolic checkers (using timed automata) such as Uppaal would outperform it. In addition, Uppaal is continuous time (although timing constants in Uppaal are integers) whereas TTMs are discrete time. Nevertheless, the assertion notation of TTMs is more expressive than Uppaal (see Sect. 5 and Table 3) and its event-based syntax is amenable to formal reasoning and compositional reasoning.

A comparison was performed in [9] between RTS (a PAT plugin) and Uppaal using the Fischer's mutual exclusion algorithm. We compare the performance of the TTM/PAT tool to RTS and Uppaal using the same example. For a proper comparison of the three tools, many more examples would be needed.

Our experiment shows that, in determining that properties **P1** (a safety property) and **P2** (a liveness property stating that a process requesting access to its critical section leads it to wait) are valid, the clock zone mode of RTS is faster than Uppaal (see Table 2). The speed of TTM/PAT is within a factor between 3 and 4 of the digitization mode of RTS. TTM/PAT is almost as fast as Uppaal in producing counterexamples for property **P3** (expressing the starvation freedom property). Results in Table 2 (with n the number of processes put in parallel) suggest that the techniques used in clock zones of RTS and those of Uppaal would provide enhancements for more efficient verification of TTMs.

5   Conclusion

We introduce a convenient, expressive textual syntax for event-based TTMs, and its operational semantics for building the TTM/PAT tool in the PAT framework. The TTM assertion language, linear-time temporal logic (LTL), allows references to event occurrences, including clock ticks (thus allowing for checking non-Zeno behaviours). The tool supports type checking, graphical simulation, and LTL verification. The tool performs significantly better on a nuclear shutdown system than the manually encoded versions in Uppaal and SAL.

The TTM tool is an explicit state model checker (with a discrete time domain) that has comparable performance to the digitization mode of RTS [9] (see end of Sect. 4). We can improve the performance of the tool by considering a continuous time domain and using symbolic analysis, e.g., the clock zone algorithms of RTS or the timed automata of Uppaal. In either case, this would come at the cost of expressiveness. Table 3 shows that Uppaal's TCTL assertion language is less expressive than that of TTM notation. There are temporal properties such as $\lozenge\square p$ that can be specified and verified in TTM/PAT but not in Uppaal. Also, non-Zenoness and timer monotonicity can be checked directly in the TTM assertion language. In RTS, the construct "P within $[l, u]$", which forces process P to terminate between l and u units of time, is not supported by the clock zone algorithms; the lower time bound is the problematic part to implement. Also, RTS does not allow explicit timers which are important for verifying global timing properties.

The TTM/PAT tool already supports an assume-guarantee style of compositional reasoning (discussed in an extended report [8]). The use of LTL better supports compositional reasoning than branching time logic [11]. Event actions specified as before-after predicates allow us, in the future, to enhance compositional reasoning using axiomatic methods (as in [2]). We intend to explore the clock zone algorithms of RTS as these are already directly available in the PAT toolset. We also intend to explore the use of SMT solvers for axiomatic reasoning about TTMs. We expect that the use of before-after predicates, for specifying the semantics of events in TTMs, will facilitate this type of formal reasoning.

Acknowledgments. The authors would like to thank NSERC and ORF for their generous financial support.

References

1. Abrial, J.-R.: Modeling in Event-B. Cambridge University Press, Cambridge (2010)
2. Chandy, K.M., Misra, J.: Parallel Program Design—a Foundation. Addison-Wesley, Reading (1989)
3. de Moura, L., Owre, S., Ruess, H., Rushby, J., Shankar, N., Sorea, M., Tiwari, A.: SAL 2. In: Alur, R., Peled, D.A. (eds.) CAV 2004. LNCS, vol. 3114, pp. 496–500. Springer, Heidelberg (2004)

4. Jee, E., Lee, I., Sokolsky, O.: Assurance cases in model-driven development of the pacemaker software. In: Margaria, T., Steffen, B. (eds.) ISoLA 2010, Part II. LNCS, vol. 6416, pp. 343–356. Springer, Heidelberg (2010)
5. Larsen, K.G., Pettersson, P., Yi, W.: Uppaal in a nutshell. Int. J. Softw. Tools Technol. Transf. **1**(1–2), 134–152 (1997)
6. Lawford, M., Pantelic, V., Zhang, H.: Towards integrated verification of timed transition models. Fund. Inform. **70**(1–2), 75–110 (2006)
7. Ostroff, J.S.: Composition and refinement of discrete real-time systems. ACM Trans. Softw. Eng. Methodol. **8**(1), 1–48 (1999)
8. Ostroff, J.S., Wang, C.-W., Hudon, S.: TTM/PAT: a tool for modelling and verifying timed transition models. Technical Report CSE-2013-05, York University (2013)
9. Sun, J., Liu, Y., Dong, J.S., Liu, Y., Shi, L., André, É.: Modeling and verifying hierarchical real-time systems using stateful timed CSP. ACM Trans. Softw. Eng. Methodol. **22**(1), 3:1–3:29 (2013)
10. Sun, J., Liu, Y., Dong, J.S., Pang, J.: PAT: towards flexible verification under fairness. In: Bouajjani, A., Maler, O. (eds.) CAV 2009. LNCS, vol. 5643, pp. 709–714. Springer, Heidelberg (2009)
11. Vardi, M.Y.: Branching vs. linear time: final showdown. In: Margaria, T., Yi, W. (eds.) TACAS 2001. LNCS, vol. 2031, pp. 1–22. Springer, Heidelberg (2001)

Formalizing and Verifying Function Blocks Using Tabular Expressions and PVS

Linna Pang[✉], Chen-Wei Wang, Mark Lawford, and Alan Wassyng

McMaster Centre for Software Certification, McMaster University,
Hamilton L8S 4K1, Canada
{pangl,wangcw,lawford,wassyng}@mcmaster.ca

Abstract. Many industrial control systems use programmable logic controllers (PLCs) since they provide a highly reliable, off-the-shelf hardware platform. On the programming side, function blocks (FBs) are reusable components provided by the PLC supplier that can be combined to implement the required system behaviour. A higher quality system may be realized if the FBs are pre-certified to be compliant with an international standard such as IEC 61131-3. We present an approach to formalizing FB requirements using tabular expressions, and to verifying the correctness of the FBs implementations in the PVS proof environment. We applied our approach to the example FBs of IEC 61131-3 and identified issues in the standard: ambiguous behavioural descriptions, missing assumptions, and erroneous implementations.

Keywords: Critical systems · Formal specification · Formal verification · Function blocks · Tabular expressions · IEC 61131-3 · PVS

1 Introduction

Many industrial control systems have replaced traditional analog equipment by components that are based upon programmable logic controllers (PLCs) to address increasing market demands for high quality [1]. Function blocks (FBs) are basic design units that implement the behaviour of a PLC, where each FB is a reusable component for building new, more sophisticated components or systems. The search for higher quality may be realized if the FBs are pre-certified with respect to an international standard such as IEC 61131-3 [8,9]. Standards such as DO-178C (in the aviation domain) and IEEE 7-4.3.2 (in the nuclear domain) list acceptance criteria of mission- or safety-critical systems for practitioners to comply with. Two important criteria are that (1) the system requirements are precise and complete; and that (2) the system implementation exhibits behaviour that conforms to these requirements. In one of its supplements, DO-178C advocates the use of formal methods to construct, develop, and reason about the mathematical models of system behaviours.

Tabular expressions [20,21] are a way to document system requirements that have proven to be both practical and effective in industry [13,25]. PVS [18]

C. Artho and P.C. Ölveczky (Eds.): FTSCS 2013, CCIS 419, pp. 125–141, 2014.
DOI: 10.1007/978-3-319-05416-2_9, © Springer International Publishing Switzerland 2014

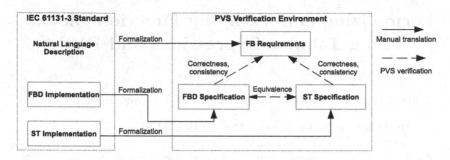

Fig. 1. Framework

is a non-commercial theorem prover, and provides an integrated environment with mechanized support for writing specifications using tabular expressions and (higher-order) predicates, and for (interactively) proving that implementations satisfy the tabular requirements using sequent-style deductions. In this paper we report on using tabular expressions to formalize the requirements of FBs and on using PVS to verify their correctness (with respect to tabular requirements).

As a case study, we have formalized[1] 23 of 29 FBs listed in IEC 61131-3 [8,9], an important standard with over 20 years of use on critical systems running on PLCs. There are two compelling reasons for formalizing the existing behavioural descriptions of FBs supplied by IEC 61131-3. First, formal descriptions such as tabular expressions force tool vendors and users of FBs to have the same interpretations of the expected system behaviours. Second, formal descriptions are amenable to mechanized support such as PVS to verify the conformance of candidate implementations to the high-level, input-output requirements. Currently IEC 61131-3 lacks an adequate, formal language for describing the behaviours of FBs and for arguing about their correctness. Unfortunately, IEC 61131-3 uses FB descriptions that are too close to the level of hardware implementations. For the purpose of this paper, we focus on FBs that are described in the more commonly used languages of structured text (ST) and function block diagrams (FBDs). Note that two versions of IEC 61131-3 are cited here. The earlier version [8] has been in use since 2003. Most of the work reported on in this paper relates to this version. When the new version [9] was issued, we expected to find that the problems we had discovered in the earlier version had been corrected. However, we found that many of the example FBs had been removed from the standard and the remaining FBs are still problematic.

We now summarize our approach and contributions with reference to Fig. 1. As shown on the left, a function block will typically have a natural language description of the block behaviour accompanied by a detailed implementation in the ST or FBD description, or in some cases both. Based upon all of this information we create a black box tabular requirements specification in PVS for the

---

[1] PVS files are available at http://www.cas.mcmaster.ca/~lawford/papers/ FTSCS2013. All verifications are conducted using PVS 5.0.

behaviour of the FB as described in Sect. 3.2. The ST and FBD implementations are formalized as predicates in PVS, again making use of tables, as described in Sect. 3.1. In the case when there are two implementations for an FB, one in FBD and the other in ST, we attempt to prove their (functional) equivalence in PVS. For any implementation we attempt to prove the *correctness* and *consistency* with respect to the FB requirements in PVS (Sect. 4).

Using our approach, we have identified a number of issues in IEC 61131-3 and suggested resolutions (Sect. 5), which are summarized below:

1. The behaviour of the *pulse* timer is characterized through a timing diagram with at least two scenarios unspecified.
2. The description of the *sr* block (a set-dominant latch) lacks an explicit time delay on the intermediate values being computed and fed back. By introducing a delay FB, we verified the correctness of *sr*.
3. The description of the up-down counter *ctud* permits unintuitive behaviours. We eliminate them by incorporating a relation on its three inputs (i. e., low limit, high limit, and preset value) in the tabular requirement of *ctud*.
4. The description of the *limits_alarm* block allows the low limit and high limit alarms to be tripped simultaneously. We resolve this by explicitly constraining the two hysteresis zones to be both disjoint and ordered.
5. The ST and FBD implementations for the *stack_int* block (stack of integers) failed the equivalence proof. We identified a missing FB in the FBD implementation, and then discharged the proof.

We will discuss issues (1), (2), and (3) in further detail in Sect. 5. Details of the remaining issues that we omit are available in an extended report [19]. In the next section we discuss background materials: the IEC 61131-3 Standard, tabular expressions, and PVS.

2   Preliminaries

2.1   IEC 61131-3 Standard Function Blocks

Programmable logic controllers (PLCs) are digital computers that are widely utilized in real-time and embedded control systems. In the light of unifying the syntax and semantics of programming languages for PLCs, the International Electrotechnical Committee (IEC) first published IEC 61131-3 in 1993 with revisions in 2003 [8] and 2013 [9]. The issues of ambiguous behaviours, missing assumptions, and erroneous behavioural descriptions that we found have not been resolved in the latest edition.

We applied our methodology to the standard functions and function blocks listed in Annex F of IEC 61131-3 (1993). FBs are more flexible than standard functions in that they allow internal states, feedback paths and time-dependent behaviours. We distinguish between *basic* and *composite* FBs: the former consist of standard functions only, while the latter can be constructed from standard functions and any other pre-developed basic or composite FBs. We focus on two

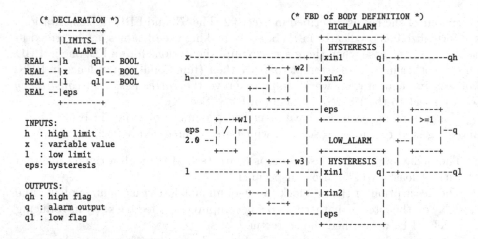

Fig. 2. *Limits_alarm* standard declaration and FBD implementation [8]

programming languages that are covered in IEC 61131-3 for writing behavioural descriptions of FBs: structured text (ST) and function block diagrams (FBDs). ST syntax is block structured and resembles that of Pascal, while FBDs visualize inter-connections or data flows between inputs and outputs of block components.

Figure 2 shows the FBD of the *limits_alarm* block, consisting of declarations of inputs and outputs, and the definition of computation. An alarm monitors the quantity of some variable x, subject to a low limit l and a high limit h, with the hysteresis band of size *eps*. The body definition visualizes how ultimate and intermediate outputs are computed, e. g., output ql is obtained by computing $HYSTERESIS(l + (eps/2.0), x, eps/2.0)$. There are five internal component blocks of *limits_alarm*: addition (+), subtraction(−), division (/), logical disjunction (≥ 1), and the hysteresis effect (*hysteresis*). The internal connectives are w_1, w_2 and w_3. Section 3.2 presents the precise input-output tabular requirement.

2.2 Tabular Expressions

Tabular expressions [20, 21] (a. k. a. function tables) are an effective approach to describing conditionals and relations, thus ideal for documenting many system requirements. They are arguably easier to comprehend and to maintain than conventional mathematical expressions. Tabular expressions have well-defined formal semantics (e. g., [10]), and they are useful both in inspections and in testing and verification [25]. For our purpose of capturing the input-output requirements of function blocks in IEC 61131-3, the tabular structure in Fig. 3 suffices: the input domain and the output range are partitioned into rows of, respectively, the first column (for input conditions) and the second column (for output results). The input column may be sub-divided to specify sub-conditions.

We may interpret the above tabular structure as a list of "if-then-else" predicates or logical implications. Each row defines the input circumstances under

Condition	Result f
$C_{1.1}$	res_1
C_1 $C_{1.2}$	res_2
...	...
$C_{1.m}$	res_m
...	...
C_n	res_n

```
IF  C₁
    IF       C₁.₁ THEN f = res₁
    ELSEIF   C₁.₂ THEN f = res₂
    ...
    ELSEIF   C₁.ₘ THEN f = resₘ
ELSEIF  ...
ELSEIF    Cₙ   THEN f = resₙ
```

Fig. 3. Semantics of horizontal condition table (HCT)

which the output f is bound to a particular result value. For example, the first row corresponds to the predicate $(C_1 \land C_{1.1} \Rightarrow f = res_1)$, and so on. In documenting input-output behaviours using horizontal condition tables (HCTs), we need to reason about their *completeness* and *disjointness*. Suppose there is no sub-condition, completeness ensures that at least one row is applicable to every input, i.e., $(C_1 \lor C_2 \lor \cdots \lor C_n \equiv True)$. Disjointness ensures that the rows do not overlap, e.g., $(i \neq j \Rightarrow \neg(C_i \land C_j))$. Similar constraints apply to the sub-conditions, if any. These properties can often be easily checked automatically using SMT solvers or a theorem prover such as PVS [6].

2.3   PVS

Prototype Verification System (PVS) [18] is an interactive environment for writing specifications and performing proofs. The PVS specification language is based on classical higher-order logic. The syntactic constructs that we use the most are "if-then-else" predicates and tables, which we will explain as we use them. An example of using tabular expressions to specify and verify the Darlington Nuclear Shutdown System (SDS) in PVS can be found in [13].

PVS has a powerful interactive proof checker to perform sequent-style deductions. The completeness and disjointness properties are generated automatically as Type Correctness Conditions (TCCs) to be discharged. We will discuss a found issue (Sect. 5) where the ST implementation supplied by IEC 61131-3 is formalized as a PVS table but its disjointness TCC failed to be discharged. In this paper we omit proof details that are available in an extended report [19].

As PLCs are commonly used in real-time systems, time modelling is a critical aspect in our formalization. We consider a discrete-time model in which a time series consists of equally spaced sample times or "ticks" in PVS:

```
delta_t: posreal
time: TYPE+ = nonneg_real
tick: TYPE = {t: time | EXISTS (n: nat): t = n * delta_t}
```

Constant `delta_t` is a positive real number. Here `time` is the set of nonnegative real numbers, and `tick` is the set of time samples [7].

3   Formalizing Function Blocks Using Tabular Expressions

Below we present a formal approach to defining standard functions and function blocks in IEC 61131-3 using tabular expressions.

3.1   Formalizing IEC 61131-3 Function Block Implementations

We perform formalization at levels of standard functions, basic function blocks (FBs), and composite FBs. Similar to [4], we formulate each standard function or function block as a predicate, characterizing its input-output relation.

Standard Functions. IEC 61131-3 defines eight groups of standard functions, including: (1) data type conversion; (2) numerical; (3) arithmetic; (4) bit-string; (5) selection and comparison; (6) character string; (7) time and date types; and (8) enumerated data types. In general, we formalize the behaviour of a standard function f as a Boolean function:

$$f(i_1, i_2, \ldots, i_m, o_1, o_2, \ldots, o_n) : bool \equiv R(i_1, i_2, \ldots, i_m, o_1, o_2, \ldots, o_n)$$

where predicate R characterizes the precise relation on the m inputs and the n outputs of standard function f. Our formalization covers both timed and untimed behaviours of standard functions. As an example of a timed function, consider function *move* that takes as inputs an enabling condition *en* and an integer *in*, and that outputs an integer *out*. The behaviour of *move* is time-dependent: at the very first clock tick, *out* is initialized to zero; otherwise, at time instant t $(t > 0)$, *out* is either equal to *in* at time t, if condition *en* holds at t, or otherwise *out* is equal to *in* at time $t - \alpha * \delta$ $(\alpha = 1, 2, \ldots)$ where *en* was last enabled (i. e., a case of "no change" for *out*). More precisely, we translate the input-output relation of function *move* into PVS:

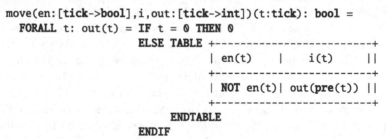

We characterize the temporal relation between *in* and *out* as a universal quantification over discrete time instants. Functions [tick->bool] and [tick->int] capture the input and output values at different time instants. The behaviour at each time instant t is expressed as an IF...THEN...ELSE...ENDIF statement. Construct TABLE...ENDTABLE that appears in the ELSE branch exemplifies the use of tabular expressions as part of a predicate. The main advantage of embedding tables in predicates is that the PVS prover will generate proof obligations for completeness and disjointness accordingly.

Untimed behaviour, on the other hand, abstracts from the input-output relation at the current time instant, which makes first-order logic suffice for the formalization. For example, consider the standard function *add* that is used as an internal component of the FB *limits_alarm* (see Fig. 2), which has the obvious formalization: $add(in_1, in_2, out : int) : bool \equiv out = in_1 + in_2$. Incorporating the output value *out* as part of the function parameters makes it possible to formalize basic FBs with internal states, or composite FBs. For basic FBs with no internal states, we formalize them as function compositions of their internal blocks. As a result, we also support a version of *add* that returns an integer value: $add(in_1, in_2 : int) : int = in_1 + in_2$.

Basic Function Blocks. A basic function block (FB) is an abstraction component that consists of standard functions. When all internal components of a basic FB are functions, and there are no intermediate values to be stored, we formalize the output as the result of a functional composition of the internal functions. For example, given FB *weigh*, which takes as inputs a gross weight *gw* and a tare weight *tw* and returns the net weight *nw*, we formalize weigh by defining the output *nw* as $nw = int2bcd(subtract(bcd2int(gross), tare))$, where *int2bcdandbcd2int* are standard conversion functions between binary-coded decimals and integers. On the other hand, to formalize a basic FB that has internal states to be stored, we take the conjunction of the predicates that formalize its internal functions. We formalize composite FBs in a similar manner.

Composite Function Block. Each composite FB contains as components standard functions, basic FBs, or other pre-developed composite FBs. For example, *limits_alarm* (Sect. 2) is a composite FB consisting of standard functions and two instances of the pre-developed composite FB *hysteresis*. Our formalization of each component as a predicate results in *compositionality*: a predicate that formalizes a composite FB is obtained by taking the conjunction of those that formalize its components. IEC 61131-3 uses ST and FBD to describe composite FBs.

Remark. Predicates that formalize basic or composite FBs represent their black-box input-output relations. Since we use function tables in PVS to specify these predicates, their behaviours are deterministic. This allows us to easily compose their behaviours using logical conjunction. The conjunction of deterministic components is functionally deterministic.

Formalizing Composite FB Implementation: ST. We translate an ST implementation supplied by IEC 61131-3 into its equivalent expression in PVS. We illustrate (parts of[2]) our ST-to-PVS translation using concrete examples.

---

[2] Other translation patterns can be found in [19].

Pattern 1 illustrates that we transform sequential compositions (;) into logical conjunctions (&). We write a_{-1} to denote the value of variable a at the previous time tick (i. e., before the current function block is executed). In general, we constrain the relationship between each variable v and v_{-1} to formalize the effect of its containing function block.

#	ST expressions	PVS predicates
1	*basic assignments*	
	`a := a + b; c := NOT (a > 0)`	`a = a_-1 + b & c = NOT (a > 0)`

Pattern 2 illustrates that we reconstruct conditional statement by taking the conjunction of the assignment effect of each variable; each variable assignment is formalized via a tabular expression. How variables are used in the tables is used to derive the order of evaluation. For example, b is evaluated before c to compute $c = a + b$.

2	*conditional assignments*	

	``IF z THEN``
	``  b := c * 3; c := a + b;``
	``ELSE``
	``  b := b + c; e := b - 1;``
	``END_IF``
		``b = TABLE | z        | c_-1 * 3 ||``
		``          | NOT z | b_-1 + c ||``
		``   ENDTABLE &``
		``c = TABLE | z        | a + b    ||``
		``          | NOT z | c_-1     ||``
		``   ENDTABLE &``
		``e = TABLE | NOT z | b - 1    ||``
		``          | z        | e_-1     ||``
		``   ENDTABLE``

For the above example, an "if-then-else" conditional that returns the conjunction of the variable update predicates more closely correspond to the original ST implementation may instead be used. In general though when assignment conditions become more complicated, we feel it is clearer to isolate the update of each variable.

Pattern 3 illustrates that we translate each invocation of a function block `FB` into an instantiation of its formalizing predicate `FB_REQ`, where the return value of `FB` (i. e., `FB.output`) is incorporated as an argument of `FB_REQ`.

3	*function block invocations, reuse*	

	``FB1(in_1 := a, in_2 := b);``
	``FB2(in_1 := FB1.output);``
	``out := FB2.output;``
		``FB1_REQ(a, b, fb1_out) &``
		``FB2_REQ(fb1_out, fb2_out) &``
		``out = fb2_out``

Formalizing Composite FB Implementation: FBD. To illustrate the case of formalizing a FBD implementation supplied by IEC 61131-3, let us consider the following FBD of a composite FB and its formalizing predicate in Fig. 4:

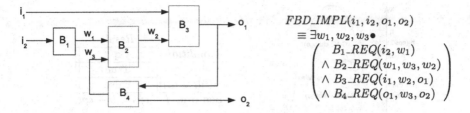

Fig. 4. Composite FB implementation in FBD and its formalizing predicate

Figure 4 consists of four internal blocks, B_1, B_2, B_3, and B_4, that are already formalized (i. e., their formalizing predicates $B_1\_REQ,\ldots,B_4\_REQ$ exist). The high-level requirement (as opposed to the implementation supplied by IEC 61131-3) for each internal FB constrains upon its inputs and outputs, documented by tabular expressions (see Sect. 3.2). To describe the overall behaviour of the above composite FB, we take advantage of our formalization being *compositional*. In other words, we formalize a composite FB by existentially quantifying over the list of its inter-connectives (i. e., w_1, w_2 and w_3), such that the conjunction of predicates that formalize the internal components hold.

For example, we formalize the FBD implementation of block *limits_alarm* (Sect. 2) as a predicate LIMITS_ALARM_IMPL in PVS:

```
LIMITS_ALARM_IMPL(h,x,l,eps,qh,q,ql)(t): bool =
 FORALL t:
  EXISTS (w1,w2,w3):
    div(eps(t),2.0,w1(t)) & sub(h(t),w1(t),w2(t)) &
    add(l(t),w1(t),w3(t)) & disj(qh(t),ql(t),q(t)) &
    HYSTERESIS_req_tab(x,w2,w1,qh)(t) & HYSTERESIS_req_tab(w3,x,w1,ql)(t)
```

We observe that predicate LIMITS_ALARM_IMPL, as well as those for the internal components, all take a time instant $t \in tick$ as a parameter. This is to account for the time-dependent behaviour, similar to how we formalized the standard function *move* in the beginning of this section.

The above predicates that formalize the internal components, e. g., predicate HYSTERESIS_req_tab, do not denote those translated from the ST implementation of IEC 61131-3. Instead, as one of our contributions, we provide high-level, input-output requirements that are missing from IEC 61131-3 (to be discussed in the next section). Such formal, compositional requirement are developed for the purpose of formalizing and verifying sophisticated, composite FBs.

3.2   Formalizing Requirements of Function Blocks

As stated, IEC 61131-3 supplies low-level, implementation-oriented ST or FBD descriptions for function blocks. For the purpose of verifying the correctness of

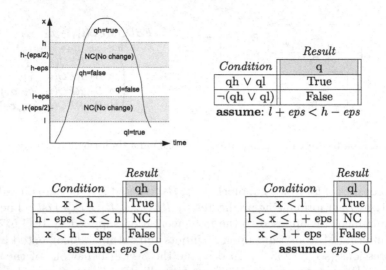

Fig. 5. *Limits_alarm* requirement in tabular expression

the supplied implementation, it is necessary to obtain requirements for FBs that are both complete (on the input domain) and disjoint (on producing the output). Tabular expressions (in PVS) are an excellent notation for describing such requirements. Our method for deriving the tabular, input-output requirement for each FB is to partition its input domain into equivalence classes, and for each such input condition, we consider what the corresponding output from the FB should be.

As an example, we consider the requirement for function block *limits_alarm* (Sect. 2). The expected input-output behaviour and its tabular requirement (which constrains the relation between inputs x, h, l, eps and outputs q, qh, ql) is depicted in Fig. 5. We use "NC" to denote "No Change", i.e., the value of variable qh is equal to the value at previous time tick qh_{-1}. Our formalization process revealed the need for two missing assumptions from IEC 61131-3: $eps > 0$ and $l + eps < h - eps$. They allow us to ensure that the two hysteresis zones $[l, l + eps]$ and $[h - eps, h]$ are non-empty, disjoint and ordered [19].

Let predicates f_qh, f_ql, and f_q be those that formalize, respectively, the table for qh, ql and q, we then translate the above requirement into PVS as:

```
LIMITS_ALARM_REQ(h,x,l,eps,qh,q,ql)(t): bool =
    f_qh(x,h,eps,qh)(t) & f_ql(x,l,eps,ql)(t) & f_q(qh,ql,q)(t)
```

By using the function definitions of q, qh and ql, we can verify the correctness of the FBD implementation of *limits_alarm*, formalized as the predicate above. This process can be generalized to verify other FBDs in IEC 61131-3.

4   Verifying Function Blocks in PVS

We now present the two kinds of verification we perform.

4.1   Verifying the Correctness of an Implementation

Given an implementation predicate I, our correctness theorem states that, if I holds for all possible inputs and outputs, then the corresponding requirement predicate R also holds. This corresponds to the proofs of *correctness* shown in Fig. 1. For example, to prove that the FBD implementation of block *limits_alarm* in Sec. 3.1 is *correct* with respect to its requirement in Sec. 3.2, we must prove the following in PVS:

$$\vdash \forall h, x, l, eps \bullet \forall qh, q, ql \bullet limits\_alrm\_impl(h, x, l, eps, qh, q, ql) \Rightarrow \tag{1}$$
$$limits\_alrm\_req(h, x, l, eps, qh, q, ql)$$

Furthermore, we also need to ensure that the implementation is consistent or feasible, i.e., for each input list, there exists at least one corresponding list of outputs, such that I holds. Otherwise, the implementation trivially satisfies any requirements. This is shown in Fig. 1 as proofs of *consistency*. In the case of *limits_alarm*, we must prove the following in PVS:

$$\vdash \forall h, x, l, eps \bullet \exists qh, q, ql \bullet limits\_alrm\_impl(h, x, l, eps, qh, q, ql) \tag{2}$$

4.2   Verifying the Equivalence of Implementations

In IEC 61131-3, block *limits_alarm* is supplied with ST only. In theory, when both ST and FBD implementations are supplied for the same FB (e.g., *stack_int*), it may suffice to verify that each of the implementations is *correct* with respect to the requirement. However, as the behaviour of FBs is intended to be deterministic in most cases, it would be worth proving that the implementations (if they are given at the same level of abstraction) are equivalent, and generate scenarios, if any, where they are not. This is also labelled in Fig. 1 as proofs of *equivalence*.

In Sect. 3.1 we discussed how to obtain, for a given FB, a predicate for its ST description (say FB_st_impl) and one for its FBD description (say FB_fbd_impl). Both predicates share the same input list $i_1, \dots, i_m$ and output list $o_1, \dots, o_n$. Consequently, to verify that the two supplied implementations are equivalent, we must prove the following in PVS:

$$\vdash \forall i_1, \dots, i_m \bullet \forall o_1, \dots, o_n \bullet$$
$$FB\_st\_impl(i_1, \dots, i_m, o_1, \dots, o_n) \equiv FB\_fbd\_impl(i_1, \dots, i_m, o_1, \dots, o_n) \tag{3}$$

However, the verification of block *stack_int* is an exception. Its ST and FBD implementations are at different levels of abstraction: the FBD description is closer to the hardware level as it declares additional, auxiliary variables to indicate system errors (Appendix E of IEC 61131-3) and thus cause interrupts. Consequently, we are only able to prove a refinement (i.e., implication) relationship instead (i.e., the FBD implementation implies the ST implementation).

Although IEC 61131-3 (2003) had been in use for almost 10 years, while performing this verification on *stack_int*, we found an error (of a missing FB in the FBD implementation) that made the above implication unprovable [19].

5   Case Study: Issues Found in Standard IEC 61131-3

To justify the value of our approach (Sects. 3 and 4), we have formalized and verified 23 of 29 FBs from IEC 61131-3. Our coverage so far has revealed a number of issues that are listed in the introduction. We briefly discuss the first three and our reactions to them. The complete discussion is available in [19].

5.1   Ambiguous Behaviour: Pulse Timer in Timing Diagrams

Block *pulse* is a timer defined in IEC 61131-3, whose graphical declaration is shown on the LHS of Fig. 6. It takes two inputs (a boolean condition *in* and a length *pt* of time period) and produces two outputs (a boolean value *q* and a length *et* of time period). It acts as a pulse generator: as soon as the input condition *in* is detected to hold, it generates a pulse to let output *q* remain *true* for a constant *pt* of time units. The elapsed time that *q* has remained *true* can also be monitored via output *et*. IEC 61131-3 presents a timing diagram[3] as depicted on the RHS of Fig. 6, where the horizontal time axis is labelled with time instants t_i ($i \in 0..5$), to specify (an incomplete set of) the behaviour of block *pulse*.

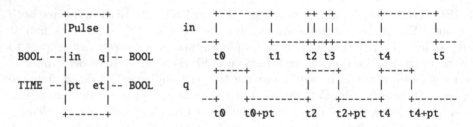

Fig. 6. *pulse* timer declaration and definition in timing diagram

The above timing diagram suggests that when a rising edge of the input condition *in* is detected at time t, another rising edge that occurs before time $t + pt$ may not be detected, e. g., the rising edge occurring at t_3 might be missed as $t_3 < t_2 + pt$.

The use of timing diagrams to specify behaviour is limited to a small number of use cases; subtle or critical boundary cases are likely to be missing. We formalize the *pulse* timer using tabular expressions that ensure both completeness and disjointness. We found that there are at least two scenarios that are not covered by the above timing diagram supplied by IEC 61131-3. *First*, if a rising

---

[3] For presenting our found issues, it suffices to show just the parts of *in* and *q*.

	Condition	Result q
¬q_{-1}	¬in_{-1} ∧ in	true
	in_{-1} ∨ ¬in	false
q_{-1}	**Held_For(q,pt)**	**false**
	¬Held_For(q,pt)	true

Condition	Result pulse_start_time
¬q_{-1} ∧ q	t
q_{-1} ∨ ¬q	NC

	Condition			Result et
	q			t − pulse_start_time
¬q	¬Held_For_ts(in,pt,pulse_start_time)			0
	Held_For_ts **(in,pt,pulse_start_time)**	**in**	t − pulse_start_time ≥ pt	**pt**
			t − pulse_start_time < pt	t − pulse_start_time
		¬in		0

Fig. 7. Requirement of *pulse* timer using tabular expressions

edge of condition *in* occurred at $t_2 + pt$, should there be a pulse generated to let output q remain *true* for another pt time units? If so, there would be two connected pulses: from t_2 to $t_2 + pt$ and from $t_2 + pt$ to $t_2 + 2pt$. Second, if the rising edge that occurred at t_3 stays high until some time t_k, $(t_2 + pt \le t_k \le t_4)$, should the output *et* be default to 0 at time $t_2 + pt$ or at time t_k?

We use the three tables in Fig. 7 to formalize the behaviour of the *pulse* timer, where outputs q and *et* and the internal variable *pulse_start_time* are initialized to, respectively, *false*, 0, and 0. The tables have their obvious equivalents in PVS. To make the timing behaviour precise, we define two auxiliary predicates *Held_For* and *Held_For_ts* which are based on the work presented in [7]:

```
Held_For(P:pred[tick],duration:posreal)(t:tick): bool =
  EXISTS(t_j:tick): (t-t_j >= duration) &
                  (FORALL (t_n: tick | t_n >= t_j & t_n <= t): P(t_n))
Held_For_ts(P:pred[tick],duration:posreal,ts:tick)(t:tick): bool =
  (t-ts >= duration) & (FORALL (t_n: tick | t_n >= ts & t_n <= t): P(t_n))
```

Predicate *Held_For(P, duration)* holds when the input predicate P holds for at least *duration* units of time. Predicate *Held_For_ts(P, duration, ts)* is more restricted, insisting that the starting time of *duration* is *ts*. As a result, we make explicit assumptions to disambiguate the above two scenarios. Scenario 1 would match the condition row (in bold) in the upper-left table for output q, where q at the previous time tick holds (i. e., q_{-1}) and q has already held for pt time units, so the problematic rising edge that occurred at $t_2 + pt$ would be missed. Due to our resolution to Scenario 1, at time $t2+pt$, Scenario 2 would match the condition row (in bold) in the lower table for output *et*, where q at the current time tick does not hold (i. e., $¬q$), condition *in* has held for more than pt time units, so the value of *et* remains as pt without further increasing.

As *pulse* timer is not supplied with implementation, there are no correctness and consistency proofs to be conducted. Nonetheless, obtaining a precise, complete, and disjoint requirement is valuable for future concrete implementations.

5.2   Ambiguous Behaviour: Implicit Delay Unit

PLC applications often use feedback loops: outputs of a FB are connected as inputs of either another FB or the FB itself. IEC 61131-3 specifies feedback loops through either a connecting line or shared names of inputs and outputs. However, feedback values (or of intermediate output values) cannot be computed instantaneously in reality. We address this issue by introducing a delay block Z_{-1} and its formalization below:

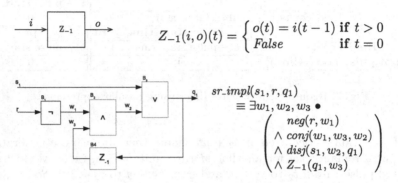

$$Z_{-1}(i,o)(t) = \begin{cases} o(t) = i(t-1) & \text{if } t > 0 \\ False & \text{if } t = 0 \end{cases}$$

$$sr\_impl(s_1, r, q_1)$$
$$\equiv \exists w_1, w_2, w_3 \bullet \begin{pmatrix} neg(r, w_1) \\ \wedge \; conj(w_1, w_3, w_2) \\ \wedge \; disj(s_1, w_2, q_1) \\ \wedge \; Z_{-1}(q_1, w_3) \end{pmatrix}$$

Fig. 8. Block sr implementation in FBD and its formalizing predicate

There is an explicit, one-tick delay between the input and output of block Z_{-1}, making it suitable for denoting feedback values as output values produced in the previous execution cycle. The types of i and o must match. For example, block sr creates a set-dominant latch (a. k. a. flip-flop), takes as inputs a boolean set flag s_1 and a boolean reset flag r, and returns a boolean output q_1. The value of q_1 is fed back as another input of block sr. Value of q_1 remains *true* as long as the set flag s_1 is enabled, and q_1 is reset to *false* only when both flags are disabled. There should be a delay between the value of q_1 is computed and passed to the next execution cycle. We formalize this by adding the explicit delay block Z_{-1} and conjoining predicates for the internal blocks (as shown in Fig. 8). Blocks B_1 (formalized by predicate neg), B_2 ($conj$), B_3 ($disj$), and B_4 (Z_{-1}) in Fig. 8 denote the FB of, respectively, logical negation, conjunction, disjunction, and delay. Arrows w_1, w_2, and w_3 are internal connectives. Adding an explicit delay block Z_{-1} to formalize feedback loops led us to discharge the correctness and consistency theorems (Sect. 4) of the FBD implementation in Fig. 8.

5.3   Missing Assumption: Limit on Counters FBs

An up-down counter (*ctud*) in IEC 61131-3 is composed of an up counter (*ctu*) and a down counter (*ctd*). The output counter value cv is incremented (using the up counter) if a rising edge is detected on an input condition cu, or cv is decremented (using the down counter) if a rising edge is detected on the input cd. Actions of increment and decrement are subject to, respectively, a high limit

$PVmax$ and a low limit $PVmin$. The value of cv is loaded to a preset value pv if a load flag ld is $true$; and it is default to 0 if a reset condition r is enabled. Two Boolean outputs are produced to reflect the change on cv: $qu \equiv (cv > pv)$ and $qd \equiv (cv <= 0)$.

As we attempted to formalize and verify the correctness of the ST implementation of block $ctud$ supplied by IEC 61131-3, we found two missing assumptions.

First, the relationship between the high and low limits is not stated. Let $PVmin$ be 10 and $PVmax$ be 1, then the counter can only increment when $cv < 1$, decrement when $cv > 10$ (disabled when $1 \leq cv \leq 10$). This contradicts with our intuition about how low and high limits are used to constrain the behaviour of a counter. Consequently, we introduce a new assumption[4]: $PVmin < PVmax$.

Condition				Result
				cv
r				0
¬r	ld			pv
	¬ld	cu ∧ cd		NC
		cu∧¬cd	$cv_{-1} < PVmax$	$cv_{-1}+1$
			$cv_{-1} \geq PVmax$	NC
		¬cu∧cd	$cv_{-1} > PVmin$	$cv_{-1}-1$
			$cv_{-1} \leq PVmin$	NC
		¬cu ∧ ¬cd		NC

assume: $PVmin < pv < PVmax$

Fig. 9. Tabular requirement of $ctud$

Second, the range of the preset value pv, with respect to the limits $PVmin$ and $PVmax$, is not clear. If cv is loaded by the value of pv, such that $pv > PVmax$, the output qu can never be $true$, as the counter increments when $cv < PVmax$. Similarly, if pv is such that $pv < PVmin$ and $pv = 1$, the output qd can never be $true$, as the counter decrements when $cv > PVmin$. As a result, we introduce another assumption: $PVmin < pv < PVmax$. Our tabular requirement for the up-down counter that incorporates the missing assumption is shown in Fig. 9. Similarly, we added $pv < PVmax$ and $PVmin < pv$ as assumptions for, respectively, the up and down counters.

6   Related Work

There are many works on formalizing and verifying PLC programs specified by programming languages covered in IEC 61131-3, such as sequential function charts (SFCs). Some approaches choose the environment of model checking: e.g., to formalize a subset of the language of instruction lists (ILs) using timed automata, and to verify real-time properties in Uppaal [15]; to automatically transform SFC programs into the synchronous data flow language of Lustre, amenable to mechanized support for checking properties [12]; to transform FBD specifications to Uppaal formal models to verify safety applications in the industrial automation domain [23]; to provide the formal operational semantics of ILs which is encoded into the symbolic model checker Cadence SMV, and to verify rich behavioural properties written in linear temporal logic (LTL) [5]; and to provide the formal verification of a safety procedure in a nuclear power plant

---

[4] If the less intuitive interpretation is intended, we fix the assumption accordingly.

(NPP) in which a verified Coloured Petri Net (CPN) model is derived by reinterpretation from the FBD description [17]. There is also an integration of SMV
and Uppaal to handle, respectively, untimed and timed SFC programs [2].

Some other approaches adopt the verification environment of a theorem
prover: e. g., to check the correctness of SFC programs, automatically generated from a graphical front-end, in Coq [3]; and to formalize PLC programs
using higher-order logic and to discharge safety properties in HOL [24]. These
works are similar to ours in that PLC programs are formalized and supported
for mechanized verifications of implementations. An algebra approach for PLC
programs verification is presented in [22]. In [14], a trace function method (TFM)
based approach is presented to solve the same problem as ours.

Our work is inspired by [16] in that the overall system behaviour is defined by
taking the conjunction of those of internal components (circuits in [16] or FBs in
our case). Our resolutions to the timing issues of the *pulse* timer are consistent
with [11]. However, our approach is novel in that (1) we also obtain tabular
requirements to be checked against, instead of writing properties directly for the
chosen theorem prover or model checker; and (2) our formalization makes it easier
to comprehend and to reason about properties of disjointness and completeness.

7   Conclusion and Future Work

We present an approach to formalizing and verifying function blocks (FBs) using
tabular expressions and PVS. We identified issues concerning ambiguity, missing
assumptions, and erroneous implementations in the IEC 61131-3 standard of
FBs. As future work, we will apply the same approach to the remaining FBs in
IEC 61131, and possibly to IEC 61499 that fits well with distributed systems.

References

1. Bakhmach, E., Siora, O., Tokarev, V., Reshetytskyi, S., Kharchenko, V., Bezsalyi,
   V.: FPGA - based technology and systems for I&C of existing and advanced reac-
   tors. International Atomic Energy Agency, p. 173 (2009), IAEA-CN-164-7S04
2. Bauer, N., Engell, S., Huuck, R., Lohmann, S., Lukoschus, B., Remelhe, M.,
   Stursberg, O.: Verification of PLC programs given as sequential function charts.
   In: Ehrig, H., Damm, W., Desel, J., Große-Rhode, M., Reif, W., Schnieder, E.,
   Westkämper, E. (eds.) INT 2004. LNCS, vol. 3147, pp. 517–540. Springer, Heidelberg (2004)
3. Blech, J.O., Biha, S.O.: On formal reasoning on the semantics of PLC using Coq.
   CoRR abs/1301.3047 (2013)
4. Camilleri, A., Gordon, M., Melham, T.: Hardware verification using higher-order
   logic. Technical Report UCAM-CL-TR-91, Cambridge University Computer Lab
   (1986)
5. Canet, G., Couffin, S., Lesage, J.J., Petit, A., Schnoebelen, P.: Towards the automatic verification of PLC programs written in instruction list. In: IEEE International Conference on Systems, Man and Cybernetics, pp. 2449–2454 (2000)

6. Eles, C., Lawford, M.: A tabular expression toolbox for Matlab/Simulink. In: NASA Formal Methods, pp. 494–499 (2011)
7. Hu, X., Lawford, M., Wassyng, A.: Formal verification of the implementability of timing requirements. In: Cofer, D., Fantechi, A. (eds.) FMICS 2008. LNCS, vol. 5596, pp. 119–134. Springer, Heidelberg (2009)
8. IEC: 61131-3 Ed. 2.0 en:2003: Programmable Controllers – Part 3: Programming Languages. International Electrotechnical Commission (2003)
9. IEC: 61131-3 Ed. 3.0 en:2013: Programmable Controllers – Part 3: Programming Languages. International Electrotechnical Commission (2013)
10. Jin, Y., Parnas, D.L.: Defining the meaning of tabular mathematical expressions. Sci. Comput. Program. **75**(11), 980–1000 (2010)
11. John, K.H., Tiegelkamp, M.: IEC 61131-3: Programming Industrial Automation Systems Concepts and Programming Languages, Requirements for Programming Systems, Decision-Making Aids, 2nd edn. Springer, Heidelberg (2010)
12. Kabra, A., Bhattacharjee, A., Karmakar, G., Wakankar, A.: Formalization of sequential function chart as synchronous model in Lustre. In: NCETACS, pp. 115–120 (2012)
13. Lawford, M., McDougall, J., Froebel, P., Moum, G.: Practical application of functional and relational methods for the specification and verification of safety critical software. In: Rus, T. (ed.) AMAST 2000. LNCS, vol. 1816, p. 73. Springer, Heidelberg (2000)
14. Liu, Z., Parnas, D., Widemann, B.: Documenting and verifying systems assembled from components. Front. Comput. Sci. China **4**(2), 151–161 (2010)
15. Mader, A., Wupper, H.: Timed automaton models for simple programmable logic controllers. In: ECRTS, pp. 114–122. IEEE (1999)
16. Melham, T.: Abstraction mechanisms for hardware verification. VLSI Specification, Verification and Synthesis, pp. 129–157. Kluwer Academic Publishers, Boston (1987)
17. Németh, E., Bartha, T.: Formal verification of safety functions by reinterpretation of functional block based specifications. In: Cofer, D., Fantechi, A. (eds.) FMICS 2008. LNCS, vol. 5596, pp. 199–214. Springer, Heidelberg (2009)
18. Owre, S., Rushby, J.M., Shankar, N.: PVS: a prototype verification system. In: Kapur, D. (ed.) CADE 1992. LNCS, vol. 607, pp. 748–752. Springer, Heidelberg (1992)
19. Pang, L., Wang, C.W., Lawford, M., Wassyng, A.: Formalizing and verifying function blocks using tabular expressions and PVS. Technical Report 11, McSCert, Aug 2013
20. Parnas, D.L., Madey, J.: Functional documents for computer systems. Sci. Comput. Program. **25**(1), 41–61 (1995)
21. Parnas, D.L., Madey, J., Iglewski, M.: Precise documentation of well-structured programs. IEEE Trans. Softw. Eng. **20**, 948–976 (1994)
22. Roussel, J.M., Faure, J.: An algebraic approach for PLC programs verification. In: 6th International Workshop on Discrete Event Systems, pp. 303–308 (2002)
23. Soliman, D., Thramboulidis, K., Frey, G.: Transformation of function block diagrams to Uppaal timed automata for the verification of safety applications. Ann. Rev. Control **36**, 338–345 (2012)
24. Völker, N., Krämer, B.J.: Automated verification of function block-based industrial control systems. Sci. Comput. Program. **42**(1), 101–113 (2002)
25. Wassyng, A., Janicki, R.: Tabular expressions in software engineering. In: Proceedings of ICSSEA'03, Paris, France, vol. 4, pp. 1–46 (2003)

Reflections on Verifying Software with Whiley

David J. Pearce$^{(\boxtimes)}$ and Lindsay Groves

Victoria University of Wellington, Wellington, New Zealand
{djp,lindsay}@ecs.vuw.ac.nz

Abstract. An ongoing challenge for computer science is the development of a tool which automatically verifies that programs meet their specifications, and are free from runtime errors such as divide-by-zero, array out-of-bounds and null dereferences. Several impressive systems have been developed to this end, such as ESC/Java and Spec#, which build on existing programming languages (e.g. Java, C#). Unfortunately, such languages were not designed for this purpose and this significantly hinders the development of practical verification tools for them. For example, soundness of verification in these tools is compromised (e.g. arithmetic overflow is ignored). We have developed a programming language specifically designed for verification, called Whiley, and an accompanying verifying compiler. In this paper, we reflect on a number of challenges we have encountered in developing a practical system.

1 Introduction

The idea of verifying that a program meets a given specification for all possible inputs has been studied for a long time. Hoare's Verifying Compiler Grand Challenge was an attempt to spur new efforts in this area to develop practical tools [1]. A verifying compiler *"uses automated mathematical and logical reasoning to check the correctness of the programs that it compiles"*. Hoare's intention was that verifying compilers should fit into the existing development tool chain, *"to achieve any desired degree of confidence in the structural soundness of the system and the total correctness of its more critical components"*. For example, commonly occurring errors could be automatically eliminated, such as: *division-by-zero, integer overflow, buffer overruns* and *null dereferences*.

The first systems that could be reasonably considered as verifying compilers were developed some time ago, and include that of King [2], Deutsch [3], the Gypsy Verification Environment [4] and the Stanford Pascal Verifier [5]. Following on from these, was the Extended Static Checker for Modula-3 [6]. Later, this became the Extended Static Checker for Java (ESC/Java) — a widely acclaimed and influential work in this area [7]. Building on this success was the Java Modeling Language (and its associated tooling) which provided a standard notation for specifying functions in Java [8,9]. More recently, the Spec# language [10–12] was developed on top of C#, whilst Dafny was developed from scratch to simplify verification [13,14].

C. Artho and P.C. Ölveczky (Eds.): FTSCS 2013, CCIS 419, pp. 142–159, 2014.
DOI: 10.1007/978-3-319-05416-2_10, © Springer International Publishing Switzerland 2014

Continuing this line of work, we are developing a verifying compiler for the Whiley programming language [15–18]. Whiley is an imperative language designed to simplify verification and to be suitable for safety-critical systems. For example, Whiley uses unbounded integer and rational arithmetic in place of e.g. IEEE 754 floating point (which is notoriously difficult to reason about [19]). Likewise, pure (i.e. mathematical) functions are distinguished from those which may have side-effects. Our goal is to develop a verifying compiler which can automatically establish a Whiley program as: *correct with respect to its declared specifications*; and, *free from runtime error* (e.g. divide-by-zero, array index-out-of-bounds, etc.). More complex properties, such as establishing termination, are not considered (although would be interesting future work). Finally, the Whiley verifying compiler is released under an open source license (BSD), can be downloaded from http://whiley.org and forked at http://github.com/DavePearce/Whiley/. Note that development of the language and compiler is ongoing and should be considered a work-in-progress.

Contribution. The seminal works by Floyd [20], Hoare [21], Dijkstra [22], and others provide a foundation upon which to develop tools for verifying software. However, in developing a verifying compiler for Whiley, we have encountered some gaps between theory and practice. In this paper, we reflect on our experiences using Whiley to verify programs and, in particular, highlight a number of challenges we encountered.

2   Language Overview

We begin by exploring the Whiley language and highlighting some of the choices made in its design. For now, we stick to the basic issues of syntax, semantics and typing and, in the following section, we will focus more specifically on using Whiley for verification. Perhaps one of our most important goals was to make the system as accessible as possible. To that end, the language was designed to superficially resemble modern imperative languages (e.g. Python), and this decision has significantly affected our choices.

Overview. Languages like Java and C# permit arbitrary side-effects within methods and statements. This presents a challenge when such methods may be used within specifications. Systems like JML and Spec# require that methods used in specifications are *pure* (i.e. side-effect free). An important challenge here is the process of checking that a function is indeed pure. A significant body of research exists on checking functional purity in object-oriented languages (e.g. [23,24]). Much of this relies on interprocedural analysis, which is too costly for a verifying compiler. To address this, Whiley is a hybrid object-oriented and functional language which divides into *a functional core* and an *imperative outer layer*. Everything in the functional core can be modularly checked as being side-effect free.

Value Semantics. The prevalence of pointers — or references — in modern programming languages (e.g. Java, C++, C#) has been a major hindrance in the development of verifying compilers. Indeed, Mycroft recently argued that (unrestricted) pointers should be "considered harmful" in the same way that Dijkstra considered goto harmful [25]. To address this, all compound structures in Whiley (e.g. lists, sets, and records) have *value semantics*. This means they are passed and returned by-value (as in Pascal, MATLAB or most functional languages). But, unlike functional languages (and like Pascal), values of compound types can be updated in place. Whilst this latter point may seem unimportant, it serves a critical purpose: to give Whiley the appearance of a modern *imperative* language when, in fact, the functional core of Whiley is pure. This goes towards our goal of making the language as accessible as possible.

Value semantics implies that updates to a variable only affect that variable, and that information can only flow out of a function through its return value. Consider:

```
int f([int] xs):
    ys = xs
    xs[0] = 1
    ...
```

Here, [int] represents a list of ints (i.e. a variable-length array). The semantics of Whiley dictate that, having assigned xs to ys as above, the subsequent update to xs does not affect ys. Arguments are also passed by value, hence xs is updated inside f() and this does not affect f's caller. That is, xs is not a *reference* to a list of int; rather, it *is* a list of ints and assignments to it do not affect state visible outside of f().

Unbounded Arithmetic. Modern languages typically provide fixed-width numeric types, such as 32 bit twos-complement integers, or 64-bit IEEE 754 floating point numbers. Such data types are notoriously difficult for an automated theorem prover to reason about [19]. Systems like JML and Spec# assume (unsoundly) that numeric types do not overflow or suffer from rounding. To address this, Whiley employs *unbounded integers* and *rationals* in place of their fixed-width alternatives and, hence, does not suffer the limitations of soundness discussed above.

Flow Typing & Unions. An unusual feature of Whiley is the use of a *flow typing system* (see e.g. [18,26,27]) coupled with *union types* (see e.g. [28,29]). This gives Whiley the look-and-feel of a dynamically typed language (e.g. Python). For example, local variables are never explicitly declared; rather, they are declared by assignment. To illustrate, we consider null references. These have been a significant source of error in languages like Java and C#. The issue is that, in such languages, one can treat *nullable* references as though they are *non-null* references [30] (Hoare calls this his billion dollar mistake [31]). Although many approaches have been proposed (e.g. [32–36]), Whiley's type system provides an elegant solution:

```
int|null indexOf(string str, char c):
   ...

[string] split(string str, char c):
   idx = indexOf(str,c)
   // idx has type null|int
   if idx is int:
      // idx now has type int
      below = str[0..idx]
      above = str[idx..]
      return [below,above]
   else:
      // idx now has type null
      return [str]
```

Here, `indexOf()` returns the first index of a character in the string, or **null** if there is none. The type **int|null** is a union type, meaning it is either an **int** *or* **null**. After the assignment "idx = indexOf(str,c)" variable idx has type **int|null**. The system ensures **null** is never dereferenced because the type **int|null** cannot be treated as an **int**. Instead, one must first check it *is* an **int** using e.g. "idx **is int**" (similar to `instanceof` in Java). Furthermore, Whiley's flow type system automatically retypes variables through such conditionals. In the example above, the variable idx is automatically retyped by "idx **is int**" to have type **int** on the true branch, and type **null** on the false branch. This prevents the needs for explicit casts after a type test (as required in e.g. Java).

As another example, we consider unions of the same kind (e.g. a union of record types, or a union of list types). These expose commonality and are called *effective unions* (e.g. an effective record type). In the case of a union of records, fields common to all records are exposed:

```
define Circle as { int x, int y, int radius }
define Rectangle as { int x, int y, int width, int height }
define Shape as Circle | Rectangle
```

A Shape is either a Rectangle or a Circle (which are both record types). Any variable of type Shape exposes fields x and y *because these are common to all cases*. Finally, it's interesting to note that the notion of an effective record type is similar, in some ways, to that of the *common initial sequence* found in C [37].

Recursive Data Types. Whiley provides recursive types which are similar to the abstract data types found in functional languages (e.g. Haskell, ML, etc.). For example:

```
define LinkedList as null | {int data, LinkedList next}

int length (LinkedList l):
   if l is null:
      // l now has type null
      return 0
```

```
else:
    // l now has type {int data, LinkedList next}
    return 1 + length (l.next)
```

Here, we again see how flow typing gives an elegant solution. More specifically, on the false branch of the type test "`l is null`", variable `l` is automatically retyped to `{int data, LinkedList next}` — thus ensuring the subsequent dereference of `l.next` is safe. No casts are required as would be needed for a conventional imperative language (e.g. Java). Finally, like all compound structures, the semantics of Whiley dictates that recursive data types are passed by value (or, at least, appear to be from the programmer's perspective).

Performance. Many of our choices (e.g. value semantics and unbounded arithmetic) have a potentially detrimental effect on performance. Whilst this is a trade-off we accept, there are existing techniques which can help. For example, we can use reference counting to minimise unnecessary cloning of compound structures (see e.g. [38]). Furthermore, we can exploit the specifications that are an integral part of Whiley programs. That is, when the compiler can prove an integer will remain within certain bounds, it is free to use a fixed-width type (e.g. a 32 bit **int**).

3   Verification

A key goal of the Whiley project is to develop an open framework for research in automated software verification. As such, we now explore verification in Whiley.

Example 1 — Preconditions and Postconditions. The following Whiley code defines a function accepting a positive integer and returning a non-negative integer (i.e. natural number):

```
int f(int x) requires x > 0, ensures $ >= 0 && $ != x:
    return x-1
```

Here, the function `f()` includes a **requires** and **ensures** clause which correspond (respectively) to its *precondition* and *postcondition*. In this context, $ represents the return value, and must only be used in the **ensures** clause. The Whiley compiler statically verifies that this function meets its specification.

A slightly more unusual example is the following:

```
int f(int x) requires x >= 0, ensures 2*$ >= $:
    return x
```

In this case, we have two alternative (and completely equivalent) definitions for a natural number. We can see that the precondition is equivalent to the postcondition by subtracting $ from both sides. The Whiley compiler is able to reason that these are equivalent and statically verifies that this function is correct.

Example 2 — Conditionals. Variables in Whiley are described by their underlying type and those constraints which are shown to hold. As the automated
theorem prover learns more about a variable, it automatically takes this into
consideration when checking constraints are satisfied. For example:

```
int abs (int x) ensures $ >= 0:
    if x >= 0:
        return x
    else:
        return -x
```

The Whiley compiler statically verifies that this function always returns a non-
negative integer. This relies on the compiler to reason correctly about the implicit
constraints implied by the conditional. A similar, but slightly more complex
example is that for computing the maximum of two integers:

```
int max(int x, int y)
        ensures $ >= x && $ >= y && ($==x || $==y):
    if x > y:
        return x
    else:
        return y
```

Again, the Whiley compiler statically verifies this function meets its specification. Here, the body of the function is almost completely determined by the
specification — however, in general, this it not the case.

Example 3 — Bounds Checking. An interesting example which tests the automated theorem prover more thoroughly is the following:

```
null|int indexOf (string str, char c):
    for i in 0..|str|:
        if str[i] == c:
            return i
    return null
```

The access `str[i]` must be shown as within the bounds of the list `str`. Here,
the range constructor `x..y` returns a list of consecutive integers from `x` upto,
but not including `y` (and, futhermore, if `x >= y` then the empty list is returned).
Hence, this function cannot cause an out-of-bounds error and the Whiley compiler statically verifies this.

In fact, the specification for `indexOf()` could be made more precise as follows:

```
null|int indexOf (string str, char c)
    ensures $ == null || (0 <= $ && $ < |str|):
    . . .
```

In this case, we are additionally requiring that, when the return value is an **int**,
then it is a valid index into `str`. Again, the Whiley compiler statically verifies
this is the case.

Example 4 — Loop Invariants. Another example illustrates the use of *loop invariants* in Whiley:

```
int sum([int] list)
        requires all { item in list | item >= 0 },
        ensures $ >= 0:
    r = 0
    for v in list where r >= 0:
        r = r + v
    return r
```

Here, a bounded quantifier is used to enforce that sum() accepts a list of natural numbers. Also, an explicit loop invariant has been given through a `where` clause. The key constraint is that summing a list of natural numbers yields a natural number (recall arithmetic is unbounded and does not overflow in Whiley). The Whiley compiler statically verifies that sum() does indeed meet this specification. The loop invariant is necessary to help the compiler generate a sufficiently powerful verification condition to prove the function meets the post condition (more on this later).

Example 5 — Recursive Structures. The Whiley language supports invariants over recursive structures, as the following illustrates:

```
define Tree as null | Node

define Node as { int data, Tree lhs, Tree rhs } where
                (lhs == null || lhs.data < data) &&
                (rhs == null || rhs.data > data)
```

This defines something approximating the notion of an unbalanced binary search tree. Unfortunately, the invariant permits e.g. data < lhs.rhs.data for a given tree node and, thus, is not sufficient to properly characterise binary search trees. Whilst our focus so far has been primarily on array programs and loop invariants, in the future we plan to place more emphasis on handling recursive structures, such as binary search trees.

4   Hoare Logic

We now briefly review Hoare logic [21] and Dijkstra's predicate transformers [22], before examining in Sect. 5 a number of challenges we encountered putting them into practice. Hoare logic provides some important background to understanding how the Whiley verifying compiler works, and why certain difficulties manifest themselves. Our discussion here is necessarily brief and we refer to Frade and Pinto for an excellent survey [39].

4.1   Overview

The rules of Hoare logic are presented as judgements involving triples of the form: $\{p\}$ s $\{q\}$. Here, p is the precondition, s the statement to be executed and q is the postcondition. Figure 1 presents the rules of Hoare Logic which, following Whiley, we have extended to include explicit loop invariants. To better understand these rules, consider the following example:

$$\left\{x \geq 0\right\} \ x = x + 1 \ \left\{x > 0\right\}$$

Here we see that, if $x \geq 0$ holds immediately before the assignment then, as expected, it follows that $x > 0$ holds afterwards. However, whilst this is intuitively true, it is not so obvious how this triple satisfies the rules of Fig. 1. For example, as presented it does not immediately satisfy H-ASSIGN. However, rewriting the triple is helpful here:

$$\left\{x + 1 > 0\right\} \ x = x + 1 \ \left\{x > 0\right\}$$

The above triple clearly satisfies H-ASSIGN and, furthermore, we can obtain the original triple from it via H-CONSEQUENCE (i.e. since $x + 1 > 0 \implies x \geq 0$). The following illustrates a more complex example:

```
int f(int i) requires i >= 0, ensures $ >= 10:
```
$$\left\{i \geq 0\right\}$$
```
  while i < 10 where i >= 0:
```
$$\left\{i < 10 \wedge i \geq 0\right\}$$
```
    i = i + 1
```
$$\left\{i \geq 0\right\}$$
$$\left\{i \geq 10 \wedge i \geq 0\right\}$$
```
  return i
```

Here, we have provided the intermediate assertions which tie the Hoare triples together (note, these are not part of Whiley syntax). These assertions reflect the internal information a verifying compiler might use when establishing this function is correct.

4.2 Verification Condition Generation

Automatic program verification is normally done with a *verification condition generator* [7]. This converts the program source into a series of logical conditions — called *verification conditions* — to be checked by the automated theorem prover. There are two basic approaches: propagate *forward* from the precondition; or, propagate *backwards* from the postcondition. We now briefly examine these in more detail.

Weakest Preconditions. Perhaps the most common way to generated verification conditions is via the *weakest precondition transformer* [22]. This determines the weakest precondition (written $wp(s,q)$) that ensures a statement s meets a given postcondition q. Roughly speaking, this corresponds to propagating the postcondition backwards through the statement. For example, consider verifying this triple:

$$\frac{}{\{p[x/e]\}\; \mathtt{x = e}\; \{p\}}\;(\text{H-Assign})$$

$$\frac{\{p\}\; \mathtt{s_1}\; \{r\}\; \{r\}\; \mathtt{s_2}\; \{q\}}{\{p\}\; \mathtt{s_1; s_2}\; \{q\}}\;(\text{H-Sequence})$$

$$\frac{\{p_1\}\; \mathtt{s}\; \{q_1\}}{\{p_2\}\; \mathtt{s}\; \{q_2\}}\quad p_2 \implies p_1 \quad q_1 \implies q_2\;(\text{H-Consequence})$$

$$\frac{\{p \wedge e_1\}\; \mathtt{s_1}\; \{q\}\quad \{p \wedge \neg e_1\}\; \mathtt{s_2}\; \{q\}}{\{p\}\; \mathtt{if\ e_1:\ s_1\ else:\ s_2}\; \{q\}}\;(\text{H-If})$$

$$\frac{\{e_1 \wedge e_2\}\; \mathtt{s}\; \{e_2\}}{\{e_2\}\; \mathtt{while\ e_1\ where\ e_2:\ s}\; \{\neg e_1 \wedge e_2\}}\;(\text{H-While})$$

Fig. 1. Hoare logic.

$$\{x \geq 0\}\; \mathtt{x = x + 1}\; \{x > 0\}$$

Propagating $x > 0$ backwards through $\mathtt{x = x + 1}$ gives $x + 1 > 0$ via H-Assign. From this, we can generate a verification condition to check that the given pre-condition implies this calculated weakest precondition (i.e. $x \geq 0 \implies x + 1 > 0$). To understand this process better, let's consider verifying a Whiley function:

```
int f(int x) requires x >= 0, ensures $ >= 0:
    x = x - 1
    return x
```

The implementation of this function does not satisfy its specification. Using weakest preconditions to determine this corresponds to the following chain of reasoning:

$$x \geq 0 \implies wp(\mathtt{x = x - 1}, x \geq 0)$$
$$\hookrightarrow x \geq 0 \implies x - 1 \geq 0$$
$$\hookrightarrow \mathtt{false}$$

Here, the generated verification condition is $x \geq 0 \implies wp(\mathtt{x = x - 1}, x \geq 0)$. This is then reduced to a contradiction (e.g. by the automated theorem prover) which indicates the original program did not meet its specification.

Strongest Postconditions. By exploiting Floyd's rule for assignment [20], an alternative formulation of Hoare logic can be developed which propagates in a forward direction and, thus, gives a *strongest postcondition transformer* [39,40]. This determines the strong postcondition (written $sp(\mathtt{p,s})$) that holds after a given statement s with pre-condition p. For example, propagating $x = 0$ forwards through $\mathtt{x = x + 1}$ yields $x = 1$. Using strongest postconditions to verify functions is similar to using weakest preconditions, except operating in the opposite direction. Thus, for a triple $\{p\}\, \mathtt{s}\, \{q\}$, we generate the verification condition $sp(\mathtt{p, s}) \implies q$. For example, consider:

$$\{x = 0\}\; \mathtt{x = x + 1}\; \{x > 0\}$$

In this case, the generated verification condition will be $x = 1 \implies x > 0$, which can be trivially established by an automated theorem prover.

5 Experiences

In the previous section, we outlined the process of automatic verification using Hoare logic and Dijkstra's predicate transformers. This was the starting point for developing our verifying compiler for Whiley. However, whilst Hoare logic provides an excellent foundation for reasoning about programs, there remain a number of hurdles to overcome in developing a practical tool. We now reflect on our experiences in this endeavour using examples based on those we have encountered in practice.

5.1 Loop Invariants

The general problem of automatically determining loop invariants is a hard algorithmic challenge (see e.g. [41–43]). However, we want to cover as many simple cases as possible to reduce programmer burden. We now examine a range of simple cases that, in our experience, appear to occur frequently.

Challenge 1 — Loop Invariant Variables. From the perspective of a practical verification tool, the rule H-WHILE from Fig. 1 presents something of a hurdle. This is because it relies on the programmer to completely specify the loop invariant *even in cases where this appears unnecessary.* For example, consider the following Whiley program:

```
int f(int x) requires x > 0, ensures $ >= 10:
    i = 0
    while i < 10 where i >= 0:
        i = i + x
    return i
```

Intuitively, we can see this program satisfies its specification. Unfortunately, this program cannot be shown as correct under the rules of Fig. 1 because the loop invariant is too weak. Unfortunately, rule H-WHILE only considers those facts given in the loop condition and the declared loop invariant — hence, all information about x is discarded. Thus, under H-WHILE, the verifier must assume that x could be negative within the loop body — which may seem surprising because x is not modified by the loop!

   We refer to x in the example above as a *loop invariant variable.* To verify this program under rule H-WHILE, the loop invariant must be strengthened as follows:

```
int f(int x) requires x > 0, ensures $ >= 10:
    i = 0
    while i < 10 where i >= 0 && x >= 0:
        i = i + x
    return i
```

Now, one may say the programmer made a mistake here in not specifying the loop invariant well enough; however, our goal in developing a practical tool is to reduce programmer effort as much as possible. Therefore, in the Whiley verifying compiler, *loop invariant variables are identified automatically so that the programmer does not need to respecify their invariants.*

Challenge 2 — Simple Synthesis. As mentioned above, generating loop invariants in the general case is hard. However, there are situations where loop invariants can easily be determined. The following illustrates an interesting example:

```
int sum([int] xs)
    requires all { x in xs | x >= 0 }, ensures $ >= 0:
  i = 0
  r = 0
  while i < |xs| where r >= 0:
      r = r + xs[i]
      i = i + 1
  return r
```

This function computes the sum of a list of natural numbers, and returns a natural number. The question to consider is: *did the programmer specify the loop invariant properly?* Unfortunately, the answer again is: *no.* In fact, the loop invariant needs to be strengthened as follows:

```
  ...
  while i < |xs| where r >= 0 && i >= 0:
      r = r + xs[i]
      i = i + 1
  return r
```

The need for this is frustrating as, intuitively, it is trivial to see that i >= 0 holds throughout. In the future, we aim to automatically synthesize simple loop invariants such as this.

Observation. The Whiley language also supports the notion of a *constrained type* as follows:

```
define nat as int where $ >= 0
```

Here, the **define** statement includes a **where** clause constraining the permissible values for the type ($ represents the variable whose type this will be). Thus, nat defines the type of non-negative integers (i.e. the natural numbers).

An interesting aspect of Whiley's design is that local variables are not explicitly declared. This gives Whiley the look-and-feel of a dynamically typed language and goes towards our goal of making the language accessible. In fact, permitting variable declarations would provide an alternative solution to the above issue with sum():

```
int sum([int] xs)
    requires all { x in xs | x >= 0 }, ensures $ >= 0:
  nat i = 0
  nat r = 0
```

```
while i < |xs|:
    r = r + xs[i]
    i = i + 1
return r
```

Here, variable declarations are used to restrict the permitted values of variables i and r throughout the function. Unfortunately, Whiley does currently not permit local variable declarations and, hence, the above is invalid. In the future, we plan to support them for this purpose, although care is needed to integrate them with flow typing.

Challenge 3 — Loop Invariant Properties. Whilst our verifying compiler easily handles loop invariant variables, there remain situations when invariants need to be needlessly respecified. Consider the following:

```
[int] add([int] v1, [int] v2)
    requires |v1| == |v2|, ensures |$| == |v1|:
    i = 0
    while i < |v1| where i >= 0:
        v1[i] = v1[i] + v2[i]
        i = i + 1
    return v1
```

This example adds two vectors of equal size. Unfortunately, this again does not verify under the rule H-WHILE because the loop invariant is too weak. The key problem is that v1 is modified in the loop and, hence, our above solution for loop invariant variables does not apply. Following rule H-WHILE, the verifying compiler can only reason about what is specified in the loop condition and invariant. Hence, it knows nothing about the size of v1 after the loop. This means, for example, it cannot establish that $|v1| == |v2|$ holds after the loop. Likewise (and more importantly in this case), it cannot establish that the size of v1 is unchanged by the loop (which we refer to as a *loop invariant property*). Thus, it cannot establish that the size of the returned vector equals that held in v1 on entry, and reports the function does not meet its postcondition.

In fact, it is possible to specify a loop invariant which allows the above function to be verified by our compiler. Since v2 is a loop invariant variable and $|v1| == |v2|$ held on entry, we can use i >= 0 && |v1| == |v2| as the loop invariant.

Observation. The example above presents an interesting challenge that, by coincidence, can be resolved by exploiting a loop invariant variable. However, it raises a more general question: *how can we specify that the size of a list is loop invariant?* Unfortunately, this is impossible in the Whiley language developed thus far because it requires some notion of a variable's value *before* and *after* the loop body is executed. To illustrate, consider the following hypothetical syntax in Whiley:

```
    ...
    while i < |v1| where i >= 0 && |v1'| == |v1|:
        v1[i] = v1[i] + v2[i]
```

```
      i = i + 1
   return v1
```

Here, v1` represents the value of v1 on the previous iteration. Unfortunately, this syntax is not yet supported in Whiley and, furthermore, its semantics are unclear. For example, on entry to the loop it's unclear how |v1`| == |v1| should be interpreted.

Challenge 4 — Overriding Invariants. In most cases, the loop condition and invariant are used independently to increase knowledge. However, in some cases, they need to be used in concert. The following illustrates:

```
[int] create(int count, int value)
   requires count >= 0, ensures |$| == count:
   r = []
   i = 0
   while i < count:
      r = r + [value]
      i = i + 1
   return r
```

This example uses the list append operator (i.e. r + [value]) and is surprisingly challenging. An obvious approach is to connect the size of r with i as follows:

```
   ...
   while i < count where |r| == i:
      r = r + [value]
      i = i + 1
   return r
```

Unfortunately, this is insufficient under the rule H-WHILE from Fig. 1. This is because, after the loop is complete, the rule establishes the invariant and the *negated* condition. Thus, after the loop, we have $i \geq count \wedge |r| == i$, but this is insufficient to establish that $|r| == count$. In fact, we can resolve this by using an *overriding loop invariant* as follows:

```
   ...
   while i < count where i <= count && |r| == i:
      r = r + [value]
      i = i + 1
   return r
```

In this case, $i \geq count \wedge i \leq count \wedge |r| == i$ holds after the loop, and the automated theorem prover will trivially establish that $|r| == count$. We say that the loop invariant *overrides* the loop condition because i <= count implies i < count.

5.2 Error Reporting

Error reporting is an important practical consideration for any verification tool, as we want error messages which are as meaningful, and precise, as possible. We now consider how the two approaches to verification condition generation affect this.

Weakest Preconditions. An unfortunate side-effect of operating in a backwards direction, as $wp(\mathsf{s},\mathsf{q})$ does, is that reporting useful errors in the source program is more difficult. For example, consider this example which performs an integer division:

```
int f(int x) requires x > 0, ensures $ > 0:
    x = 1 / (x - 1)
    return x
```

This function contains a bug which can cause a division-by-zero failure (i.e. if x==1 on entry). Using $wp(\mathsf{s},\mathsf{q})$, a single verification condition is generated for this example:

$$x > 0 \implies (x - 1 \neq 0 \wedge \frac{1}{x-1} > 0) \tag{1}$$

A modern automated theorem prover (e.g. [44,45]) will quickly establish this condition does not hold. At this point, the verifying compiler should report a helpful error message. Unfortunately, during the weakest precondition transform, information about where exactly the error arose was lost. To identify where the error occurred, there are two intrinsic questions we need to answer: *where exactly in the program code does the error arise?* and, *which execution path(s) give rise to the error?* The $wp(\mathsf{s},\mathsf{q})$ transform fails to answer both because it generates a single verification condition for the entire function which is either shown to hold, or not [46,47]. One strategy for resolving this issue is to embed attributes in the verification condition identifying where in the original source program particular components originated [7]. Unfortunately, this requires specific support from the automated theorem prover (which is not always available).

Strongest Postconditions. Instead of operating in a backwards direction, our experience suggests it is inherently more practical to generate verification conditions in a forwards direction (and there is anecdotal evidence to support this [39]). Recall that this corresponds to generating strongest postconditions, rather than weakest preconditions. The key advantage is that verification conditions can be emitted at the specific points where failures may occur. In the above example, there are two potential failures: (1) 1/(x-1) should not cause division-by-zero; (2) the postcondition $ > 0 must be met. A forward propagating verification condition generator can generate separate conditions for each potential failure. For example, it can emit the following verification conditions:

$$x > 0 \implies x - 1 \neq 0 \tag{2}$$

$$x > 0 \implies \frac{1}{x-1} > 0 \tag{3}$$

Each of these can be associated with the specific program point where it originated and, in the case it cannot be shown, an error can be reported at that point. For example, since the first verification condition above does not hold, an error can be reported for the statement $x = 1/(x - 1)$. When generating verification conditions based on $wp(s, q)$, it is hard to report errors at the specific point they arise because, at each point, only the weakest precondition for *subsequent* statements is known.

6   Related Work

Hoare provided the foundation for formalising work in this area with his seminal paper introducing *Hoare Logic* [21]. This provides a framework for proving that a sequence of statements meets its postcondition given its precondition. Unfortunately Hoare logic does not tell us how to *construct* such a proof; rather, it gives a mechanism for *checking* a proof is correct. Therefore, to actually verify a program is correct, we need to construct proofs which satisfy the rules of Hoare logic.

The most common way to automate the process of verifying a program is with a verification condition generator. As discussed in Sect. 4.2, such algorithms propagate information in either a forwards or backwards direction. However, the rules of Hoare logic lend themselves more naturally to the latter [39]. Perhaps for this reason, many tools choose to use the weakest precondition transformer. For example, the widely acclaimed ESC/Java tool computes weakest preconditions [7], as does the Why platform [48], Spec# [49], LOOP [50], JACK [51] and SnuggleBug [52]. This is surprising given that it leads to fewer verification conditions and, hence, makes it harder to generate useful error messages (recall our discussion from Sect. 4.2). To workaround this, Burdy *et al.* embed path information in verification conditions to improve error reporting [51]. A similar approach is taken in ESC/Java, but requires support from the underlying automated theorem prover [45]. Denney and Fischer extend Hoare logic to formalise the embedding of information within verification conditions [53]. Again, their objective is to provide useful error messages.

The Dafny language has been developed with similar goals in mind to Whiley [14]. In particular, Dafny was designed to simplify verification and, to this end, makes similar choices to Whiley. For example, all arithmetic is unbounded and a strong division is made between functional and imperative constructs. Here, pure functions are supported for use in specifications and directly as code, whilst methods may have side-effects and can describe pointer-based algorithms. These two aspects are comparable (respectively) to Whiley's functional core and imperativer outer layer. Finally, Dafny supports explicit pre- and post-conditions for functions and methods which are discharged using Z3 [44].

7   Conclusion

In this paper, we reflected on our experiences using the Whiley verifying compiler. In particular, we identified a number of practical considerations for any verifying compiler which are not immediately obvious from the underlying theoretical foundations.

Acknowledgements. This work is supported by the Marsden Fund, administered by the Royal Society of New Zealand.

References

1. Hoare, C.A.R.: The verifying compiler: a grand challenge for computing research. JACM **50**(1), 63–69 (2003)
2. King, S.: A program verifier. Ph.D. thesis, Carnegie-Mellon University (1969)
3. Peter Deutsch, L.: An interactive program verifier. Ph.D. thesis, University of California (1973)
4. Good, D.I.: Mechanical proofs about computer programs. In: Hoare, C.A.R., Shepherdson, J.C. (eds.) Mathematical Logic and Programming Languages, pp. 55–75. Prentice Hall, Englewood Cliffs (1985)
5. Luckham, D.C., German, S.M., von Henke, F.W., Karp, R.A., Milne, P.W., Oppen, D.C., Polak, W., Scherlis, W.L.: Stanford pascal verifier user manual. Technical report CS-TR-79-731, Department of Computer Science, Stanford University (1979)
6. Detlefs, D.L., Leino, K.R.M., Nelson, G., Saxe, J.B.: Extended static checking. SRC Research report 159, Compaq Systems Research Center (1998)
7. Flanagan, C., Leino, K.R.M., Lillibridge, M., Nelson, G., Saxe, J.B., Stata, R.: Extended static checking for Java. In: Proceedings of PLDI, pp. 234–245 (2002)
8. Leavens, G.T., Cheon, Y., Clifton, C., Ruby, C., Cok, D.R.: How the design of JML accommodates both runtime assertion checking and formal verification. Sci. Comput. Program. **55**(1–3), 185–208 (2005)
9. Cok, D.R., Kiniry, J.R.: ESC/Java2: uniting ESC/Java and JML. In: Barthe, G., Burdy, L., Huisman, M., Lanet, J.-L., Muntean, T. (eds.) CASSIS 2004. LNCS, vol. 3362, pp. 108–128. Springer, Heidelberg (2005)
10. Barnett, M., Rustan, K., Leino, M., Schulte, W.: The Spec# programming system: an overview. Technical report, Microsoft Research (2004)
11. Barnett, M., DeLine, R., Fähndrich, M., Leino, K.R.M., Schulte, W.: Verification of object-oriented programs with invariants. J. Object Technol. **3**(6), 27–56 (2004)
12. Barnett, M., Evan Chang, B.-Y., DeLine, R., Jacobs, B., Leino, K.R.M.: Boogie: a modular reusable verifier for object-oriented programs. In: de Boer, F.S., Bonsangue, M.M., Graf, S., de Roever, W.-P. (eds.) FMCO 2006. LNCS, vol. 4111, pp. 364–387. Springer, Heidelberg (2006)
13. Leino, K.R.M.: Dafny: an automatic program verifier for functional correctness. In: Clarke, E.M., Voronkov, A. (eds.) LPAR-16 2010. LNCS, vol. 6355, pp. 348–370. Springer, Heidelberg (2010)
14. Rustan, K., Leino, M.: Developing verified programs with Dafny. In: Joshi, R., Müller, P., Podelski, A. (eds.) VSTTE 2012. LNCS, vol. 7152, p. 82. Springer, Heidelberg (2012)
15. The whiley programming language. http://whiley.org
16. Pearce, D.J., Groves, L.: Whiley: a platform for research in software verification. In: Erwig, M., Paige, R.F., Van Wyk, E. (eds.) SLE 2013. LNCS, vol. 8225, pp. 238–248. Springer, Heidelberg (2013)
17. Pearce, D., Noble, J.: Implementing a language with flow-sensitive and structural typing on the JVM. Electron. Notes Theoret. Comput. Sci. **279**(1), 47–59 (2011)
18. Pearce, D.J.: Sound and complete flow typing with unions, intersections and negations. In: Giacobazzi, R., Berdine, J., Mastroeni, I. (eds.) VMCAI 2013. LNCS, vol. 7737, pp. 335–354. Springer, Heidelberg (2013)

19. Bryant, R.E., Kroening, D., Ouaknine, J., Seshia, S.A., Strichman, O., Brady, B.A.: Deciding bit-vector arithmetic with abstraction. In: Grumberg, O., Huth, M. (eds.) TACAS 2007. LNCS, vol. 4424, pp. 358–372. Springer, Heidelberg (2007)
20. Floyd, R.W.: Assigning meaning to programs. In: Proceedings AMS, vol. 19, pp. 19–31. American Mathematical Society (1967)
21. Hoare, C.A.R.: An axiomatic basis for computer programming. CACM **12**, 576–580 (1969)
22. Dijkstra, E.W.: Guarded commands, nondeterminancy and formal derivation of programs. CACM **18**, 453–457 (1975)
23. Rountev, A.: Precise identification of side-effect-free methods in Java. In: Proceedings of ICSM, pp. 82–91. IEEE Computer Society (2004)
24. Sălcianu, A., Rinard, M.: Purity and side effect analysis for Java programs. In: Cousot, R. (ed.) VMCAI 2005. LNCS, vol. 3385, pp. 199–215. Springer, Heidelberg (2005)
25. Mycroft, A.: Programming language design and analysis motivated by hardware evolution. In: Riis Nielson, H., Filé, G. (eds.) SAS 2007. LNCS, vol. 4634, pp. 18–33. Springer, Heidelberg (2007)
26. Tobin-Hochstadt, S., Felleisen, M.: Logical types for untyped languages. In: Proceedings of ICFP, pp. 117–128 (2010)
27. Guha, A., Saftoiu, C., Krishnamurthi, S.: Typing local control and state using flow analysis. In: Barthe, G. (ed.) ESOP 2011. LNCS, vol. 6602, pp. 256–275. Springer, Heidelberg (2011)
28. Barbanera, F., Dezani-Cian Caglini, M.: Intersection and union types. In: Proceedings of the TACS, pp. 651–674 (1991)
29. Igarashi, A., Nagira, H.: Union types for object-oriented programming. J. Object Technol. **6**(2), 31–52 (2007)
30. Pierce, B.C.: Types and Programming Languages. MIT Press, Cambridge (2002)
31. Hoare, T.: Null references: The billion dollar mistake, presentation at QCon (2009)
32. Fähndrich, M., Leino, K.R.M.: Declaring and checking non-null types in an object-oriented language. In: Proceedings of the OOPSLA, pp. 302–312. ACM Press (2003)
33. Ekman, T., Hedin, G.: Pluggable checking and inferencing of non-null types for Java. J. Object Technol. **6**(9), 455–475 (2007)
34. Chalin, P., James, P.R.: Non-null references by default in Java: alleviating the nullity annotation burden. In: Ernst, E. (ed.) ECOOP 2007. LNCS, vol. 4609, pp. 227–247. Springer, Heidelberg (2007)
35. Male, C., Pearce, D.J., Potanin, A., Dymnikov, C.: Java bytecode verification for @NonNull types. In: Hendren, L. (ed.) CC 2008. LNCS, vol. 4959, pp. 229–244. Springer, Heidelberg (2008)
36. Hubert, L.: A non-null annotation inference for Java bytecode. In: Proceedings of the PASTE, pp. 36–42. ACM (2008)
37. ISO/IEC. international standard ISO/IEC 9899, programming languages – C (1990)
38. Lameed, N., Hendren, L.: Staged static techniques to efficiently implement array copy semantics in a MATLAB JIT compiler. In: Knoop, J. (ed.) CC 2011. LNCS, vol. 6601, pp. 22–41. Springer, Heidelberg (2011)
39. Frade, M.J., Pinto, J.S.: Verification conditions for source-level imperative programs. Comput. Sci. Rev. **5**(3), 252–277 (2011)
40. Gordon, M., Collavizza, H.: Forward with Hoare. In: Roscoe, A.W., Jones, C.B., Wood, K.R. (eds.) Reflections on the Work of C.A.R. Hoare, History of Computing, pp. 101–121. Springer, London (2010)

41. Chadha, R., Plaisted, D.A.: On the mechanical derivation of loop invariants. J. Symbolic Comput. **15**(5 & 6), 705–744 (1993)
42. Leino, K.R.M., Logozzo, F.: Loop invariants on demand. In: Yi, K. (ed.) APLAS 2005. LNCS, vol. 3780, pp. 119–134. Springer, Heidelberg (2005)
43. Furia, C.A., Meyer, B.: Inferring loop invariants using postconditions. CoRR, abs/0909.0884 (2009)
44. de Moura, L., Bjørner, N.: Z3: An efficient SMT solver. In: Proceedings of the TACAS, pp. 337–340, (2008)
45. Detlefs, D.L., Nelson, G., Saxe, J.B.: Simplify: a theorem prover for program checking. JACM **52**, 365–473 (2005)
46. Leino, K.R.M., Millstein, T.D., Saxe, J.B.: Generating error traces from verification-condition counterexamples. Sci. Comput. Program. **55**(1–3), 209–226 (2005)
47. Jager, I., Brumley, D.: Efficient directionless weakest preconditions. Technical Report CMU-CyLab-10-002, Carnegie Mellon University (2010)
48. Filliâtre, J.-C., Marché, C.: The Why/Krakatoa/Caduceus platform for deductive program verification. In: Damm, W., Hermanns, H. (eds.) CAV 2007. LNCS, vol. 4590, pp. 173–177. Springer, Heidelberg (2007)
49. Barnett, M., Rustan M. Leino, K.: Weakest-precondition of unstructured programs. In: Proceedings of the PASTE, pp. 82–87. ACM Press (2005)
50. Jacobs, B.: Weakest pre-condition reasoning for Java programs with JML annotations. JLAP **58**(1–2), 61–88 (2004)
51. Burdy, L., Requet, A., Lanet, J.-L.: Java applet correctness: a developer-oriented approach. In: Araki, K., Gnesi, S., Mandrioli, D. (eds.) FME 2003. LNCS, vol. 2805, pp. 422–439. Springer, Heidelberg (2003)
52. Chandra, S., Fink, S.J., Sridharan, M.: Snugglebug: a powerful approach to weakest preconditions. In: Proceedings of the PLDI, pp. 363–374. ACM Press (2009)
53. Denney, E., Fischer, B.: Explaining verification conditions. In: Meseguer, J., Roşu, G. (eds.) AMAST 2008. LNCS, vol. 5140, pp. 145–159. Springer, Heidelberg (2008)

Compositional Nonblocking Verification
with Always Enabled Events
and Selfloop-Only Events

Colin Pilbrow and Robi Malik$^{(\boxtimes)}$

Department of Computer Science, University of Waikato, Hamilton, New Zealand
colinpilbrow@gmail.com, robi@waikato.ac.nz

Abstract. This paper proposes to improve compositional nonblocking verification through the use of always enabled and selfloop-only events. Compositional verification involves abstraction to simplify parts of a system during verification. Normally, this abstraction is based on the set of events not used in the remainder of the system, i.e., in the part of the system not being simplified. Here, it is proposed to exploit more knowledge about the system and abstract events even though they are used in the remainder of the system. Abstraction rules from previous work are generalised, and experimental results demonstrate the applicability of the resulting algorithm to verify several industrial-scale discrete event system models, while achieving better state-space reduction than before.

1 Introduction

The *nonblocking property* is a weak liveness property commonly used in *supervisory control theory* of discrete event systems to express the absence of livelocks or deadlocks [6,22]. This is a crucial property of safety-critical control systems, and with the increasing size and complexity of these systems, there is an increasing need to verify the nonblocking property automatically. The standard method to check whether a system is nonblocking involves the explicit composition of all the automata involved, and is limited by the well-known *state-space explosion* problem. *Symbolic model checking* has been used successfully to reduce the amount of memory required by representing the state space symbolically rather than enumerating it explicitly [2].

  Compositional verification [10,27] is an effective alternative that can be used independently of or in combination with symbolic methods. Compositional verification works by simplifying individual automata of a large synchronous composition, gradually reducing the state space of the system and allowing much larger systems to be verified in the end. When applied to the nonblocking property, compositional verification requires very specific abstraction methods [9,17]. A suitable theory is laid out in [18], where it is argued that abstractions used in nonblocking verification should preserve a process-algebraic equivalence called *conflict equivalence*. Various abstraction rules preserving conflict equivalence have been proposed and implemented [9,17,20,25].

C. Artho and P.C. Ölveczky (Eds.): FTSCS 2013, CCIS 419, pp. 160–177, 2014.
DOI: 10.1007/978-3-319-05416-2_11, © Springer International Publishing Switzerland 2014

Conflict equivalence is the most general process equivalence for use in compositional nonblocking verification [18]. If a part of a system is replaced by a conflict equivalent abstraction, the nonblocking property is guaranteed to be preserved independently of the other system components. While this is easy to understand and implement, more simplification is possible by considering the other system components. This paper proposes simplification rules that take into account that certain events are always enabled or only selfloops in the rest of the system, and shows how this additional information can achieve further state-space reduction.

In the following, Sect. 2 introduces the background of nondeterministic automata, the nonblocking property, and conflict equivalence. Next, Sect. 3 describes compositional verification and always enabled and selfloop-only events. Section 4 presents simplification rules that exploit such events, and Sect. 5 shows how these events are found algorithmically. Afterwards, Sect. 6 presents the experimental results, and Sect. 7 adds concluding remarks. Further details and formal proofs of technical results can be found in [21].

2 Preliminaries

2.1 Events and Languages

Event sequences and languages are a simple means to describe discrete system behaviours [6,22]. Their basic building blocks are *events*, which are taken from a finite *alphabet* $\mathbf{A}$. In addition, two special events are used, the *silent event* τ and the *termination event* ω. These are never included in an alphabet $\mathbf{A}$ unless mentioned explicitly using notation such as $\mathbf{A}_\tau = \mathbf{A} \cup \{\tau\}$, $\mathbf{A}_\omega = \mathbf{A} \cup \{\omega\}$, and $\mathbf{A}_{\tau,\omega} = \mathbf{A} \cup \{\tau, \omega\}$.

$\mathbf{A}^*$ denotes the set of all finite *traces* of the form $\sigma_1\sigma_2 \cdots \sigma_n$ of events from $\mathbf{A}$, including the *empty trace* ε. The *concatenation* of two traces $s, t \in \mathbf{A}^*$ is written as st. A subset $L \subseteq \mathbf{A}^*$ is called a *language*. The *natural projection* $P \colon \mathbf{A}_{\tau,\omega}^* \to \mathbf{A}_\omega^*$ is the operation that deletes all silent (τ) events from traces.

2.2 Nondeterministic Automata

System behaviours are modelled using finite automata. Typically, system models are deterministic, but abstraction may result in nondeterminism.

Definition 1. A (nondeterministic) *finite automaton* is a tuple $G = \langle \mathbf{A}, Q, \to, Q^\circ \rangle$ where $\mathbf{A}$ is a finite set of *events*, Q is a finite set of *states*, $\to \subseteq Q \times \mathbf{A}_{\tau,\omega} \times Q$ is the *state transition relation*, and $Q^\circ \subseteq Q$ is the set of *initial states*.

The transition relation is written in infix notation $x \xrightarrow{\sigma} y$, and is extended to traces $s \in \mathbf{A}_{\tau,\omega}^*$ in the standard way. For state sets $X, Y \subseteq Q$, the notation $X \xrightarrow{s} Y$ means $x \xrightarrow{s} y$ for some $x \in X$ and $y \in Y$, and $X \xrightarrow{s} y$ means $x \xrightarrow{s} y$ for some $x \in X$. Also, $X \xrightarrow{s}$ for a state or state set X denotes the existence of a state $y \in Q$ such that $X \xrightarrow{s} y$.

The termination event $\omega \notin \mathbf{A}$ denotes completion of a task and does not appear anywhere else but to mark such completions. It is required that states reached by ω do not have any outgoing transitions, i.e., if $x \xrightarrow{\omega} y$ then there does not exist $\sigma \in \mathbf{A}_{\tau,\omega}$ such that $y \xrightarrow{\sigma}$. This ensures that the termination event, if it occurs, is always the final event of any trace. The traditional set of *terminal* states is $Q^\omega = \{ x \in Q \mid x \xrightarrow{\omega} \}$ in this notation. For graphical simplicity, states in Q^ω are shown shaded in the figures of this paper instead of explicitly showing ω-transitions.

To support silent events, another transition relation $\Rightarrow \subseteq Q \times \mathbf{A}_\omega^* \times Q$ is introduced, where $x \xRightarrow{s} y$ denotes the existence of a trace $t \in \mathbf{A}_{\tau,\omega}^*$ such that $P(t) = s$ and $x \xrightarrow{t} y$. That is, $x \xrightarrow{s} y$ denotes a path with *exactly* the events in s, while $x \xRightarrow{s} y$ denotes a path with an arbitrary number of τ events shuffled with the events of s. Notations such as $X \xRightarrow{s} Y$ and $x \xRightarrow{s}$ are defined analogously to $\rightarrow$.

Definition 2. Let $G = \langle \mathbf{A}_G, Q_G, \rightarrow_G, Q_G^\circ \rangle$ and $H = \langle \mathbf{A}_H, Q_H, \rightarrow_H, Q_H^\circ \rangle$ be two automata. The *synchronous composition* of G and H is

$$G \parallel H = \langle \mathbf{A}_G \cup \mathbf{A}_H, Q_G \times Q_H, \rightarrow, Q_H^\circ \times Q_H^\circ \rangle, \tag{1}$$

where

- $(x_G, x_H) \xrightarrow{\sigma} (y_G, y_H)$ if $\sigma \in (\mathbf{A}_G \cap \mathbf{A}_H) \cup \{\omega\}$, $x_G \xrightarrow{\sigma}_G y_G$, and $x_H \xrightarrow{\sigma}_H y_H$;
- $(x_G, x_H) \xrightarrow{\sigma} (y_G, x_H)$ if $\sigma \in (\mathbf{A}_G \setminus \mathbf{A}_H) \cup \{\tau\}$ and $x_G \xrightarrow{\sigma}_G y_G$;
- $(x_G, x_H) \xrightarrow{\sigma} (x_G, y_H)$ if $\sigma \in (\mathbf{A}_H \setminus \mathbf{A}_G) \cup \{\tau\}$ and $x_H \xrightarrow{\sigma}_H y_H$.

Automata are synchronised using lock-step synchronisation [12]. Shared events (including ω) must be executed by all automata synchronously, while other events (including τ) are executed independently.

2.3   The Nonblocking Property

The key liveness property in supervisory control theory is the *nonblocking* property. An automaton is nonblocking if, from every reachable state, a terminal state can be reached; otherwise it is *blocking*. When more than one automaton is involved, it also is common to use the terms *nonconflicting* and *conflicting*.

Definition 3. [18] An automaton $G = \langle \mathbf{A}, Q, \rightarrow, Q^\circ \rangle$ is *nonblocking* if, for every state $x \in Q$ and every trace $s \in \mathbf{A}^*$ such that $Q^\circ \xRightarrow{s} x$, there exists a trace $t \in \mathbf{A}^*$ such that $x \xRightarrow{t\omega}$. Two automata G and H are *nonconflicting* if $G \parallel H$ is nonblocking.

To reason about conflicts in a compositional way, the notion of *conflict equivalence* is developed in [18]. According to process-algebraic testing theory, two automata are considered as equivalent if they both respond in the same way to tests [7]. For *conflict equivalence*, a *test* is an arbitrary automaton, and the *response* is the observation whether the test composed with the automaton in question is nonblocking or not.

Definition 4. [18] Two automata G and H are *conflict equivalent*, written $G \simeq_{\text{conf}} H$, if, for any automaton T, $G \parallel T$ is nonblocking if and only if $H \parallel T$ is nonblocking.

3   Compositional Verification

When verifying whether a composed system of automata

$$G_1 \parallel G_2 \parallel \cdots \parallel G_n , \tag{2}$$

is nonblocking, compositional methods [9,17] avoid building the full synchronous composition immediately. Instead, individual automata G_i are simplified and replaced by smaller conflict equivalent automata $H_i \simeq_{\text{conf}} G_i$. If no simplification is possible, a subsystem of automata $(G_j)_{j \in J}$ is selected and replaced by its synchronous composition, which then may be simplified.

The soundness of this approach is justified by the *congruence* properties [18] of conflict equivalence. For example, if G_1 in (2) is replaced by $H_1 \simeq_{\text{conf}} G_1$, then by considering $T = G_2 \parallel \cdots \parallel G_n$ in Definition 4, it follows that the abstracted system $H_1 \parallel T = H_1 \parallel G_2 \parallel \cdots \parallel G_n$ is nonblocking if and only if the original system (2) is.

Previous approaches for compositional nonblocking verification [9,17] are based on *local* events. A component G_1 in a system such as (2) typically contains some events that appear only in G_1 and not in the remainder $T = G_2 \parallel \cdots \parallel G_n$ of the system. These events are called local and are abstracted using hiding, i.e., they are replaced by the silent event τ. Conflict equivalence uses τ as a placeholder for events not used elsewhere, and in this setting is the coarsest conflict-preserving abstraction [18].

Yet, in practice, the remainder $T = G_2 \parallel \cdots \parallel G_n$ is known. This paper proposes ways to use additional information about T to inform the simplification of G_1 and produce better abstractions. In addition to using the τ events, it can be examined how other events are used by T. There are two kinds of events that are easy to detect: *always enabled* events and *selfloop-only* events.

Definition 5. Let $G = \langle A, Q, \rightarrow, Q^\circ \rangle$ be an automaton. An event $\sigma \in A$ is *always enabled* in G, if for every state $x \in Q$ it holds that $x \overset{\sigma}{\Rightarrow}$.

An event is always enabled in an automaton if it can be executed from every state—possibly after some silent events. If during compositional verification, an event is found to be always enabled in every automaton except the one being simplified, this event has similar properties to a silent event. Several abstraction methods that exploit silent events to simplify automata can be generalised to exploit always enabled events also.

Definition 6. Let $G = \langle A, Q, \rightarrow, Q^\circ \rangle$ be an automaton. An event $\sigma \in A$ is *selfloop-only* in G, if for every transition $x \overset{\sigma}{\rightarrow} y$ it holds that $x = y$.

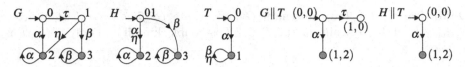

Fig. 1. Two automata G and H such that $G \simeq_{\{\eta\},\emptyset} H$ but not $G \simeq_{\mathrm{conf}} H$.

Selfloops are transitions that have the same start and end states. An event is selfloop-only if it only appears on selfloop transitions. As the presence of self-loops does not affect the nonblocking property, the knowledge that an event is selfloop-only can help to simplify the system beyond standard conflict equivalence. In the following definition, conflict equivalence is generalised by considering sets **E** and **S** of events that are always enabled or selfloop-only in the rest of the system, i.e., in the test T.

Definition 7. Let G and H be two automata, and let **E** and **S** be two sets of events. G and H are *conflict equivalent* with respect to **E** and **S**, written $G \simeq_{\mathbf{E},\mathbf{S}} H$, if for every automaton T such that **E** is a set of always enabled events in T and **S** is a set of selfloop-only events in T, it holds that $G \parallel T$ is nonblocking if and only if $H \parallel T$ is nonblocking.

Clearly, standard conflict equivalence implies conflict equivalence with respect to **E** and **S**, as the latter considers fewer tests T. Yet, both equivalences have the same useful properties for compositional nonblocking verification. The following results are immediate from the definition.

Proposition 1. Let G and H be two automata.

(i) $G \simeq_{\mathrm{conf}} H$ if and only if $G \simeq_{\emptyset,\emptyset} H$.
(ii) If $\mathbf{E} \subseteq \mathbf{E}'$ and $\mathbf{S} \subseteq \mathbf{S}'$ then $G \simeq_{\mathbf{E},\mathbf{S}} H$ implies $G \simeq_{\mathbf{E}',\mathbf{S}'} H$.

Proposition 2. Let $G_1,\ldots,G_n$ and H_1 be automata such that $G_1 \simeq_{\mathbf{E},\mathbf{S}} H_1$, where **E** and **S** are sets of events that respectively are always enabled and selfloop-only for $G_2 \parallel \cdots \parallel G_n$. Then $G_1 \parallel \cdots \parallel G_n$ is nonblocking if and only if $H_1 \parallel G_2 \parallel \cdots \parallel G_n$ is nonblocking.

Proposition 1 confirms that conflict equivalence with respect to **E** and **S** is coarser than standard conflict equivalence and considers more automata as equivalent. Thus, the modified equivalence has the potential to achieve better abstraction. At the same time, Proposition 2 shows that the modified equivalence can be used in the same way as standard conflict equivalence to replace automata in compositional verification, provided that suitable event sets **E** and **S** can be determined.

Example 1. Automata G and H in Fig. 1 are *not* conflict equivalent as demonstrated by the test automaton T. On the one hand, $G \parallel T$ is blocking because the state $(1,0)$ is reachable by τ from the initial state $(0,0)$, and $(1,0)$ is a deadlock state, because G disables event α in state 1 and T disables events β and η in state 0. On the other hand, $H \parallel T$ is nonblocking.

Note that η is not always enabled in T since $0 \overset{\eta}{\Rightarrow}_T$ does not hold. In composition with a test T that has η always enabled, G will be able to continue from state 1, and H will be able to continue from state 01. It follows from Proposition 4 below that $G \simeq_{\{\eta\},\emptyset} H$.

4   Simplification Rules

To exploit conflict equivalence in compositional verification, it is necessary to algorithmically compute a conflict equivalent abstraction of a given automaton. Several abstraction rules are known for standard conflict equivalence [9,17]. This section generalises some of these and proposes four computationally feasible rules to simplify automata under the assumption of always enabled and selfloop-only events. Before that, Subsect. 4.1 introduces general terminology to describe all abstractions.

4.1   Automaton Abstraction

A common method to simplify an automaton is to construct its *quotient* modulo an equivalence relation. The following definitions are standard.

An *equivalence relation* is a binary relation that is reflexive, symmetric and transitive. Given an equivalence relation $\sim$ on a set Q, the *equivalence class* of $x \in Q$ with respect to $\sim$, denoted $[x]$, is defined as $[x] = \{\, x' \in Q \mid x' \sim x \,\}$. An equivalence relation on a set Q partitions Q into the set $Q/\!\sim\, = \{\, [x] \mid x \in Q \,\}$ of its equivalence classes.

Definition 8. Let $G = \langle A, Q, \rightarrow, Q^\circ \rangle$ be an automaton, and let $\sim \subseteq Q \times Q$ be an equivalence relation. The *quotient automaton* $G/\!\sim$ of G with respect to $\sim$ is $G/\!\sim\, = \langle A, Q/\!\sim, \rightarrow/\!\sim, \tilde{Q}^\circ \rangle$, where $\tilde{Q}^\circ = \{\, [x^\circ] \mid x^\circ \in Q^\circ \,\}$ and $\rightarrow/\!\sim\, = \{\, ([x], \sigma, [y]) \mid x \overset{\sigma}{\rightarrow} y \,\}$.

When constructing a quotient automaton, classes of equivalent states in the original automaton are combined or *merged* into a single state. A common equivalence relation to construct quotient automata is *observation equivalence* or *weak bisimulation* [19].

Definition 9. [19] Let $G = \langle A, Q, \rightarrow, Q^\circ \rangle$ be an automaton. A relation $\approx \subseteq Q \times Q$ is an *observation equivalence* relation on G if, for all states $x_1, x_2 \in Q$ such that $x_1 \approx x_2$ and all traces $s \in A_\omega^*$ the following conditions hold:

(i) if $x_1 \overset{s}{\Rightarrow} y_1$ for some $y_1 \in Q$, then there exists $y_2 \in Q$ such that $y_1 \approx y_2$ and $x_2 \overset{s}{\Rightarrow} y_2$;
(ii) if $x_2 \overset{s}{\Rightarrow} y_2$ for some $y_2 \in Q$, then there exists $y_1 \in Q$ such that $y_1 \approx y_2$ and $x_1 \overset{s}{\Rightarrow} y_1$.

Two states are observation equivalent if they have got exactly the same sequences of enabled events, leading to equivalent successor states. Observation equivalence is a well-known equivalence with efficient algorithms that preserves all temporal logic properties [5]. In particular, an observation equivalent abstraction is conflict equivalent to the original automaton.

Proposition 3. [17] Let G be an automaton, and let $\approx$ be an observation equivalence relation on G. Then $G \simeq_{\mathrm{conf}} G/\approx$.

A special case of observation equivalence-based abstraction is τ-*loop removal*. If two states are mutually connected by sequences of τ-transitions, it follows from Definition 9 that these states are observation equivalent, so by Proposition 3 they can be merged preserving conflict equivalence. This simple abstraction results in a τ-*loop free* automaton, i.e., an automaton that does not contain any proper cycles of τ-transitions.

Definition 10. Let $G = \langle \mathbf{A}, Q, \rightarrow, Q^\circ \rangle$ be an automaton. G is τ-*loop free*, if for every path $x \xrightarrow{t} x$ with $t \in \{\tau\}^*$ it holds that $t = \varepsilon$.

While τ-loop removal and observation equivalence are easy to compute and produce good abstractions, there are conflict equivalent automata that are not observation equivalent. Several other relations are considered for conflict equivalence [9,17].

Definition 11. [9] Let $G = \langle \mathbf{A}, Q, \rightarrow, Q^\circ \rangle$ be an automaton. The *incoming equivalence* relation $\sim_{\mathrm{inc}} \subseteq Q \times Q$ is defined such that $x \sim_{\mathrm{inc}} y$ if,

(i) $Q^\circ \xRightarrow{\varepsilon} x$ if and only if $Q^\circ \xRightarrow{\varepsilon} y$;
(ii) for all states $w \in Q$ and all events $\sigma \in \mathbf{A}$ it holds that $w \xRightarrow{\sigma} x$ if and only if $w \xRightarrow{\sigma} y$.

Two states are incoming equivalent if they have got the same incoming transitions from the exactly same source states. (This is different from reverse observation equivalence, which accepts *equivalent* rather than identical states.) Incoming equivalence alone is not enough for conflict-preserving abstraction. It is combined with other conditions in the following.

4.2   Enabled Continuation Rule

The Enabled Continuation Rule is a generalisation of the Silent Continuation Rule [9], which allows to merge incoming equivalent states in a τ-loop free automaton provided they have both have an outgoing τ-transition. The reason for this is that, if a state has an outgoing τ-transition, then the other outgoing transitions are "optional" [9] for a test that is to be nonblocking with this automaton. Only continuations from states without further τ-transitions must be present in the test. Using always enabled events, the condition on τ-transitions can be relaxed: it also becomes possible to merge incoming equivalent states if they have outgoing always enabled transitions instead of τ.

Rule 1 (Enabled Continuation Rule). In a τ-loop free automaton, two states that are incoming equivalent and both have an outgoing *always enabled* or τ-transition are conflict equivalent and can be merged.

Example 2. Consider automaton G in Fig. 1 with $\mathbf{E} = \{\eta\}$. States 0 and 1 are both "initial" since they both can be reached silently from the initial state 0. This is enough to satisfy $\sim_{\text{inc}}$ in this case, since neither state is reachable by any event other than τ. Moreover, G has no τ-loops, state 0 has an outgoing τ-transition, and state 1 has an outgoing always enabled event η. Thus, by the Enabled Continuation Rule, states 0 and 1 in G are conflict equivalent and can be merged into state 01 as shown in H.

Note that states 0 and 1 are not observation equivalent because $0 \xrightarrow{\alpha} 2$ while state 1 has no outgoing α-transition. The Silent Continuation Rule [9] also is not applicable because state 1 has no outgoing τ-transition. Only with the additional information that η is always enabled, it becomes possible to merge states 0 and 1.

Proposition 4. Let $G = \langle \mathbf{A}, Q, \to_G, Q^\circ \rangle$ be a τ-loop free automaton, let $\mathbf{E} \subseteq \mathbf{A}$, and let $\sim \subseteq Q \times Q$ be an equivalence relation such that $\sim \subseteq \sim_{\text{inc}}$, and for all $x, y \in Q$ such that $x \sim y$ it holds that either $x = y$, or $x \xrightarrow{\eta_1}$ and $y \xrightarrow{\eta_2}$ for some events $\eta_1, \eta_2 \in \mathbf{E} \cup \{\tau\}$. Then $G \simeq_{\mathbf{E}, \emptyset} G/\sim$.

Proposition 4 confirms that the nonblocking property of the system is preserved under the Enabled Continuation Rule, provided that $\mathbf{E}$ is a set of always enabled events for the remainder of the system.

4.3   Only Silent Incoming Rule

The Only Silent Incoming Rule [9] is a combination of observation equivalence and the Silent Continuation Rule. Since the Silent Continuation Rule has been generalised to use always enabled events, the Only Silent Incoming Rule can as well.

The original Only Silent Incoming Rule [9] makes it possible to remove a state with only τ-transitions incoming and merge it into its predecessors, provided that the removed state has got at least one outgoing τ-transition. Again, the requirement for an outgoing τ-transition can be relaxed to allow an always enabled transition also.

Rule 2 (Only Silent Incoming Rule). If a τ-loop free automaton has a state q with only τ-transitions entering it, and an always enabled or τ-transition outgoing from state q, then all transitions outgoing from q can be copied to originate from the states with τ-transitions to q. Afterwards, the τ-transitions to q can be removed.

Example 3. In Fig. 2 it holds that $G \simeq_{\{\eta\}, \emptyset} H$. State 3 in G has only τ-transitions incoming and the always enabled event η outgoing. This state can be removed in two steps. First, state 3 is split into two observation equivalent states $3a$ and $3b$ in G', and afterwards the Silent Continuation Rule is applied to merge these states into their incoming equivalent predecessors, resulting in H. Note that states 1, 2, and 3 are not observation equivalent because of the β- and γ-transitions from states 1 and 2.

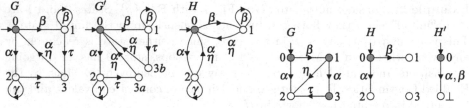

Fig. 2. Only silent incoming rule.

Fig. 3. Limited certain conflicts rule.

Proposition 5. Let $G = \langle \mathbf{A}, Q, \to_G, Q^\circ \rangle$ be a τ-loop free automaton, and let $\mathbf{E} \subseteq \mathbf{A}$. Let $q \in Q$ such that $q \xrightarrow{\eta}_G$ for some $\eta \in \mathbf{E} \cup \{\tau\}$, and for each transition $x \xrightarrow{\sigma}_G q$ it holds that $\sigma = \tau$. Further, let $H = \langle \mathbf{A}, Q, \to_H, Q^\circ \rangle$ with

$$\to_H = \{\, (x, \sigma, y) \mid x \xrightarrow{\sigma}_G y \text{ and } y \neq q \,\} \cup \{\, (x, \sigma, y) \mid x \xrightarrow{\tau}_G q \xrightarrow{\sigma}_G y \,\} \,. \qquad (3)$$

Then $G \simeq_{\mathbf{E}, \emptyset} H$.

It is shown in [9] that the Only Silent Incoming Rule can be expressed as a combination of observation equivalence and the Silent Continuation Rule as suggested in Example 3. The same argument can be used to prove Proposition 5.

4.4 Limited Certain Conflicts Rule

If an automaton contains blocking states, i.e., states from where no state with an ω-transition can be reached, then a lot of simplification is possible. Once a blocking state is reached, all further transitions are irrelevant. Therefore, all blocking states can be merged into a single state, and all their outgoing transitions can be deleted [16].

In fact, this rule does not only apply to blocking states. For example, consider state 3 in automaton G in Fig. 3. Despite the fact that state 3 is a terminal state, if this state is ever reached, the composed system is necessarily blocking, as nothing can prevent it from executing the silent transition $3 \xrightarrow{\tau} 2$ to the blocking state 2. State 3 is a state of *certain conflicts*, and such states can be treated like blocking states for the purpose of abstraction.

It is possible to calculate all states of certain conflicts, but the algorithm to do this is exponential in the number of states of the automaton to be simplified [16]. To reduce the complexity, the Limited Certain Conflicts Rule [9] approximates the set of certain conflicts. If a state has a τ-transition to a blocking state, then the source state also is a state of certain conflicts. This can be extended to include always enabled events, because if an always enabled transition takes an automaton to a blocking state, then nothing can disable this transition and the composed system is necessarily blocking.

Rule 3 (Limited Certain Conflicts Rule). If an automaton contains an always enabled or τ-transition to a blocking state, then the source state of this transition is a state of certain conflicts, and all its outgoing transitions can be deleted.

Example 4. Consider automaton G in Fig. 3 with $\mathbf{E} = \{\eta\}$. States 1, 2, and 3 are states of certain conflicts. State 2 is already blocking, and states 1 and 3 have a τ- or an always enabled η-transition to the blocking state 2. All outgoing transitions from these states are removed, including the ω-transitions from states 1 and 3. This results in automaton H. Now state 3 is unreachable and can be removed, and states 1 and 2 can be merged using observation equivalence to create H'. It holds that $G \simeq_{\{\eta\},\emptyset} H \simeq_{\mathrm{conf}} H'$.

Proposition 6. Let $G = \langle \mathbf{A}, Q, \rightarrow_G, Q^\circ \rangle$ be an automaton and $\mathbf{E} \subseteq \mathbf{A}$, let $q \in Q$ be a blocking state, and let $p \xrightarrow{\eta} q$ for some $\eta \in \mathbf{E} \cup \{\tau\}$. Furthermore, let $H = \langle \mathbf{A}, Q, \rightarrow_H, Q^\circ \rangle$ where $\rightarrow_H = \{\, (x, \sigma, y) \in \rightarrow \mid x \neq p \,\}$. Then $G \simeq_{\mathbf{E},\emptyset} H$.

Proposition 6 confirms that a state with a τ- or always enabled transitions to some other blocking state can also be made blocking, by deleting all outgoing transitions (including ω) from it. The Limited Certain Conflicts Rule should be applied repeatedly, as the deletion of transitions may introduce new blocking states and thus new certain conflicts.

4.5 Selfloop Removal Rule

The final abstraction rule concerns selfloop-only events. To verify nonblocking, it is enough to check if every state in the final synchronous composition of all automata can reach a terminal state. Selfloops in the final synchronous composition have no effect on the blocking nature of the system, since any path between two states still passes the same states when all selfloops are removed from the path. So the final synchronous composition is nonblocking if and only if it is nonblocking with all selfloops removed.

Based on this observation, if an event is known to be selfloop-only in all automata except the one being simplified, then selfloops with that event can be added or removed freely to the automaton being simplified.

Rule 4 (Selfloop Removal Rule). If an event λ is selfloop-only in all other automata, then selfloop transitions $q \xrightarrow{\lambda} q$ can be added to or removed from any state q.

This rule can be used to remove selfloops and save memory, sometimes reducing the amount of shared events or allowing other rules to be used. If an event only appears on selfloops in all automata, then it can be removed entirely. Furthermore, the addition of selfloops to certain states may also be beneficial.

Example 5. Figure 4 shows a sequence of conflict-preserving changes to an automaton containing the selfloop-only event λ. First, the λ-selfloop in G_1 is removed to create G_2. In G_2, states 0 and 1 are close to observation equivalent, as they both have a β-transition to state 2; however 0 has a λ-transition to 1 and 1 does not. Yet, it is possible to add a λ-selfloop to state 1 and create G_3. Now states 0 and 1 are observation equivalent and can be merged to create G_4. Finally, the λ-selfloop in G_4 is removed to create G_5.

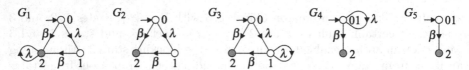

Fig. 4. Removal and addition of selfloops.

Proposition 7. Let $G = \langle \mathbf{A}, Q, \rightarrow_G, Q^\circ \rangle$ and $H = \langle \mathbf{A}, Q, \rightarrow_H, Q^\circ \rangle$ be automata with $\rightarrow_H = \rightarrow_G \cup \{(q, \lambda, q)\}$ for some $\lambda \in \mathbf{A}$. Then $G \simeq_{\emptyset, \{\lambda\}} H$.

Proposition 7 shows that the addition of a single selfloop preserves conflict equivalence. It can be applied in reverse to remove selfloops, and it can be applied repeatedly to add or remove several selfloops in an automaton or in the entire system.

The implementation in Sect. 6 uses selfloop removal whenever applicable to delete as many selfloops as possible. In addition, observation equivalence has been modified to assume the presence of selfloops for all selfloop-only events in all states, so as to achieve the best possible state-space reduction.

5   Finding Always Enabled and Selfloop-Only Events

While the simplification rules in Sect. 4 are straightforward extensions of known rules for standard conflict equivalence [9], their application requires the knowledge about always enabled and selfloop-only events. Assume the system (2) encountered during compositional verification is

$$G_1 \parallel G_2 \parallel \cdots \parallel G_n \,, \tag{4}$$

and automaton G_1 is to be simplified. Then it is necessary to know always enabled and selfloop-only events in $T = G_2 \parallel \cdots \parallel G_n$. For each component automaton G_i, such events are easy to detect based on Definitions 5 and 6. It also is a direct consequence of the definitions that these properties carry over to the synchronous product.

Proposition 8. Let G_1 and G_2 be two automata. If an event σ is always enabled (or selfloop-only) in G_1 and G_2, then σ is always enabled (or selfloop-only) in $G_1 \parallel G_2$.

Given Proposition 8, an event can be considered as always enabled or selfloop-only if it has this property for every automaton in (4) except the automaton being simplified. When checking the individual automata, selfloop-only events are easily found by checking whether an event in question only appears on selfloop transitions. For always enabled events, it is checked whether the event in question is enabled in every state, but additional considerations can help to find more always enabled events.

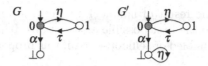

Fig. 5. Finding an always enabled event.

Example 6. Consider automaton G in Fig. 5. It clearly holds that $0 \xrightarrow{\eta}$, and $1 \xrightarrow{\tau} 0 \xrightarrow{\eta}$ and thus $1 \xRightarrow{\eta}$. Although η is not enabled in state $\perp$, this state is a blocking state and the set of enabled events for blocking states is irrelevant—it is known [16] that G is conflict equivalent to G'. Then η can be considered as always enabled in G' and thus also in G.

By definition, an always enabled event η must be possible in every state of the environment T, except for blocking states according to Example 6. However, this condition is stronger than necessary, as η typically is not always possible in the automaton G being simplified. This observation leads to *conditionally* always enabled events.

Definition 12. Let $G = \langle \mathbf{A}, Q_G, \to_G, Q_G^\circ \rangle$ and $T = \langle \mathbf{A}, Q_T, \to_T, Q_T^\circ \rangle$ be two automata. An event $\sigma \in \mathbf{A}$ is *conditionally always enabled* for G in T, if for all $s \in \mathbf{A}^*$ such that $Q_G^\circ \xRightarrow{s\sigma}_G$ and all states $x_T \in Q_T$ such that $Q_T^\circ \xRightarrow{s}_T x_T$, it holds that $x_T \xRightarrow{\sigma}_T$.

An event is conditionally always enabled if the environment T enables it in all states where it is possible in the automaton G to be simplified. The following Proposition 9 shows that the result of compositional nonblocking verification is also preserved with events that are only conditionally always enabled.

Proposition 9. Let G, H, and T be automata, and let $\mathbf{E}$ and $\mathbf{S}$ be event sets such that $G \simeq_{\mathbf{E},\mathbf{S}} H$, and $\mathbf{E}$ is a set of conditionally always enabled events for G in T, and $\mathbf{S}$ is a set of selfloop-only events for T. Then $G \parallel T$ is nonblocking if and only if $H \parallel T$ is nonblocking.

Conditionally always enabled events can be used like general always enabled events, but they are more difficult to find. To check the condition of Definition 12, it is necessary to explore the state space of $G \parallel T$, which has the same complexity as a nonblocking check. Yet, the condition is similar to *controllability* [6], which can often be verified quickly by an *incremental controllability check* [4]. The incremental algorithm gradually composes some of the automata of the system (4) until it can be ascertained whether or not a given event is conditionally always enabled. In many cases, it gives a positive or negative answer after composing only a few automata.

By running the incremental controllability check for a short time, some conditionally always enabled events can be found, while for others the status remains inconclusive. Fortunately, it is not necessary to find all always enabled events. If the status of an event is not known, it can be assumed that this event is *not* always enabled. The result of nonblocking verification will still be correct, although it may not use the best possible abstractions. It is enough to only consider events as always enabled or selfloop-only, if this property can be established easily.

6   Experimental Results

The compositional nonblocking verification algorithm has been implemented in the discrete event systems tool Waters/Supremica [1], which is freely available for download [26]. The software is further developed from [17] to support always enabled and selfloop-only events.

The new implementation has been applied to all models used for evaluation in [17] with at least $5 \cdot 10^8$ reachable states. The test suite includes complex industrial models and case studies from various application areas such as manufacturing systems, communication protocols, and automotive electronics. The following list gives some details about these models.

aip Model of the automated manufacturing system of the Atelier Inter-établissement de Productique [3]. The tests consider two early versions (**aip0**) based on [14], and a more detailed version (**aip1**) according to [24], which has been modified for a parameterisable number of pallets.
profisafe PROFIsafe field bus protocol model [15]. The task considered here is to verify nonblocking of the communication partners and the network in input-slave configuration with sequence numbers ranging up to 4, 5, and 6.
tbed Model of a toy railroad system [13] in three different designs.
tip3 Model of the interaction between a mobile client and event-based servers of a Tourist Information System [11].
verriegel Car central locking system, originally from the KORSYS project [23].
6link Models of a cluster tool for wafer processing [28].

Compositional verification repeatedly chooses a small set of automata, composes them, applies abstraction rules to the synchronous composition, and replaces the composed automata with the result. This is repeated until the remaining automata are considered too large, or there are only two automata left. The last two automata are not simplified, because it is easier to check the nonblocking property directly by explicitly constructing and exploring the synchronous composition.

A key aspect for a compositional verification algorithm is the way how automata are selected to be composed. The implementation considered here follows a two-step approach [9]. In the first step, some *candidate* sets of automata are formed, and in the second a most promising candidate is selected. For each event σ in the model, a candidate is formed consisting of all automata with σ in their alphabet. Among these candidates, the candidate with the smallest estimated number of states after abstraction is selected. The estimate is obtained by multiplying the product of the state numbers of the automata forming the candidate with the ratio of the numbers of events in the synchronous composition of the candidate after and before removing any local events. This strategy is called **MustL/MinS** [9,17].

After identification of a candidate, its automata are composed, and then a sequence of abstraction rules is applied to simplify it. First, τ-loops (Definition 10) and observation equivalent redundant transitions [8] are removed from the automaton. This is followed by the Only Silent Incoming Rule (Proposition 5), the Only Silent Outgoing Rule [9], the Limited Certain Conflicts Rule (Proposition 6), Observation Equivalence (Proposition 3), the Non-α Determinisation Rule [17], the Active Events Rule [9], and the Silent Continuation Rule (Proposition 4).

During simplification, all selfloops with selfloop-only events are deleted, and observation equivalence and the removal of observation equivalent redundant transitions exploit selfloop-only events for further simplification. Furthermore, the Only Silent Incoming Rule, the Limited Certain Conflicts Rule, and the Silent Continuation Rule take always enabled events into account. For the experiments, the detection of always enabled events and selfloop-only events can be turned on and off separately, producing four strategies **None** (no special events), **SL** (selfloop-only events), **AE** (always enabled events), and **SL/AE** (selfloop-only and always enabled events).

The strategies **AE** and **SL/AE** consider events as always enabled if they are always enabled in every automaton except the one being simplified. Two further strategies **SL/AE** ⟨200⟩ and **SL/AE** ⟨1000⟩ also search for events that are conditionally always enabled (Definition 12). This is done using an incremental controllability check [4] that tries to compose an increasing part of the model until it is known whether or not an event is always enabled, or until a state limit of 200 or 1000 states is exceeded; in the latter case, the check is abandoned and the event is assumed to be not always enabled.

The results of the experiments are shown in Table 1 and Fig. 6. The table shows for each model the total number of reachable states in the synchronous composition (Size) if known, and whether or not the model is nonblocking (Res). Then it shows for each strategy, the number of states in the largest automaton encountered during abstraction (Peak States), the number of states in the synchronous composition explored after abstraction (Final States), and the total verification time (Time). The best result in each category is highlighted in bold in the table. Figure 6 displays the final state numbers and runtimes for six representative experiments graphically.

In some cases, compositional nonblocking verification terminates early, either because all reachable states of all automata are known to be terminal, or because some automaton has no reachable terminal states left. In these cases, the final synchronous composition is not constructed and the final states number is shown as 0 in the table.

All experiments are run on a standard desktop computer using a single core 3.3 GHz CPU and 8 GB of RAM. The experiments are controlled by state limits. If during abstraction the synchronous composition of a candidate has more than

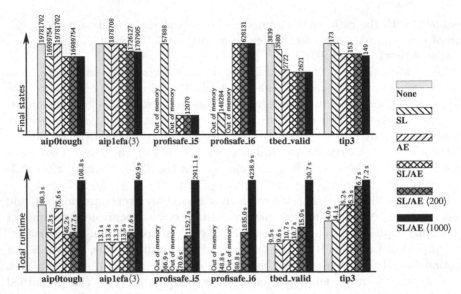

Fig. 6. Final state numbers and runtimes for representative experiments.

100,000 states, it is discarded and another candidate is chosen instead. The state limit for the final synchronous composition after abstraction is 10^8 states. If this limit is exceeded, the run is aborted and the corresponding table entries are left blank.

The experiments show that compositional verification can check the non-blocking property of systems with up to 10^{14} states in a matter of seconds. The exploitation of always enabled and selfloop-only events reduces the peak or final state numbers in many cases. This is important as these numbers are the limiting factors in compositional verification.

The runtimes tend to increase slightly when always enabled or selfloop-only events are used, because the smaller state numbers are outweighed by the effort to find the special events. The search has to be repeated after each abstraction step, because each abstraction can produce new always enabled or selfloop-only events, and the cost increases with the number of steps and events. Conditionally always enabled events can produce better abstractions, but as shown in Fig. 6, it takes a lot of time to find them.

There are also cases where the state numbers increase with always enabled and selfloop-only events. A decrease in the final state number after simplification can come at the expense of increase in the peak state number during simplification. With more powerful simplification algorithms, originally larger automata may fall under the state limits. Also, different abstractions may trigger different candidate selections in following steps, which are not always optimal, and in some cases, the merging of states may prevent observation equivalence from becoming applicable in later steps.

Table 1. Experimental results.

Model	Size	Res	None Peak states	None Final states	None Time [s]	SL Peak states	SL Final states	SL Time [s]	AE Peak states	AE Final states	AE Time [s]
aip0aip	$1.02 \cdot 10^9$	yes	1090	5	1.4	1090	5	**1.4**	1090	5	1.4
aip0tough	$1.02 \cdot 10^{10}$	no	96049	19781702	80.3	96049	**16989754**	47.3	96049	19781702	75.6
aip1efa⟨3⟩	$6.88 \cdot 10^8$	yes	40290	1878708	13.1	40290	1878708	13.4	40290	1878708	13.3
aip1efa⟨16⟩	$9.50 \cdot 10^{12}$	no	65520	13799628	22.2	65520	13799628	**22.2**	65520	13799628	22.9
aip1efa⟨24⟩	$1.83 \cdot 10^{13}$	no	6384	13846773	18.4	6384	13846773	18.6	6384	13846773	18.7
profisafe_i4		yes				74088	**409**	82.3			
profisafe_i5		yes				98304	57888	66.9			
profisafe_i6		yes				55296	**148284**	48.8			
tbed_ctct	$3.94 \cdot 10^{13}$	no	43825	0	**14.5**	43825	0	14.8	43825	0	16.6
tbed_hisc	$5.99 \cdot 10^{12}$	yes	1757	33	2.7	1757	33	**2.7**	1705	33	2.8
tbed_valid	$3.01 \cdot 10^{12}$	yes	50105	3839	9.5	50105	3580	9.6	50105	2722	10.7
tip3	$2.27 \cdot 10^{11}$	yes	**6399**	173	4.0	**6399**	173	4.1	12303	153	5.2
tip3_bad	$5.25 \cdot 10^{10}$	no	1176	14	1.0	1032	14	1.0	1176	**0**	1.1
verriegel3	$9.68 \cdot 10^8$	yes	3303	2	2.0	3303	2	1.7	3349	2	1.8
verriegel3b	$1.32 \cdot 10^9$	no	**1764**	0	**1.2**	1764	0	1.3	1795	0	1.2
verriegel4	$4.59 \cdot 10^{10}$	no	**2609**	2	1.4	2609	2	1.5	2644	2	1.7
verriegel4b	$6.26 \cdot 10^{10}$	no	**1764**	0	1.4	1764	0	1.4	1795	0	**1.4**
6linka	$2.45 \cdot 10^{14}$	no	64	0	**0.4**	64	0	0.4	64	0	0.5
6linki	$2.75 \cdot 10^{14}$	no	61	0	0.3	61	0	0.3	61	0	0.3
6linkp	$4.43 \cdot 10^{14}$	no	32	0	0.3	32	0	**0.3**	32	0	0.3
6linkre	$6.21 \cdot 10^{13}$	no	118	12	0.5	118	12	0.5	**106**	**0**	0.5

Model	Size	Res	SL/AE Peak states	SL/AE Final states	SL/AE Time [s]	SL/AE (200) Peak states	SL/AE (200) Final states	SL/AE (200) Time [s]	SL/AE (1000) Peak states	SL/AE (1000) Final states	SL/AE (1000) Time [s]
aip0aip	$1.02 \cdot 10^9$	yes	1090	5	1.4	892	5	24.5	892	5	32.0
aip0tough	$1.02 \cdot 10^{10}$	no	96049	**16989754**	45.2	96049	**16989754**	47.7	96049	**16989754**	108.8
aip1efa⟨3⟩	$6.88 \cdot 10^8$	yes	40290	1878708	13.5	32980	1726127	17.6	31960	1707905	40.9
aip1efa⟨16⟩	$9.50 \cdot 10^{12}$	no	65520	13799628	22.9	65520	13799628	28.6	65520	13799628	47.5
aip1efa⟨24⟩	$1.83 \cdot 10^{13}$	no	6384	13846773	19.2	5313	13846773	24.0	**5292**	13846773	41.9
profisafe_i4		yes	49152	9864	**61.6**	49152	9864	638.4	49152	9864	2848.9
profisafe_i5		yes	98304	**12070**	70.6	98304	**12070**	1152.7	98304	**12070**	2911.1
profisafe_i6		yes	52224	628131	80.8	52224	628131	1835.0	52224	628131	4238.9
tbed_ctct	$3.94 \cdot 10^{13}$	no	43825	0	16.4	43825	0	20.9	43825	0	43.7
tbed_hisc	$5.99 \cdot 10^{12}$	yes	1705	33	3.0	1705	33	24.5	1705	138	81.5
tbed_valid	$3.01 \cdot 10^{12}$	yes	50105	**2621**	10.7	50105	**2621**	15.0	50105	**2621**	30.7
tip3	$2.27 \cdot 10^{11}$	yes	12303	153	5.3	12303	153	6.7	12303	149	7.2
tip3_bad	$5.25 \cdot 10^{10}$	no	1096	**0**	1.1	1096	**0**	2.9	1096	**0**	3.8
verriegel3	$9.68 \cdot 10^8$	yes	3349	2	**1.5**	2644	2	6.0	2644	2	9.6
verriegel3b	$1.32 \cdot 10^9$	no	1795	0	1.3	1795	0	5.8	1795	0	8.3
verriegel4	$4.59 \cdot 10^{10}$	yes	2644	2	1.6	2644	2	8.6	2644	2	17.3
verriegel4b	$6.26 \cdot 10^{10}$	no	1795	0	1.6	1795	0	8.1	1795	0	13.6
6linka	$2.45 \cdot 10^{14}$	no	64	0	0.5	64	0	2.2	64	0	2.7
6linki	$2.75 \cdot 10^{14}$	no	61	0	0.3	61	0	1.7	61	0	2.0
6linkp	$4.43 \cdot 10^{14}$	no	32	0	0.3	32	0	1.6	32	0	2.0
6linkre	$6.21 \cdot 10^{13}$	no	**106**	**0**	**0.5**	**106**	**0**	2.3	**106**	**0**	2.8

Yet, the large PROFIsafe models [15] can only be verified compositionally with selfloop-only events. By adding always enabled and selfloop-only events to the available tools, it becomes possible to solve problems that are not solvable otherwise.

7   Conclusions

It has been shown how conflict-preserving abstraction can be enhanced by taking into account additional information about the context in which an automaton to be abstracted is used. Specifically, *always enabled* and *selfloop-only* events are easy to discover and help to produce simpler abstractions. Experimental results demonstrate that these special events can make it possible to verify the non-blocking property of more complex discrete event systems. In future work, it is of interest whether the algorithms to detect and use always enabled and selfloop-only events can be improved, and whether other conflict-preserving abstraction methods can also be generalised.

References

1. Åkesson, K., Fabian, M., Flordal, H., Malik, R.: Supremica—an integrated environment for verification, synthesis and simulation of discrete event systems. In: Proceedings of the 8th International Workshop on Discrete Event Systems, WODES '06, Ann Arbor, MI, USA, pp. 384–385 (2006)
2. Baier, C., Katoen, J.P.: Principles of Model Checking. MIT Press, Cambridge (2008)
3. Brandin, B., Charbonnier, F.: The supervisory control of the automated manufacturing system of the AIP. In: Proceedings of Rensselaer's 4th International Conference on Computer Integrated Manufacturing and Automation Technology, Troy, NY, USA, pp. 319–324 (1994)
4. Brandin, B.A., Malik, R., Malik, P.: Incremental verification and synthesis of discrete-event systems guided by counter-examples. IEEE Trans. Control Syst. Technol. **12**(3), 387–401 (2004)
5. Brookes, S.D., Rounds, W.C.: Behavioural equivalence relations induced by programming logics. In: Diaz, J. (ed.) ICALP 1983. LNCS, vol. 154, pp. 97–108. Springer, Heidelberg (1983)
6. Cassandras, C.G., Lafortune, S. (eds.): Introduction to Discrete Event Systems, 2nd edn. Springer, Heidelberg (2008)
7. De Nicola, R., Hennessy, M.C.B.: Testing equivalences for processes. Theor. Comput. Sci. **34**(1–2), 83–133 (1984)
8. Eloranta, J.: Minimizing the number of transitions with respect to observation equivalence. BIT **31**(4), 397–419 (1991)
9. Flordal, H., Malik, R.: Compositional verification in supervisory control. SIAM J. Control Optim. **48**(3), 1914–1938 (2009)
10. Graf, S., Steffen, B.: Compositional minimization of finite state systems. In: Clarke, E.M., Kurshan, R.P. (eds.) CAV 1990. LNCS, vol. 531, pp. 186–6. Springer, Heidelberg (1991)
11. Hinze, A., Malik, P., Malik, R.: Interaction design for a mobile context-aware system using discrete event modelling. In: Proceedings of the 29th Australasian Computer Science Conference, ACSC '06, pp. 257–266. Australian Computer Society, Hobart (2006)
12. Hoare, C.A.R.: Communicating Sequential Processes. Prentice-Hall, Upper Saddle River (1985)

13. Leduc, R.J.: PLC implementation of a DES supervisor for a manufacturing testbed: an implementation perspective. Master's thesis. Department of Electrical Engineering, University of Toronto, ON, Canada. http://www.cas.mcmaster.ca/~leduc (1996)

14. Leduc, R.J.: Hierarchical interface-based supervisory control. Ph.D. thesis, Department of Electrical Engineering, University of Toronto, ON, Canada. http://www.cas.mcmaster.ca/~leduc (2002)

15. Malik, R., Mühlfeld, R.: A case study in verification of UML statecharts: the PROFIsafe protocol. J. Univ. Comput. Sci. 9(2), 138–151 (2003)

16. Malik, R.: The language of certain conflicts of a nondeterministic process. Working Paper 05/2010, Department of Computer Science, University of Waikato, Hamilton, New Zealand. http://hdl.handle.net/10289/4108 (2010)

17. Malik, R., Leduc, R.: Compositional nonblocking verification using generalised nonblocking abstractions. IEEE Trans. Autom. Control 58(8), 1–13 (2013)

18. Malik, R., Streader, D., Reeves, S.: Conflicts and fair testing. Int. J. Found. Comput. Sci. 17(4), 797–813 (2006)

19. Milner, R.: Communication and Concurrency. Series in Computer Science. Prentice-Hall, Upper Saddle River (1989)

20. Pena, P.N., Cury, J.E.R., Lafortune, S.: Verification of nonconflict of supervisors using abstractions. IEEE Trans. Autom. Control 54(12), 2803–2815 (2009)

21. Pilbrow, C.: Compositional nonblocking verification with always enabled and selfloop-only events. Working Paper 07/2013, Department of Computer Science, University of Waikato, Hamilton, New Zealand. http://hdl.handle.net/10289/8187 (2013)

22. Ramadge, P.J.G., Wonham, W.M.: The control of discrete event systems. Proc. IEEE 77(1), 81–98 (1989)

23. KorSys Project. http://www4.in.tum.de/proj/korsys/

24. Song, R.: Symbolic synthesis and verification of hierarchical interface-based supervisory control. Master's thesis, Department of Computing and Software, McMaster University, Hamilton, ON, Canada. http://www.cas.mcmaster.ca/~leduc (2006)

25. Su, R., van Schuppen, J.H., Rooda, J.E., Hofkamp, A.T.: Nonconflict check by using sequential automaton abstractions based on weak observation equivalence. Automatica 46(6), 968–978 (2010)

26. Supremica. http://www.supremica.org

27. Valmari, A.: Compositionality in state space verification methods. In: Billington, J., Reisig, W. (eds.) Application and Theory of Petri Nets 1996. LNCS, vol. 1091, pp. 29–56. Springer, Heidelberg (1996)

28. Yi, J., Ding, S., Zhang, M.T., van der Meulen, P.: Throughput analysis of linear cluster tools. In: Proceedings of the 3rd International Conference on Automation Science and Engineering, CASE 2007, Scottsdale, AZ, USA, pp. 1063–1068 (2007)

Formal Semantics and Analysis
of Timed Rebeca in Real-Time Maude

Zeynab Sabahi-Kaviani[1], Ramtin Khosravi[1(✉)], Marjan Sirjani[1,2],
Peter Csaba Ölveczky[3], and Ehsan Khamespanah[1]

[1] School of Electrical and Computer Engineering, University of Tehran, Tehran, Iran
r.khosravi@ut.ac.ir
[2] School of Computer Science, Reykjavik University, Reykjavik, Iceland
[3] Department of Informatics, University of Oslo, Oslo, Norway

Abstract. The actor model is one of the main models for distributed
computation. Timed Rebeca is a timed extension of the actor-based
modeling language Rebeca. Although Rebeca is supported by a rich
verification toolset, Timed Rebeca has not had an executable formal
semantics, and has therefore had limited support for formal analysis.
In this paper, we provide a formal semantics of Timed Rebeca in Real-
Time Maude. We have automated the translation from Timed Rebeca
to Real-Time Maude, allowing Timed Rebeca models to be automatically analyzed using Real-Time Maude's reachability analysis tool and
timed CTL model checker. This enables a formal model-based methodology which combines the convenience of intuitive modeling in Timed
Rebeca with formal verification in Real-Time Maude. We illustrate this
methodology with a collision avoidance protocol for wireless networks.

1 Introduction

The importance of formal modeling and analysis for ensuring the dependability
and correctness of safety-critical systems has long been acknowledged. However, the lack of formal modeling languages close to programming and modeling
languages used by practitioners has limited the use of formal methods. Timed
Rebeca [1] is an actor-based [2] modeling language that extends the Rebeca language [17] to support the modeling of distributed real-time systems. Because
of its Java-like syntax and its simple and intuitive message-driven and object-
based computational model, Timed Rebeca is an easy-to-learn language for system developers, thereby bridging the gap between formal methods and practical
software engineering.

Although Rebeca is supported by a rich model checking toolset [15], model
checking of Timed Rebeca models has not been supported until now. Even
though Timed Rebeca has an SOS semantics, it lacks an executable formal
semantics that would enable automated analysis methods such as simulation
and temporal logic model checking.

However, providing an executable formal semantics for Timed Rebeca is quite
challenging. For example, since Timed Rebeca has a rich expression/statement

C. Artho and P.C. Ölveczky (Eds.): FTSCS 2013, CCIS 419, pp. 178–194, 2014.
DOI: 10.1007/978-3-319-05416-2_12, © Springer International Publishing Switzerland 2014

language that allows the values of state variables to grow beyond any bound, and since the message queues can become arbitrarily long, Timed Rebeca cannot be translated into popular real-time formalisms such as, e.g., timed automata.

In this paper, we provide a formal Real-Time Maude semantics for Timed Rebeca. Real-Time Maude [12] is a specification formalism and analysis tool for real-time systems based on rewriting logic [11]. With its natural time model and expressive formalism, which is particularly suitable for formally specifying distributed real-time systems in an object-oriented way, Real-Time Maude should be ideally suited for this challenging task. Real-Time Maude is supported by a high-performance toolset providing a spectrum of analysis methods, including simulation through timed rewriting, reachability analysis, and (untimed) linear temporal logic model checking as well as timed CTL model checking.

We have automated the translation from Timed Rebeca to Real-Time Maude, so that the user gets Real-Time Maude simulation and model checking of his/her Timed Rebeca model for free. Furthermore, such formal analysis is being integrated into the Rebeca toolset. This would of course not be very useful if the user would need to understand the Real-Time Maude representation of his/her Timed Rebeca model, and/or would need to define state properties in Real-Time Maude, in order to model check his/her Timed Rebeca model. We have therefore taken advantage of Real-Time Maude's support for *parametric* state propositions to predefine useful generic state propositions, so that the user can define his/her (possibly timed) temporal logic properties *without* having to know Real-Time Maude or understand how the mapping from Timed Rebeca works.

Altogether, this enables a formal model-engineering methodology that combines the convenience of modeling in an intuitive actor language with Java-like syntax with formal verification in Real-Time Maude. We illustrate this methodology with a collision avoidance protocol case study.

The rest of the paper is structured as follows. Section 2 briefly introduces Timed Rebeca and Real-Time Maude. Section 3 explains the Real-Time Maude formalization of the Timed Rebeca semantics. Section 4 defines some useful generic atomic state propositions that allows the user to easily define his/her temporal logic formulas without knowing Real-Time Maude. Section 5 illustrates our methodology on a collision avoidance protocol. Finally, Section 6 discusses related work and Sect. 7 gives some concluding remarks.

2   Preliminaries

2.1   Timed Rebeca

Since Timed Rebeca is an extension of the Rebeca modeling language, we first introduce Rebeca and then explain Timed Rebeca in more detail.

Rebeca [17] is a pure actor-based modeling language suitable for specifying distributed systems. Rebeca is supported by a rich model checking toolset [15].

A Rebeca model consists of a set of actors (called *rebecs*) that communicate asynchronously by message passing. Each actor maintains a queue of messages

$$
\begin{aligned}
Model &::= Class^*\ Main \\
Main &::= \mathbf{main}\ \{\ InstanceDcl^*\ \} \\
InstanceDcl &::= className\ rebecName(\langle rebecName\rangle^*) : (\langle literal\rangle^*); \\
Class &::= \mathbf{reactiveclass}\ className\ \{\ KnownRebecs\ Vars\ Constr\ MsgSrv^*\ \} \\
KnownRebecs &::= \mathbf{knownrebecs}\ \{\ VarDcl^*\ \} \\
Vars &::= \mathbf{statevars}\ \{\ VarDcl^*\ \} \\
VarDcl &::= type\ \langle v\rangle^+; \\
Constr &::= className\ methodName(\langle type\ v\rangle^*)\ \{\ Stmt^*\ \} \\
MsgSrv &::= \mathbf{msgsrv}\ methodName(\langle type\ v\rangle^*)\ \{\ Stmt^*\ \} \\
Stmt &::= v = e;\ |\ v =?(e_1,\dots,e_n)\ |\ Send;\ |\ \mathbf{if}\ (e)\ \{\ Stmt^*\ \}\ [\mathbf{else}\ \{\ Stmt^*\ \}]\ | \\
&\qquad \mathbf{delay}(e);\ |\ \mathbf{for}\ (Stmt_1;\ e;\ Stmt_2)\ \{\ Stmt^*\ \} \\
Send &::= rebecName.methodName(\langle e\rangle^*)\ [\mathbf{after}(e)]\ [\mathbf{deadline}(e)]
\end{aligned}
$$

Fig. 1. Abstract syntax of Timed Rebeca. Angle brackets $\langle\dots\rangle$ are used as meta paren-thesis. Identifiers *className*, *rebecName*, *methodName*, *v*, *literal*, and *type* denote class name, rebec name, method name, variable, literal, and type, respectively; and *e* denotes an (arithmetic or boolean) expression. In *for* loops, $Stmt_1$ is the initialization state-ment, e_2 is a boolean expression (the loop execution condition), and $Stmt_2$ is the update statement (executed after each iteration).

that it has received but not yet processed. An actor repeatedly takes a mes-sage from the beginning of its queue and executes the corresponding *message server*, which may involve sending messages to other actors and changing the actor's local state. Execution is non-preemptive: the actor does not take the next message from its queue before the running message server is finished.

A Rebeca specification defines a number of *reactive classes* and a *main* block. A reactive class defines an actor type and its behavior as well as its relationship to other actors. The body of a reactive class definition has three sections: *known rebecs*, *state variables*, and *message servers*. A rebec can only send messages to its known rebecs. The local state of a rebec is given by the values of its state variables. The type of state variables can be integer types, Boolean, and arrays.

The message servers specify how the rebecs respond to incoming messages. They may have parameters and may define local variables. The body of a message server consists of a number of statements, including assignments, conditionals, loops, and sending messages. The expressions contains common arithmetic and logical operators. The nondeterministic assignment $v =?(e_1,\dots,e_k)$ nondeter-ministically assigns (the current evaluation of) one of the expressions e_i to the variable v. Each class has a constructor (with the same name as the class) which initializes the state variables of its instances.

Timed Rebeca [1] is a timed extension of Rebeca whose abstract syntax is given in Fig. 1. The following timed features have been added for specifying distributed real-time systems:

- *delay* is a statement used to model *computation times*. Since we assume that the execution times of the other statements to be zero, the computation time must be specified by the modeler using the delay statement.
- *after* is a time tag attached to a message and defines the earliest time the message can be served, *relative* to the time when the message was sent.
- *deadline* is a time tag attached to a message which determines the expiration time of the messages, *relative* to the time when the message was sent.

When a message with tag *after t* is sent, it is added to the set of *undelivered messages* and resides there until *t* time units have elapsed. Then, it is *delivered*, i.e., appended to the receiving rebec's message queue. The messages in a rebec's queue are therefore ordered according to their delivery time (if the delivery time of two messages are the same, the order in which they are delivered is selected nondeterministically). If the deadline of a message is reached, regardless of whether it is delivered or not, the message is purged. A rebec takes a message from its queue as soon as it can (i.e., when it has finished processing the previous message, and there are some messages in the queue).

Figure 2 shows a Timed Rebeca model of a simple thermostat system composed of two actors t and h of reactive classes **Thermostat** and **Heater**, respectively. The actors are instantiated in the **main** block; e.g., **Heater h(t):();** creates an instance h of **Heater**, passing t as its known rebec, and invoking its constructor (with empty parameter list). The goal of the system is to keep the temperature between 25 and 30 degrees. The **Thermostat** actor checks the temperature every 5 time units, by sending a **checkTemp** message to itself (line 19). If the temperature is not in the acceptable range, it sends the **Heater** actor h the proper **on** or **off** message, which expires after 20 time units (lines 16 and 18). It takes two time units for the heater to turn itself on or off. The heater also models the change in the environment by nondeterministically changing the temperature by 1 to 3 degrees every 10 time units (lines 47–49), and sending the delta to the heater (line 50).

2.2   Real-Time Maude

Real-Time Maude [12,13] extends the rewriting-logic-based Maude language and tool [5] to support the formal specification and analysis of real-time systems. A Real-Time Maude timed module is a tuple (Σ, E, IR, TR), where:

- (Σ, E) is a membership equational logic [5] theory where Σ is an algebraic signature, declaring the sorts, subsorts, and functions of the system, and E a set of confluent and terminating conditional equations. (Σ, E) specifies the system's states as an algebraic data type, and must contain a specification of a sort **Time** modeling the (discrete or dense) time domain.

```
 1 | reactiveclass Thermostat {        30 |   statevars {
 2 |   knownrebecs {                    31 |     boolean on;
 3 |       Heater heater;               32 |     int delta;
 4 |   }                                33 |   }
 5 |   statevars {                      34 |   Heater() {
 6 |     int period;                    35 |     on = false;
 7 |     int temp;                      36 |     self.run();
 8 |   }                                37 |   }
 9 |   Thermostat() {                   38 |   msgsrv on() {
10 |     period = 5;                    39 |     delay(2);
11 |     temp = 25;                     40 |     on = true;
12 |     self.checkTemp();              41 |   }
13 |   }                                42 |   msgsrv off() {
14 |   msgsrv checkTemp() {             43 |     delay(2);
15 |     if (temp >= 30)                44 |     on = false;
16 |       heater.off() deadline(20);   45 |   }
17 |     if (temp <= 25)                46 |   msgsrv run(){
18 |       heater.on() deadline(20);    47 |     delta = ?(1,2,3);
19 |     self.checkTemp()               48 |     if (on == false)
20 |         after(period);            49 |       delta = -1 * delta;
21 |   }                                50 |     thermostat.changeTemp(delta);
22 |   msgsrv changeTemp(int delta) {   51 |     self.run() after(10);
23 |     temp = temp + delta;           52 |   }
24 |   }                                53 | }
   | }
                                       55 | main {
26 | reactiveclass Heater {             56 |   Thermostat t(h):();
27 |   knownrebecs {                    57 |   Heater h(t):();
28 |     Thermostat thermostat;         58 | }
29 |   }
```

Fig. 2. The Timed Rebeca model for a simple thermostat/heater system.

- *IR* is a set of (possibly conditional) *labeled instantaneous rewrite rules* specifying the system's *instantaneous* (i.e., zero-time) local transitions, written with syntax rl [*l*] : *u* => *v*, where *l* is a label. Such a rule specifies a *one-step transition* from an instance of the term *u* to the corresponding instance of the term *v*. The rules are applied *modulo* the equations E.
- *TR* is a set of (usually conditional) *tick rules*, written with syntax crl [*l*] : {*t*} => {*t'*} in Time τ if *cond*, that model time elapse. {_} is a built-in constructor of sort GlobalSystem, and τ is a term of sort Time that denotes the *duration* of the rewrite.

The initial state must be a ground term of sort GlobalSystem and must be reducible to a term of the form {*u*} using the equations in the specification.

The Real-Time Maude syntax is fairly intuitive. A function symbol f in Σ is declared with the syntax op f : s_1 ... s_n -> s, where $s_1...s_n$ are the sorts of its arguments, and s is its result *sort*. Equations are written with syntax eq $u = v$, and ceq $u = v$ if *cond* for conditional equations. The mathematical variables in such statements are declared with the keywords var and vars. An equation

$f(t_i, \ldots, t_n) = t$ with the `owise` (for "otherwise") attribute can be applied to a subterm $f(\ldots)$ only if no other equation with left-hand side $f(u_1, \ldots, u_n)$ can be applied.

A *class* declaration `class` $C \mid att_1 : s_1 , \ldots , att_n : s_n$ declares a class C with attributes att_1 to att_n of sorts s_1 to s_n, respectively. An *object* of class C is represented as a term $< O : C \mid att_1 : val_1 , \ldots , att_n : val_n >$ where O, of sort `Oid` is the object's *identifier*, and where val_1 to val_n are the current values of the attributes att_1 to att_n. The state is a term of sort `Configuration`, and has the structure of a *multiset* of objects and *messages*, with multiset union denoted by a juxtaposition operator that is declared associative and commutative, so that rewriting is *multiset rewriting*.

The dynamic behavior of concurrent object systems is axiomatized by specifying each of its transition patterns by a rewrite rule. For example, the rule

```
rl [1] :
  m(O,W)
  < O : C | a1 : X, a2 : O', a3 : Z >
  =>
  < O : C | a1 : X + W, a2 : O', a3 : Z >
  dly(m'(O'),X) .
```

defines a parameterized family of transitions in which a message `m`, with parameters `O` and `W`, is read and consumed by an object `O` of class `C`. The transitions change the attribute `a1` of the object `O` and send a new message `m'(O')` with delay `X`.

Formal Analysis. The Real-Time Maude tool provides a spectrum of analysis methods, including:

- *timed rewriting* that simulates one behavior of the system *up to certain duration* from an initial state;
- *timed search* analyzes whether a state matching a state pattern is reachable from the initial state within a certain time interval;
- *model checking* to check whether each possible behavior from the initial state satisfies a temporal logic formula. Real-Time Maude extends Maude's *linear temporal logic model checker*. *State proposition* are terms of sort `Prop`, and their semantics should be given by (possibly conditional) equations of the form $\{statePattern\} \mid= prop = b$, for a b a term of sort `Bool`, which defines the state proposition *prop* to hold in a state $\{t\}$ if $\{t\} \mid= prop$ evaluates to `true`. A temporal logic *formula* is constructed by state propositions and temporal logic operators such as `True`, `False`, $\sim$ (negation), $/\backslash$, $\backslash/$, `->` (implication), `[]` ("always"), `<>` ("eventually"), and `U` ("until"). The time-bounded model checking command has the syntax `mc` $\{t\}$ `|=t` φ `in time <=` τ `.` for initial state $\{t\}$ and temporal logic formula φ. Real-Time Maude has also recently been equipped with a model checker for *timed* computation tree logic (TCTL) properties [10].

3   Real-Time Maude Semantics of Timed Rebeca

This section explains how we have formalized the semantics of Timed Rebeca in Real-Time Maude in an object-oriented style.

Specifying the Static Parts. In the Real-Time Maude semantics of a Timed Rebeca model we need to keep track of (i) the *declarations* of the (message servers of the) reactive classes; (ii) the rebecs in their current states; and (iii) the set of as-yet undelivered messages.

Since the message servers do not change dynamically, we do not need to carry them around in the state. Instead, the message servers are modeled by a function

```
op msgServer : ClassName MsgHeader -> Statements .
```

where `msgServer`(c, m) defines the code to be executed by a rebec of reactive class c when it treats a message with header m. The sort `Statements` is a straight-forward representation of the body of a message server. For example, in our thermostat example, `msgServer(Thermostat, Thermostat)` equals

```
(period := 5) ; (temp := 25) ;
(sendSelf checkTemp with noArg deadline INF after 0)
```

and `msgServer(Thermostat, checkTemp)` equals

```
(if( temp >= 30 ) then (send off with noArg to "heater" deadline 20 after 0)) ;
(if( temp <= 25 ) then (send on  with noArg to "heater" deadline 20 after 0)) ;
(sendSelf checkTemp with noArg deadline INF after 5)
```

We also have a function `formalParams` such that `formalParams`(c, m) returns the list of the formal parameters of the message server for m in reactive class c.

We mostly omit the details of how basic Rebeca statements (e.g., assignments and evaluation of expressions) are formalized in Real-Time Maude, and refer to [3] for a thorough treatment of the Real-Time Maude formalization of the evaluation of expressions in a fairly sophisticated language. The only expression we mention is due to the possibility of having *nondeterministic assignments*. We formalize the expression list $?\,(e_1, e_2, \ldots, e_n)$ in a nondeterministic assignment as a list $e_1\,?\,e_2\,?\,\ldots\,?\,e_n$ using the following list data type:

```
sort NDExpr .    subsort Expr < NDExpr .
op nil : -> NDExpr .
op _?_ : NDExpr NDExpr -> NDExpr [assoc id: nil] .
```

Since `nil` is the identity element for lists, Maude considers l and `nil ?` l and l `? nil` to be identical lists. In particular, a single expression e is considered by Maude to be identical to the lists `nil ?` e and e `? nil` and `nil ?` e `? nil`.

The state of the Real-Time Maude representation of a Timed Rebeca model is a multiset consisting of one `Rebec` object for each rebec in the system and one message for each message in the set of undelivered messages.

A rebec is modeled by an object instance of the following class `Rebec`:

```
class Rebec | stateVars : Valuation,      queue : MsgList,
              classId : ClassName,        toExecute : Statements,
              knownRebecs : KnownList .
```

where **stateVars** represents the state variables of the rebec and the formal parameters of the message server being treated, together with their current values,
as a set of terms of the form *var-name* |-> *value*; **queue** is a ':::'-separated list
of messages representing the message queue of the rebec; **classId** is the name
of the reactive class of the rebec; **toExecute** denotes the remaining statements
the rebec has to execute (and is **noStatements** if the rebec is not executing a
message server); and **knownRebecs** denotes the "known rebecs" of the rebec.

For example, the following term models the rebec **"t"** of class **Thermostat**
right after completing its constructor. Its state variables have the values 5 and
25, there is only one message in its queue (sent by itself), and the rebec is not
executing any message server.

```
< "t" : Rebec | stateVars : ('period |-> 5) ('temp |-> 25),
                queue : (checkTemp with noArg from "t" to "t" deadline INF),
                classId : Thermostat,
                toExecute : noStatements,
                knownRebecs : (Heater heater --> "h") >
```

Communication between rebecs takes place when a rebec sends a message
to another rebec (or to itself). The message is put into the multiset of undelivered messages until its message delay ends. It is then delivered to the receiver's
message queue. *Delivered messages* are modeled using the constructor

```
msg _with_from_to_deadline_ : MsgHeader Valuation Oid Oid TimeInf -> Msg .
```

A delivered message therefore contains a header (the message name), its arguments, the id of the sender rebec, the id of the receiver, and the time remaining
until the expiration (deadline) of the message. *Delayed messages* have the form
$dly(m, t)$, where m is a message as above and t is the remaining delay of the
message, and where $dly(m, 0)$ is considered to be identical to m [12].

Instantaneous Transitions. We next formalize the instantaneous actions of a
Timed Rebeca rebec using rewrite rules. We show 9 of the 16 rewrite rules that
define our semantics of the Timed Rebeca.

In the following rule, an idle rebec takes the first message from its queue and
starts executing the statements in the corresponding message server by putting
those statements into its **toExecute** attribute. Some additional bookkeeping is
also required: the formal parameters of the message server must be initialized to
the values in the message and added to the state variables; to clean up at the
end of the execution, we add a new statement **removeVars** to execute *after* the
statements in the message server have been executed:[1]

---

[1] In this paper we follow the Maude convention that variables are written with (only)
capital letters, and do not show the variable declarations.

```
rl [takeMessage] :
   < O : Rebec | stateVars : SVARS,
                 queue : (M with VAL from O' deadline DL) :: MSGLIST,
                 classId : C, toExecute : noStatements >
  =>
   < O : Rebec | stateVars : SVARS  VAL ('sender |-> O'),
                 queue : MSGLIST,
                 toExecute : msgServer(C,M) ; removeVars(VAL ('sender |-> O')) >.
```

Because of the possibility of having nondeterministic assignments, the rewrite rule modeling (both deterministic and nondeterministic) assignment is interesting. The following rule uses pattern matching and the fact that the list concatenation operator ? is declared to be associate and to have identity **nil** to nondeterministically select *any* possibly expression **EX** from a list of expressions. This rule also covers *deterministic* assignment, since the list variables LIST1 and LIST2 may both match the empty list **nil**. In addition, the rebec updates its **toExecute** attribute to only execute the remaining statements:

```
rl [detAndNondetAssignment]  :
   < O : Rebec | stateVars : (VAR |-> VAL) SVARS,
                 toExecute : (VAR := LIST1 ? EX ? LIST2) ; STMTLIST >
  =>
   < O : Rebec | stateVars : (VAR |-> evalExp(EX, (VAR |-> VAL) SVARS)) SVARS,
                 toExecute : STMTLIST > .
```

We next describe the semantics of loops **for** (*init*; *cond*; *update*){*body*}, where *init* is a statement executed once in the beginning, *cond* is a Boolean expression that must be true to continue the iterations, *update* is a statement executed after each iteration, and *body* is a statement list executed in each iteration. The semantics of loops is formalized in a standard "unfolding" style:

```
rl [forLoop] :
   < O : Rebec | toExecute : for(INIT, COND, UPDATE, BODY) ; STMTLIST >
  =>
   < O : Rebec | toExecute : INIT ; iterate(COND, UPDATE, BODY) ; STMTLIST > .

rl [iterate] :
   < O : Rebec | stateVars : SVARS,
                 toExecute : iterate(COND, UPDATE, BODY) ; STMTLIST >
  =>
   < O : Rebec | toExecute : if evalBoolExp(COND, SVARS) then
                               BODY ; UPDATE ; iterate(COND, UPDATE, BODY) ; STMTLIST
                             else STMTLIST fi > .
```

If the first statement is a send statement, the rebec creates a delayed message which is added to the undelivered message soup.

```
rl [sendMessage] :
   < O : Rebec | stateVars : SVARS,
                 toExecute : (send M with ARGS to REC deadline DL after AFT)
                             ; STMTLIST , knownRebecs : (CN NK --> RCVR) NL >
  =>
```

```
< 0 : Rebec | toExecute :  STMTLIST >
dly(M with getVals(ARGS, SVARS, formalParams(CN,M)) from 0 to RCVR
        deadline evalIntExp(DL,SVARS),
      evalIntExp(AFT,SVARS)) .
```

Both DL and AFT are expressions evaluated using evalIntExp in the context
of the current variable assignment SVARS. The created message is added to the
system configuration; when its remaining delay becomes 0, the message becomes
"undelayed" as explained above, and can be received by the intended recipient,
which puts the message into its message queue:

```
rl [readMessage] :
  (M with ARGS from 0 to 0' deadline DL )
  < 0' : Rebec | queue : MSGLIST >
=>
  < 0' : Rebec | queue : MSGLIST :: (M with ARGS from 0 deadline DL) > .
```

Another interesting case is the execution of a delay statement, which is
treated as follows: When the rebec encounters the delay statement, it evaluates
the delay expression using the current values of the variables. Once it has done
that, it leaves the delay statement in the beginning of its toExecute attribute
until the remaining delay becomes 0, when the rebec just continues with the next
statement. Decreasing the remaining delay is done by the tick rule below. The
following rules then, respectively, evaluate the delay expression at the beginning
of the delay, and finish the delay when the remaining delay is 0:

```
crl [evaluateDelayExpression] :
  < 0 : Rebec | stateVars : SVARS, toExecute : delay(EX) ; STMTLIST >
  =>
  < 0 : Rebec | toExecute :  delay(evalIntExp(EX, SVARS)) ; STMTLIST  >
  if not (EX :: Int) .

rl [endDelay] :
  < 0 : Rebec | toExecute : delay(0) ; STMTLIST >
  =>
  < 0 : Rebec | toExecute :  STMTLIST  > .
```

Timed Behavior. The following "standard" object-oriented tick rule [12] is
used to model time advance until the next time when something must "happen":

```
var SYSTEM : Configuration .
crl [tick] : {SYSTEM}  => {elapsedTime(SYSTEM, mte(SYSTEM))} in time mte(SYSTEM)
             if mte(SYSTEM) > 0 .
```

The variable SYSTEM matches the entire state of the system. The function mte
(*m*aximal *t*ime *e*lapse) determines how much time can advance in a given state.
If an instantaneous rule is enabled, it must be executed immediately; therefore,
mte of a state must be zero when an instantaneous rule is enabled in that state.

The function mte is the minimum of the mte of each rebec and each message
in the soup. As mentioned above, the mte must be 0 when the rebec has a

statement to execute which does not have the form **delay**(i), for an integer i; in the latter case, the mte equals i. If there are no statements to be executed, the mte equals 0 if the rebec has a message in its queue, and equals the infinity value INF if the message queue is empty:

```
op mte : Configuration -> TimeInf [frozen (1)] .
eq mte(none) = INF.
eq mte(dly(M,T)  CONF) = min(T, mte(CONF)) .
ceq mte(OBJECT CONF) = min(mte(OBJECT), mte(CONF)) if CONF =/= none .
eq mte(< O : Rebec | toExecute : noStatements, queue : empty >) = INF .
eq mte(< O : Rebec | toExecute : delay(T) ; STMTLIST >) = T .
eq mte(< O : Rebec | >) = 0 [owise] .
```

The function `elapsedTime` models the effect of time elapse on a state as follows: The effect of time elapse on a rebec is that the remaining time until the message deadline is decreased according to the elapsed time for each message in the queue. Furthermore, the remaining delay of a delay statement being executed is also decreased according to the elapsed time. For messages traveling between rebecs, their remaining delays and deadline are decreased according to the elapsed time. In both cases, if the deadline expires before the message is treated, the message is purged (i.e., becomes the empty configuration **none**):

```
op elapsedTime : Configuration Time -> Configuration [frozen (1)] .
eq elapsedTime(none, T) = none .
eq elapsedTime(dly(M with ARGS from O to O' deadline T1, T2)  CONF, T)
 = (if T2 <= T1 then dly(M with ARGS from O to O' deadline (T1 - T), T2 - T)
    else none fi)  elapsedTime(CONF, T) .
eq elapsedTime(< O : Rebec | toExecute : STMTLIST, queue : MSGLIST > CONF, T)
 = < O : Rebec | toExecute : decreaseDelay(STMTLIST, T),
                 queue : decreaseDeadline(MSGLIST, T) >  elapsedTime(CONF, T) .

op decreaseDelay : StatementList Time -> StatementList .
eq decreaseDelay(delay(T1) ; STMTLIST, T) = delay(T1 - T) ; STMTLIST .
eq decreaseDelay(STMTLIST, T) = STMTLIST [owise] .
op decreaseDeadlines : MsgList Time -> MsgList .
eq decreaseDeadlines(nil, T) = nil .
eq decreaseDeadlines((M with ARGS from O to O' deadline T1) :: MSGLIST, T)
 = (if T <= T1 then (M with ARGS from O to O' deadline T1 - T) else none fi)
   decreaseDeadlines(MSGLIST, T) .
```

4   Formal Analysis of Timed Rebeca Models

We have automated the translation of Timed Rebeca models to Real-Time Maude. The translator is currently being integrated into RMC (Rebeca Model Checker) [15] to support Real-Time Maude simulation, reachability analysis, and untimed LTL and timed CTL model checking of Timed Rebeca models from within the Rebeca toolset. To allow the Timed Rebeca modeler to define his/her LTL and TCTL formulas without having to know anything about the Real-Time Maude representation of his/her model, and without having to know how to define atomic state propositions in Real-Time Maude, we have predefined a number of useful generic atomic propositions. LTL and TCTL formulas can then be defined using these propositions and the usual logical operators such as ~ (not), /\ (conjunction), etc., linear temporal logic operators such as [] (always), <> (eventually), etc., and timed CTL operators such as AG (always), AF[<= than t] (always reachable within time t), etc.

We have defined atomic propositions on the *state variables* of the rebecs. The value of a state variable can be compared to constants of the same type using common relational operators such as is (equality) and <= . For example, the proposition   *variable* of *rebec* <= *value*   holds if the current value of the state variable *variable* in the rebec *rebec* is less than or equal to *value*:

```
ops _of_is_ _of_<=_ _of_<_ ... : IntVar Oid Int -> Prop .
eq {CONF < O : Rebec | stateVars : (V |-> I) VAL >} |= V of O is J = I == J .
eq {CONF < O : Rebec | stateVars : (V |-> I) VAL >} |= V of O <= J = I <= J .
```

As an example, temp of "h" <= 30 is true if the temp state variable of the rebec h is less than or equal to 30.

Likewise, we have defined generic propositions o hasSent m to o', denoting that rebec o has sent a message with header m to the rebec o' and that the message is still in the network; and o hasReceived m from o' (the message with header m is already in o's queue), and the more generic o hasReceived m:

```
ops _hasSent_to_ _hasReceived_from_ : Oid MsgHeader Oid -> Prop .
eq {CONF dly((MN with VAL from O to O' deadline T), T')}
    |= O hasSent MN to O' = true .
eq {CONF  < O : Rebec | queue : ML1 :: (MN with VAL from O' to O deadline T) :: ML2 >}
    |= O hasReceived MN from O' = true .
op _hasReceived_ : Oid MsgHeader -> Prop [ctor] .
eq {CONF < O : Rebec | queue : ML1 :: (MN with VAL from O' to O deadline T) :: ML2 >}
    |= O hasReceived MN = true .
```

We can now easily define temporal logic properties of our Timed Rebeca models:

```
[] ((temp of "t" >= 30) -> <> (on of "h" is false))
```

5   Case Study: A Collision Avoidance Protocol

This section illustrates our modeling and verification methodology on the IEEE 802.11 RTS/CTS protocol for collision avoidance in wireless networks [7]. When a node decides to send data to another node, it sends a *Request to Send* (RTS) message to the destination node, which is expected to reply with a *Clear to Send* (CTS) message. Other nodes in the network which receive RTS or CTS messages wait for a certain amount of time, making the medium free for the two communicating nodes. This mechanism also solves the *hidden node problem*, which occurs when two nodes want to send data to the same node. The destination node is in the range of both senders, but the senders are out of the range of each other (hence, unaware of each other's decision to send a message). In the protocol, the destination node sends a CTS message to only one of the senders. The other sender waits for a random amount of time, and then sends an RTS message to the destination node. Furthermore, this protocol solves the *exposed node problem* as well, where two adjacent nodes send data to two different destination nodes, so that the interference of data transfer of adjacent senders results in message collision. The problem is solved by preventing the senders from sending data after receiving the CTS message from other sender nodes.

We have analyzed the following properties of our Timed Rebeca model:

- *Collision freedom:* there are not data messages from two different senders at the same time.
- *Starvation avoidance:* A node that wants to send data to any destination will eventually be able to do so.
- *Delivery time bound:* There must be an upper time bound on the data transfer to a node that is not in the radio transmission range of the sender; this time bound depends on the network topology and delays.

Our model uses the reactive classes `Node` and `RadioTransfer`. Each `Node` knows a `RadioTransfer` rebec, which is responsible for broadcasting its messages to all nodes in the node's transmission range. To transmit data, the sender sends an RTS message to the receiver (through its `RadioTransfer` rebec) and waits for the response. When an RTS message is delivered, the receiver checks wether the network is busy. If so, it sends an RTS message to itself after a random `backOff` (modeled by a nondeterministic choice among the values $\{2, 3, 4\}$). If the receiver is not the target of the message, it marks the status of the network as busy. Otherwise, it sends a CTS message to the sender. Receiving an RTS message is handled by the following message server:

```
msgsrv rcvRTS(byte sndr, byte rcvr) {
    if (rcvr == id)
        if (channelIdle)  radioTransfer.passCTS(id, sndr);
        else  self.rcvRTS(sndr,rcvr) after(backOff);
    else
        channelIdle = false;
}
```

When a node receives a CTS message, it checks whether it is the target of the message. If so, it sends its data. If not, it sets the network status to idle:

```
msgsrv rcvCTS(byte sndr,byte rcvr) {
    if (rcvr == id)  self.sendData();
    else  channelIdle = true;
}
```

We have performed the analysis on a 2.53 GHz Intel processor with 2 GB RAM, running Ubuntu 10.10. The case examined has four nodes in a ring topology (each node has two adjacent nodes in its communication range). We have analyzed different transmission topologies to also analyze the hidden node and the exposed node problems.

To verify collision freedom, we must ensure that no two messages with different senders exist in radio transfer range, which can be verified for all behaviors up to time 1000 using the following model checking command:

```
(mc initState |=t
  []  ~  (  (("node1" hasSent passData) /\ ("node2" hasSent passData))
       \/ (("node2" hasSent passData) /\ ("node3" hasSent passData))
       \/ (("node3" hasSent passData) /\ ("node4" hasSent passData))
       \/ (("node4" hasSent passData) /\ ("node1" hasSent passData)) )
  in time <= 1000 .)
```

The model checking result reported by Real-Time Maude in 5 min was true.

To analyze starvation freedom we use the following command, which states that each node will eventually (within time 1000) be able to send a data message:

```
(mc initState |=t (<> ("node1" hasSent passData to "radioTransfer1")) /\
    (<> ("node2" hasSent passData to "radioTransfer2")) /\
    (<> ("node3" hasSent passData to "radioTransfer3")) /\
    (<> ("node4" hasSent passData to "radioTransfer4")) in time <= 1000 .)
```

This model checking command returns a counterexample, since the protocol suffers from starvation.

To analyze whether the upper time bound for a transmission from node 1 to node 3 via node 2 is less than t, we can use the TCTL formula $\forall\Box(s_{12} \to \forall\Diamond^{\leq t}r_{32})$, where s_{12} is true if node 1 has just sent a message to node 2, and r_{32} is true if node 3 has just received the message from node 2. This can be verified using the following command for $t = 6$:

```
(mc-tctl initState |= AG ( ("node1" hasSent passData to "node2") implies
           (AF[<= than 6] ("node3" hasRcv rcvData from "node2")) ) .)
```

The protocol fails to satisfy this property, because of the starvation. But changing AF to EF makes the property hold; i.e., for all possible behaviors from the initial state, there exists a path where the transmission can take place in less than 6 time units. Model checking this property took around 20 hours.

6   Related Work

Timed Actor Models. Although there are some actor-based modeling languages for real-time systems, their lack of effective analysis tools is a significant obstacle to applying formal verification to real systems. In some cases, assertion-based verification is suggested to analyze invariance and other safety properties. However, there is need for more general verification methods, such as model checking liveness properties and other (timed or untimed) temporal logic properties.

One real-time actor-based modeling language is RTSynchronizer [16]. The formalism specifies the model in terms of a number of actors and a global synchronizer which simulates the timed behavior of the actors. Each actor is extended with timing assumptions which are used by the synchronizer to figure out the ready-to-execute messages of the actor. In contrast with the "pure" actor language Timed Rebeca, the computation in RTSynchronizer takes place through interactions between the synchronizer and the actors. RTSynchronizer provides limited verification by placing the desired invariant properties in the body of the actors, but this approach does not support the model checking of more general temporal logic properties. (See also below.)

Creol is an actor-based language for modeling concurrent objects enriched by synchronization patterns and type system [8]. Jaghouri et al. add timing features to Creol in [4], where they also develop a schedulability analysis technique, but, again, there is no support for temporal logic verification of such models.

Work on Timed Rebeca. Aceto et al. in [1] suggested a mapping from Timed Rebeca models to Erlang for simulation (but not further formal analysis) purposes. A semantics based on *floating-time transition system* was recently proposed for Timed Rebeca [9]. Schedulability and deadlock-freedom can be checked efficiently using this semantics, but no state-based property can be verified.

Real-Time Maude as a Semantic Framework. Because of its expressiveness and natural object-oriented model of distributed real-time systems, Real-Time Maude has proved to be a suitable semantic framework in which a number of formal modeling languages have been given a formal semantics. Examples of such modeling languages include Ptolemy II discrete-event models, the Orc web orchestration language, subsets and synchronous versions of the avionics modeling standard AADL, timed model transformation frameworks, and so on (see [14] for an overview). However, the only work on Real-Time Maude semantics for timed actor languages is the work by Ding et al. [6] on the above-mentioned quite different RTSynchronizer model. Unfortunately, no details about the Real-Time Maude semantics are given in [6], and it seems that their work does not define the semantics for the entire language, but only for the case study of a Simplex architecture modeled using RTSynchronizer. Furthermore, no attempts at temporal logic model checking were performed in [6].

7   Conclusion

Using Real-Time Maude, we have defined the first executable formal semantics of Timed Rebeca. This enables a wide range of formal analysis methods for Timed Rebeca models, including simulation, reachability analysis, and both timed and untimed temporal logic model checking. We have integrated such Real-Time Maude analysis of Timed Rebeca models into the Rebeca toolset, and have defined a number of useful atomic propositions, allowing the Timed Rebeca user to define her desired properties without knowing Real-Time Maude. We illustrated such verification of Timed Rebeca models on a collision avoidance protocol.

Since Timed Rebeca, with its Java-like syntax and simple and intuitive actor-based communication model, should be easy to learn and use for people unfamiliar with formal methods, our work bridges the gap between practitioners and formal methods, since it enables a model-engineering methodology that combines the convenience of Timed Rebeca modeling with powerful formal analysis in Real-Time Maude.

We have focused on providing a clean and intuitive semantics. If states encountered *during* the execution of a message server do not matter for the properties we are interested in, we could significantly optimize the semantics by executing together, in one step, all the statements in a message server. This would significantly reduce the number of interleavings and would drastically improve the model checking performance. Finally, although the counterexamples from the Real-Time Maude analyses should be fairly easy to understand, we should nevertheless provide them in terms of the Timed Rebeca model.

References

1. Aceto, L., Cimini, M., Ingólfsdóttir, A., Reynisson, A.H., Sigurdarson, S.H., Sirjani, M.: Modelling and simulation of asynchronous real-time systems using Timed Rebeca. In: Proceedings of the FOCLASA'11. EPTCS, vol. 58 (2011)
2. Agha, G.: ACTORS - A Model of Concurrent Computation in Distributed Systems. MIT Press series in artificial intelligence. MIT Press, Cambridge (1990)
3. Bae, K., Ölveczky, P.C., Feng, T.H., Lee, E.A., Tripakis, S.: Verifying hierarchical Ptolemy II discrete-event models using Real-Time Maude. Sci. Comput. Program. **77**(12), 1235–1271 (2012)
4. de Boer, F., Chothia, T., Jaghoori, M.M.: Modular schedulability analysis of concurrent objects in Creol. In: Arbab, F., Sirjani, M. (eds.) FSEN 2009. LNCS, vol. 5961, pp. 212–227. Springer, Heidelberg (2010)
5. Clavel, M., Durán, F., Eker, S., Lincoln, P., Martí-Oliet, N., Meseguer, J., Talcott, C. (eds.): All About Maude. LNCS, vol. 4350. Springer, Heidelberg (2007)
6. Ding, H., Zheng, C., Agha, G., Sha, L.: Automated verification of the dependability of object-oriented real-time systems. In: Proceedings of the WORDS Fall. IEEE (2003)
7. IEEE Standard for Information Technology - Specific Requirements Part 11: Wireless LAN Medium Access Control (MAC) and Physical Layer (PHY). IEEE Std 802.11e-2005 (Amendment to IEEE Std 802.11, 1999 Edition (Reaff 2003)) (2005)
8. Johnsen, E.B., Owe, O.: An asynchronous communication model for distributed concurrent objects. Softw. Syst. Model. **6**(1), 39–58 (2007)
9. Khamespanah, E., Sabahi, Z., Khosravi, R., Sirjani, M., Izadi, M.: Timed-rebeca schedulability and deadlock-freedom analysis using floating-time transition system. In: AGERE!'12, SPLASH Workshops. ACM (2012)
10. Lepri, D., Ábrahám, E., Ölveczky, P.C.: Timed CTL model checking in Real-Time Maude. In: Durán, F. (ed.) WRLA 2012. LNCS, vol. 7571, pp. 182–200. Springer, Heidelberg (2012)
11. Meseguer, J.: Conditioned rewriting logic as a united model of concurrency. Theoret. Comput. Sci. **96**(1), 73–155 (1992)
12. Ölveczky, P.C., Meseguer, J.: Semantics and pragmatics of Real-Time Maude. High.-Order Symbolic Comput. **20**(1–2), 161–196 (2007)
13. Ölveczky, P.C., Meseguer, J.: The Real-Time Maude tool. In: Ramakrishnan, C.R., Rehof, J. (eds.) TACAS 2008. LNCS, vol. 4963, pp. 332–336. Springer, Heidelberg (2008)
14. Ölveczky, P.C.: Semantics, simulation, and formal analysis of modeling languages for embedded systems in Real-Time Maude. In: Agha, G., Danvy, O., Meseguer, J. (eds.) Formal Modeling: Actors, Open Systems, Biological Systems. LNCS, vol. 7000, pp. 368–402. Springer, Heidelberg (2011)

15. Rebeca Language Home Page. http://www.rebeca-lang.org
16. Ren, S., Agha, G.: RTsynchronizer: language support for real-time specifications in distributed systems. In: Proceedings of the LCT-RTS'95. ACM (1995)
17. Sirjani, M., Movaghar, A., Shali, A., de Boer, F.S.: Modeling and verification of reactive systems using Rebeca. Fundam. Inform. **63**(4), 385–410 (2004)

On the Cloud-Enabled Refinement Checking of Railway Signalling Interlockings

Andrew Simpson[✉] and Jaco Jacobs

Department of Computer Science, University of Oxford, Wolfson Building,
Parks Road, Oxford OX1 3QD, UK
Andrew.Simpson@cs.ox.ac.uk

Abstract. Railway signalling systems have received a great deal of attention from the formal methods community. One reason for this is that the domain is relatively accessible; another is that the safety analyses to be undertaken are often highly parallelizable. In this paper we describe a 'cloud interface' for the refinement checker, Failures Divergences Refinement (FDR), which has been motivated and validated by an approach to the modelling and analysis of railway signalling interlockings.

1 Introduction

Railway signalling systems have received a great deal of attention from the formal methods community. Early contributions include those of Hansen [1], Morley [2], and Haxthausen and Peleska [3]. More recent contributions include those of Kanso et al. [4], James and Roggenbach [5], and Haxthausen et al. [6]. In many ways, this level of attention is unsurprising. First, the domain is relatively accessible, enabling researchers to comprehend the problem at hand, and communicate their intentions and solutions to a receptive audience. Another reason for this is the fact that the safety-criticality of the domain is attractive to formal methods researchers [7]. The body of work is substantial: one only has to consider the FMERail contributions from the late 1990s,[1] the fact that such applications are considered a success story for the formal methods community (see, for example, [8]), and the forthcoming 2013 Workshop on a Formal Methods Body of Knowledge for Railway Control and Safety Systems.[2] We would argue that another reason for this relative success is that the safety analyses that can be undertaken are — depending on the model and the approach used — often highly parallelizable. To this end, decomposition approaches have been proposed by Winter and Robinson [9] and Simpson et al. [10], as well as others.

In this paper we revisit the contribution of [10] — which utilised Communicating Sequential Processes (CSP) [11,12] and the associated refinement checker Failures Divergences Refinement (FDR) [13,14] — as a means of motivating and validating a cloud-enabled approach to refinement checking. Specifically,

---

[1] See http://www2.imm.dtu.dk/~dibj/fmerail/fmerail/.
[2] See http://ssfmgroup.wordpress.com/.

C. Artho and P.C. Ölveczky (Eds.): FTSCS 2013, CCIS 419, pp. 195–211, 2014.
DOI: 10.1007/978-3-319-05416-2_13, © Springer International Publishing Switzerland 2014

we utilise the open source Eucalyptus framework [15] to demonstrate how the theoretical decomposition approach described in [10] can be made practical — enabling the checking of systems consisting of billions of states in a matter of minutes.

The structure of the remainder of this paper is as follows. In Sect. 2 we provide necessarily brief introductions to CSP, FDR, and our case study. Then, in Sect. 3, we discuss our cloud-enabled interface for FDR. We present our case study in Sect. 4. Finally, in Sect. 5, we summarise our contribution, and outline our plans for future work in this area.

2   On CSP, FDR, and GDL

2.1   CSP and FDR

The language of CSP is a notation for describing the behaviour of concurrently-evolving objects, or *processes*, in terms of their interaction with their environment. This interaction is modelled in terms of *events*: abstract, instantaneous, synchronisations that may be shared between several processes. We denote the set of all events within a given context as Σ; we can also give consideration to the *alphabet* of a process — the events that it can perform.

We use compound events to represent communication. The event name $c.x$ may represent the communication of a value x on a *channel* named c. At the event level, no distinction is made between *input* and *output*: the willingness to engage in a variety of similar events — the readiness to accept input — is modelled at the process level; the same is true of output, which corresponds to an insistence upon a particular event from a range of possibilities.

A *process* describes the pattern of availability of certain events. The prefix process $e \to P$ is ready to engage in event e; should this event occur, the subsequent behaviour is that of the process P.

An external (or deterministic) choice of processes $P \,\square\, Q$ is resolved through interaction with the environment — the first event to occur will determine the subsequent behaviour. If this event was possible for only one of the two alternatives, then the choice will go on to behave as that process. If it was possible for both, then the choice becomes non-deterministic. This form of choice exists in an indexed form: $\square\ i : I \bullet P(i)$ is an external choice between processes $P(i)$, where i ranges over the (finite) indexing set I.

We may denote input in one of two ways. The process $c?x \to P$ is willing initially to accept any value (of the appropriate type) on channel c. Alternatively, if we wish to restrict the set of possible input values to a subset of the type associated with the channel c, then we may write $\square\ x : X \bullet c.x \to P$.

There are various flavours of parallel combinations, but in this paper we limit ourselves to only one: we write $P \parallel Q$ to denote that the component processes P and Q cooperate upon the events appearing in the alphabets of both P and Q, with the events falling outside the intersection occurring independently.

The standard notion of refinement for CSP processes, which is defined in [16], is based upon the failures/divergences model of CSP. In this model, each process is associated with a set of behaviours: tuples of sequences and sets that record the occurrence and availability of events.

The *traces* of a process P, denoted *traces* $[P]$, are finite sequences of events in which P may participate *in that order*; the *failures* of P, denoted *failures* $[P]$, are pairs of the form (tr, X), such that tr is a trace of P and X is a set of events which may be refused by P after the trace tr has been observed. (We shall not concern ourselves with divergences.)

We write $P \sqsubseteq_M Q$ when the process Q refines the process P under the model M: Q is 'at least as good as' P. With respect to failures, the formal definition is as follows:

$$P \sqsubseteq_F Q \Leftrightarrow traces\,[\![Q]\!] \subseteq traces\,[\![P]\!] \wedge failures\,[\![Q]\!] \subseteq failures\,[\![P]\!]$$

It is the relationship that exists between refinement and parallel composition that makes the combination of CSP and FDR an attractive choice for the task at hand: namely, it allows us to decompose large problems into a larger number of smaller ones. In the following, we rely upon the fact that, if we know that $P \sqsubseteq_F Q$ holds, then — provided that R has nothing to say about the events of P (that is to say, that its alphabet doesn't contain any of those events) — we can conclude that $P \sqsubseteq_F Q \parallel R$ holds also.

The refinement checker FDR — which utilises the machine-readable dialect of CSP, CSP_M (see, for example, [17]) — uses this theory of refinement to investigate whether a potential design meets its specification.

2.2   Solid State Interlocking

Given the safety-critical nature of railway interlockings, it is important to be able to guarantee a range of safety properties. The complexity of automating this task is characterised by Ferrari *et al.* thus:

> "It is a well known fact that interlocking systems, due to their inherent complexity related to the high number of variables involved, are not amenable to automatic verification, typically incurring the state space explosion problem." [18]

Following [10], we consider *Solid State Interlocking* (SSI) [19] as a case study. SSI is a computer-based control system, the software of which can be divided into generic and specific components. The latter (our concern) varies between locations and describes the signalling functions for that particular instance. We shall use the simple junction of Fig. 1 to illustrate a manageable (but still meaningful) subset of the components of interest.

The track is divided into segments by *track circuits* (TAA, etc.), with each circuit being fitted with a detection device that informs the interlocking if a specific segment is *occupied* (o) or *clear* (c). *Sets of points* help trains navigate junctions and can be either *controlled normal* (cn) or *controlled reverse* (cr).

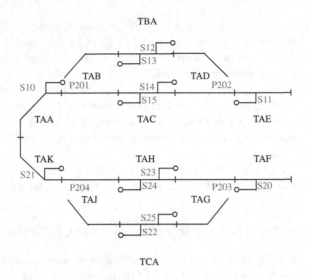

Fig. 1. The Open Alvey interlocking

As an example (and with respect to Fig. 1), if a train is travelling over track circuit TAK towards track circuit TAJ and points P204 are in controlled reverse position, then the train will follow the section of track covering track circuit TCA. Conversely, if points P204 are in the controlled normal position, the train will continue along track circuit TAJ towards TAH. Boolean checks may be performed on a set of points: these checks indicate whether it is free to move into the controlled normal (*free to go normal*) or controlled reverse (*free to go reverse*) directions. A set of points is *controlled free to go normal* (cfn) if it is free to go normal or if it is already in controlled normal; a set of points is *controlled free to go reverse* (cfr) if it is free to go reverse or if it is already in controlled reverse. A *signal* grants a requesting train entry onto the particular section of track that is under its control. Signal S11, for example, is concerned with track circuits TAD, TAC and TBA. A *route* is a section of track between two signals: route R13 is the section of track between the entry signal S13 and the exit signal S21, running over three track circuits (TAB, TAA and TAK) and one set of points (P201). A route can be *requested* (req), *set* (s), or *unset* (xs). *Subroutes* are sections of routes associated with track circuits; there may exist several subroutes over a particular track circuit. Track circuit TAB, for example, has three entry/exit points (TAA, TAC and TBA), which are labelled clockwise from a 12:00 position. Entry (or exit) from (or to) circuit TBA is labelled A, entry (exit) from (to) TAC is labelled B, and C is associated with entry (exit) from (to) TAA. Subroute UAB_AC is associated with track circuit TAB, with entry from track circuit TBA and exit at track circuit TAA. A subroute can either be *locked* (l) or *free* (f).

The *Geographic Data Language* (GDL) [20] describes conditions for setting routes, releasing subroutes, etc. We restrict ourselves to a subset of GDL in the following.

As an example, route R14 runs from signal S14 over track circuits TAD and TAE and points P202. The condition for setting this route is written

$$\text{Q14 } \textbf{if} \quad \text{P202 cfn} \quad \text{UAE\_AB f} \quad \text{UAD\_AB f}$$
$$\textbf{then } \text{R14 s} \quad \text{P202 cn} \quad \text{UAD\_BA l} \quad \text{UAE\_BA l}$$

This tests if points P202 are controlled free to go normal and if subroutes UAE_AB and UAD_AB are free. If they are, the route can be set: points P202 are set to controlled normal, and subroutes UAD_BA and UAE_BA are locked.

Our second type of conditional check pertains to subroutes becoming free. Consider again route R14. When this route is set, subroutes UAD_BA and UAE_BA are both locked. The condition for releasing UAE_BA is written

$$\text{UAE\_BA f } \textbf{if} \quad \text{TAE c} \quad \text{UAD\_BA f} \quad \text{UAD\_CA f}$$

Here, UAE_BA becomes free when track circuit TAE is clear, and subroutes UAD_BA and UAD_CA are both free.

There are minor variations on this pattern. For example, for UAD_BA to become free, track circuit TAD must be clear and route R14 must be unset:

$$\text{UAD\_BA f } \textbf{if} \quad \text{TAD c} \quad \text{R14 xs}$$

In [21] a number of safety invariants are listed, including:

1. If a route is set, then all of its subroutes are locked.
2. For every track circuit, at most one of subroutes passing over it should be locked for a route at any time.
3. If a subroute over a track circuit containing points is locked for a route, then the points are correctly aligned with that subroute.
4. If a track circuit containing points are occupied, then the points are locked.
5. If a subroute is locked for a route, then all subroutes ahead of it on that route are also locked.

In [10,21] an approach to the modelling, decomposition and analysis of GDL representations is described. By taking advantage of the relationship that exists between refinement and process composition in the failures model of CSP (as outlined in Sect. 2.1), it is shown how safety checks of potentially billions of states might be decomposed into hundreds of thousands of checks of hundreds or thousands of states — giving rise to the potential for a parallelized refinement-checking process. In the following, we show how that largely theoretical process has been made practical via a cloud-enabled interface for FDR.

3 A Cloud-Enabled FDR

3.1 Eucalyptus

Cloud computing — an aggregate of multi-core, multi-processor, distributed compute nodes — enables access to a range of configurable and reliable computing resources that can scale on demand, which, from an automated verification perspective, is extremely desirable. The nature of such activity is bursty: large quantities of computing resources, particularly memory and processing power, are required only when checks are being executed. It follows that the notion of having significant quantities of resources available 'on demand' sits comfortably with automated verification: it provides a viable approach to alleviate the state space explosion problem and has the potential to increase throughput. The notion of computing resources as a utility that can be provisioned and relinquished as needed is a powerful one: it creates the illusion of infinite computing resources, available on-demand, with no prior commitment as to how long they are used. Moreover, when the computing resources are no longer required, they can be released without incurring any penalties.

Cloud computing provision is typically characterised as one of *Infrastructure as a Service* (IaaS), *Platform as a Service* (PaaS), and *Software as a Service* (SaaS). The first of these is our concern, with the core idea being that computing resources should behave like physical hardware. Users select, control and configure an entire virtualised server, consisting of the operating system kernel, plus all required applications and data; administrative tasks are typically automated. By having computing instances at such a low level we place few limitations on the software that can ultimately be deployed in this context.

Eucalyptus is an open source cloud computing platform that provides an API for provisioning, managing and relinquishing virtual machines in an IaaS cloud [15]. A virtual machine, or *instance*, runs on top of a *hypervisor*, which provides the capabilities necessary in order to provide an isolated computing environment. When a user wishes to start a new instance in the Eucalyptus cloud, they do so using a pre-defined machine image, which includes the operating system and any other pre-built software required. It is possible to customise these, create a new image, and then launch the instance using the custom image; this is a *Eucalyptus Machine Image* (EMI).

Eucalyptus is composed of several components that interact through SOAP interfaces. These components are: *node controllers* (NC in Fig. 2), which control VM-related activities on a compute node; *cluster controllers* (CC), which manage the node controllers within their clusters; *storage controllers* (SC), which can be attached to an instance file system as a volume; *Walrus*, a service that provides a mechanism for cloud-based persistent storage; and the *cloud controller* (CLC), which facilitates the management of the cloud as a whole.

3.2   A Cloud Interface for FDR

Parallel model checking techniques typically partition the state space. Our approach involves partitioning the problem not at the level of the state space, but, rather, at the level of the model. Conceptually, we have a CSP model, with a requirement being that the model is such that it allows for checks (expressed as refinements) to be broken down into several, smaller refinements. Once this partitioning is achieved, the refinement checks can then be allocated to a farm of processors to be either confirmed or refuted. (We readily acknowledge that

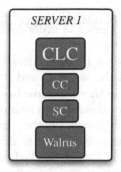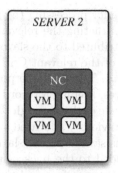

Fig. 2. Eucalyptus set-up

only certain classes of problem will be amenable to such an approach. In particular, its relevance is limited to safety properties; liveness properties could not be checked in this way.)

Thus, our process is as follows.

1. Take as input a text file containing a CSP problem description.
2. Automatically derive process definitions from the input file.
3. Automatically extract appropriate process definitions and generate refinement checks by composing the process definitions relevant to the particular refinement check.
4. Distribute the refinement checks to compute nodes (each running a server version of FDR).
5. Collect the results and display the end result.

Our case study is characteristic of a problem that can be decomposed into independent refinement checks and then distributed to various processing nodes: input to the model checker is a text file representing data for a particular railway interlocking; the CSP model is then automatically derived (along with refinement checks) to assert various safety conditions. These checks can then be distributed to the various processing nodes.

Eucalyptus is used to provide the private infrastructure as a service cloud.[3] The set-up of Fig. 2 consists of two physical machines: the first server is configured as the cloud controller, cluster controller, Walrus and storage controller; the second is configured as a node controller capable of booting virtual instances. While this is a relatively straightforward set-up, the approach can be scaled to incorporate as many node controllers as necessary.

The node controllers host the virtual instances which boot the machine image containing the FDR binary. Sitting above FDR is the software used to coordinate the scheduling of refinement checks and the processing of results. We utilise a single master node and several slave nodes. The role of the master node is to distribute refinements to, and collect results from, slaves. Additionally, the master

---

[3] We use the Ubuntu Enterprise Cloud, which uses KVM as the default hypervisor.

node is responsible for processing the input file, deriving suitable process definitions, and then extracting the relevant processes in order to form refinements;
these are then distributed to the slave nodes.

A *job* consists of the relevant CSP code and a refinement to check; jobs are
stored in a *jobqueue*. The available pool of slaves are stored in a *slavepool* — a
circular list of slaves, keeping a record of whether the slave has been allocated a
job. The master node cycles through the list of slaves in a round-robin fashion. If
a slave has been previously allocated a job, it checks whether the job is complete.
If it is, the result is saved and the slave's state is marked as *idle*; if it is not, the
slave is simply added to the back of the list, to be checked on the next cycle.
Alternatively, if a slave is free and there are jobs in the job queue, the slave is
allocated the next available job, and its state is set to busy. A slave node simply
waits for a job from the master. Additionally, it responds to periodic status
requests (from the master) as to whether a refinement check is complete or not.

The basic pseudocode executed on the master node is shown below.

```
while (length(jobQueue) > 0)
{
    slave = slavepool.pop()
    if (slave.isBusy()) /*refinement check assigned*/
        {
            refinement = slave.getRefinement()
            if (refinement.complete())
                {
                    result = refinement.getResult()
                    resultQueue.append(result)
                    slave.reset()
                    slavepool.append(slave)
                }
            else
                {
                    /*not done*/
                    slavepool.append(slave)
                }
        }
    else /*slave is idle*/
        {
            if (length(jobQueue>0))
                {
                    job = jobQueue.pop()
                    slave.assignJob(job)
                }
        }
}
```

Four types of data are of interest to us: *application data* (the binary of the
model checker, and any other associated applications or scripts); *input data*

(CSP$_M$ scripts describing concurrent interactions of processes along with refinements we wish to prove or refute); *non-persistent application-generated data* (data required only for as long as the CSP$_M$ script is loaded and a refinement check is executed); and *persistent application-generated data* (the result of a refinement check (and, if appropriate, counter-examples)).

4   The Case Study

We have used the approach of Sect. 3 to model various interlockings; as a means of illustration, we consider the model of [21] and the example of Fig. 1.

4.1   Translating GDL into CSP

To translate (ASCII-based) GDL models to CSP$_M$, we have used the lexical analyser and parser generator *PLY* (a lex–yacc parsing tool for Python).[4]

During the parsing phase, we record semantic information regarding the GDL: this is used to construct process definitions and to decide which processes need to be combined for a particular refinement check. In particular, we record: the set of track circuits, *Circuit*; the set of sets of points, *Points*; the set of routes, *Route*; and the set of subroutes, *Subroute*. In addition, we build a syntax tree that relates the various interlocking components; we also construct various functions that relate different interlocking components. For example, the following functions relate track circuits to the subroutes associated with them, return the set of all sets of points associated with a given route, and map each route to its constituent sequence of subroutes, respectively:

$$subroutesOfCircuit : Circuit \rightarrow \mathbb{P}\, Subroute$$

$$pointsOfRoute : Route \rightarrow \mathbb{P}\, Points$$

$$subroutesOfRoute : Route \rightarrow seq\, Subroute$$

The translation tool reads the whole file and then translates it, which involves building tree structures. Once all the input is parsed we can then transform this into corresponding CSP process definitions.

4.2   The CSP Model

The components involved in setting route R14 are the subroutes UAE_AB, UAD_AB, UAD_BA and UAE_BA, and points P202. The process *R14true* characterises the preconditions for setting route R14: points P202 should be controlled free to go normal, and subroutes UAD_AB and UAE_AB should be free. If any of the conditions necessary to set the route becomes false, then the process state is updated and the process subsequently behaves as *R14false*. Should there be a request to set the route, points P202 are locked in the controlled normal position, UAD_BA and UAE_BA are both locked, and route R14

---

[4] See http://www.dabeaz.com/ply.

is set. The process *R14false* models when it is not possible to set route R14, i. e. when one or more of the conditional checks evaluates to false. The variable x represents the state of points P202 (controlled free to go normal or not); y and z are concerned with the states of subroutes UAE_AB and UAD_AB (free or locked). Changes in state for P202, UAE_AB and UAD_AB may be observed. Once all conditions are met, the process behaves as *R14true*.

$R14true =$

$routeState.R14.req \rightarrow pointPosition.P202.cn \rightarrow$

$\qquad subrouteState.UAD\_BA.l \rightarrow subrouteState.UAE\_BA.l \rightarrow$

$\qquad\qquad routeState.R14.s \rightarrow R14true$

$\square$

$pointState.P202.cfn.false \rightarrow R14false(false, f, f)$

$\square$

$subrouteState.UAE\_AB.l \rightarrow R14false(true, l, f)$

$\square$

$subrouteState.UAD\_AB.l \rightarrow R14false(true, f, l)$

$R14false(x, y, z) =$

if $x = true \wedge y = f \wedge z = f$ then $R14true$

else $(\, pointState.P202.cfn?i \rightarrow R14false(i, y, z)$

$\qquad \square$

$\qquad subrouteState.UAE\_AB?i \rightarrow R14false(x, i, z)$

$\qquad \square$

$\qquad subrouteState.UAD\_AB?i \rightarrow R14false(x, y, i)\,)$

In the process *UAE_BAlocked*, variable x represents the state of track circuit TAE, and y and z represent the states of UAD_BA and UAD_CA respectively. If the conditions are met, the subroute can be freed and the process then behaves as *UAE_BAfree*. The process also allows changes to the relevant components, updating the relevant variable accordingly.

$UAE\_BAlocked(x, y, z) =$

if $x = c \wedge y = f \wedge z = f$ then

$\qquad subrouteState.UAE\_BA.f \rightarrow UAE\_BAfree(x, y, z)$

else $(\, circuitState.TAE?i \rightarrow UAE\_BAlocked(i, y, z)$

$\qquad \square$

$\qquad subrouteState.UAD\_BA?i \rightarrow UAE\_BAlocked(x, i, z)$

$\qquad \square$

$\qquad subrouteState.UAD\_CA?i \rightarrow UAE\_BAlocked(x, y, i)\,)$

$$UAE\_BAfree(x, y, z) =$$
$$subrouteState.UAE\_BA.l \rightarrow UAE\_BAlocked(x, y, z)$$

$\square$

$$circuitState.TAE?i \rightarrow UAE\_BAfree(i, y, z)$$

$\square$

$$subrouteState.UAD\_BA?i \rightarrow UAE\_BAfree(x, i, z)$$

$\square$

$$subrouteState.UAD\_CA?i \rightarrow UAE\_BAfree(x, y, i)$$

Subroute-release data depending on a route rather than subroutes (which is usually the case for the first subroute of a route) are modelled slightly differently. For example, in the case of subroute UAD_BA we have the following:

$$UAD\_BAlocked(x, y) =$$
if $x = c \wedge y = xs$ then
$$\qquad subrouteState.UAD\_BA.f \rightarrow UAD\_BAfree(x, y)$$
else $(\ circuitState.TAD?i \rightarrow UAD\_BAlocked(i, y)$

$\qquad\quad \square$

$\qquad\quad \square\ i : \{req, xs\} \bullet routeState.R14.i \rightarrow UAD\_BAlocked(x, i)\ )$

$$UAD\_BAfree(x, y) =$$
$$subrouteState.UAD\_BA.l \rightarrow UAD\_BAlocked(x, y)$$

$\square$

$$circuitState.TAD?i \rightarrow UAD\_BAfree(i, y)$$

$\square$

$\square\ i : \{req, xs\} \bullet routeState.R14.i \rightarrow UAD\_BAfree(x, i)$

4.3 Decomposing the Problem

We now consider how our model can be decomposed into a series of independent checks by considering the second of our safety invariants: "For every track circuit, at most one of subroutes passing over it should be locked for a route at any time."

A subroute becomes locked when a route passing over it is set. Given a track circuit, t, we need take into account only the route-setting data for those routes which may lock subroutes over running it. As an example, four routes travel over track circuit TAK: R13, R15, R22, and R24, with the route-setting data for these routes being as follows.

Q13 **if**   P201 cfr   UAA_BA f   UAB_CA f
     then R13 s P201 cr   UAB_AC l   UAA_AB l   UAK_AB l

Q15 **if**   P201 cfn   UAA_BA f   UAB_CB f
     then R15 s P201 cn   UAB_BC l   UAA_AB l   UAK_AB l

Q22 **if**   P204 cfr   UAJ_CB f   UAK_AB f
     then R22 s P204 cr   UAJ_BC l   UAK_BA l   UAA_BA l

Q24 **if**   P204 cfn   UAJ_CA f   UAK_AB f
     then R24 s P204 cn   UAJ_AC l   UAK_BA l   UAA_BA l

Only routes R22 and R24 can lock subroute UAK_BA, and, before this subroute can be locked by either, subroute UAK_AB must be free. As such, we need take no other processes into account in ensuring that UAK_AB and then UAK_BA cannot be locked: if subroute UAK_AB is locked, then neither route R22 nor route R24 can be set, and, therefore, subroute UAK_BA cannot be locked.

Examining the conditions for routes R13 and R15 to be set, we see that before either route can be set, subroute UAA_BA must be free. The subroute-release data for this subroute is given by

UAA_BA f   **if**   TAA c UAK_BA f

It follows that we need take into account only processes representing route-setting data for routes R13 and R15, and subroute-release data for subroute UAA_BA to ensure that UAK_BA and then UAK_AB cannot be locked.

In this case, then, only five processes need to be considered to ensure that safety invariant 1 holds for track circuit TAK. The justification for this is based upon the fact that the events with which we are concerned can only ever occur with the co-operation of processes representing route-setting data for routes R13, R15, R22 and R24. Composition with further processes will only serve to reduce the set of possible behaviours for these components, while expanding the state space of the check to be performed. Thus, the task of checking this safety invariant reduces to one of tractable size — as shown in Table 1. (Track circuits TAE and TAF do not appear as they are both associated with exactly

Table 1. The complexity of verifying invariant 2 for our simple interlocking

Track circuit	States
TAA	14592
TAB	3532
TAC	232
TAD	3312
TAG	3312
TAH	232
TAJ	3532
TAK	14592
TBA	232
TCA	232

one route.) The automation of this dependency-establishing process is at the heart of our approach.

4.4   Safety Invariants in CSP

We now demonstrate how we can model safety invariants. We illustrate this via the first of our invariants: *if a route is set, then all of its subroutes are locked.*
    For any route r, we define

$$U = \{u : Subroute \mid u \in set(subroutesOfRoute(r))\}$$

where *set* converts a sequence into a set.
    We represent the invariant as a process thus:

$S_1(r, U, locked) =$
    if $locked = U$ then
            $\Box\, u : locked \bullet subrouteState.u.f \rightarrow S_1(r, U, locked \setminus \{u\})$

            $\Box$

            $\Box\, routeState.r.s \rightarrow routeState.r.xs \rightarrow S_1(r, U, locked)$
    else
            $\Box\, u : U \setminus locked \bullet subrouteState.u.l \rightarrow S_1(r, U, locked \cup \{u\})$

            $\Box$

            $\Box\, u : locked \bullet subrouteState.u.f \rightarrow S_1(r, U, locked \setminus \{u\})$

It is clear that we can only set a route r when all the subroutes along that route are locked; we also require the route to become unset before any associated subroutes can become free.

    With respect to our CSP model, we need to derive a suitable implementation process, which, as per the previous subsection, involves extracting relevant process descriptions from the GDL and then combining them using parallel composition. The following determines the necessary processes to be composed for $r \in Route$.

1. Include the processes representing route-setting data for r.
2. Consider all processes related to subroute-release data for each subroute along r, i.e. for each element in the set $set(subroutesOfRoute(r))$.
3. The process $Train(r, subroutesOfRoute(r), pointsOfRoute(r))$ models a train moving along route r.

    It is the first of these steps — "include the processes representing route setting data for r" — that allows us to decompose the checking of safety invariant 1 into smaller, independent checks. Consider, for example, route $R10A$, where

$$set\,(subroutesOfRoute\,(R10A)) = \{UAB\_CA, UBA\_BA\}$$

Combining the above, we have

$$I_1 (R10A) =$$
$$R10A \parallel UAB\_CA \parallel UBA\_BA \parallel Train(R10A, \langle TAB, TBA \rangle, \{P201\})$$

as the implementation process for safety invariant 1 and route $R10A$. Via FDR, we can verify

$$S_1 (R10A, \{UAB\_CA, UBA\_BA\}, \{UAB\_CA, UBA\_BA\}) \sqsubseteq_F I_1 (R10A)$$

Crucially, as all of the relevant communications are present, it follows that

$$S_1 (R10A, \{UAB\_CA, UBA\_BA\}, \{UAB\_CA, UBA\_BA\}) \sqsubseteq_F System$$

By verifying similar refinements for the other routes, we can assert that safety invariant 1 holds for that interlocking. The proof of this relies on the fact that all relevant behaviours relevant to the verification of the safety invariant for route r can be observed in the implementation process $I_1 (r)$ (see [21]).

The round-trip execution times for checking each of the 16 routes of Fig. 1 are typically in the range 3–5 s; this results in a cumulative time of under 1 min to check this safety invariant for the example interlocking, which consists of $4.84662992 \times 10^{22}$ states;[5] the cumulative times for the other safety invariants are of a similar order.

5   Conclusions

We have described how a cloud-enabled interface for FDR gives rise to a means of parallelized safety checks on railway interlockings. For the sake of readability, we have based our account on a relatively simple scenario; [21] shows how the theoretical approach — which we have now made practical — is scalable to 'real-life' interlockings. We have concentrated on CSP and FDR, rather than other approaches, as the relationship between parallel composition and refinement means that it is feasible to decompose large problems into smaller ones in an elegant fashion — making it an exceptional candidate for a cloud computing style approach.

One of the biggest challenges of model checking in a practical setting is handling the enumeration of the state space in an efficient manner. Various approaches to alleviate the state space explosion problem are known from the literature: partial order reduction techniques (see, for example, [22]) are one approach; the local search approach proposed by Roscoe et al. [23], whereby states spaces are partitioned into 'blocks', is another. An experimental parallel implementation of FDR is described in [24]: states are randomly allocated between different computing nodes using a hash function; the state space is explored using a breadth-first search algorithm, and at the end of each level successor states are

---

[5] 12 track circuits, 4 points, 16 routes and 30 subroutes, giving rise to $2^{12} \times 4^4 \times 3^{16} \times 2^{30}$ states.

exchanged between the compute nodes. An alternative approach is that taken by FDR Explorer [25], whereby an API "makes possible to create optimised CSP code to perform refinement checks that are more space or time efficient, enabling the analysis of more complex and data-intensive specifications."

Our approach involves partitioning the problem not at the level of the state space, but at the level of the CSP model — which means it is applicable only in certain contexts, with one being the scenario considered in this paper. All of the refinement checks are generated automatically and subsequently sent to slave nodes for processing. There are clearly limitations, though. Crucially, we rely upon the existence of models being of a form that can be decomposed into smaller subproblems; once this partitioning is done, the refinement checks can then be allocated to a farm of processors to either be confirmed or refuted. While deconstructing the problem at the model level in the way that we have done can work for safety properties, it is of no use when considering liveness properties, for example.

The initial prototype implementation of the software that schedules the checks between processing nodes can be extended in several ways. At the moment, there is a single point of failure: should the master node die, there would be no way to schedule more refinement checks or to collect the results. Another point to consider would be the costing model used by the cloud provider: given that virtual instances are priced per hour, if many of the refinement checks are similar (as per the case study of this paper), we can try and optimise the cost by considering the execution time of a single check. The most pressing item of future work, however, is the consideration of further case studies — with a view to identifying other classes of problems that may benefit from this approach. Initial ares of interest in this respect are asynchronous hardware circuits and automatic test case generation.

Acknowledgements. The authors would like to thank the anonymous reviewers for their helpful comments and constructive criticisms.

References

1. Hansen, K.M.: Validation of a railway interlocking model. In: Naftalin, M., Denvir, T., Bertran, M. (eds.) FME 1994. LNCS, vol. 873, pp. 582–601. Springer, Heidelberg (1994)
2. Morley, M.J.: Safety in railway signalling data: a behavioural analysis. In: Joyce, J., Seger, C. (eds.) HUG 1993. LNCS, vol. 780, pp. 465–474. Springer, Heidelberg (1994)
3. Haxthausen, A.E., Peleska, J.: Formal development and verification of a distributed railway control system. IEEE Trans. Softw. Eng. **26**(8), 687–701 (2000)
4. Kanso, K., Moller, F., Setzer, A.: Automated verification of signalling principles in railway interlocking systems. Electron. Notes Theoret. Comput. Sci. **250**(2), 19–31 (2009)
5. James, P., Roggenbach, M.: Automatically verifying railway interlockings using SAT-based model checking. In: Proceedings of the 10th International Workshop

on Automated Verification of Critical Systems (AVoCS 2010), Electronic Communication of the European Association of Software, Science and Technology, vol. 35 (2010)

6. Haxthausen, A.E., Peleska, J., Kinder, S.: A formal approach for the construction and verification of railway control systems. Form. Asp. Comput. **23**(2), 191–219 (2011)

7. Fantechi, A., Fokkink, W., Morzenti, A.: Some trends in formal methods applications to railway signalling. In: Gnesi, S., Margaria, T. (eds.) Formal Methods for Industrial Critical Systems: A Survey of Applications, pp. 63–82. Wiley, Hoboken (2013)

8. Bacherini, S., Fantechi, A., Tempestini, M., Zingoni, N.: A story about formal methods adoption by a railway signaling manufacturer. In: Misra, J., Nipkow, T., Sekerinski, E. (eds.) FM 2006. LNCS, vol. 4085, pp. 179–189. Springer, Heidelberg (2006)

9. Winter, K., Robinson, N.J.: Modelling large interlocking systems and model checking small ones. In: Oudshoorn, M. (ed.) Proceedings of the 26th Australasian Computer Science Conference (ACSC 2003), Australian Computer Science, Communications, vol. 16, pp. 309–316 (2003)

10. Simpson, A.C., Woodcock, J.C.P., Davies, J.W.M.: The mechanical verification of solid state interlocking geographic data. In: Groves, L., Reeves, S. (eds.) Proceedings of Formal Methods Pacific 1997, pp. 223–242. Springer, Wellington (1997)

11. Hoare, C.A.R.: Communicating Sequential Processes. Prentice Hall, London (1985)

12. Roscoe, A.W.: Understanding Concurrent Systems. Springer, London (2010)

13. Roscoe, A.W.: Model checking CSP. In: Roscoe, A.W. (ed.) A Classical Mind: Essays in Honour of C.A.R. Hoare. Prentice Hall, London (1994)

14. Roscoe, A.W., Gardiner, P.H.B., Goldsmith, M.H., Hulance, J.R., Jackson, D.M., Scattergood, J.B.: Hierarchical compression for model-checking CSP or how to check 10^{20} dining philosophers for deadlock. In: Brinksma, E., Cleaveland, W.R., Larsen, K.G., Margaria, T., Steffen, B. (eds.) TACAS 1995. LNCS, vol. 1019, pp. 133–152. Springer, Heidelberg (1995)

15. Nurmi, D., Wolski, R., Grzegorczyk, C., Obertelli, G., Soman, S., Youseff, L., Zagorodnov, D.: The eucalyptus open-source cloud-computing system. In: Proceedings of the 9th IEEE/ACM International Symposium on Cluster Computing and the Grid (CCGRID 2009), pp. 124–131 (2009)

16. Brookes, S.D., Roscoe, A.W.: An improved failures model for communicating processes. In: Brookes, S.D., Roscoe, A.W., Winskel, G. (eds.) NSF-SERC 1985. LNCS, vol. 197, pp. 281–305. Springer, Heidelberg (1985)

17. Roscoe, A.W.: The Theory and Practice of Concurrency. Prentice Hall, London (1997)

18. Ferrari, A., Magnani, G., Grasso, D., Fantechi, A.: Model checking interlocking control tables. In: Schnieder, E., Tarnai, G. (eds.) Proceedings of Formal Methods for Automation and Safety in Railway and Automotive Systems 2010 (FORMS/FORMAT 2010), pp. 107–115. Springer, Heidelberg (2011)

19. Cribbens, A.: Solid state interlocking (SSI): an integrated electronic signalling system for mainline railways. IEE Proc. **134**(3), 148–158 (1987)

20. British Rail Research: SSI data preparation guide. Published by British Railways Board. ELS-DOC-3080, Issue K of SSI8003-INT and supplements (1990)

21. Simpson, A.C.: Safety through security. DPhil thesis, Oxford University Computing Laboratory (1996)

22. Godefroid, P.: Partial-Order Methods for the Verification of Concurrent Systems: An Approach to the State-Explosion Problem. LNCS, vol. 1032. Springer, Heidelberg (1996)

23. Roscoe, A.W., Armstrong, P.J., Pragyesh, : Local Search in Model Checking. In: Liu, Z., Ravn, A.P. (eds.) ATVA 2009. LNCS, vol. 5799, pp. 22–38. Springer, Heidelberg (2009)

24. Goldsmith, M.H., Martin, J.M.R.: The parallelisation of FDR. In: Proceedings of Workshop on Parallel and Distributed Model Checking (PDMC 2002) (2002)

25. Freitas, L., Woodcock, J.C.P.: FDR explorer. Form. Asp. Comput. 21(1–2), 133–154 (2009)

Parametric Schedulability Analysis of Fixed Priority Real-Time Distributed Systems

Youcheng Sun[1], Romain Soulat[2], Giuseppe Lipari[1,2], Étienne André[3(✉)], and Laurent Fribourg[2]

[1] Scuola Superiore Sant'Anna, Pisa, Italy
[2] LSV, ENS Cachan & CNRS, Cachan Cedex, France
[3] Université Paris 13, Sorbonne Paris Cité, LIPN, CNRS, Villetaneuse, France
Etienne.Andre@univ-paris13.fr

Abstract. In this paper, we address the problem of parametric schedulability analysis of distributed real-time systems scheduled by fixed priority. We propose two different approaches to parametric analysis. The first one is a novel analytic technique that extends single-processor sensitivity analysis to the case of distributed systems. The second approach is based on model checking of Parametric Stopwatch Automata (PSA): we generate a PSA model from a high-level description of the system, and then we apply the Inverse Method to obtain all possible behaviours of the system. Both techniques have been implemented in two software tools, and they have been compared with classical holistic analysis on two meaningful test cases. The results show that the analytic method provides results similar to classical holistic analysis in a very efficient way, whereas the PSA approach is slower but covers the entire space of solutions.

1 Introduction and Motivation

Designing and analysing distributed real-time systems is a very challenging task. The main source of complexity arises from the large number of parameters to consider: tasks priorities, computation times and deadlines, synchronisation, precedence and communication constraints, etc. Finding the optimal values for the parameters is not easy and often a small change in one parameter may completely change the behaviour of the system and even compromise its correctness. For these reasons, designers are looking for analysis methodologies that allow incremental design and exploration of the parameter space.

Task computation times are particularly important parameters. In modern processor architectures, it is very difficult to precisely compute worst-case computation times of tasks, thus estimations derived by previous executions are often used in the analysis. However, estimations may turn out to be optimistic, hence an error in the estimation of a worst-case execution time may compromise the schedulability of the entire system.

In this paper we investigate the problem of doing parametric analysis of real-time distributed systems scheduled by fixed priority. We consider an application

C. Artho and P.C. Ölveczky (Eds.): FTSCS 2013, CCIS 419, pp. 212–228, 2014.
DOI: 10.1007/978-3-319-05416-2_14, © Springer International Publishing Switzerland 2014

modelled by a set of pipelines (also called *transactions* in [19]), where each pipeline is a sequence of periodic tasks to be executed in order, and all tasks in a pipeline must complete before an end-to-end deadline. We consider that all processors in the distributed system are connected by one or more CAN bus [13], a network standard used in automotive applications.

The first contribution of the paper (Sect. 4) is to propose a new method for doing parametric analysis of the system, using the worst-case computation times of the tasks as parameters. The method extends the sensitivity analysis proposed by Bini *et al.* [9] by considering distributed systems and non-preemptive scheduling.

The proposed analytical method is not exact, as it sometimes overestimates the interference of higher priority tasks and of previous tasks in the pipeline on the response time of a task. Therefore, the second contribution of the paper (Sect. 5) is to propose also an exact schedulability analysis by modelling a distributed real-time system as a set of parametric timed automata; then we apply a model checking methodology using the Inverse Method [7,14].

Finally, in Sect. 6 we compare these two approaches with the MAST tool [16], a state-of the art tool for classical schedulability analysis. Comparison is performed on two case studies from the research literature on which we measured run-time and effectiveness of the three analyses. Results show that the analytical approach can very efficiently compute the feasible space of parameters with a good precision.

2   Related Work

Many research papers have already addressed the problem of parametric schedulability analysis, especially on single processor systems. Bini and Buttazzo [9] proposed an analysis of fixed priority single processor systems, which is used as a basis for this paper.

Parameter sensitivity can also be carried out by repeatedly applying classical schedulability tests, like the holistic analysis [19]. One example of this approach is used in the MAST tool, in which it is possible to compute the *slack* (i.e. the percentage of variation) with respect to one parameter for single processor and for distributed systems by applying binary search in that parameter space [19].

A similar approach is followed by the SymTA/S tool [17], which is based on the *event-stream* model [20]. Another interesting approach is the Modular Performance Analysis (MPA) [23], which is based on Real-Time Calculus. In both cases, the analysis is compositional, therefore less complex than the holistic analysis. Nevertheless, these approaches are not fully parametric, in the sense that it is necessary to repeat the analysis for every combination of parameter values in order to obtain the schedulability region.

Model checking of *parametric timed automata* (PTA) or *parametric stop-watch automata* (PSA) can be used for parametric schedulability analysis [12]. In particular, thanks to generality of the PTA and PSA modelling language, it is possible to model a larger class of constraints, and perform parametric analysis on many different variables, for example task offsets. This approach has been recently extended to distributed real-time systems [18].

Also grounded on PTA and PSA is the Inverse Method [7], applied in particular to schedulability analysis [14]. This method is very general because it permits to perform analysis on any system parameter. However, this generality may be paid in terms of complexity of the analysis.

In this paper, we aim at performing fully parametric analysis of real-time distributed systems. We first present extensions of the methods proposed in [9] to the case of distributed real-time systems. We also present a model of a distributed real-time systems using PSA, and compare the two approaches against classical analysis in MAST.

3   System Model

We consider distributed real-time systems consisting of several computational nodes, each one hosting one single processor, which are connected by one or more shared networks. Without loss of generality, from now on we will use the term *task* to denote both tasks and messages, and the term *processor* to denote both processors and networks.

A distributed real-time system consists of a set of task pipelines $\{\mathcal{P}^1, \ldots, \mathcal{P}^n\}$ to be executed on a set of processors. A *pipeline* is a chain of tasks $\mathcal{P}^j = \{\tau_1^j, \ldots, \tau_n^j\}$ to be executed in order, and each task is allocated on one (possibly different) processor. In order to simplify the notation, in the following we sometimes drop the pipeline superscript when there is no possibility of misinterpretation.

A pipeline is assigned two fixed parameters: T^j is the pipeline period and D_{e2e}^j is the end-to-end deadline. This means that all tasks of the pipeline are activated together every T^j units of time; and all tasks should be completed within a time interval of D_{e2e}^j.

A task in the pipeline can be a piece of code to be executed on a processor or a message to be sent over a network. More precisely, a real-time periodic task is a tuple $\tau_i = (C_i, T_i, D_i, R_i, q_i, p_i, J_i)$.

This task model contains the following fixed parameters:

- T_i is the task period. All tasks in the same pipeline have period equal to the pipeline period T;
- D_i is the task relative deadline;
- q_i is the task priority; the larger q_i, the higher the priority;
- p_i is the index of the processor (or network) on which the task executes.

Also, a task is characterised by the following free parameters (variables):

- C_i is the worst-case computation time (or worst-case transmission time, in case it models a message). It is the worst-case time the task needs to complete one periodic instance when executed alone on a dedicated processor (or network). In this paper we want to characterise the schedulability of a distributed system in the space of the computation times, so C_i is a free parameter.

- R_i is the *task worst-case response time*, i.e. the worst case finishing time of any task instance relative to the activation of its pipeline.
- J_i is the task worst-case activation jitter, i.e. the greatest time since its activation that a task must wait for all preceding tasks to complete their execution.

Every task activation is an *instance* (or *job*) of the task. We denote the kth instance of task τ_i as $\tau_{i,k}$. An instance $\tau_{i,k}$ of a task in the pipeline can start executing only after the corresponding instance of the preceding task $\tau_{i-1,k}$ has completed. Finally, the last task in the pipeline must complete every instance before D_{e2e} units of time from its pipeline's activation. For a job $\tau_{i,k}$ we define the following notation:

- $a_{i,k}$ is $\tau_{i,k}$'s arrival time (coincident with the activation time of the pipeline).
- $s_{i,k}$ is the start time of the instance, i.e. the first time the instance executes on the processor.
- $f_{i,k}$ is the job's finishing time.
- $r_{i,k}$ the task release time. The first task of a pipeline is released immediately at the time of its arrival $r_{0,k} = a_{0,k}$; successive tasks are released at the finishing time of the preceding tasks: $r_{i,k} = f_{i-1,k}$. The following relationship holds: $\forall i, k \ a_{0,k} = a_{i,k} \leq r_{i,k} \leq s_{i,k} < f_{i,k}$.
- The maximum difference between arrival and release time is the worst-case activation jitter of the task: $J_i = \max_k (r_{i,k} - a_{i,k})$.
- The maximum difference between finishing time and arrival time is the worst-case response time of the task: $R_i = \max_k (f_{i,k} - a_{i,k})$.

Parameters R_i and J_i depend on the other tasks parameters and on the scheduling policy according to a complex set of equations. Of course, they cannot be considered parameters that the programmer can modify: nevertheless, for our purposes it is useful to consider them as variables to help us write the set of constraints that define the schedulability space (the exact role of such variables will be detailed in Sect. 4.3).

A scheduling algorithm is *fully preemptive* if the execution of a lower priority job can be suspended at any instant by the release of a higher priority job, which is then executed in its place. A scheduling algorithm is *non-preemptive* if a lower priority job, once it has started executing, can complete its execution regardless of the release of higher priority jobs. In this paper, we consider fully preemptive fixed priority scheduling for processors, and non-preemptive fixed priority scheduling for networks.

4   Analytic Method

In this section we present a novel method for parametric analysis of distributed system. The method extends the sensitivity analysis by Bini *et al.* [9,21] to include jitter and deadline parameters.

In Sects. 4.1 and 4.2, we only consider the scheduling of independent periodic tasks in a single processor. Then, in Sect. 4.3, we extend the schedulability analysis to distributed systems.

4.1   Preemptive Tasks with Constrained Deadlines

There are many ways to test the schedulability of a set of real-time periodic tasks scheduled by fixed priority on a single processor. In the following, we will use the test proposed by Seto *et al.* [21] because it is amenable to parametric analysis of computation times, jitters and deadlines.

The original theorem was formulated for tasks with deadlines equal to periods. For the moment, we generalise it to tasks with constrained deadlines (i.e. $D_i \leq T$), while in Sect. 4.2 we deal with unconstrained deadlines, jitter and non-preemptive scheduling.

Definition 1. *The set of* scheduling points $\mathbb{P}^{i-1}(t)$ *for a task τ_i is the set of all vectors corresponding to multiples of the period of any task τ_j with priority higher than τ_i, until the maximum possible value of the deadline. It can be computed as follows. Let $\eta_j(t) = \left\lceil \frac{t}{T_j} \right\rceil$, and let $\eta^{i-1}(t)$ be the corresponding vector of $i - 1$ elements with $j = 0, \ldots, i - 1$. Then:*

$$\mathbb{P}^{i-1}(t) = \{\eta^{i-1}(t)\} \cup \{\eta^{i-1}(kT_h) \mid 0 < kT_h < t, h < i\} \tag{1}$$

Theorem 1 ([21]). *Consider a system of periodic tasks $\{\tau_1, \ldots, \tau_n\}$ with constrained deadlines and zero jitter, executed on a single processor by a fixed priority preemptive scheduler. Assume all tasks are ordered in decreasing order of priorities, with τ_1 being the highest priority task.*

Task τ_i is schedulable if and only if:

$$\exists \mathbf{n} \in \mathbb{P}^{i-1}(D_i) \begin{cases} C_i + \displaystyle\sum_{j=1}^{i-1} n_j C_j \leq n_k T_k \quad \forall k = 1, \ldots, i-1 \\[3mm] C_i + \displaystyle\sum_{j=1}^{i-1} n_j C_j \leq R_i \\[3mm] R_i \leq D_i \end{cases} \tag{2}$$

where $\mathbf{n}$ is a vector of $i-1$ integers, and $\mathbb{P}^{i-1}(D_i)$ is the set of scheduling points.

Notice that, with respect to the original formulation, we have separated the case of $k = i$ from the rest of the inequalities and we introduced variable R_i.

The theorem allows us to only consider sets of linear inequalities, because the non-linearity has been encoded in the variables n_j. Each vector $\mathbf{n}$ defines a convex region (maybe empty) with variables $C_1, \ldots, C_i$ and $R_1, \ldots, R_i$. The "*exists*" quantifier means that the region for each task τ_i is the union of convex regions, hence it may be non-convex. Since we have to check the schedulability of all tasks, we must intersect all such regions to obtain the final region of schedulable parameters. The resulting system is a disjunction of sets of conjunctions of inequalities. Geometrically, this corresponds to a non-convex polyhedron in the space of the variables C and R of tasks.

It is worth to note that, using this formulation, we can compute the response time of a task by simply minimising the corresponding variable R_i under the constraints of Eq. (2). As an example, consider the following task set (the same as in [10]): $\tau_1 = (C = 1, T = 3), \tau_2 = (C = 2, T = 8), \tau_3 = (C = 4, T = 20)$, in decreasing order of priority, to be scheduled by preemptive fixed priority scheduling on a single processor.

We consider the response time R_3 as a parameter and set up the system of inequalities according to Eq. (2). After reduction of the non-useful constraints, we obtain $12 \leq R_3 \leq 20$. Therefore, the response time is $R_3 = 12$, which is the same that can be obtained by classical response time analysis.

4.2   Extensions to the Model

We now extend Seto's test to unconstrained deadlines and variable jitters, and non-preemptive scheduling. Non-preemptive scheduling can be modelled by considering an initial *blocking time*, due to the fact that a task cannot preempt lower-priority executing tasks.

The worst case response time for a non preemptive task τ_i can be found in its longest i-level active period [11]. An i-level active period L_i is an interval $[a, b)$ such that the amount of processing that needs to be performed due to jobs with priority higher than or equal to τ_i (including τ_i itself) is larger than 0 for all $t \in (a, b)$, and equal to 0 at instants a and b. The longest L_i can be found by computing the lowest fixed point of a recursive function. Notice that, by considering non-preemption and tasks with deadline greater than periods, the worst-case response time may be found in any instance of the active period, not necessarily in the first one (as with the classical model of constrained deadline preemptive tasks).

Unfortunately, the longest busy period cannot be computed when tasks have parametric worst-case computation times. However, under the assumption that there is at least an idle-time in the hyperperiod (i.e. its utilisation is strictly less than 100%) a sufficient feasibility test can be derived by computing the worst-case response time for every instance of the task set in the hyperperiod H_n. Therefore, we can extend our model as follows.

Theorem 2. *A non preemptive task τ_i is schedulable if $\forall h = 1, \ldots, \frac{H_n}{T_i}$, $\exists \mathbf{n} \in \mathbb{P}^{i-1}((h-1)T_i + D_i)$ such that*

$$- B_i + (h-1)C_i + \sum_{j=1}^{i-1} n_j C_j \leq n_l T_l - J_l \quad \forall l = 1, \ldots, i-1;$$

$$- B_i + (h-1)C_i + \sum_{j=1}^{i-1} n_j C_j \leq (h-1)T_i + R_i - C_i - J_i;$$

$- R_i \leq D_i$ *and* $B_i \leq C_j - 1$ *for all* $j > i$.

Proof 1. See [22].

Term B_i is an additional internal variable used to model the blocking time that a task suffers from lower priority tasks. It is possible to avoid the introduction of this additional variable by substituting it in the inequalities with a simple Fourier-Motzkin elimination.

Notice that the introduction of unconstrained deadlines adds a great amount of complexity to the problem. In particular, the number of non-convex regions to intersect is now $\mathcal{O}(\sum_{i=1}^{n} \frac{H_n}{T_i})$, which is dominated by $\mathcal{O}(nH_n)$. So, the proposed problem representation is pseudo-polynomial in the size of the hyperperiod. However, in real applications, we expect the periods to have "nice" relationships: for example, in many cases engineers choose periods that are multiples of each others. Therefore, we expect the set of inequalities to have manageable size for realistic problems.

4.3   Distributed Systems

Until now, we have considered the parametric analysis of independent tasks on single processor systems, with computation times, response times, blocking times and jitters as free variables.

One key observation is that a precedence constraint between two consecutive tasks τ_i and τ_{i+1} in the same pipeline can be expressed as $R_i \leq J_{i+1}$. This relationship derives directly from the definition of response time and jitter in Sect. 3. Using this elementary property, we can now build the parametric space for a distributed system as follows.

1. For each processor and network, we build the constraint system of Theorem 2. Notice that the set of constraints for the individual single processor systems are independent of each other (because they are constraints on different tasks).
2. For each pipeline $\mathcal{P}^a$:
   – two successive tasks τ_i^a and τ_{i+1}^a must fulfil the constraint $R_i^a \leq J_{i+1}^a$;
   – for the initial task we impose $J_1^a = 0$.

Such pipeline constraints must intersect the combined system to produce the final system of constraints. However, simply adding the above precedence constraints can lead to pessimistic solutions. In fact, if two tasks from the same pipeline are assigned to the same processor, the interference they may cause on each other and on the other tasks may be limited.

Suppose τ_i^a and τ_j^a are allocated to the same processor and $q_i^a > q_j^a$. Then, τ_i^a can at most interfere with the execution of a job from τ_j^a a number of times equal to $\xi = \left\lceil \frac{\max\{0, D_{e2e}^a - T^a\}}{T^a} \right\rceil$. So, we impose that $\forall \mathbf{n} \in \mathbb{P}^{j-1}$, $n_i \leq \xi$.

The analytic method proposed in this section has been implemented in a software tool, called RTSCAN, which is based on the PPL (Parma Polyhedra Library) [8], a library specifically designed and optimised to represent and operate on polyhedra. The library efficiently operates on rational numbers with arbitrary precision: therefore, in this work we make the assumption that all variables (computations times, response times and jitter) are defined in the domain of rationals (rather than reals).

We observed that the complexity of the methodology for generating the parameter space strongly depends on the number of free parameters considered in the analysis. Therefore, as a preliminary step, the tool requires the user to select a subset of the computation times on which the analysis will be performed, whereas the other parameters will be assigned fixed values. During construction of the polyhedron we have to keep R_i, J_i and B_i for each task as variables. Therefore, the number of variables to be managed is $nV = 4 \cdot N + F$, where N is the number of tasks and F is the number of variables to analyse. At the end, we can eliminate the R_i, J_i and B_i variables, hence the final space consists of F dimensions. An evaluation of this tool and of the run-time complexity of the analysis will be presented in Sect. 6.

The analytic method described so far is not exact. In fact, when dealing with pipelines in a distributed system we may sometimes overestimate the interference of higher priority-tasks on lower priority ones. For this reason, we now present an exact parametric analysis based on PSA and model checking.

5   The Inverse Method Approach

5.1   Parametric Timed Automata with Stopwatches

Timed automata are finite-state automata augmented with clocks, i.e., real-valued variables increasing uniformly, that are compared within guards and invariants with timing delays [3]. Parametric timed automata (PTA) [4] extend timed automata with parameters, i.e., unknown constants, that can be used in guards and invariants. We will use here an extension of PTA with *stopwatches* [2], where clocks can be stopped in some control states of the automaton.

Given a set X of clocks and a set U of parameters, a constraint C over X and U is a conjunction of linear inequalities on X and U^1. Given a parameter valuation (or point) π, we write $\pi \models C$ when the constraint where all parameters within C have been replaced by their value as in π is satisfied by a non-empty set of clock valuations.

Definition 2. *A parametric timed automaton with stopwatches (PSA) $\mathcal{A}$ is $(\Sigma, Q, q_0, X, U, K, I, slope, \rightarrow)$ with Σ a finite set of actions, Q a finite set of locations, $q_0 \in Q$ the initial location, X a set of h clocks, U a set of parameters, K a constraint over U, I the invariant assigning to every $q \in Q$ a constraint over X and U, slope : $Q \rightarrow \{0, 1\}^h$ assigns a constant slope to every location, and $\rightarrow$ a step relation consisting of elements (q, g, a, ρ, q'), where $q, q' \in Q$, $a \in \Sigma$, $\rho \subseteq X$ is the set of clocks to be reset, and the guard g is a constraint over X and U.*

The semantics of a PSA $\mathcal{A}$ is defined in terms of states, i.e., pairs (q, C) where $q \in Q$ and C is a constraint over X and U. Given a point π, we say that a state (q, C) is π-compatible if $\pi \models C$. Runs are alternating sequences of states and actions, and traces are time-abstract runs, i.e., alternating sequences of *locations* and actions. The trace set of $\mathcal{A}$ corresponds to the traces associated with all the runs of $\mathcal{A}$. Given $\mathcal{A}$ and π, we denote by $\mathcal{A}[\pi]$ the (non-parametric)

---

[1] Note that this is a more general form than the strict original definition of PTA [4]; since most problems for PTA are undecidable anyway, this has no practical incidence, and increases the expressiveness of the formalism.

timed stopwatch automaton where each occurrence of a parameter has been replaced by its constant value as in π. Details can be found in, e.g., [7].

The Inverse Method for PSA [7] exploits the knowledge of a reference point of timing values for which the good behaviour of the system is known. The method synthesises automatically a dense space of points around the reference point, for which the discrete behaviour of the system, that is the set of all the admissible sequences of interleaving events, is guaranteed to be the same.

The Inverse Method IM proceeds by exploring iteratively longer runs from the initial state. When a π-incompatible state is met (that is a state (q, C) such that $\pi \not\models C$), a π-incompatible inequality J is selected within the projection of C onto U. This inequality is then negated, and the analysis restarts with a model further constrained by $\neg J$. When a fixpoint is reached, that is when no π-incompatible state is found and all states have their successors within the set of reachable states, the intersection of all the constraints onto the parameters is returned.

Although the principle of IM shares similarities with sensitivity analysis, IM proceeds by iterative state space exploration. Furthermore, its result comes under the form of a fully parametric constraint, in contrast to sensitivity analysis. By repeatedly applying the method, we are able to decompose the parameter space into a covering set of "tiles", which ensure a uniform behaviour of the system: it is sufficient to test only one point of the tile in order to know whether or not the system behaves correctly on the whole tile. This is known as the *behavioural cartography* [5].

5.2   Modelling the System Using Parametric Stopwatch Automata

Timed Automata with Stopwatches have been used for modelling scheduling problems in the past. Our model technique is similar to [1,2], except that we model pipelines of tasks, and that we use PSA for obtaining the space of feasible computation times. In the current implementation, we only model pipelines with end-to-end deadlines no larger than their periods. This allows us to simplify the model and reduce the complexity of the analysis. The extension to deadlines larger than the period is discussed at the end of the section.

We illustrate our model with the help of an example of two pipelines $\mathcal{P}^1, \mathcal{P}^2$ with $\mathcal{P}^1 = \{\tau_1, \tau_2\}$, $\mathcal{P}^2 = \{\tau_3, \tau_4\}$, $p(\tau_1) = p(\tau_4) = p_1$, $p(\tau_2) = p(\tau_3) = p_2$, p_1 being a preemptive processor and p_2 being non-preemptive. We have that $q_1 > q_4$ and $q_3 > q_2$.

Figure 1 shows the PSA model of a pipeline. A pipeline is a sequence of tasks that are to be executed in order: when a task completes its instance, it instantly releases the next task in the pipeline. Since we assume constrained deadlines, once every task in the pipeline has completed, the pipeline waits for the next period to start. This PSA contains one local clock $x_{\mathcal{P}^1}$, one parameter T_1 (the pipeline's period), and synchronises on 5 actions: "τ_1 release", "τ_1 completed", "τ_2 release", "τ_2 completed", and "$\mathcal{P}^1$ restart". The order of these events imposes that task τ_1 must be entirely executed before task τ_2. The initialisation of the pipeline's local clock $x_{\mathcal{P}^1}$ and the invariant $x_{\mathcal{P}^1} \leq T_1$ ensure that the pipeline's

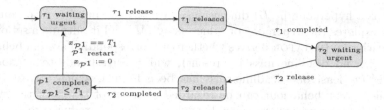

Fig. 1. PSA modelling a pipeline $\mathcal{P}^1$ with two tasks τ_1, τ_2

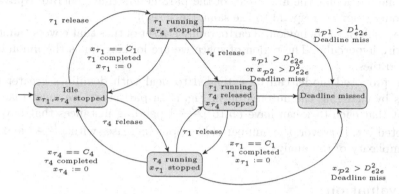

Fig. 2. PSA modelling a preemptive processor with two tasks τ_1, τ_4

execution terminates within its period T_1. The guard $x_{\mathcal{P}^1} == T_1$ ensures that the pipeline restarts after exactly T_1 units of time.

Figure 2 shows the model of a preemptive processor with 2 tasks τ_1 and τ_4, where task τ_1 has higher priority over task τ_4. The processor starts by being *idle*, waiting for a task release. As soon as a request has been received (e.g. action "τ_4 release"), it moves to one of the states where the corresponding task is running ("τ_4 running"). If it receives another release request ("τ_1 release"), it moves to the state corresponding to the higher priority task running ("τ_1 release, τ_4 released"). The fact that τ_1 does not execute anymore is modelled by the blocking of the clock x_{τ_4} corresponding to task τ_4. Moreover, while a task executes, the scheduler automaton checks if the corresponding pipeline misses its deadline (e.g. guard $x_{\mathcal{P}^1} > D_{e2e}^1$, where D_{e2e}^1 is τ_1's deadline). In the case of a deadline miss, the processor moves to a special failure state ("deadline missed") and stops any further computation.

The model of a non-preemptive processor is very similar to the model of preemptive processor: the central state in Fig. 2 which accounts for the fact that τ_4 is stopped when τ_1 is released, in the non-preemptive case must not stop τ_4, but simply remember that τ_1 has been released, so that we can move to the top state when τ_4 completes its instance.

We use the IMITATOR software tool [6] implementing the behavioural cartography, to perform the analysis of the PSA. The tool takes as input a textual description of the PSA and an interval of values for each parameter, which can be seen as a hypercube in $|U|$ dimensions, with $|U|$ the number of parameters. Then, it explores the hypercube of values using IM, and it outputs a set of tiles.

For each tile, IMITATOR derives whether the corresponding system behaviour is valid (i.e. no deadline miss is present), which corresponds to a good tile, or invalid (at least one deadline miss has been found), which corresponds to a bad tile. Every behaviour can be regarded as a set of traces of the system. Although deadline misses are *timed* behaviours, they are reduced to (untimed) traces thanks to the "deadline miss" location of the processor PSA. All points inside one particular tile are values of the parameters that generate equivalent behaviours (they correspond to the same trace set).

The result of the behavioural cartography is a set of tiles that covers "almost"[2] the entire hypercube. The region of space we are looking for is the union of all the good tiles.

The proposed model can be extended to deal with deadlines greater than periods by changing the automaton in Fig. 1. In particular, we must take into account that each task can have up to $\lceil \frac{D_{e2e}}{T} \rceil$ pending instances that have not completed yet. However, the number of locations increases with $\lceil \frac{D_{e2e}}{T} \rceil$ and thus the complexity of the analysis.

6   Evaluation

In this section we evaluate the effectiveness and the running time of the two proposed tools on two case studies. As a baseline comparison, we choose to also run the same kind of analysis on the same case studies using MAST.

In order to simplify the visualisation of the results, for each test case we present the 2D region generated for two parameters only. However, all three methods are general and can be applied to any number of parameters. In Sect. 6.3 we will present the execution times of the three tools on the test-cases.

MAST [15] is a software tool implemented and maintained by the CTR group at the *Universidad de Cantabria* that allows to perform schedulability analysis for distributed real-time systems. It provides the user with several different kinds of analysis. For our purposes, we have selected the "Offset Based analysis" [19], an improvement over classical holistic analysis that takes into account some of the relationships between tasks belonging to the same pipeline.

6.1   Test Case 1

The first test case (TC1) has been adapted from [19] (we reduced the computation times of some tasks to position the system in a more interesting schedulability region). It consists of three simple periodic tasks and one pipeline, running on two processors (p_1 and p_3), connected by a CAN bus (p_2). The parameters

---

[2] Technically, a part might be non-covered in some cases at the border between the good and the bad subspace; this part has a width of at most ϵ, where ϵ is an input of the tool; of course, the smaller ϵ, the more costly the analysis (see [5,7]).

Table 1. Test case 1; all numbers in "ticks"

Pipeline/Task	T	D_{e2e}	Tasks	C	q	p
τ_1	20	20	–	Free	9	1
P^1	150	150	τ_1^1	Free	3	1
			τ_2^1	10	9	2
			τ_3^1	8	5	3
			τ_4^1	15	2	2
			τ_5^1	25	2	1
τ_2	30	30	–	6	9	3
τ_3	200	200	–	40	2	3

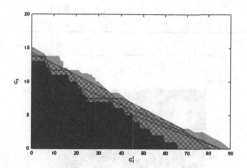

Fig. 3. TC1: Schedulability regions produced by RTSCAN (hatched), MAST (dark blue, below), and IMITATOR (light green, above) (Color figure online)

are listed in Table 1. The pipeline models a remote procedure call from processor 1 to processor 3. All tasks have deadlines equal to periods, and also the pipeline has end-to-end deadline equal to its period. Only two messages are sent on the network, and according to our optimisation rule for building parametric space, if the pipeline is schedulable, they cannot interfere with each other. We performed parametric schedulability analysis with respect to C_1 and C_1^1.

The resulting regions of schedulability from the three tools are reported in Fig. 3. In this particular test, RTSCAN dominates MAST. After some debugging, we discovered that the analysis algorithm currently implemented in MAST does not consider the fact that the two messages τ_2^1 and τ_4^1 cannot interfere with each other, and instead considers a non-null blocking time on the network.

As expected, the region computed by IMITATOR dominates the other two tools. This means that there is much space for improvement in the analysis even for such simple systems.[3]

---

[3] By zooming in the figure, it looks like in some very small areas, the region produced by RTSCAN goes over the region produced by IMITATOR. However, remember that both tools only deal with integer numbers; that small region does not contain any integer point.

Table 2. Test case 2: periods and deadlines are in milliseconds, computation times in micro-seconds.

Pipeline	T	D_{e2e}	Tasks	C	q	p
P^1	200 (30)	200	τ_1^1	4,546	10	1
			τ_2^1	445	10	2
			τ_3^1	9,091	10	4
			τ_4^1	445	9	2
			τ_5^1	Free	9	1
P^2	3,000	1,000	τ_1^2	Free	9	4
			τ_2^2	889	8	2
			τ_3^2	44,248	10	3
			τ_4^2	889	7	2
			τ_5^2	22,728	8	1

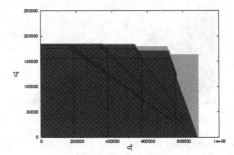

Fig. 4. Schedulability regions for test case 2a, produced by RTSCAN (hatched), MAST (dark blue, below), and IMITATOR (light green, above) (Color figure online)

6.2 Test Case 2

The second test case is taken from [23]. It consists of two pipelines on 3 processors (with id 1, 3 and 4) and one network (with id 2). We actually consider two versions of this test case: in the first version (a) pipeline P^1 is periodic with period 200 ms and end-to-end deadline equal to the period. In the second version (b), the period of the first pipeline is reduced to 30 ms (as in the original specification in [23]). The full set of parameters is reported in Table 2, where all values are expressed in microseconds. We perform parametric analysis on C_5^1 and C_1^2.

For version (a) we run all tools and we report the regions of schedulability in Fig. 4. Once again IMITATOR dominates the other two. Also, MAST dominated RTSCAN. The reason is due to the offset-based analysis methodology used in MAST, which reduces the interference on one task from other tasks belonging to the same pipeline.

For version (b) we run only RTSCAN and MAST, because in the current version we only model constrained deadline systems with IMITATOR. The results

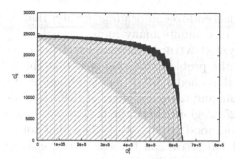

Fig. 5. Schedulability regions for test case 2b, produced by RTSCAN (grey, below) and MAST (dark blue, above) (Color figure online)

Table 3. Execution times of the tools

Test case	RTSCAN	MAST	IMITATOR
1	0.27s	7s	19min42
2a	0.47s	40min13	2h08
2b	1min11	33min19	–

for version (b) are reported in Fig. 5. In this case, MAST dominates RTSCAN. Again, this is due to the fact that MAST implements the offset-based analysis.

6.3 Execution Times

Before looking at the execution times of the three tools in the three different test cases, it is worth to discuss some details about their implementation.

IMITATOR produces a disjunction of convex regions. However, these regions are typically small and disjoints. Moreover, to produce a region, IMITATOR needs to start from a candidate point on which to call *IM*, and then move to close-by regions. One key factor here is how this search is performed. Currently, IMITA-TOR searches for a candidate point in the neighbourhood of the current region. This is a very general strategy that works for any kind of PSA. However, the particular structure of schedulability problems would probably require an ad-hoc exploration algorithm.

MAST can perform sensitivity analysis on one parameter (called *slack compu-tation* in the tool), using binary search on a possible interval of values. Therefore, to run the experiments, we performed a cycle on all values of one parameter (with a predefined step) and we asked MAST to compute the interval of feasible values for the other parameter.

All experiments have been performed on an Intel Core I7 quad-core processor (800 MHz per processor) with 8 GiB of RAM. The execution times of the tools in the three test cases are reported in Table 3. RTSCAN is the fastest method in all test-cases. In test case 2b, the execution time of RTSCAN is much larger than the one obtained from test case 2a. This is due to the fact that in test case 2b one pipeline has end-to-end deadline greater than the period, and therefore RTSCAN needs to compute many more inequalities (for all points in the hyperperiod). Finally, IMITATOR is the slowest of the three and does not scale well with the size of the problem. We observed that the tool spends a few seconds for computing the schedulability region around each point. However, the regions are quite small, and there are many of them: for example, in test case 2a IMITATOR analysed 257 regions. Also, the tool spends a large amount of time in searching for neighbourhood points. We believe that some improvement in the computation time of IMITATOR can be achieved by coming up with a different exploration strategy more specialised to our problem.

We also evaluated the scalability of RTSCAN with respect to the number of parameters. To do this, we run the tool on test case 2b with a varying number of parameters. The computation time went from 1min11 for $F = 2$ parameters, up to 20min15 for the case of $F = 6$. With $F = 6$, the memory used by our program took a peak utilisation of 7.2 GiB, close to the memory limit of our PC. However, we believe that 6 parameters are sufficient for many practical engineering uses.

7 Conclusions and Future Work

In this paper we presented two different approaches to perform parametric analysis of distributed real-time systems: one based on analytic methods of classic schedulability analysis; the other one based on model checking of PSA. We compared the two approached with classical holistic analysis.

The results are promising, and we plan to extend this work along different directions. Regarding the analytic method, we want to enhance the analysis including static and dynamic offsets, following the approach of [19]. Also, we want to test the scalability of our approach on industrial test-cases.

As of IMITATOR, we plan to improve the algorithm to explore the parameters space: a promising idea is to use the analytic method to find an initial approximation of the feasible space, and then extend the border of the space using PSA.

Acknowledgements. We would like to express our gratitude to Michael González Harbour and Juan M. Rivas, from the Universidad de Cantabria, for their support to installing and using the MAST tool.

The research leading to these results has received funding from the European Union Seventh Framework Programme (FP7/2007-2013) under grant agreement No. 246556.

References

1. Abdeddaïm, Y., Asarin, E., Maler, O.: Scheduling with timed automata. Theoret. Comput. Sci. **354**(2), 272–300 (2006)
2. Abdeddaïm, Y., Maler, O.: Preemptive job-shop scheduling using stopwatch automata. In: Katoen, J.-P., Stevens, P. (eds.) TACAS 2002. LNCS, vol. 2280, pp. 113–126. Springer, Heidelberg (2002)

3. Alur, R., Dill, D.L.: A theory of timed automata. Theoret. Comput. Sci. **126**(2), 183–235 (1994)
4. Alur, R., Henzinger, T.A., Vardi, M.Y.: Parametric real-time reasoning. In: STOC, pp. 592–601. ACM (1993)
5. André, É., Fribourg, L.: Behavioral cartography of timed automata. In: Kučera, A., Potapov, I. (eds.) RP 2010. LNCS, vol. 6227, pp. 76–90. Springer, Heidelberg (2010)
6. André, É., Fribourg, L., Kühne, U., Soulat, R.: IMITATOR 2.5: a tool for analyzing robustness in scheduling problems. In: Giannakopoulou, D., Méry, D. (eds.) FM 2012. LNCS, vol. 7436, pp. 33–36. Springer, Heidelberg (2012)
7. André, É., Soulat, R.: The Inverse Method. FOCUS Series in Computer Engineering and Information Technology. ISTE/Wiley, London/New York (2013)
8. Bagnara, R., Hill, P.M., Zaffanella, E.: The Parma Polyhedra Library: toward a complete set of numerical abstractions for the analysis and verification of hardware and software systems. Sci. Comput. Program. **72**(1–2), 3–21 (2008)
9. Bini, E.: The design domain of real-time systems. Ph.D. thesis, Scuola Superiore Sant'Anna (2004)
10. Bini, E., Buttazzo, G.C.: Schedulability analysis of periodic fixed priority systems. IEEE Trans. Comput. **53**(11), 1462–1473 (2004)
11. Bril, R.J., Lukkien, J.J. , Verhaegh, W.F.J.: Worst-case response time analysis of real-time tasks under fixed-priority scheduling with deferred preemption revisited. In: ECRTS, pp. 269–279. IEEE Computer Society (2007)
12. Cimatti, A., Palopoli, L., Ramadian, Y.: Symbolic computation of schedulability regions using parametric timed automata. In: RTSS, pp. 80–89 (2008)
13. Davis, R.I., Burns, A., Bril, R.J., Lukkien, J.J.: Controller area network (CAN) schedulability analysis: refuted, revisited and revised. Real-Time Syst. **35**, 239–272 (2007)
14. Fribourg, L., Lesens, D., Moro, P., Soulat, R.: Robustness analysis for scheduling problems using the inverse method. In: TIME, pp. 73–80. IEEE Computer Society Press (2012)
15. Gonzalez Harbour, M., Gutierrez Garcia, J.J., Palencia Gutierrez, J.C., Drake Moyano, J.M.: Mast: modeling and analysis suite for real time applications. In: ECRTS, pp. 125–134 (2001)
16. Grupo de Computadores y Tiempo Real, Universidad de Cantabria. MAST: Modeling and analysis suite for real-time applications. http://mast.unican.es/
17. Henia, R., Hamann, A., Jersak, M., Racu, R., Richter, K., Ernst, R.: System level performance analysis – the SymTA/S approach. IEE Proc. Comput. Dig. Tech. **152**(2), 148–166 (2005)
18. Le, T.T.H., Palopoli, L., Passerone, R., Ramadian, Y.: Timed-automata based schedulability analysis for distributed firm real-time systems: a case study. Int. J. Softw. Tools Technol. Transfer **15**(3), 211–228 (2013)
19. Palencia, J.C., Gonzalez Harbour, M.: Schedulability analysis for tasks with static and dynamic offsets. In: RTSS, pp. 26–37 (1998)
20. Richter, K., Ernst, R.: Event model interfaces for heterogeneous system analysis. In: DATE, pp. 506–513. IEEE Computer Society (2002)
21. Seto, D., Lehoczky, D.P., Sha, L.: Task period selection and schedulability in real-time systems. In: RTSS (1998)

22. Sun, Y., Soulat, R., Lipari, G., André, É, Fribourg, L.: Parametric schedulability analysis of fixed priority real-time distributed systems. Research report LSV-13-03, Laboratoire Spécification et Vérification, ENS Cachan, France (2013)
23. Wandeler, E., Thiele, L., Verhoef, M., Lieverse, P.: System architecture evaluation using modular performance analysis: a case study. Int. J. Softw. Tools Technol. Transfer **8**(6), 649–667 (2006)

Wind Turbine System: An Industrial Case Study in Formal Modeling and Verification

Jagadish Suryadevara[1](✉), Gaetana Sapienza[2], Cristina Seceleanu[1],
Tiberiu Seceleanu[2], and Stein-Erik Ellevseth[2], and Paul Pettersson[1]

[1] Mälardalen Real-Time Research Centre, Mälardalen University, Västerås, Sweden
{jagadish.suryadevara,cristina.seceleanu,paul.pettersson}@mdh.se
[2] ABB Corporate Research, Billingstad, Norway
{gaetana.sapienza,tiberiu.seceleanu}@se.abb.com,
stein-erik.ellevseth@no.abb.com

Abstract. In the development of embedded systems, the formal analysis of system artifacts, such as structural and behavioral models, helps the system engineers to understand the overall functional and timing behavior of the system. In this case study paper, we present our experience in applying formal *verification and validation* (V&V) techniques, we had earlier proposed, for an industrial *wind turbine system* (WTS). We demonstrate the complementary benefits of formal verification in the context of existing V&V practices largely based on *simulation* and *testing*. We also discuss some modeling *trade-offs* and challenges we have identified with the case-study, which are worth being emphasized. One issue is related, for instance, to the *expressiveness* of the system artifacts, in view of the known limitations of rigorous verification, e.g. *model-checking*, of industrial systems.

Keywords: Industrial case-study · Wind turbine system · MARTE/ CCSL · EAST-ADL · Verification · Model checking · UPPAAL

1 Introduction

The increasing complexity and criticality of real-time embedded systems (RTES), in domains such as industrial automation, automotive and avionics, stresses the need for applying systematic design phases, combined with rigorous *verification and validation* (V&V) techniques, during system development [3]. A well-defined design process with necessary tool support leads to ensuring system *predictability*, w.r.t intended functional and timing behavior. Nevertheless, meeting such a clear objective has several challenges. One of pre-requisites is well-defined system artifacts representing system *structure* as well as *behavior* with *reactive*, *continuous*, *discrete*, and *real-time* features, or a combination thereof, at suitable *levels-of-abstraction*. For complex industrial systems, the above design by-products, while necessary, may lead to additional issues such as ensuring *traceability*, *analyzability* as well as *reusability* of the system artifacts. In this

C. Artho and P.C. Ölveczky (Eds.): FTSCS 2013, CCIS 419, pp. 229–245, 2014.
DOI: 10.1007/978-3-319-05416-2_15, © Springer International Publishing Switzerland 2014

context, model-based development approaches, which enable continuous V&V throughout the development process, have become a feasible solution to tackle some of the challenges. However, formal verification techniques such as *model checking*, while useful for the exhaustive analysis of system behavior, are challenging to apply for complex system models. A related issue is choosing a suitable level of *granularity* and *expressiveness* for system artifacts, given the well-known limitations of model-checking, such as the *state-space explosion* problem. In this paper, we address some of these challenges in the context of applying modeling and formal verification techniques using a *wind turbine system* case-study, a complex industrial RTES.

The Unified Modeling Language (UML) provides a modeling profile called MARTE (Modeling and Analysis of Real-Time and Embedded systems) [7] to support the *performance* and *schedulability* analysis of system models. MARTE also includes CCSL – a time model and a *clock constraint specification language* [1] for specifying logical and chronometric constraints for system models. On the other hand, EAST-ADL [2], an emerging standard for automotive systems, provides an integrated model-based development for RTES, through well-defined phases, as well as support for *traceability*. Recently, EAST-ADL has been integrated with *model-checking* support for component-based designs, e.g. the ViTAL tool [4] based on the timed automata technology for verification [5,10,11].

In this paper, we target the verification of functionality and timing behavior of a *wind turbine* system developed in the context of the iFEST (industrial Framework for Embedded Systems Tools), an ARTEMISIA project. In Sect. 2.2, we overview a simplified version of the *wind turbine system* (WTS), and describe its functionality and timing behavior. Rest of the paper is organized as follows: In Sect. 3, we briefly recall CCSL and timed automata. In Sect. 4, we describe a modeling methodology for the WTS to enable verification using *model checking*. The analysis results of simulating, as well as model checking the WTS model are presented in Sect. 5. In Sect. 6, we discuss our experience with the case study with respect to the challenges and limitations in applying formal techniques to complex industrial systems. We conclude the paper in Sect. 7.

2   Windturbine System (WTS) : An Overview

Wind energy sources are fast-growing and in line with the technological advancement. Modern wind turbine systems require sophisticated and effective control functionalities in order to fulfill *performance*, *safety*, and *maintainability* requirements. The main purpose of a wind turbine system is to convert the rotational mechanical energy of the rotor blades (i.e. mechanical components of a wind turbine) caused by the wind into electrical energy to be redistributed via a power grid. Given the system's complexity, the iFEST (industrial Framework for Embedded Systems Tools) project[1] aims at providing a model-based approach

---

[1] http://www.artemis-ifest.eu/

for system development, to ensure the system *predictability* w.r.t the specified functional and timing behavior.

2.1 Development Process and Environment

In the iFEST project, we have carried out the system development by adopting the V-model based software development approach, as follows:

During *Requirement and Analysis* phase, we have documented the WTS requirements, both functional and extra-functional including timing behavior. For the *Design* phase, we have combined component- and model-based approaches, keeping in view the overall system *analyzability* and *reusability* requirements. During the *Implementation* phase, we have applied automatic code generation technologies. Subsequently, the implemented system, a combined FPGA and CPU solution, has been deployed on a heterogenous hardware platform (XilinX ZynQ 7000 product family). For the *Verification and Validation* (V&V), we have used model-based techniques as follows: (i) simulation of the WTS functionality using Simulink and related toolboxes, and (ii) automatic model-based test-case generation with MaTeLo tool. However, the above techniques are not sufficient to ensure system *predictability* w.r.t to all possible system executions, hence formal verification is desirable to complement the current analysis methods. To address the above open issue, in this paper, we present a verification technique towards enhanced system validation. And, our contributions are as below:

- As enhanced system validation, we apply verification technique to establish system properties, (partially) based on simulation results of Simulink-based system models.
- We are able to verify safety requirements that involve timing behavior (e.g. "the wind turbine moves to Park mode, within 30 s of detecting that the wind speed has crossed the upper limit of 20 m/s").

2.2 The Wind Turbine System Model

The wind turbine system is modeled as a *closed-loop* control system, as shown in Fig. 1. The key components are the *Plant* and the *Controller* subsystems. The *Controller* dynamically regulates the rotor blades of the *wind turbine* w.r.t the specified wind profile, to maximize the generation of electrical energy and also to avoid damage to the plant in case of turbulent wind scenarios. It automatically changes the *Controller Output* signal to regulate the plant, based on the wind and the plant's actual conditions, which are received by the *Controller* via the *Sensor Input* signals. The *Wind Profile* and the *Resistive Load* are used to simulate and test the behavior of the plant and the controller, under specific wind and resistive load conditions. Further details of the plant and controller subsystems are described below.

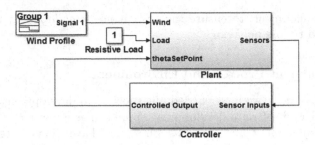

Fig. 1. Wind turbine system model

2.2.1 Plant Model

As shown in Fig. 2 (in Sect. 4), it consists of three main components; *Servo*, *Rotor*, and *Generator*. The pitch of the turbine, determined by the *Controller* (described below), is actuated by the *Servo*. The *Rotor* produces the required *torque* to maximize the angular speed of the *Generator* (which produces the final voltage), based on the pitch value as well as the current wind speed (we assume a fixed *resistive load*). The *Rotor* optimizes the produced torque value based on the current angular speed of the *Generator*.

2.2.2 Controller Model

As shown in Fig. 3 (in Sect. 4), it consists of four main components: the *Filter*, the *Main Controller*, the *Pitch Controller*, and the *Park and Brake Controller*. The *Filter Subsystem* is responsible for transducing, filtering and scaling the wind signal and plant signal (for instance the rotational speed of the turbine), which are used by the *Main Controller* and the *Pitch Controller*. Based on the inputs received through the *Filter*, the *Main Controller* directs the overall control. It oversees the performance and operations of the turbine in order to maximize the energy production and prevent any damage to the plant. Based on the wind and plant state, the controller determines the operational mode (i.e. park, start-up, generating, or brake) of the turbine. The *Pitch Control* calculates the proper pitch i.e. angle to steer the rotor blades when the turbine starts up or generates power. The *Pitch and Brake* controller determines if the turbine needs to brake or park, to ensure the safety of the wind turbine, for instance, during wind turbulences.

3 Preliminaries

In this section, we present an overview of the preliminaries needed for modeling of the wind turbine system. We have used EAST-ADL modeling framework for structural modeling of the WTS. The timed causality behavior of the system is specified using CCSL. To provide the verification using the UPPAAL, a model checking tool, we have developed the timed automata based semantic models of the system, based on the corresponding EAST-ADL models and the CCSL specifications.

3.1 EAST-ADL

The modeling process in EAST-ADL framework, developed in the context of the EAST-EEA project, is structured into different abstraction levels such as *feature level, analysis level, design level* etc. At both analysis and design levels, the system is described by a *FunctionalArchitecture* that consists of a number of inter-connected *FunctionPrototypes* (instantiation of *FunctionType* components). FunctionProtoype components are either *event-* or *time-*triggered. The execution semantics of the EAST-ADL components is as follows; components interact through single buffer, *rewritable, non-consumable* ports, and execute in *read-execute-write* phases in *run-to-completion* fashion. The detailed timing behavior as well as timing constraints for an EAST-ADL model can be specified using TADL2, the Timing Augmented Description Language (ver 2), currently being integrated with EAST-ADL framework [8]. In related works, we have proposed verification techniques for TADL2-based EAST-ADL models [5,10,11].

3.2 CCSL

CCSL is used to specify the constraints imposed on the logical *clocks* (activation conditions) of a model. A CCSL clock is defined as a sequence of *instants* (event occurrences). CCSL constraints are of three kinds: (i) *Synchronous* constraints rely on the notion of *coincidence*. For example, the constraint "a coincidesWith b", denoted by a = b, specifies that each instant of a coincides with the corresponding instant of b. Another example of a synchronous constraint is "a isPeriodicOn bperiod n", which specifies the subclock a whose 'ticks' correspond to every n^{th} 'tick' of b. (ii) *Asynchronous* constraints are based on instant *precedence*; the constraint "a isFasterThan b" (denoted by a $\preceq$ b) specifies that clock a is (non-strictly) faster than clock b. (iii) *Mixed* constraints combine *coincidence* and *precedence*; the constraint "c = a delayedFor n on b" specifies that c 'ticks' synchronously with the nth 'tick' of b following a 'tick'.

3.3 Timed Automata

A timed automaton is a tuple $< L, l_0, C, A, E, I >$, where L is a set of *locations*, $l_0 \in L$ is the initial location, C is the set of clocks, A is the set of actions, synchronization actions and the internal τ-action, $E \subseteq L \times A \times B(C) \times 2^C \times L$ is a set of edges between locations with an action, a guard, a set of clocks to be reset, and $I : L \to B(C)$ assigns clock *invariants* to locations. A location can be marked *urgent* (u) or *committed* (c) to indicate that the time is not allowed to progress in the specified location(s), the latter being a stricter form indicating further that the next transition can only be taken from the corresponding location(s) only. Also, synchronization between two automata is modeled via *channels* (e.g., **x**! and **x**?) with rendezvous or broadcast semantics.

The UPPAAL model-checker extends the timed automata language with a number of features such as global and local (bounded) integer variables, arithmetic operations, arrays, and a C-like programming language. The tool consists of three parts: a graphical editor for modeling timed automata, a simulator for trace generation, and a verifier for the verification of a system modeled as a network of timed automata. A subset of CTL (computation tree logic) is used as the input language for the verifier. For further details, we refer to UPPAAL tutorial [6].

4   WTS: Formal Specification and Modeling

In this section, we present a formal specification and modeling approach for WTS, an *aposteriori* modeling technique, that is, the specification and modeling artifacts are based on existing design artifacts such as Simulink models, requirements documents etc. However, we apply an *abstraction* strategy to obtain the corresponding real-time semantic models that represent the system functionality as well as the timing behavior. Further, the strategy attempts to preserve the models' *tractability* to make the exhaustive verification feasible. The overall modeling strategy, based on design principles such as *separation-of-concerns* and *correctness-by-construction*, captures the underlying *model-of-computation* and the execution behavior of the WTS. Below, we outline some generic views/assumptions on which we base our formal modeling:

– **Plant models and Instantaneous executions**. A *Plant* model represents physical devices such as *sensors* and *actuators* with the corresponding *model-of-computation* based on *reactivity* and *instantaneity*.
– **Controller models and Timed executions**. *Controllers* contain software components based on timed *model-of-computation*, with explicit timing aspects, such as *delay, execution time, end-to-end deadline* etc., to be formally specified and modeled.
– **Time and event triggering**. The activation or triggering of RTES components is generally based on specific *time* or *event*[2] occurrences. *Plant* components are event-triggered (i.e. in response to occurrence of input data), whereas *controller* components are time- or event-triggered, this primarily being a design-choice.
– **Run-to-completion**. RTES components execute in *run-to-completion* steps, that is, in terms of *read-execute-write* cycles.
– **Data and value semantics**. Due to the associated *models-of-computation*, as described above, a data entity at a given 'instant', in the *Plant* or *Controller*, may correspond to two distinct value instants.
– **Real-time features**. The structural and behavioral models of RTES often fail to model real-time features, such as *urgency, priority*, and *synchrony* (explained later) w.r.t to the underlying execution model.

---

[2] While time is also an 'event', we differentiate this in this paper explicitly.

– **Environment modeling.** An *environment* is external to the system, representing physical parameters such as *temperature, pressure, wind speed* etc. To support formal verification, a modeling strategy based on *non-determinism* as well as the properties to be verified, is needed.

To obtain an *expressive* and *verifiable* semantic model of the WTS, we employ a component-based modeling approach, based on real-time formalisms such as CCSL and timed automata. The overall modeling approach is as follows:

– Data and event representations are made based on the structural models.
– The timed causality behavior of the system components, w.r.t the associated *model-of-computation*, is formally specified using CCSL constraints.
– The functional behavior of the components is modeled using an abstract finite-state-machine notation, and transformed into timed automata.
– The CCSL constraints are transformed into timed automata, and composed using the notion of *synchronization product* (described later).

Finally, a real-time semantic model of the overall system is obtained as a network (i.e., a *parallel composition*) of timed automata described above.

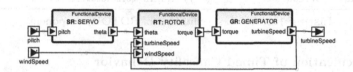

Fig. 2. Structural modeling: a *plant* model for the WTS.

In Fig. 2, we present the structural model of *plant* and *controller* for the WTS (based on the corresponding Simulink models), using the EAST-ADL modeling framework (in MetaEdit+[3]). The main components of the plant, that is SERVO, ROTOR, and GENERATOR are modeled as `FunctionalDevice` prototypes in EAST-ADL. In Fig. 3, we present the structural model of the Controller. It models the three sub-controllers MainControl, PitchRegulation, and ParkBrake, modeled as `AnalysisFunctionTypes`. For further details of the functionality of these components, we refer to Sect. 2.2. We demonstrate the overall modeling approach for WTS, using the ROTOR and the MainControl components, below. We will also discuss some related modeling issues.

4.1   Data and Events

As shown in Fig. 2, the ROTOR prototype, denoted by RT, receives input *pitch* (`theta`), *turbine speed* (`omega`), and *wind speed* (`ws`) and produces the corresponding `torque` value as the output. Hence, we define the local variables $theta_l$,

---
[3] www.metacase.com

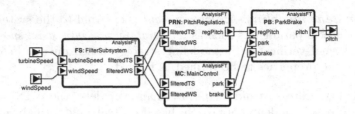

Fig. 3. Structural modeling: a *controller* model of the WTS.

$omega_l$, and ws_l and the corresponding global variables ws_g, $omega_g$, $theta_g$. The local variables are updated at the activation of the RT using the corresponding global values. This is consistent with the data semantics discussed previously.

```
1 CCSLclock  RT_in;              // read (input) instants
  CCSLclock  RT_out;             // write (output) instants
3 CCSLclock  RT_omega;           // activation (trigger) instants

5 CCSLconstraint
  RT_omega  =  RT_in;            // RT_omega coincidesWith RT_in
7 RT_in  =  RT_out;              // RT_in coincidesWith RT_out
```

Listing 1.1. CCSL specification of ROTOR component.

4.2   Specification of Timed Causality Behavior

The timed causality behavior of real-time components, w.r.t the corresponding *model-of-computation*, can be specified precisely using CCSL logical clocks and CCSL constraints. We use CCSL (logical) clocks to represent events corresponding to 'read', 'execute', and 'write' instants of a component. In Listing 1.1 and Listing 1.2, we present the CCSL specification of ROTOR (RT) and MainControl (MC) prototypes, respectively. The constraints specify the timed causality behavior of the components w.r.t to the corresponding *model-of-computation*. For instance, the CCSL constraints for RT specify the *reactivity* and *instantaneity* behavior of RT execution within the *Plant* model. On the other hand, the CCSL constraints for MC specify the time-triggered behavior of the *controller* execution. The timing attributes of the controller components are given in Table 1. The CCSL specifications provide a basis for constructing real-time semantic models e.g. timed automata based models, as well as *observers* to establish the system properties, as presented later in this section.

```
1 CCSLclock  MC_in               //read (input) instants
  CCSLclock  MC_out              //write (output) instants
3
  CCSLconstraint
5 MC_in delayedFor 10 on SysClk ≼ MC_out   //Minimum execution time
  MC_out ≼ MC_in delayedFor 15 on SysClk   //Maximum execution time
7 MC_in isPeriodicWith period 100 on SysClk //Time triggering
```

Listing 1.2. CCSL specification of MainControl component.

Table 1. Timing attributes of *Controller* components.

Component	Period (ms)	Min. execution time (ms)	Max. execution time (ms)
MainControl	100	10	15
PitchRegulation	50	35	45
ParkBrake	50	15	20
Filter	–	20	25

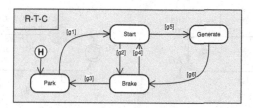

Fig. 4. Functional behavior of the MainControl component.

4.3   Modeling Functional Behavior of Real-Time Components

In Fig. 4, we present the behavior modeling for the MainControl protoype (based on the corresponding Simulink model). The behavior is specified using a *finite-state-machine* (FSM) notation. It represents the overall system behavior (stateful) in terms of control states PARK, START, BRAKE, and GENERATE. The states represent the operational *modes* of the WTS, based on the *wind speed* and the *turbine speed*; the mode transitions corresponding to mode-change behavior are triggered by boolean conditions (guards) *g1*, *g2*, .. etc. Further, we simply annotate the behavior model to denote the execution semantics such as *run-to-completion* (R-T-C) and *history* (denoted by the control node H). The functionality of other components in the WTS are stateless computations, that is partial functions between input and corresponding output values, for instance as represented by the *writeTorque()* function of the ROTOR.

4.4   Formal Modeling of *Plant* Components

In this subsection, we present formal modeling approach, based on CCSL, for the plant components of the WTS. We had earlier proposed, in a previous work [10], transformation of CCSL constraints into timed automata. The transformations can be used to derive timed automata based models that represent the timed causality behavior of the system. For instance, in Fig. 5(a) and (b), we present the timed automata semantics of CCSL constraints that specify the timed causality behavior of ROTOR executions (see Listing 1.1), using events RT_in and RT_out representing component activation and termination respectively. Note that an event e.g. RT_in is modeled using synchronization channels i.e. send/receive signals RT_in! and RT_out!. Also note that the *synchronous* occurrence of event

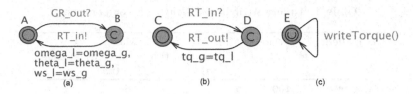

Fig. 5. Timed automata modeling: (a) `RT_omega = RT_in`   (b) `RT_in = RT_out`   (c) Computation RT.

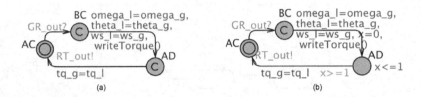

Fig. 6. Timed automata model for (event-triggered) ROTOR.

signals, e.g. `GR_out?` and `RT_in!` in Fig. 5(a), is specified using *committed* locations. A *committed* location indicates that the corresponding enabled transitions from the location are 'forced' before time can progress. This facilitates precise modeling of overall timing behavior of the system.

The above automata can be composed, using the notion of *synchronization product* (based on common labels or synchronization signals), as shown in Fig. 6(a). For instance, locations B and C in the automata in Fig. 5(a) and (b) respectively, are mapped to the location BC in Fig. 6(a), due to the synchronization of signals `RT_in!` and `RT_in?`.

It can be noted that the composed location 'BD' is not possible in the synchronized product automaton, as the location is *non-reachable* due to the synchronization at B and C, leading to location AD (i.e. location A, and D simultaneously in resp. automata) in the synchronized product, instead. Further, as shown in Fig. 6(a), we associate the transitions corresponding to component activation, with data updates and the corresponding computation; the `RT_in` event denotes input as well as execution of the corresponding functionality, during a transition from location BC to location AD. However, to make the overall automata model of the WTS system *tractable* (time-wise), and hence formally verifiable, we need to relax the notion of *instantaneity* for the automata models of the *Plant* components. This can be done by introducing a minimum time delay for each component, if not specified already. This is done by assigning a timing *invariant*, the delay of one time unit, for instance at location AD in Fig. 6(b).

4.5   Formal Modeling of *Controller* Components

In this subsection, we describe the timed automata modeling of the *Controller* components for the WTS. In Fig. 7, we present the timed automata semantics

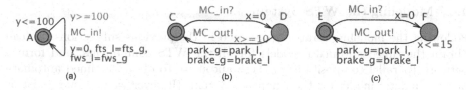

Fig. 7. Semantic modeling: (a) Periodic triggering   (b) Min. exec. time   (c) Max. exec. time

of the CCSL constraints (Listing 1.2) that specify the time-triggered execution behavior of the MainControl (MC) prototype. We have composed these automata, as shown in Fig. 8(a), based on the notion of *synchronization product* (as described in the previous subsection). This consists of following steps; we have composed the automata in Fig. 7(b) and (c), and then finally with the automaton in Fig. 7(a) (note the invariant $y \leq 100$ at every location in the product automaton).

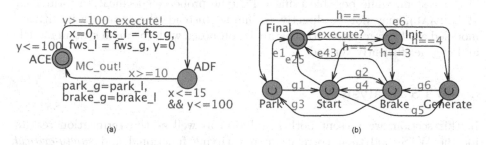

Fig. 8. Timed automata modeling of MainControl: (a) time-triggering (b) functional behavior.

As shown in Fig. 8(b), we have also transformed the behavior (functional) model of the MainControl (Fig. 4) component into corresponding timed automaton, following the mapping techniques proposed previously [9]. We briefly outline the transformation as follows; we have mapped the control states to automaton locations. Further, using additional locations *Init* and *Final* and the history variable '*h*', we have modeled the execution semantics, that is, *run-to-completion*, and preserving the *history*. For model readability, we have not shown the data updates for the transitions; also, the boolean guards of the form 'eij' correspond to actual expression (¬gi && ¬gj). It can be noted that all the locations of the transformed automaton are marked 'urgent' indicating the behavior model does not consume time, which has been separately modeled using the timed causality model discussed above. Finally, we 'connect' the transformed behavior model of the MainControl prototype, as described above, with the automata model of the corresponding timing behavior (Fig. 8(b)), using synchronization channel 'execute'.

4.6   Modeling the WTS System

Following the modeling strategy presented in the previous subsections, we can obtain the timed automata models for all the WTS components, and form a network (parallel composition) of these automata to obtain a timed automata based semantic model for the complete system. However, some issues exist as discussed below:

Modeling the Environment: The plant model described previously, models the components such as sensors and actuators constituting an *environment* model for the WTS *controller*. However, this is not sufficient to obtain a 'closed' model of the system that is necessary to enable exhaustive verification of the WTS model. For instance, modeling external parameters such as WindSpeed, while necessary, is not feasible using timed automata. In view of this, as well as the hybrid nature of the plant components e.g. ROTOR, GENERATOR etc., we choose to integrate the simulation data of the corresponding Simulink models, to construct the partial functions that represent the computations of the components.

Modeling 'observer' automata: The formal specification of complex properties of the system, while possible using CTL (the property specification formalism of UPPAAL), may not be directly verifiable. Instead, these can be intuitively modeled as *observer* automata, (parallel) composed with the main system model, and can be efficiently verified.

5   WTS Analysis

In this section, we present both simulation as well as the verification results for the WTS, and their correlation in verifying functional and *safety-critical* properties w.r.t the overall timing behavior of the system.

5.1   Simulation

The main purpose of simulating the WTS, using the MathWorks Simulink and StateFlow[4], is to analyze the system behavior under normal operating conditions, and to validate the system (in particular the *Controller*) when the *wind speed* exceeds the designed limit. The simulation results are presented in Fig. 9.

The simulation time is step-wise incremented from 0 up to 80 s, with a fixed sample time equal to 1 ms. For the simulation, a specific wind speed profile has been created. According to this, the system is simulated for normal operating limits, i.e., 5–20 m/s up to 30 s, then up to 30 m/s above 43 s. The simulation results are analyzed w.r.t the turbine control states representing the operational modes (i.e. 0:park, 1:start, 2:generate, 3:brake).

While the simulation provides rich data representing the computation and control of the WTS w.r.t complex environment behavior, system *properties* however can not be established without analyzing the data. In the next subsection,

---

[4] http://www.mathworks.se/products/stateflow/

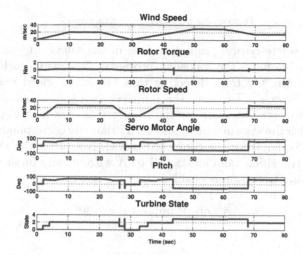

Fig. 9. Simulation results

we present a verification technique to 'exhaustively' analyze the simulation data, w.r.t the overall system timing and causality behavior, towards establishing the system properties. Below, we describe some verification results for the WTS system.

5.2   Verification

For WTS, a formal modeling of the corresponding *plant* and the *environment* parameters is not possible. Hence, we use simulation data and construct partial functions (input to output values) that represent the computations of the *plant* components, for instance ROTOR. Also, we use simulation values corresponding to the environment parameters e.g. *wind-profile* of the WTS. In the next section, we will discuss some aspects about the construction of the relevant partial functions.

Verification of functional properties: Verification of functional properties gives insight into the overall system (architectural) design. For instance, in the WTS case, it is useful to verify the following property: "if the *wind speed* is within the prescribed limits, the controller eventually moves to Generate mode". The property can be formulated as a liveness property or leads_to property (denoted by ⤳, implemented as --> in UPPAAL), as below.

$$(\text{ws>=5 \&\& ws<=20) --> state==2} \tag{1}$$

Verification of safety-critical properties: One of the safety-critical requirements for the WTS is to fulfill the following property: "the wind turbine moves to Park mode, within 30 s from detecting that the wind speed has crossed the upper limit of 20 m/s". To verify the property (w.r.t to simulation data), we construct an *observer* automata for the property as shown in Fig. 10, compose the observer with the system model, and verify that the corresponding *invariant*, the Property (2), holds for the composed model. Note that the *urgent* channel 'U!' forces the transition from location B to A without any further delay, when the corresponding transition is enabled.

$$A\square\,\text{obs.B implies } x <= 30 \tag{2}$$

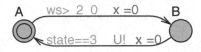

Fig. 10. An observer automata to verify the safety-property: `A[] obs.B implies x<=30`

Verifying reachability properties: We can verify *reachability* of specific control states or computation. For instance, using the Property 3, a *reachability* property, we can verify that the control state 'Park' (Fig. 8(b)) has been reached (at least once) during the simulation of the WTS. While this may be easily validated using the simulation trace, we can use similar properties to verify specific 'error' states e.g. by extending the behavior model with special 'locations' that are reached if the corresponding 'error' is detected. The presence of these error locations in the simulation data can then be 'exhaustively' verified.

$$\exists <> \text{MC.Park} \tag{3}$$

Verifying deadlock-freeness: Using the Property 4, we can verify that the system is *deadlock-free*, w.r.t overall timed causality behavior of the WTS, as modeled by the corresponding timed automata model. The property is an important validation of the system, which can not be achieved using simulation only, as the corresponding Simulink model does not represent the timing behavior of the system explicitly. Also, the property, when satisfied, verifies the correctness (i.e. *consistency*) of the timing attributes (Table 1) associated with the system (architectural) design.

$$A\square\,(\text{not deadlock}) \tag{4}$$

6   Discussion and Lessons-Learned

In this paper, we have presented a formal modeling and verification approach for an industrial system, namely a *wind turbine system*. The main goal of the work has been to provide formal verification as a complementary analysis method to existing validation techniques based primarily on simulation. We have successfully addressed the following challenges:

- *Abstract but expressive system models*: Using real-time formalisms such as CCSL and timed automata, we were able to construct intuitive system models amenable for exhaustive verification (w.r.t to timing). With the separation of timing and functional modeling, the technique is scalable to complex system models.

- *Verification as complementary analysis to simulation*: The verification is based on 'exhaustively' analyzing the simulation data w.r.t the timing behavior of the system. While verification models are expressive in terms of system structure and precise timing behavior, simulation models are suitable to specify *plant* and the *environment*, e.g. 'wind profile' modeling in the case of WTS simulation. Thus, the verification approach provides an enhanced simulation-based validation.

The formal modeling approach for the *wind turbine system* considers the corresponding simulation results to model a suitable abstraction of the *plant* model. It facilitates constructing a formal model of the WTS, including the plant behavior. This was primarily one of the obstacles in earlier efforts to achieve formal verification of the system. Besides, the formal models were only possible due to expressiveness of real-time semantic formalisms such as CCSL and modeling flexibility in timed automata, as demonstrated in this paper. Further, we believe that the modeling approach is scalable to large complex systems, due to parallel composition of semantic models (timed automata) representing system components. For the verification results, we have considered only the control properties of the system with respect to the overall timed causality behavior. However, we can also consider the data values in the verification, due to timed automata variables. Thus, we have combined the expressiveness of CCSL with modeling capabilities of timed automata.

However, some limitations of our approach do exist. The exhaustiveness of the verification is limited to partial functions constructed using specific instance(s) of simulation. Hence, the approach may be similar to testing-based analysis (albeit model-based). Hence, we need strategies, e.g. choosing suitable simulation *step* and data profiles, to generate simulation data w.r.t the system properties to be verified. Further, it may be noted that the simulation-extended verification approach presented above may be suitable for data-intensive control systems (e.g. hybrid systems), such as the *wind turbine system* case study presented in the paper. On the other hand, control-intensive systems may be exhaustively modeled and verifiable using *model-checking* independent of simulation.

7   Conclusion

In this paper, we have presented a formal modeling and verification approach for an industrial case-study, namely an example *wind turbine system*. The architectural and behavioral modeling, partially based on the existing system artifacts such as Simulink-models, additionally captures precise timing behavior of the system. The modeling approach, based on the real-time formalisms such as CCSL and timed automata, also integrates simulation data to model *plant* and *environment* behavior. Based on this, the proposed verification technique using *model-checking*, enhances the simulation-based system *validation*. Besides verifying functional properties that validate correctness of the system design, *safety-critical* properties w.r.t the overall system timing behavior can also be verified. This is clearly an important analysis step forward within existing validation approaches for industrial applications. Thus the paper addresses V&V challenges in the industrial context, by combining both simulation and verification techniques, paving the way towards scalable application of *model-checking* for an enhanced validation process. As future work, we intend to investigate *requirement*-driven strategies to derive the simulation criteria for generating relevant partial functions. This leads to enhanced validation process that can verify useful classes of system properties.

Acknowledgment. This work was partially funded by Swedish Research Council (project ARROWS), Mälardalen University (Sweden), and ARTEMISIA project iFEST.

References

1. André, C., Mallet, F., de Simone, R.: Modeling time(s). In: Engels, G., Opdyke, B., Schmidt, D.C., Weil, F. (eds.) MODELS 2007. LNCS, vol. 4735, pp. 559–573. Springer, Heidelberg (2007)
2. ATESST (Advancing Traffic Efficiency through Software Technology): East-ADL2 specification. http://www.atesst.org (2008)
3. Bouyssounouse, B., Sifakis, J.: Embedded Systems Design: The ARTIST Roadmap for Research and Development. LNCS. Springer, Heidelberg (2005)
4. Enoiu, E.P., Marinescu, R., Seceleanu, C., Pettersson, P.: Vital : a verification tool for east-adl models using uppaal port. In: ICECCS'12, July 2012 (2012)
5. Goknil, A., Suryadevara, J., Peraldi-Frati, M.A., Mallet, F.: Analysis support for TADL2 timing constraints on EAST-ADL models. In: Drira, K. (ed.) ECSA 2013. LNCS, vol. 7957, pp. 89–105. Springer, Heidelberg (2013)
6. Larsen, K.G., Pettersson, P., Yi, W.: Uppaal in a Nutshell. Int. J. Softw. Tools Technol. Transfer **1**(1–2), 134–152 (1997)
7. OMG: UML Profile for MARTE, v1.0. Object Management Group, formal/2009-11-02 (November 2009)
8. Peraldi-Frati, M.A., Goknil, A., Deantoni, J., Nordlander, J.: A timing model for specifying multi clock automotive systems: the timing augmented description language V2. In: ICECCS 2012, pp. 230–239 (2012)

9. Slutej, D., Håkansson, J., Suryadevara, J., Seceleanu, C., Pettersson, P.:Analyzing a pattern-based model of a real-time turntable system. In: Jens Happe, B.Z. (ed.) 6th International Workshop on Formal Engineering approaches to Software Components and Architectures (FESCA), ETAPS'09, York, UK, March 2009. Electronic Notes in Theoretical Computer Science (ENTCS), vol. 253, pp. 161–178. Elsevier (2009)
10. Suryadevara, J., Seceleanu, C., Mallet, F., Pettersson, P.: Verifying MARTE/CCSL mode behaviors using UPPAAL. In: Hierons, R.M., Merayo, M.G., Bravetti, M. (eds.) SEFM 2013. LNCS, vol. 8137, pp. 1–15. Springer, Heidelberg (2013)
11. Suryadevara, J.: Validating EAST-ADL timing constraints using UPPAAL. In: 39th Euromicro Conference on Software Engineering and Advanced Applications, SEAA 2013 (2013)

Refinement Tree and Its Patterns: A Graphical Approach for Event-B Modeling

Kriangkrai Traichaiyaporn[(⊠)] and Toshiaki Aoki

School of Information Science, Japan Advanced Institute of Science and Technology
(JAIST), Ishikawa, Japan
{kriangkrai.tr,toshiaki}@jaist.ac.jp

Abstract. Event-B is a famous formal approach for verifying the
requirements specification of safety-critical systems. Even though Event-
B is a good formal approach which is successful in applying to several
practical case studies, we think that additional methods are needed to
apply it to the safety critical systems. Once we identify the requirements, Event-B allows us to formally describe the requirements. However,
Event-B does not explicitly support analysing and elaborating requirements themselves. Although refinement mechanisms provided by Event-
B is useful to stepwise model concrete requirements from abstract ones,
guideline of the refinements is not provided. This paper aims to propose a refinement tree diagram and its refinement patterns to provide
the requirements analysis and elaboration, and the guideline for Event-
B. The diagram and the patterns are partially derived from the KAOS
method, a goal-oriented requirements engineering method. The utility of
the diagram and the patterns is successfully shown by applying them to
three practical case studies.

1 Introduction

In the development of safety-critical systems, most of the typical approaches,
to guarantee that the systems are sufficiently safe, start from ensuring the correctness of requirements specifications. Formal methods are recommended for
verifying the correctness by the functional safety standards such as ISO26262
[8]. It is common that the requirements specifications are too complex to be
formally verified all at once. Thus, refinement techniques are applied to reduced
the complexity by stepwise transforming an abstract specification into a concrete
specification. Among the refinement techniques, the refinement mechanism provided by Event-B is a more flexible one comparing to the related languages such
as Z [15] and VDM [9].

Event-B [3] is a formal specification language for modeling and verifying
system requirements through the refinement mechanism. Event-B has been successfully applied to several practical safety-critical systems. Some examples are a
train controller system [16], hybrid systems [17], and a metro system [14]. Event-
B can be regarded as a method for correct-by-construction system development.

C. Artho and P.C. Ölveczky (Eds.): FTSCS 2013, CCIS 419, pp. 246–261, 2014.
DOI: 10.1007/978-3-319-05416-2_16, © Springer International Publishing Switzerland 2014

Even though Event-B is a good formal approach which is successful in applying to several practical case studies, it lacks some methods, which are necessary for the practical development of the safety-critical systems. This paper focuses on dealing with two issues in Event-B. Firstly, Event-B provides no method for analyzing and elaborating requirements specifications. The method is needed to specify essential information of the safety-critical systems. Without sufficiently specifying the information, it is impossible to justify that a system is safe. Secondly, there is no guideline for using the refinement mechanism in Event-B effectively. Given that a complicated system is being modeled in Event-B, designers and developers of the system might have no idea how to organize the refinement steps which is a source of difficulty in the usage of refinement [2].

In this paper, we aim to fulfil what Event-B lacks by proposing a refinement tree diagram and its refinement patterns. The refinement tree diagram is to graphically show the steps of refinement of the modeled specification in the form of tree structure. The diagram is designed in a way that it can be easily transformed into the Event-B specification. The refinement patterns are proposed in addition to the diagram to guide the refinement of the Event-B specification. The diagram along with the patterns are created by adapting the concepts from the goal model and the goal refinement patterns of the KAOS method [19].

The KAOS method is a goal-oriented requirements engineering method for analyzing and elaborating requirements. Its core model, the goal model, is created through the notion of goal refinement. The goal refinement provides a nearer way to how human stepwise refines requirements and is, thus, easy to understand. The KAOS method includes a set of goal refinement patterns to efficiently refine goals by following the frequently-used refinement tactics. Seeing that the KAOS method provides what we need to fulfil Event-B, we apply the KAOS method to Event-B. However, the formal semantics of the KAOS method and the formal specification of Event-B are different. Their notions of refinement are different as well. Consequently, instead of directly using the goal model, we propose the refinement tree diagram and the refinement patterns based on the goal model and the goal refinement patterns.

The refinement tree diagram and the refinement patterns are applied to model three practical safety-critical case studies. From the case studies, we find that we can specify the necessary information, such as behavior, inputs, and output, through the refinement tree diagram in a similar manner to the KAOS method. Furthermore, the refinement patterns can guide the way to stepwise refine the specifications of the case studies well. Therefore, we conclude that the refinement tree and the refinement patterns can complement Event-B.

The remainder of this paper is organized as follows. Section 2 overviews Event-B and the KAOS method. Section 3 explains the motivation behind the creation of the refinement tree diagram. Sections 4 and 5 describe the refinement tree diagram and its patterns respectively. Section 6 briefly demonstrates the application of our diagram and patterns on three case studies, and the results. Relevant issues from the results are discussed in Sect. 7. Related works are discussed in Sect. 8. Finally, Sect. 9 concludes this paper.

2   Background

This section provides a short overview of Event-B and the KAOS method.

2.1   Event-B

Event-B [3] is a formal specification language for modeling specification of systems. The language is based on first-order predicate logic and discrete transition systems. The main feature of Event-B is its refinement mechanism to incrementally constructing a specification from an abstract one into a concrete one.

A specification described in Event-B may be divided into a static part called the *context*, and a dynamic part called the *machine*. In this paper, we simply assume that there is some context and do not mention it explicitly. Machines are for describing behavioral properties of the specifications. Machines contain all of the state *variables*. Types and properties of the variables are declared through *invariants* in a form of the predicate. The values of the variables can be changed by the execution of *events*.

From an abstract machine containing a collection of variables, invariants, and events, the refinement mechanism of Event-B allows us to refine the abstract machine into a concrete machine by adding new variables, adding new events, rewriting events description to handle new variables, strengthening the guards, and so on. To explicitly associate the abstract machine and the concrete machine, a term 'refines' following with the name of the abstract machine is written in the description of the concrete machine. Even though there are many ways to refine a machine, they are restricted by the syntactic rules and the proof obligations of Event-B. This is for preventing the description of the concrete machine from contradicting the description of the abstract machine.

Describing a specification in Event-B is always in a top-down style. The Event-B specification always start from describing the most abstract machine called 'initial machine'. Then, the initial machine is gradually refined into the first refinement, the second refinement, and so on.

An event in a machine can be represented by the following form:

$$evt \mathrel{\hat{=}} \textbf{refines } a\_evt \textbf{ any } p \textbf{ when } G \textbf{ with } W \textbf{ then } S \textbf{ end}$$

where a_evt is the name of the abstract event, p denotes internal parameters of the event, G is a predicate denoting *guards*, and S denotes the *actions* that update some variables and can be executed only when G holds. When we refine an abstract event, some variables of that event might be disappeared in its concrete event. W denotes *witnesses* that are additional elements in the concrete event for indicating the disappeared variables and their values. Again, the term 'refines' is written in the description of the concrete event to explicitly associate it with the corresponding abstract event. In the semantics of Event-B, if an event does not have the term 'refines' in its description, it means that the event implicitly refine an event named *skip*, which is a blank event.

2.2   The KAOS Method

KAOS ('Knowledge Acquisition in autOmated Specification' or 'Keep All Objects Satisfied') [19] is a goal-oriented requirements engineering method with several UML-like models. The central model of the KAOS method is the goal model to show relationships among goals of a system in a tree structure.

The goal model consists of a refinement graph expressing how higher-level goals are refined into lower-level ones and, conversely, how lower-level goals contribute to higher-level goals. The higher-level goals are in general strategic and coarse-grained whereas lower-level goals are technical and fine-grained. In a refinement graph, a node represents a goal, and an AND-refinement link relates a parent goal to a set of sub-goals. A parent goal must be satisfied when all of its sub-goals are satisfied. The relationship between a parent goal and the set of its sub-goals is called *goal refinement*. The process of goal refinement is intuitive and can drive the analysis and elaboration of requirements. Formally, all goals can be represented in linear temporal logic.

An effective way to construct a goal model is by reusing goal refinement patterns [6]. The goal refinement patterns are frequently used patterns for refining a goal into sub-goals. Each pattern suggests specific refinements for instantiation to the specifics of the modeled system. For examples, *the milestone-driven refinement pattern* is for establishing a necessary intermediate step (a milestone condition) for reaching a target condition from a current condition, and *the decomposition-by-case refinement pattern* is to introduce different cases for reaching a target condition. This pattern also checks that all possible cases are determined in the decomposition, and they are disjoint. The two examples refinement patterns are shown in Fig. 1. Parameters are used in each pattern for representing conditions. Ones can instantiate a pattern by replacing each parameter with a corresponding condition from the modeled system. The patterns are proved to be complete and consistent in term of the linear temporal logic.

In the context of the KAOS method, the pattern:

$$Achieve[TargetCondition\ (If\ CurrentCondition)]$$

prescribes goals where some target properties must be eventually satisfied in the future after a current condition is satisfied. The current condition can sometimes be omitted in the pattern.

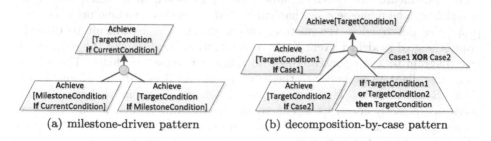

(a) milestone-driven pattern   (b) decomposition-by-case pattern

Fig. 1. KAOS goal refinement patterns

3   Motivation

The motivation behind this work comes from what we find in the existing works applying Event-B to practical case studies. An example is the work describing in [1], which is about the formalization of hybrid systems in Event-B. The hybrid systems are very important in the development of embedded systems where a piece of software, the controller, is supposed to manage an external situation, the environment. It is usual to find that most safety-critical systems are related to the hybrid systems. One hybrid system described in the article is about a system controlling trains to provide safe moves of the trains. A preliminary study is performed before the system is modeled in Event-B. From the preliminary study, some necessary invariants of the system are found, and the information needed for deciding the current acceleration of a train is specified. Without the preliminary study, those necessary information cannot be specified. This can potentially cause the system to be unsafe. The preliminary study is undoubtedly crucial, but no systematical way for the preliminary study has been proposed for Event-B.

Another notice from [1] is that even though the work focused on the hybrid systems, all of its examples have distinct ways to refine the system specifications in Event-B. The advantage of the refinement mechanism is that it provide a lot of (but limited) ways to refine an Event-B machine for widely supporting various kinds of systems. Unfortunately, the refinement mechanism is usually poorly used because it is not easy to decide how to organize the construction steps [2]. A guideline for the refinement is needed.

We find that the KAOS method provides the goal model to analyze and elaborate requirements through the intuitive notions of refinement, i.e. the goal refinement. Besides, we think the requirements analysis and elaboration can be regarded as the preliminary study. Therefore, we plan to apply the goal model to fulfil what Event-B lacks, that is, the systematical preliminary study and the guideline for using Event-B refinement.

Ideally, the most straightforward way to apply the goal model to Event-B is by using the goal model to model a system and then directly create an Event-B specification based on the goal model. However, the logic behind the two approaches are different, i.e. the linear temporal logic and the first-order predicate logic. In addition, their semantics of refinement are different. Goal refinement means that when all sub-goals are satisfied, then their parent goal is satisfied. The refinement mechanism is that a concrete machine preserves the properties described in the abstract machine. Thus, it is difficult to directly apply the goal model to Event-B. As a result, we rather propose the refinement tree diagram to assist constructing and refining Event-B machines. The refinement tree diagram is similar to the goal model, but it can be transformed into Event-B specification. Then, we propose a set of refinement patterns to help users to efficiently construct a refinement tree diagram similar to how the goal refinement patterns of KAOS guide the construction of the goal model. Some of our refinement patterns are derived from the goal refinement patterns.

4   The Refinement Tree Diagram

Refinement tree diagram is a diagram showing refinements of event from a sequence of refinements of Event-B machines in the form of tree. We design the refinement tree diagram in a way that it can graphically support:

- Demonstrating the refinements of events
- Justifying new events and invariants of a machine
- Separation of steps of refinement
- Transformation to Event-B specification

Each node of the refinement tree diagram represents either an event or an invariant. Arrows represent refinements of events and are used for separating steps of refinement. Lines among the nodes represent associations among the components. An example of the refinement tree is shown in Fig. 2. Through this example, all the details about the refinement tree diagram are gradually explained in the following subsections.

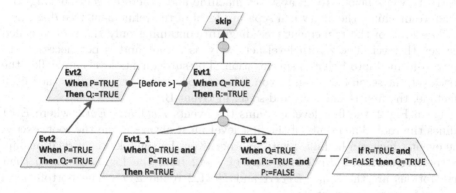

Fig. 2. An example refinement tree diagram

4.1   Nodes

In the refinement tree diagram, a parallelogram represents an Event-B event, a trapezoid represents an Event-B invariant. Note that the description written in the parallelogram strictly follows the way the event is described in Event-B specification as explained in Sect. 2.1.

Each node representing either an event or an invariant is described by using natural language. The natural language acts as identifiers for formal descriptions in Event-B. Even if it acts only as the identifiers, the meaning of the natural language should correspond to the formal specification. Therefore, the natural language that can be used in the diagram is limited to what the first-order predicate logic of Event-B can describe. For examples, if a predicate in Event-B is written as $(P = TRUE \land Q = TRUE) \Rightarrow R = FALSE$ where P, Q, R are

Boolean variables, one possible identifier of this predicate in the natural language is "If P and Q become true then R becomes false". This is up to what P, Q, R represent in the specification.

From Fig. 2, the event *skip* acts as the root of the refinement tree diagram and it is always the root of all refinement tree diagrams. Excluding the root, the example has five events; $Evt1$, $Evt2$, $Evt1\_1$, $Evt1\_2$, and $Evt2$; and an invariant. Note that there are two events written with the same descriptions. Both of them have the same name: $Evt2$.

4.2   Refinements of Events

A refinement of event is represented by an arrow with a small circle. The circle is for linking all concrete events refining the same abstract event. Here, we specify that 'refinement of event' means there are some changes in the description of a concrete event comparing to its abstract event. If the description of a concrete event is the same with its abstract event, we regard it as a 'copy' of the abstract event. In this case, the arrow directly links two events to show the copy. Because abstract events belong to an abstract machine and concrete events belong to a concrete machine, the arrow can separate level of the refinement tree diagram.

The level of the refinement tree diagram containing only the root is called the zeroth level. The zeroth level acts only as a root and is not necessary to be transformed into Event-B specification. The subsequents levels are called the first level, the second level, and so on. They respectively correspond to the initial machine, the first refinement, and so on in Event-B.

From Fig. 2, the first level contains the events $Evt1$ and $Evt2$, where $Evt1$ refines the root. The events of the first level must always refine the root, except the event which can be linked with another event by some kinds of relationship. In the bottom level, $Evt2$ is a copy of $Evt2$ from the higher level, so their descriptions are the same. $Evt1\_1$ and $Evt1\_2$ refine $Evt1$. The bottom level also contains an invariant.

Both the refinement and the copy of event can be written into Event-B specification as 'refines' relationships between abstract events and concrete events. Each event in an upper level must be pointed by at least one arrow from the subsequent level, since Event-B does not allow any abstract events to be missing in the concrete machine.

4.3   Relationships among Events and Invariants

Here, we clearly separate the links showing relationships between events and the links showing relationships between events and invariants. They are represented by plain lines and dashed lines respectively. In facts, these relationships are not shown in the original Event-B. We define the relationships to support justifying new events and invariants of a machine in the refinement tree diagram. The events and invariants which are linked by the plain lines and the dashed lines must be only in the same level of the refinement tree diagram.

In the context of this paper, 'new' events mean the events added to a concrete machine without explicitly refining an event from the abstract event. When the new events are added to a machine, it might be unclear how the new events interact with other events. The plain lines, linking two or more events, are defined for the refinement tree diagram to show the interaction among new events and others. The types of the relationship should also be written on the lines. For example, $Evt2$ and $Evt1$ in Fig. 2 are linked by a 'before' relationship, which means that $Evt2$ is necessary to be executed before $Evt1$. This is because the actions of $Evt2$ can trigger the guards of $Evt1$. Another type of relationship used in this paper is the 'parallel' relationship. The events linked by the parallel relationship means that they can interleave each other in the execution.

Invariants are needed for restricting possible values of variables. Thus, invariants also restrict the possible results of events. Conversely, events might provide us some ideas about important invariants needed to be include in a specification. These relationships between events and invariants can be shown in a refinement tree diagram through dashed lines between them as seen in Fig. 2, which contains a link from an invariant to the event $Evt1\_2$. For convention, if an invariant is related to a set of concrete events which refines the same abstract event, it should link with the small circle representing the refinement rather than linking with all the related events.

4.4   Transformation to Event-B Specification

Since we allow using natural language to be identifiers of the Event-B descriptions for events and invariants and the descriptions always contain variables, so we need to know all variables and data structure which can represent data and artifacts of a modeled system. In this paper, we assume that all needed variables have been specified before creating a refinement tree diagram. Some approaches that can be used for specifying the variables are the class diagram of KAOS [19] and the UML-B [13].

Regardless of how variables and data structures are specified, the transformation from a refinement tree diagram into Event-B specifications can be done through the following principles:

- All events and invariants within the same level of a tree must be written in the description of the same Event-B machine.
- Two consecutive levels of a refinement tree diagram means that the lower level is a concrete machine refines the abstract machine from the upper level. This refinement relationship must be written in the concrete machine as the clause *refines* followed by the abstract machine's name.
- An event in a refinement tree diagram contains the terms *any*, *when*, *with*, and *then*. Since these terms are directly derived from how an event is described in Event-B. Each term written in a parallelogram can directly map to the corresponding terms of an event in Event-B.
- Each arrow from an abstract event to a concrete event can be represented in Event-B specification through the term *refines* followed by the name of the abstract event.

The example in Fig. 2 can be easily transformed into two Event-B machines. We assume that the variables P, Q, and R are Boolean variables. The followings are parts of the machines which are derived from the example.

Initial machine:

$$Evt2 \mathrel{\hat{=}} \textbf{when } P = TRUE \textbf{ then } Q := TRUE \textbf{ end}$$
$$Evt1 \mathrel{\hat{=}} \textbf{when } Q = TRUE \textbf{ then } R := TRUE \textbf{ end}$$

First refinement:

$$Evt2 \mathrel{\hat{=}} \textbf{refines } Evt2$$
$$\textbf{when } P = TRUE \textbf{ then } Q := TRUE \textbf{ end}$$
$$Evt1\_1 \mathrel{\hat{=}} \textbf{refines } Evt1$$
$$\textbf{when } Q = TRUE \wedge P = TRUE \textbf{ then } R := TRUE \textbf{ end}$$
$$Evt1\_2 \mathrel{\hat{=}} \textbf{refines } Evt1$$
$$\textbf{when } Q = TRUE \textbf{ then } R := TRUE \wedge P := FALSE \textbf{ end}$$
$$Invariant{:}R = TRUE \wedge P = FALSE \Rightarrow Q = TRUE$$

5   The Refinement Patterns

An efficient way to create a goal model is by using the goal refinement patterns. We follow this concept by creating a set of refinement patterns for the refinement tree diagram. The refinement patterns are generic patterns to refine an abstract event into a set of concrete events with some invariants. Some refinement patterns are derived from the frequent ways to refine a machine found in the existing Event-B specifications created by others. Some refinement patterns are derived from the goal refinement patterns, since they are intuitive and complete. At the moment, we have 4 patterns in total. Our original patterns are phase-decomposition refinement pattern and event-forking refinement pattern. The KAOS-based patterns are derived from the milestone-driven refinement pattern and the decomposition-by-case pattern as described in Sect. 2.2. The descriptions of each pattern can be found in the following subsections.

5.1   The Phase-Decomposition Refinement Pattern

The phase-decomposition refinement pattern (Fig. 3) divides abstract behavior of a system into two or more phases. One phase is represented by one event. Only the transition from one phase to another is described in each event. The flow of transitions is in the form of a cycle for iterative behavior of the system. This pattern is applicable for modeling an initial specification in Event-B. The possible phases used for dividing behavior of a system are: input phase and decision phase. The input phase is for monitoring inputs of the system. The decision phase is for making a decision based on the inputs.

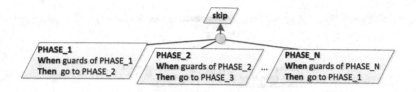

Fig. 3. The phase-decomposition-refinement pattern

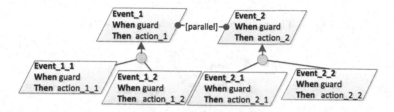

Fig. 4. The event-forking refinement pattern

5.2 The Event-Forking Refinement Pattern

This pattern (Fig. 4) is for describing environmental behavior which is usually non-deterministic and can behave in an arbitrary order. Inputs of a system can be regarded as this kind of behavior. Thus, this pattern is applicable to describe the input phase of the system. We call the creation of a group of arbitrarily ordering events as event forking. One event denotes one input. The event forking can be introduced to Event-B at both the higher level through the parallel relationship, and the lower level through the refinements without changing the guards.

5.3 The Milestone-Driven Refinement Pattern

This pattern is for decomposing an abstract event into the sequences of two or more concrete events. The decomposition is done by introducing intermediate steps (milestones) between the guard and action of the abstract event. Figure 5 shows the simplified form of the pattern, introducing just one intermediate step to an abstract event. An invariants appearing in the pattern is to ensure that after one event is executed, its action can trigger the next event to form a sequence of events.

5.4 The Decomposition-by-Case Refinement Pattern

This pattern is for refining an abstract into two or more concrete events for dealing with all possible cases of states of variables. One concrete event is supposed to deal with one case. This is to determine that which actions should be executed for each of the cases. Thus, this pattern is usually used in the decision phase. It can also be used in the input phase, if there are some restrictions on inputs which needs to be determine case-by-case. An invariant included in the

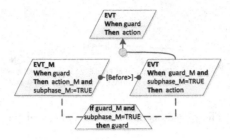

Fig. 5. The milestone-driven refinement pattern

Fig. 6. The decomposition-by-case refinement pattern

pattern is to ensure that all possible cases are determined, and they are disjoint. Figure 6 shows a simplified form of this pattern which contains only two cases.

6   Case Studies

Since our objective of this research is about the practical usage of Event-B, we utilized our model in action on three examples derived from a real-world context. The examples can show the practical utility of the refinement tree diagram along with its patterns. The examples varied on their size and types of systems in order to increase confidence in the utility of our approach.

Our approach was applied to a powered sliding door, an automatic gate controller, and Electrical Power Steering (EPS) system. The powered sliding door is derived from part 10 of ISO26262 [8]. The powered sliding door is a sliding door of a vehicle which a user can request the door to be opened or closed. The safety goal of the powered sliding door is "not to open the door while the vehicle speed is higher than 15 km/h". The automatic gate controller is derived from [20]. The goal of this system is to allow only authorized persons to enter a building through the automatic gate. Lastly, the EPS system, for controlling the electric steering of cars, was developed in collaboration with a company. The part of the EPS system which is used in this case study is the part regarding the transition to a manual steering mode. This mode is to stop the EPS system when a failure of the system is detected, and then, let the driver manually control the steering of the car. Due to limitations of space, only the simplified refinement tree diagram of the powered sliding door is shown in this

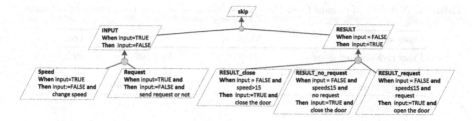

Fig. 7. The simplified refinement tree diagram of the powered sliding door

paper. If you are interested in the full diagrams of the three case studies, they can be found in the appendixes of [18].

Figure 7 shows the simplified refinement tree diagram of the powered sliding door. We modeled the first level of the refinement tree diagram of the system by, firstly, dividing the system into two phases, i.e. the input phase and the decision phase, with the phase-decomposition pattern. a Boolean variable named *input* was used to represent two phases. Then, the next level of the tree was constructed by introducing the speed of vehicle, opening request, and the door. The event-forking pattern was applied to introduce the speed and the request to the diagram as two inputs of the system. The decomposition-by-case pattern was used for determining that the door is opened or closed depending on the speed and the request. It is trivial in the figure that all cases are determined, so we omit the invariant of the pattern. We can extend the simplified diagram with another level by introducing a switch. The door will be opened only when the switch is on. The milestone-driven refinement pattern was applied to introduce the step of turning the switch on before opening the door as shown in Fig. 8.

We created the refinement tree diagrams for the other two case studies in a similar way. Roughly, we started with dividing the systems with the phase-decomposition pattern. Then, we applied our refinement patterns to gradually introduce new inputs and concepts into subsequent levels of their trees. However, some nodes in some levels of their diagrams had to be determined manually. Most of the manual events are the events which the variables in their descriptions are replaced by new variables.

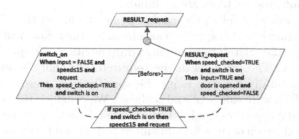

Fig. 8. Turning the switch on to open the door

Table 1. Number of events from the case studies according to sources of creation

Case study	Manual	Patterns	Total
Powered sliding door	0 (0 %)	19 (100 %)	19
Automatic gate controller	8 (34.8 %)	15 (65.2 %)	23
EPS system	18 (32.7 %)	37 (67.3 %)	55

The full refinement tree diagrams of the powered sliding door, the automatic gate controller, and the EPS system have 4 levels, 5 levels, and 8 levels respectively. To discuss about the results, we counted the total number of events from all levels of each resulted diagram. Those number are presented in Table 1. Here, we divided the events into two types according to their sources. 'Manual' means that the events are obtained manually, whereas 'Patterns' refers to the events that are derived from the refinement patterns. Note that the number of the copying events are omitted here. This is because the copying events are easily derived and, thus, are irrelevant to the difficulty of the refinement.

7 Discussion

From Table 1, we found that, at least, around two-thirds of the events in the resulted refinement tree diagrams can be derived from our proposed refinement patterns. The 'Manual' events were mostly for the replacement of variables with the new ones. This kind of refinement can be regarded as vertical refinement for enriching the structure of a model to bring it closer to an implementation structure [5]. Seeing that our approach focuses on specifying necessary information for the safety requirements specification and the vertical refinement is just a supplement to the identified necessary information. Thus, it was acceptable that the patterns cannot handle the vertical refinement at the moment. Therefore, we can conclude that the patterns are sufficient for modeling requirements specification of the safety-critical systems. Besides, the applicability of the patterns did not decrease when the specification was bigger. This fact can be discussed from the percentage of the pattern-derived events of the automatic gate controller and the EPS system that did not decrease much, even if the EPS system was a lot larger. As a result, the patterns are scalable.

In our experience modeling the case studies, we found that it was easy to justify and structure Event-B specifications by using the refinement tree diagram. This was because the relationships among components of the specifications were graphically shown. The concepts of the requirements analysis and elaboration and how to structurally stepwise refine the specifications were also provided by the patterns, which were sufficient and scalable. We conclude that the refinement tree diagram and its patterns can fulfil what Event-B lacks as described in Sect. 3.

Since the mechanism of the goal refinement is designed for decomposing a goal into two or more sub-goals, one-to-one refinement, i.e. a goal is decomposed into a single sub-goal, rarely occurs in KAOS. However, the one-to-one refinement is possible in Event-B, e.g. we can just adding guards and/or actions into an event for dealing with new variables of a concrete specification. Consequently, the notations of the refinement tree diagram cannot handle the one-to-one refinement well. This leads to the difficulty to create refinement patterns for the one-to-one refinement in the form of the refinement tree. The incompetency to well handle the one-to-one refinement is the current limitation of our approach. Actually, the vertical refinement are often the one-to-one refinement.

8 Related Work

There are many approaches aiming to use the capabilities of the KAOS method to guide Event-B modeling. All of them focus on the direct application of the goal model to Event-B, whereas our approach presents a new diagram based on the goal model. The approach in [11] directly applied the goal refinement patterns of KAOS to model a specification in Event-B. A way to describe and prove the KAOS goal refinement patterns in Event-B was defined. However, due to the differences between KAOS and Event-B, it is not possible to represent and prove all the goal refinement patterns in Event-B. This approach limits the creation of a goal model to the application of only the compatible goal refinement patterns. Rather, our approach provides a wider way to use patterns to guide the refinement by allowing the adaptation of the goal refinement patterns and the creation of new patterns for Event-B itself. The approaches described in [4,12] avoided the differences between the two frameworks by using only the leaf goals of the goal model for modeling an initial specification in Event-B. This can be done by regarding one leaf achieve goal as an event and/or an invariant. Then, developers have to use other approaches to refine the initial specification further. From this, the goal refinement does not relate to Event-B refinement. While, our approach uses the whole proposed diagram to model an initial Event-B specification along with the subsequent refinement steps.

We defined the refinement patterns of the refinement tree diagram for assisting the Event-B modeling. In [7], Hoang, Furst, and Abrial proposed that it is possible to create design patterns for Event-B. They proved this fact by proposing provably-correct design pattern for a synchronous communication protocol and applied it to model another synchronous communication protocol. The purpose of the creation of their design patterns is to efficiently model a specification in Event-B by reusing the existing Event-B specifications, which is similar to our purposes. Hence, this work supports the creation of our refinement patterns. Nonetheless, the refinements in their patterns are mostly the vertical refinement which are different from the refinements in our refinement patterns.

In 2012, Kobayashi and Honiden [10] proposed an approach to plan what models are constructed in each abstraction level of Event-B. The advantage of this approach is that it can calculate how well a plan can mitigate the complexity of a specification. This calculation is useful for selecting a plan from a set of plans. However, to make a set of plans, their approach needs that all details of a system, such as behavior, are already identified before the calculation. Our approach lacks such calculation, but it is able to identify the necessary details, together with the guideline for Event-B refinement. Thus, their work and our approach can complement each other.

9   Conclusion

By observing the applications of Event-B in modeling specification of the safety-critical systems, we found that Event-B lacks the requirements analysis and elaboration, and the guideline for its refinement mechanism. To deal with the issues, we adapted the concepts of the goal model and the goal refinement patterns from the KAOS method to create the refinement tree diagram and the refinement patterns. The refinement tree diagram can graphically demonstrate the relationships among components of an Event-B specification. Thus, it is easier to understand and justify the specification. The diagram was useful because it can be directly transformed into Event-B specifications. The refinement patterns were capable to guide how to stepwise refine Event-B specifications. Then, we successfully applied the refinement tree diagram and the patterns to three case studies to model and verify them in Event-B. Therefore, the refinement tree diagram and the refinement patterns can complement Event-B. We believe that the approach described in this paper can encourage the use of the formal methods like Event-B in the practical development of the safety-critical systems.

References

1. Abrial, J.-R., Su, W., Zhu, H.: Formalizing hybrid systems with Event-B. In: Derrick, J., Fitzgerald, J., Gnesi, S., Khurshid, S., Leuschel, M., Reeves, S., Riccobene, E. (eds.) ABZ 2012. LNCS, vol. 7316, pp. 178–193. Springer, Heidelberg (2012)
2. Abrial, J.R.: Formal methods in industry: achievements, problems, future. In: Proceedings of the 28th International Conference on Software Engineering, pp. 761–768. ACM (2006)
3. Abrial, J.R.: Modeling in Event-B: System and Software Engineering. Cambridge University Press, Cambridge (2010)
4. Aziz, B., Arenas, A., Bicarregui, J., Ponsard, C., Massonet, P.: From goal-oriented requirements to Event-B specifications. In: First NASA Formal Method Symposium (NFM 2009), Moffett Field, CA, USA, April 2009
5. Damchoom, K., Butler, M.: Applying event and machine decomposition to a flash-based filestore in Event-B. In: Oliveira, M.V.M., Woodcock, J. (eds.) SBMF 2009. LNCS, vol. 5902, pp. 134–152. Springer, Heidelberg (2009)
6. Darimont, R., Van Lamsweerde, A.: Formal refinement patterns for goal-driven requirements elaboration. ACM SIGSOFT Softw. Eng. Notes 21(6), 179–190 (1996)
7. Hoang, T.S., Furst, A., Abrial, J.-R.: Event-B patterns and their tool support. In: Software Engineering and Formal Methods, 2009 Seventh IEEE International Conference on, pp. 210–219. IEEE (2009)
8. CD ISO. 26262, Road vehicles-functional safety (2011)
9. Jones, C.B.: Systematic Software Development Using VDM, vol. 2. Prentice Hall, Englewood Cliffs (1990)

10. Kobayashi, T., Honiden, S.: Towards refinement strategy planning for Event-B. arXiv preprint arXiv:1210.7036 (2012)
11. Matoussi, A., Gervais, F., Laleau, R.: A goal-based approach to guide the design of an abstract Event-B specification. In: Engineering of Complex Computer Systems (ICECCS), 2011 16th IEEE International Conference on, pp. 139–148. IEEE (2011)
12. Ponsard, C., Devroey, X.: Generating high-level Event-B system models from KAOS requirements models. In: Actes du XXIIéme Congrés INFORSID, pp. 317–332, Lille, France (2011)
13. Said, M.Y., Butler, M., Snook, C.: Language and tool support for class and state machine refinement in UML-B. In: Cavalcanti, A., Dams, D.R. (eds.) FM 2009. LNCS, vol. 5850, pp. 579–595. Springer, Heidelberg (2009)
14. Silva, R.: Lessons learned/sharing the experience of developing a metro system case study. arXiv preprint arXiv:1210.7030 (2012)
15. Michael Spivey, J.: The Z Notation, vol. 1992. Prentice Hall, New York (1989)
16. Su, W., Abrial, J.-R., Huang, R., Zhu, H.: From requirements to development: methodology and example. In: Qin, S., Qiu, Z. (eds.) ICFEM 2011. LNCS, vol. 6991, pp. 437–455. Springer, Heidelberg (2011)
17. Su, W., Abrial, J.-R., Zhu, H.: Complementary methodologies for developing hybrid systems with Event-B. In: Aoki, T., Taguchi, K. (eds.) ICFEM 2012. LNCS, vol. 7635, pp. 230–248. Springer, Heidelberg (2012)
18. Traichaiyaporn, K.: Modeling correct safety requirements using KAOS and Event-B. Master's thesis, School of Information Science, Japan Advanced Institute of Science and Technology (JAIST). http://hdl.handle.net/10119/11496 (2013)
19. Van Lamsweerde, A.: Requirements Engineering: from System Goals to UML Models to Software Specifications, vol. 3. Wiley, New York (2009)
20. Zowghi, D., Gervasi, V.: On the interplay between consistency, completeness, and correctness in requirements evolution. Inf. Softw. Technol. 45(14), 993–1009 (2003)

Precise Documentation and Validation
of Requirements

Chen-Wei Wang$^{(\boxtimes)}$, Jonathan S. Ostroff, and Simon Hudon

Department of Electronic Engineering & Computer Science, York University,
Toronto, Canada
{jackie,jonathan,simon}@cse.yorku.ca

Abstract. Precise documentation of requirements is important for developing and certifying mission critical software. We specify cyber-physical systems via an Event-B-like machine which declar es the monitored and controlled variables and their initial condition. A machine event models the joint action of the plant and the controller. Embedded in the event action is a function table that specifies the input-output behaviour of the controller, as monitored variables are periodically updated by the plant. We extend the Event-B notation with queries and modules. The resulting machine provides us with a mathematical description of the overall system behaviour, thus allowing us to validate the requirements by proving that (1) the input-output specification of the controller is complete, disjoint and well-defined, and that (2) the machine satisfies system-wide consistency invariants elicited from domain experts. A biomedical device is used as a case study, and we mechanize proofs via a SMT solver.

Keywords: Certification · Requirements documentation and validation · Model contracts · Well-definedness · Tabular expressions

1 Introduction

The central task of system development is to design the system such that its overall behaviour satisfies the requirements. But this assumes that the requirements are precise and complete, while problems in the requirements phase will negatively impact the subsequent phases of design and implementation.

Requirements are often stated informally using natural languages, which tend to be imprecise and incomplete. It is rather difficult to reliably check that English narratives, or even semi-formal models such as use cases, address all scenarios relevant to the task at hand. Nevertheless, precise documentation of requirements is important for validating, verifying and certifying mission critical software in medical, automotive, nuclear and avionic systems [13].

Industrial standards such as IEEE 7-4.3.2 (nuclear), ISO 26262 (automotive) and DO-178C (avionics) recommend the use of formal methods. But formal methods alone do not guarantee that requirements will be complete. Tabular

C. Artho and P.C. Ölveczky (Eds.): FTSCS 2013, CCIS 419, pp. 262–279, 2014.
DOI: 10.1007/978-3-319-05416-2_17, © Springer International Publishing Switzerland 2014

expressions [20] (a.k.a. function tables) describe computer controllers as mathematical functions relating system stimuli and responses. Tabular expressions have been adopted in the nuclear domain to ensure that specifications are complete and disjoint [11,21,22].

Outline. We provide a small example to illustrate the use of tabular expressions (Sect. 1.1). The example is used to motivate our methods and contributions. The overall behaviour of a *system* is composed of the behaviour of the environment (the *plant*) together with a computer controller. We model the system behaviour with an Event-B machine extended with modules and embedded tabular expressions (Sect. 1.2). Our method produces documentation that is presented modularly, and it can be used to determine the completeness, disjointness and well-definedness (Sect. 2) of specifications for an important class of systems. Mathematically precise documents of requirements are essential: domain experts review them for correctness; programmers use them for design and coding; and regulatory authorities are assured that the software will not exhibit unintended behaviour. Our method also allows for the validation of requirements via proofs of system invariants. We report on a case study (Sect. 3) using our methods for precise documentation and validation of requirements. Section 3 shows not only that our methods are applicable to software products, but also that our methods can be applied to improve the completeness, disjointness and well-definedness of industry standards. Section 4 presents related work and conclusions.

1.1 A Small Example

Consider a computer controller embedded in a larger environment as shown in the context diagram in Fig. 1(a). In [21], stimuli from the plant (environment) are referred to as monitored variables and responses referred to as controlled variables. A variable such as z (in Fig. 1(a)) represents the current value of a monitored variable and z_{-1} refers to its value in the previous state. The system behaviour is modelled as a finite state machine. At discrete points in time, the system detects the *current* values of all monitored variables, and it uses the current state (and, possibly, the past states) of the machine to generate the current values of the controlled variables and the next state of the machine. Figure 1(b) provides an artificial example of a function table for our small system.

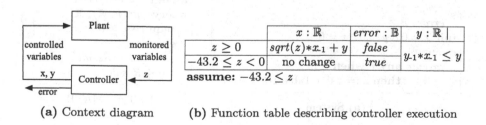

	$x : \mathbb{R}$	$error : \mathbb{B}$	$y : \mathbb{R}$
$z \geq 0$	$sqrt(z)*x_{-1} + y$	$false$	$y_{-1}*x_{-1} \leq y$
$-43.2 \leq z < 0$	no change	$true$	

assume: $-43.2 \leq z$

(a) Context diagram   (b) Function table describing controller execution

Fig. 1. Specification of a small system using the method in [21]

For example, if the current value of z is non-negative ($z \geq 0$), then output x is described by the before-after predicate $x = sqrt(z) * x_{-1} + y$, i.e., the predicate expresses how the current value of output x depends on the current values of y and input z and the previous value of x.

Periodically, the plant generates a new value, say $z \in \mathbb{R}$, which is monitored by the controller. In response, the controller generates a new value for the controlled variables $x, y \in \mathbb{R}$ based on the monitored variables and the past state. Of course, a real system will have many more monitored and controlled variables than shown in Fig. 1(a).

The above system description is an idealized view of the system behaviour that is suitable for a requirements document: outputs are generated instantaneously once inputs are received. In later refinements, accuracy and timing tolerances must be taken into account [23]. Also, we are dealing with systems where we do not have a detailed model of the plant. Our knowledge of the plant is limited to monitored and controlled variables and constraints on these variables.

In most useful systems it will not be possible to describe the controller behaviour using a single function. Instead, the requirements will include a number of interacting functions, which themselves are represented by function tables. As stated in [11, 20–22], the function tables must be complete and disjoint as formalized in Fig. 3 (p. 265). Completeness ensures that all possible inputs are covered. Disjointness ensures that there are no conflicts in the outputs.

1.2   Our Method and Contributions

Figure 2(a) describes an Event-B [1] machine *system* with event *execute* that models the joint action of the plant and the controller. The machine declares the monitored and controlled variables as well as their initial condition. The plant periodically generates new values for the monitored variable z (using the **any** construct to non-deterministically assign a value to parameter $r \in \mathbb{R}$). The function table describing the input-output behaviour of the controller is embedded in the action of the event. The Event-B notation is extended with

---

machine *system* use MATH
--machine using module MATH
variables
$x, y, z : \mathbb{R}$
error : $\mathbb{B}$
init $x = 0 \land y = 0 \land z = 0$
event
execute **any** r **when** $-43.2 \leq r$
then z := r $\parallel$ « Table 1(*b*)» **end**

(a) System

type MATH
const $\epsilon : \mathbb{R}$
axiom $0 < \epsilon \leq 0.001$
query *sqrt*$(r : \mathbb{R}) : \mathbb{R}$
require $r \geq 0$
ensure
$-\epsilon \leq r - Result^2 \leq \epsilon$
$0 \leq Result$

(b) Type MATH

Fig. 2. Description of system consisting of plant and controller

queries and modules. The resulting machine provides us with a mathematical description of the overall system behaviour, thus allowing us to validate the requirements by proving system invariants.

Input conditions		Output r
$C_1(x)$	$C_{11}(x)$	$R_1(x, r)$
	$C_{12}(x)$	$R_2(x, r)$
$C_3(x)$		$R_3(x, r)$
assume: A		

Given:
$$P_1 \triangleq C_1(x) \wedge C_{11}(x)$$
$$P_2 \triangleq C_1(x) \wedge C_{12}(x)$$
$$P_3 \triangleq C_3(x)$$
$$Q_i \triangleq R_i(x, r) \text{ for } i \in 1..3$$

(a) **Meaning of Table** : $A \wedge (\forall i \in 1..3 \bullet P_i \Rightarrow Q_i)$
(b) **Completeness** : $A \wedge (\exists i \in 1..3 \bullet P_i)$
(c) **Disjointness** : $A \wedge (\forall i, j \in 1..3 \mid i \neq j \bullet \neg(P_i \wedge P_j))$
(d) **Well-definedness** : $\mathcal{D}(A) \wedge (A \wedge (\forall i \in 1..3 \bullet \mathcal{D}(P_i) \wedge (P_i \Rightarrow \mathcal{D}(Q_i))))$

Fig. 3. Completeness, Disjointness and Well-definedness of tabular expressions

Queries (with pre/post conditions) such as *sqrt* in Fig. 2(b) are not directly supported by function tables (usually based on total functions) and Event-B. It is convenient to allow the use of partial functions (specified with preconditions). The precondition of a partial function captures in one place where the function can be applied meaningfully, thus providing a logical firewall between the specifier and the client so that functions are not misused on meaningless inputs (see the discussion on design-by-contract in [14]).

Our contributions are as follows:

1. Description of system behaviour via function tables embedded in a machine. As described, the machine event *execute* in Fig. 2(a) provides a precise description of the system behaviour involving the joint action of the plant and the controller. The event action refers to a function table that can be shown as complete and disjoint. This allows us to validate the requirements (see Item 4).

2. Queries and well-definedness. We provide a method for introducing queries defined via pre/post conditions, such as *sqrt* in Fig. 2(b). Queries facilitate the construction of complex expressions in events, invariants and function tables. A query introduces the possibility of its result being undefined if it is used in a context that does not satisfy its precondition. We thus develop a theory of well-definedness to ensure that the expressions (in function tables, guards and invariants) that involve queries are well-defined. See Sect. 2 for more details.

3. Decomposition into modules and types. We allow variables and associated queries to be collected in modules. This is particularly useful when describing complex systems. If a module does not declare variables, then we call it a type (e.g. type MATH in Fig. 2(b)). Only a machine, e.g. *system*, may declare events. Modules do not declare any events, but only related variables, queries and invariants. If module m_2 uses module m_1, then the queries and invariants of m_2 may use the variables and queries of m_1. In a large system, we partition the state into modules so as to allow a separation of concerns. We may always flatten a machine, as well as modules that it uses, into a single, larger machine.

4. Validation of requirements via proofs of invariants. To our knowledge, the literature does not discuss the proof of invariants in systems specified by function tables. These invariants may describe important system safety requirements. Using our calculus of well-definedness, we can prove these invariants in the framework developed above. Suppose we would like to prove the invariant $J(v)$ where v is the state variables of the system. As in Event-B, the proof obligation is $J(v_{-1}) \wedge G_{execute}(v_{-1}) \wedge BA_{execute}(v_{-1}, v) \Rightarrow J(v)$, where $G_{execute}$ is the event guard and $BA_{execute}$ is the before-after predicate of the event action specified by the function table.

5. E/R descriptions. In the case study, we retain informal English descriptions of system requirements (R-descriptions) and of relevant phenomena and constraints on the environment (E-descriptions). Our queries and function tables can be traced back to these descriptions.

As mentioned above in the first contribution, we embed the black-box function table describing the controller in event *execute* (see Fig. 2(a)). The domain experts may advise that there is an environmental constraint $(-42.3 \leq z)$ on the monitored variable z, which we document as an E-description. We can constrain the system behaviour accordingly via a guard $(-42.3 \leq r)$ for event *execute*. When analyzing the function table in Fig. 1(b) for completeness and disjointness, we may add an assume clause with the relevant constraint on z.

Event *execute* defines the system behaviour as follows. The action of the plant is modelled with an **any** construct. The event generates an arbitrary value for parameter r constrained only by its guard. Because of the assignment $z := r$, the event guard places constraint $(-42.3 \leq z)$ on the plant monitored variable z. Instantaneously, the event updates the controlled variables x and y (modelling the action of the controller) as specified by the function table in Fig. 1(b).

The domain experts might specify that given the controller specification, a system safety property $(0 \leq x \ \wedge \ 0 \leq y)$ holds in all states. We document this requirement as an R-description and express it as an invariant $J(x, y, z) \triangleq (0 \leq x \ \wedge \ 0 \leq y)$. The event guard is $G_{execute} \triangleq -43.2 \leq z$ and the before-after predicate is $BA_{execute} \triangleq G_{execute} \Rightarrow \beta$, where β is the BA derived from the table in Fig. 1(b): $\beta \triangleq (z \geq 0 \Rightarrow x = Sqrt(z)*x_{-1} + y) \ \wedge \ (-43.2 \leq z < 0 \Rightarrow x = x_{-1}) \ \wedge \ (y_{-1}*x_{-1} \leq y)$. The proof obligation is thus $(0 \leq x_{-1} \wedge 0 \leq y_{-1}) \wedge G_{execute} \wedge \beta \Rightarrow (0 \leq x \wedge 0 \leq y)$. In [18], we provide a calculational proof and show how it can be discharged automatically using the Z3 SMT solver [3]. For further details and the Event-B notations used in this paper, refer to [18].

2 Well-Definedness of Expressions Involving Partial Functions

It is often useful to have queries whose values are not defined for all inputs. For example, the *sqrt* query shown in Fig. 2(b) has no meaningful results for negative numbers. This raises the question of what status to give to expressions like

$sqrt(-1)$. In classical tabular expressions [19], all partial functions are totalized by extending their ranges with a special value of undefinedness. This creates various problems when using standard theorem provers, which assume that all functions are total [18]. For example, in the Z3 SMT solver [3], the expression $1/x = 1/x$ is a theorem, even though the expression is not well-defined if $x = 0$.

Given an expression exp, our extended report [17] provides a recursive definition of the predicate $\mathcal{D}(exp)$ which holds when exp is well-defined (based on [10]). The well-definedness of a query application $q(x)$ with the precondition $C_q(x)$ is defined as $\mathcal{D}(q(x)) \triangleq C_q(x)$. For example, $\mathcal{D}(1/x = 1/x) \equiv (x \neq 0)$. As shown in [17], whenever we are asked to prove predicate β_q holds, where β_q involves a query q, we need to discharge two proof obligations. First, we must show that $\mathcal{D}(\beta_q)$ holds (this is usually relatively simple). Second, we must show that β_q holds. Both proofs can be conducted using a standard theorem prover that treats all functions as total. In our framework, $\mathcal{D}(x/0 = x/0)$ is not a theorem, and thus $x/0 = x/0$ cannot be proved. The $\mathcal{D}$ operator is used in Fig. 3 (p4) to ensure that a function table using queries is well-defined.

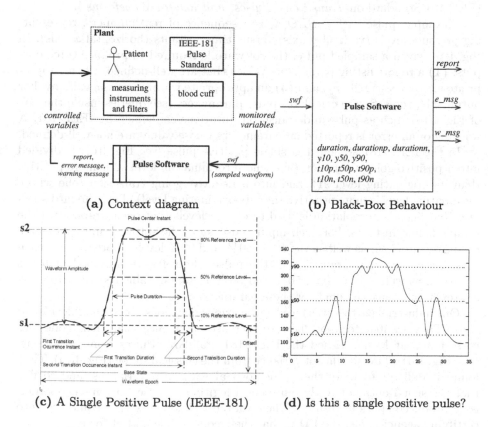

(a) Context diagram   (b) Black-Box Behaviour

(c) A Single Positive Pulse (IEEE-181)   (d) Is this a single positive pulse?

Fig. 4. The pulse software: system boundary, inputs and outputs

Table 1. Abbreviations for pulse and transition parameters

Pulse	Abb.	Pos. Tran.	Abb.	Neg. Tran.	Abb.
pulse duration	$duration$	duration	$durationp$	transition duration	$durationn$
10% level	$y10$	10% instant	$t10p$	10% instant	$t10n$
50% level	$y50$	50% instant	$t50p$	50% instant	$t50n$
90% level	$y90$	90% instant	$t90p$	90% instant	$t90n$

3   Case Study: A Biomedical Device

We report on our recent work with an industrial partner. They provided code taken from the software for a biomedical device that monitors blood pressure via a cuff. Figure 4(a) identifies the boundary of the pulse software (controller) and its operating environment (the plant). A reading from the device arrives as a sampled pulse representing blood pressure over time. Given the input pulse, the software is required to calculate parameters (see Fig. 4(c)) as defined by the IEEE-181 Standard on *Transitions, Pulses, and Related Waveforms* [7].

The input pulse $swf \in SEQ[\mathbb{R}]$ is a sequence of real numbers, representing pressure levels (vertical y axis) versus time instants (horizontal x axis). In Fig. 4(b), given a sampled pulse, the software is required to produce three outputs: **(1)** a report listing parameters values that are well-defined; **(2)** an appropriate error message, if any; and **(3)** an appropriate warning message, if any. For output (1), the software calculates pulse parameters (see queries inside the box of Fig. 4(b)) such as pulse and transition durations as defined by IEEE-181. A warning or an error is reported on parameters whose values are not well-defined.

In the IEEE-181 standard, a single positive pulse (see Fig. 4(c)) is divided into a positive-going transition (one whose terminating level $s2$ is more positive than its originating level $s1$), and into a negative-going transition (one whose terminating level is more negative than its originating level). The standard specifies that linear interpolation is used to obtain levels that occur in-between the sampled time instants. For each input pulse swf, the software must calculate the pulse duration, as well as the 10 %, 50 % and 90 % levels. Moreover, for each (positive or negative) transition of the pulse, the software must calculate its duration, as well as the 10 %, 50 % and 90 % instants. Table 1 summarizes the abbreviations that we adopt for these parameters.

Our industrial partner was faced with various questions about their developed code. They wanted to know how to increase confidence that their code was correct and at least satisfied the IEEE-181 standard. Pulses from ill patients (e.g. Fig. 4(d)) show significant variance from the classical shape (Fig. 4(c)). They found it difficult to write their code to deal with such variances, and to flag that the signal does not really represent a legitimate pulse (in some cases their code produced spurious results). They wanted to know how they could argue to certifying agencies, e.g. the FDA, that their code is safe and fit for use.

The IEEE-181 standard itself is ambiguous, thus sometimes leading to spurious calculations. For example, where there are multiple 10 % and 90 % instants, the standard specifies that we take the 10 % and 90 % instants that are closest to the 50 % instant of the standard.[1] However, for some pulses this would result in an ordering $t90p < t50p < t10p$ which gives a negative duration $(t90p - t10p)$ for the positive-going transition. The linear interpolation formula in the standard, besides being overly-complicated, does not include a description of its limitations: it includes a division, whose denominator expression might be zero, without specifying what to do in cases where it is.[2] More ambiguities and limitations both in our industrial partner's code and in the IEEE-181 standard are discussed in an extended report [17].

Our proposed methods help address the above issues. Precise documentation of requirements that is complete, disjoint and well-defined rules out issues of ambiguities and well-definedness (e.g. division by zero). For example, the limitations of the interpolation formula in IEEE-181 could have been addressed using preconditions of queries. Our version of the interpolation formula is total (see our abstract data type RFUN in Sect. 3.3). Given that the standard was not always clear, we recorded what we thought are relevant assumptions as E-descriptions (Sect. 3.1), which differentiate between valid and invalid signals, thus helping to remove ambiguities. R-descriptions (Sect. 3.2) describe the required calculation of parameters for valid pulses and the errors or warnings for invalid pulses. The complete specification is less than two pages (Fig. 6, p. 273 in Sect. 3.4 and Table 2, p.274 in Sect. 3.5). Specifying and proving a system invariant such as $t90p < t50p < t10p$ effectively validates the consistency of the requirements (see Sect. 3.7).

3.1 Atomic E-Descriptions

E-descriptions document environmental assumptions and constraints on monitored variables. An atomic description consists of two parts: (1) the description number (e.g. ENV1) allowing for traceability in the design, the code, and acceptance tests; and (2) an informal English statement.

ENV1	A *valid pulse* consists of at least 3 samples, has a unique maximum and each transition has at least one 50 % instant.

ENV2	The unique maximum partitions the waveform into a positive transition and a negative transition. The 10 %, 50 % and 90 % levels are the same for both the positive and negative transitions.

---

[1] Section 5.3.3.2 of IEEE-181: "If there is more than one reference level instant, the reference level closest to the 50 % reference level instance (see 5.3.3.1) is used, unless otherwise specified." Obviously $t90p - t10p < 0$ represents an unusual waveform. Nevertheless, the software must deal with all inputs, however unusual.

[2] Equations 5 and 6 on page 20 of IEEE-181 provide the interpolation formulas.

3.2   Atomic R-Descriptions

Having defined what a valid input pulse is (ENV1), we now document the required system input-output behaviour by considering three cases (ok, warning and error) each as an atomic R-description:

REQ3	ok: If the input pulse is *valid* and the 10 % levels of both transitions exist then output all the following parameters: **(a)** For the waveform: 10 %, 50 % and 90 % levels. **(b)** For each transition: 10 %, 50 % and 90 % instants. **(c)** For each transition: the transition duration (i.e. time from the 10 % instant to the 90 % instant). **(d)** The pulse duration (time from the 50 % instant of the positive transition to the 50 % instant of the negative transition).

REQ4	**Warning:** If the input pulse is *valid* and at least one of the 10 % levels is missing, output all the parameters except for the missing 10 % levels and instants (and associated transition duration) and issue a warning.

REQ5	**Error:** If the input pulse is *invalid* then no parameters are calculated and appropriate error messages are printed.

Furthermore, there may be multiple 50 % instants, and IEEE-181 specifies that the first one must be selected. This is appropriate for the positive transition but not for the negative transition, in which case the last 50 % seems more appropriate (if the two transitions were meant to be treated symmetrically). The 10 % and 90 % will then be defined accordingly.

REQ6	When multiple 50 % instants are present in the positive transition (respectively, negative transition), the first (respectively, the last) 50 % instant is selected.

REQ7	Output the 10 % and 90 % instants closest to the 50 % instants

Finally, we document an important system inavariant about transitions:

REQ8	- For positive transition: $t10p < t50p < t90p$ - For negative transition: $t90n < t50n < t10n$

3.3   Type RFUN for Linear Interpolation

As mentioned earlier, the linear interpolation formulas in IEEE-181 are not well-defined for all inputs. We could add a precondition to the formulas. However, we can do better. We can improve the standard by making the formulas total. We provide a re-usable type RFUN (Fig. 5) that can be used to transform the sampled input $swf : SEQ[\mathbb{R}]$ into a total, real-valued function $wf : RFUN$ (see module *waveform* in Fig. 6, p. 273) that agrees with swf on its sampled domain, and interpolates elsewhere.

---

type RFUN $\triangleq$ ($\bigcup x, y : \mathbb{R} \mid x \leq y \bullet [x, y] \to \mathbb{R}$)
query *ubound, lbound* ($rf : RFUN$): $\mathbb{R}$ --upper and lower bounds of the domain
axiom ($\forall rf : RFUN \bullet \text{dom}(rf) = [rf.lbound, rf.ubound]$)
queries
  $has(rf : RFUN; x_1, x_2, y : \mathbb{R})$: $\mathbb{B} \triangleq (\exists x : \text{dom}(rf) \mid x_1 \leq x \leq x_2 \bullet rf(x) = y)$
  --does y occur between x1 and x2?
  $first \ (rf : RFUN; x_1, x_2, y : \mathbb{R})$: $\mathbb{R} \triangleq (\downarrow x : \mathbb{R} \mid x_1 \leq x \leq x_2 \wedge rf(x) = y \bullet x)$
    --1st instant of level y in interval [x1,x2]
    require $rf.has(x_1, x_2, y)$
  $seq2rfun(s : SEQ[\mathbb{R}])$: $RFUN$ --linear interpolation
    ensure $\text{dom}(Result) = [1, s.count]$
    $\wedge \ (\forall x : [1, s.count] \bullet Result(x) = s(\lfloor x \rfloor)*(\lfloor x + 1 \rfloor - x) + \ s(\lceil x \rceil)*(x - \lfloor x \rfloor))$

Fig. 5. Abstract data type for real-valued functions RFUN

In Fig. 5, by writing $RFUN \triangleq (\bigcup x, y : \mathbb{R} \mid x \leq y \bullet [x, y] \to \mathbb{R})$, we introduce a new data type $RFUN$ that is synonymous with the set of total functions, each of which has the real-valued closed interval $[x, y]$ as its domain, and the set of real numbers as its range. The new type $RFUN$ supports a query $seq2rfun$ that converts from a finite sequence of real numbers (e.g. $swf : SEQ[\mathbb{R}]$) to a continuous function. A real-valued instant in the domain of $seq2rfun(swf)$ is projected to a value that is calculated using an improved version of linear interpolation[3] that is free from division-by-zero and avoids the need for case analysis. Given an $RFUN$ (e.g. transformed from a sampled pulse sequence) as the first argument, queries $first$ and $last$ calculate, respectively, the first and last instants where a given level y occurs within some given closed interval $[x_1, x_2]$. Symbols $\downarrow$ and $\uparrow$ are the minimum and maximum operators, respectively, extended into quantifiers.

---

[3] See the post-condition of query $seq2rfun$. Given a real t and a natural number n, $\lfloor t + n \rfloor = \lfloor t \rfloor + n$. Thus $\lfloor t + 1 \rfloor = \lfloor t \rfloor + 1$. In the definition of $seq2rfun(s)(t)$ the coefficients always add up to one, i.e. $(\lfloor t + 1 \rfloor - t) + (t - \lfloor t \rfloor) = 1$. This eliminates the possibility of division by zero and avoids the case analysis in the IEEE-181 standard. Both swf and $seq2rfun(swf)$ agree on their projected levels from the integer domain of swf, i.e. $swf = \mathbb{N} \lhd seq2rfun(swf)$.

3.4   The Machine and Its Modules

Similar to Sect. 1.1, Fig. 6 (p. 273) describes a machine *system* with an event *execute* that models the joint action of the plant and the controller. The machine declares a monitored variable (i.e., *swf*) and three controlled variables (e.g. variable *report*: $\mathbb{S} \nrightarrow \mathbb{R}$ containing the pulse and transition parameters, etc.).

The plant periodically generates a new value for the monitored variable *swf*, and the controlled variables, e.g. *report*, are updated instantaneously according to the embedded function table (« Table 2 on page 274 ») describing the controller behaviour. We organize queries used in the function table into modules as follows:

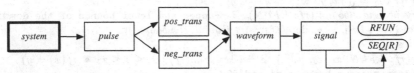

The two rounded boxes denote abstract data *types* $SEQ[G]^4$ and *RFUN*. The square box with a thick border denotes a *machine* and other square boxes denote *modules*. Each arrow corresponds to a **use** clause in Fig. 6 (p. 273). We distribute queries that calculate the pulse and transition parameters into modules that *system* uses, e.g. *duration* in the *pulse* module, *t10p* in the *pos_trans* module, etc. In those modules we also declare queries that calculate the intermediate results, e.g. *ymax* in the *signal* module. The result of each query is precisely defined either by an equality expression ($\triangleq \ldots$) or by a post-condition (an **ensure** clause). A module or a machine has access to variables and queries of all modules it directly or indirectly uses. Consequently, machine *system* has access to the monitored variable *swf* declared in module *signal*, and its embedded function table (i.e. Table 2) has access to querie *t10p* in module *pos_trans*.

A query may only be used in a context where its precondition (the **require** clause) holds; otherwise, its result is not well-defined. For example, queries *ymax* and *t50p* are only well-defined when, respectively, *s3* and *t50p*? hold. We also use a **require** clause at the module level to specify constraint that is to be included as part of the preconditions of all queries. For example, in the *waveform* module, each query should include the constraint $s3 \land um$ as part of its precondition.

3.5   Using Module Queries in Function Tables

Function Table 2 specifies the black-box relation between the outputs of the controller (the report of pulse parameters, error and warning messages) and its input (the sampled pulse *swf*). As Table 2 is embedded as part of the action of event *execute* in machine *system* its specification is facilitated by queries declared in modules that *system* uses. The table is complete, disjoint, and well-defined for any arbitrary pulse input.

---

[4] For the complete definition of type $SEQ[G] \triangleq (\bigcup n : \mathbb{N} \bullet 1..n \to G)$ that supports the standard queries *count*, *has*, *head*, and *tail*, see our extended report [18].

```
machine system use pulse
variables report, e_msg, w_msg: S
event
   execute
   any p ∈ SEQ[ℝ] then swf := p || « Table 2 on page 12 » end
```

module pulse **use** pos_trans, neg_trans
queries
  $duration$: $\mathbb{R} \triangleq t50n - t50p$
    --time between 50% instants of positive and negative transitions
    require $t50$?
  $t50$?: $\mathbb{B} \triangleq t50p? \wedge t50n?$ --do both 50% instants exist?
  $t10$?: $\mathbb{B} \triangleq t10p? \wedge t10n?$ --do both 10% instants exist?
    require $t50p? \wedge t50n?$
  $error$: $\mathbb{B} \triangleq \neg(s3 \wedge um \wedge t50?)$
  $warning$: $\mathbb{B} \triangleq \neg error \wedge \neg t10?$
  ok: $\mathbb{B} \triangleq s3 \wedge um \wedge t50? \wedge t10?$
invariant
  $complete(\langle error, warning, ok \rangle) \wedge disjoint(\langle error, warning, ok \rangle)$
  $ok \Rightarrow t10p? \wedge t10n? \wedge t50p? \wedge t50n? \wedge t90p? \wedge t90n? \wedge durationp? \wedge durationn?$
  $ok \Rightarrow (t10p < t50p < t90p) \wedge (t90n < t50n < t10p)$

module pos_trans **use** waveform
require $t50p$?
queries
  $t10p$: $\mathbb{R} \triangleq wf.last(1, t50p, y10)$
    require $t10p$?
  $t90p$: $\mathbb{R} \triangleq wf.first(t50p, tmax, y90)$
    require $t90p$?
  $durationp$: $\mathbb{R} \triangleq t90p - t10p$
    require $durationp$?
  $t10p$?: $\mathbb{B} \triangleq wf.has(1, t50p, y10)$
  $t90p$?: $\mathbb{B} \triangleq wf.has(t50p, tmax, y90)$
  $durationp$?: $\mathbb{B} \triangleq t10p? \wedge t90p?$
invariant
  $durationp? \Rightarrow t10p < t50p < t90p$

module neg_trans **use** waveform
require $t50n$?
queries
  $t10n$: $\mathbb{R} \triangleq wf.first(t50n, n, y10)$
    require $t10n$?
  $t90n$: $\mathbb{R} \triangleq wf.last(tmax, t50n, y90)$
    require $t90n$?
  $durationn$: $\mathbb{R} \triangleq (t90n - t10n)$
    require $durationn$?
  $t10n$?: $\mathbb{B} \triangleq wf.has(t50n, n, y10)$
  $t90n$?: $\mathbb{B} \triangleq wf.has(tmax, t50n, y90)$
  $durationn$?: $\mathbb{B} \triangleq t10n? \wedge t90n?$
invariant
  $durationn? \Rightarrow t90n < t50n < t10n$

module signal **use** $SEQ[\mathbb{R}]$
variable swf: $SEQ[\mathbb{R}]$
queries
  n: $\mathbb{N} \triangleq swf.count$
  $s3$: $\mathbb{B} \triangleq (n \geq 3)$
    --at least 3 samples?
  $ymax$: $\mathbb{R} \triangleq (\uparrow i | 1 \leq i \leq n \bullet swf(i))$
    --maximum level (s2 in IEEE-181)
    require $s3$
  $ymin$: $\mathbb{R} \triangleq (\downarrow i | 1 \leq i \leq n \bullet swf(i))$
    --minimum level (s1 in IEEE-181)
    require $s3$
  um: $\mathbb{B}$
    $\triangleq (\#i | 1 \leq i \leq n \bullet swf(i) = ymax) = 1$
    --is there a unique maximum?
    require $s3$

module waveform **use** signal, RFUN
require $s3 \wedge um$
queries
  $y10$: $\mathbb{R} \triangleq ymin + 0.1 * amplitude$
  $y50$: $\mathbb{R} \triangleq ymin + 0.5 * amplitude$
  $y90$: $\mathbb{R} \triangleq ymin + 0.9 * amplitude$
  $t50p$: $\mathbb{R} \triangleq wf.first(1, tmax, y50)$
    require $t50p$?
  $t50n$: $\mathbb{R} \triangleq wf.last(tmax, n, y50)$
    require $t50n$?
  wf: $RFUN \triangleq seq2rfun(swf)$
  $amplitude$: $\mathbb{R} \triangleq ymax - ymin$
  $t50p$?: $\mathbb{B} \triangleq wf.has(1, tmax, y50)$
  $t50n$?: $\mathbb{B} \triangleq wf.has(tmax, n, y50)$
  $tmax$: $\mathbb{R}$ --instant for ymax
    ensure $1 \leq Result \leq n$
      $\wedge wf(Result) = ymax$

Fig. 6. System specification: machine, modules, variables, queries, invariants

Table 2. Requirements (see Table 4 for conditions and Table 5 for messages)

This table is used in the context of machine *system* in Fig. 6 on page 273.

conditions on input				$e\_msg : 0..3$	$w\_msg : 0..2$	$report : \mathbb{S} \nrightarrow \mathbb{R}$
$s3$	um	$t50?$	$t10?$	0	0	$format \lhd S_1 \lhd S_2$
			$\neg t10?$ $\neg t10p?$	0	1	$format \lhd S_2$
			$\neg t10n?$	0	2	$format \lhd S_1$
		$\neg t50?$		1	0	$\varnothing$
	$\neg um$			2	0	
$\neg s3$				3	0	

where $S_1 = \{\text{``}t10p\text{''} \mapsto t10p, \text{``}durationp\text{''} \mapsto durationp\}$; similarly for S_2 on neg. trans.

Table 3. Formatting pulse and transition parameters ("t10p" and "t10n" left out)

p	"duration"	"y10"	"y50"	"y90"	"t50p"	"t90p"	"t50n"	"t90n"
$format(p)$	$duration$	$y10$	$y50$	$y90$	$t50p$	$t90p$	$t50n$	$t90n$

Table 4. Conditions

Ab.	Meaning
$s3$	Are there at least 3 samples?
um	Is there a unique maximum?
$t50?$	Do both $t50\,\%$ instants exist?
$t10?$	Do both $t10\,\%$ instants exist?
$t10p?$	Does $t10p$ (positive transition instant for level $y10$) exist?
$t10n?$	Does $t10n$ (negative transition instant for level $y10$) exist?

Table 5. Errors/warnings

#	Error
0	No error
1	No 50 % instant
2	No unique maximum level
3	Input lacks 3 finite floats

#	Warning
0	No warning
1	No $t10p$ instant, $durationp$
2	No $t10n$ instant, $durationn$

The first row of Table 2 specifies the report for the *ok* condition of REQ3 where the input is a valid pulse and all the pulse parameters can be calculated and reported. There are no errors or warnings to be reported. In this case $report = ((format \lhd S_1) \lhd S_2)$, where both $report$ and $format$ are partial functions of type $\mathbb{S} \nrightarrow \mathbb{R}$ and "$\lhd$" is the operator of function override. Function $format$ is defined in Table 3, and its domain equals to names of parameters whose values are well-defined where there is no error (i.e. $s3 \wedge um \wedge t50$? holds). In the first row, parameters $t10p$, $durationp$, $t10n$, and $durationn$ are well-defined and are thus added to the report. The two grey rows deal with the warning case of REQ4. The remaining rows deal with the error case of REQ5.

The first invariant in module *pulse* (Fig. 6, p. 273) ensures that the boolean conditions ok, $warning$, and $error$ are complete and disjoint. The second invariant ensures that where there are no errors or warnings, all the parameters are well-defined. The third invariant states the system safety property in REQ8 to ensure the consistency of duration calculations.

3.6 Traceability

The informal E-descriptions (Sect. 3.1) and R-descriptions (Sect. 3.2) are formalized as module queries and invariants (Fig. 6, p. 273), and entries in the tabular specification (Sect. 3.5). We discuss a number of examples. For more details, see our extended report [18].

E-descriptions. For ENV1, in the *pulse* module, we define a Boolean query ok whose definition corresponds to what qualify as a valid input pulse. Furthermore, the last two invariants in module *pulse* specify that if the input pulse is valid, then all queries that calculate the pulse and transition parameters are well-defined and the various instants appear in the right orders. For ENV2, in the *waveform* module, we define real-valued queries $y10$, $y50$, and $y90$ whose definitions are accessible by modules *pos_trans* and *neg_trans*.

R-descriptions. For REQ1, we declare queries $t50p$ and $t50n$ in module *waveform* and all other parameters as queries in modules *pos_trans*, *neg_trans*, and *pulse*. For REQ4, in the *waveform* module, query $t50p$ (and $t50n$) is defined to return the first (and the last) 50 % instant. For REQ5, in the *pos_trans* module, query $t10p$ calculates the last, and hence the closest, instant with 10 % level before the 50 % instant $t50p$. Similarly, query $t90p$ calculates the 90 % instant that is closest to $t50p$ by selecting the first one. Symmetric calculations apply to queries $t10n$ and $t90n$ in the *neg_trans* module.

3.7 Validating Tabular Expressions via Proofs

The process of decomposing queries into modules revealed the need to introduce REQ8 (on p. 270) asserting that where two 10 % (or 90 %) instants are equally close to $t50$, e.g. the first instant occurs before $t50$ and the second occurs after $t50$, the appropriate instant should be chosen on the basis that the 10 %, 50 % and 90 % instants must be in different orders for positive and negative transitions. The atomic requirement REQ8 is declared as the invariant $ok \Rightarrow (t10p < t50p < t90p) \wedge (t90n < t50n < t10n)$ in the *pulse* module (Fig. 6 on p. 273).

Tabular expressions (e.g. Table 2) and atomic requirements (e.g. REQ8) play different roles. The tabular expression ensures that the input-output black-box relation is completely specified. However, it is not obvious from the tabular expression that REQ8 holds as a global safety property. The modular specification in Fig. 6 (p. 273) is used to prove that REQ8 holds as a logical consequence of Table 2. This demonstrates the consistency between the modular specification and the atomic description REQ8, thus an important component of requirements validation. This proof follows from the invariants declared in the modules *pos_trans* and *neg_trans*. For example, in the positive transition module we have the invariant *durationp?* $\Rightarrow t10p < t50p < t90p$. Part of the proof of the above invariant declared in the *pos_trans* module is presented in Fig. 7.

Remark. In the small system of Sect. 1.1, the new state depends on previous states. In the pulse case study, the new state depends upon only new values of the monitored and controlled variables. The invariant proof obligation thus can be discharged using axioms defining the queries.

3.8   Using a SMT Solver to Discharge Proof Obligations

SMT solvers such as Z3 [3] allow us to check the satisfiability of first-order predicates involving real numbers. When proving the predicate $P(x) \Rightarrow Q(x)$ as a theorem, we check that there are no witnesses that satisfy the negation of the predicate, i.e. there are no assignments to x that make $P(x) \wedge \neg Q(x)$ true. Z3 will answer **unsat** if the negation of the predicate has no witnesses, meaning that $P \Rightarrow Q$ is a theorem; **sat** if a counterexample is found; or **unknown** if no conclusions can be reached.

Using the Z3 SMT solver, we mechanized and discharged the invariant proof in Fig. 7 (p. 276) by checking the validity of each step. We represent steps in the proof structure like Fig. 7 as $S_0, S_1, \ldots, S_n$. Each step formula S_i is formed by $F_i R_i F_{i+1}$, where $i \geq 0$, F_i and F_{i+1} are predicates, and R_i is

---

Prove: $t50p? \wedge durationp? \Rightarrow (t10p < t50p)$
   $t10p < t50p$

= ⟨ def. of $t10p$ in module *positive* in Fig. 6 (on p12) ⟩
   $wf.last(1, t50p, y10) < t50p$

= ⟨ def. of RFUN.*last* ⟩
   $(\uparrow t : \mathbb{R} \mid 1 \leq t \leq t50p \wedge wf(t) = y10 \bullet t) < t50p$

= ⟨ < over ↑; trading ⟩
   $(\forall t : \mathbb{R} \mid 1 \leq t \wedge t \leq t50p \wedge t50p \leq t \bullet wf(t) \neq y10)$

⟸ ⟨ drop first conjunct in range; anti-symmetry of ≤; one point rule ⟩
   $wf(t50p) \neq y10$

= ⟨ $wf(t50p) = y50$; def. of $t50p$ in waveform ⟩
   $\neg(y50 = y10)$

= ⟨ def. of $y50$ and $y10$ in waveform ⟩
   $\neg((ymin + 0.5 * amplitude) = (ymin + 0.1 * amplitude))$

= ⟨ arithmetic and *amplitide* $\neq 0$ ⟩
   true

Fig. 7. Proving a property of module *positive* that also validates REQ8

either an implication or an equivalence. We check that all steps are valid and they hold together to entail $H \vdash P$. For example, in Fig. 7, S_0 is $(t10p < t50p) \equiv (wf.last(1, t50p, y10) < t50p)$, and the theorem we aim to prove is $(t50p? \wedge durationp?) \vdash (t10p < t50p)$. The following proof tree structure is encoded in Z3:

$$\dfrac{\dfrac{S_0 \wedge S_1 \wedge \cdots \wedge S_{n-1} \vdash P}{H, S_0 \wedge S_1 \wedge \cdots \wedge S_{n-1} \vdash P}\ \text{MON} \qquad \dfrac{H \vdash S_0 \quad H \vdash S_1 \quad \cdots \quad H \vdash S_{n-1}}{H \vdash S_0 \wedge S_1 \wedge \cdots \wedge S_{n-1}}\ \text{SPLIT}}{H \vdash P}\ \text{CUT}$$

We use three deduction rules: CUT introduces and proves a new assumption, MON(otonicity) drops some hypotheses, and SPLIT divides the proof of a conjunction into the proofs of its constituents. The bottom sequent in the proof tree is the target theorem. The leaves are sequents stating that the steps establish the goal, and that the steps with their justifications are valid. We can ensure that the goal and the steps are well-defined by checking the sufficient condition: $\mathcal{D}(P) \wedge \mathcal{D}(F_0) \wedge \mathcal{D}(F_1) \wedge \cdots \wedge \mathcal{D}(F_n)$. See [18] for the Z3 script for proof in Fig. 7.

4   Conclusion and Related Work

In this paper we present a method for specifying an important class of systems. The overall behaviour of a system is composed of the behaviour of the environment (the plant) together with a computer controller. The informal requirements are given by E/R-descriptions. The E/R-descriptions are formalized via an Event-B-like machine that contains: (1) a set of system invariants obtained from the R-descriptions; and (2) a function table specifying the input-output behaviour of the controller. The function table uses queries organized in modules. Embedding function tables in an event system, and using queries organized in modules, allow our framework to describe the system behaviour in a way that supports precise documentation and validation of requirements. The formal requirements are validated by proving that (a) the invariants are preserved; and (b) the controller specification is complete, disjoint, and well-defined, leveraging its tabular structure. Once validated, the tabular specification serves as the basis for further design and implementation of the controller.

Using our method, the formal requirements for the biomedical device in the case study is less than two pages (Fig. 6 on p. 273 and Table 2 on p. 274). The IEEE-181 standard can also be improved using our method of precise documentation.

Our method adopts well-established software engineering principles: the separation between the controller and its operating environment using context diagrams [9], the identification of monitored and controlled variables [5,8,16], and the use of tabular expressions to capture black-box, input-output relations [11,20]. The theorem prover PVS has been used to provide tool support for tabular expressions [4,11,22]. In PVS, partial functions are converted into total functions using predicate subtyping which generates type checking proof obligations.

Our calculus of well-definedness (Sect. 2 and [17]) extends Abrial's work on model queries [2] to the specification context of tabular expressions. Authors of [12] also extend [2] to apply to equivalence rewriting. However, while our main focus is on supporting (formal) human reasoning (possibly validated by automated tools), authors of [12] target more automated reasoning. More precisely, authors of [12] create a new syntactic category, a (one-directional) rewrite rule, in order to allow users to create theories and specify identities in the context of those theories. This means that identities specified outside of such a theory (e.g., in a machine invariant or a guard) is not amenable to the same treatment as those of the rewrite rules. To combine rewrite rules with logical inference rules, authors of [12] provide a meta-theoretical justification. On the other hand, by basing our rewrite rules on a logical operator (i.e., the logical equivalence), rewriting is just one of the available inference rules. While substantial progress has been made in mechanizing proofs, there are still many challenges [6].

Since our focus is on documentation, rather than on breaking new ground on the semantics, we have not gone beyond the set of properties that can be proved in Event-B. For more expressive temporal properties, such as liveness, we may apply our method within the UNITY framework [15].

Acknowledgments. The authors would like to thank NSERC and ORF for their generous financial support.

References

1. Abrial, J.-R.: Modeling in Event-B. Cambridge University Press, New York (2010)
2. Abrial, J.-R., Mussat, L.: On using conditional definitions in formal theories. In: Bert, D., Bowen, J.P., Henson, M.C., Robinson, K. (eds.) B 2002 and ZB 2002. LNCS, vol. 2272, pp. 242–269. Springer, Heidelberg (2002)
3. de Moura, L.M., Bjørner, N.: Z3: an efficient SMT solver. In: Ramakrishnan, C.R., Rehof, J. (eds.) TACAS 2008. LNCS, vol. 4963, pp. 337–340. Springer, Heidelberg (2008)
4. Eles, C., Lawford, M.: A tabular expression toolbox for matlab/simulink. In: Bobaru, M., Havelund, K., Holzmann, G.J., Joshi, R. (eds.) NFM 2011. LNCS, vol. 6617, pp. 494–499. Springer, Heidelberg (2011)
5. Gunter, C.A., Gunter, E.L., Jackson, M., Zave, P.: A reference model for requirements and specifications. IEEE Softw. **17**(3), 37–43 (2000)
6. Hatcliff, J., Leavens, G.T., Leino, K.R.M., Müller, P., Parkinson, M.: Behavioral interface specification languages. ACM Comput. Surv. **44**(3), 16:1–16:58 (2012)
7. IEEE: IEEE standard for transitions, pulses, and related waveforms. IEEE Std 181-2011 (Revision of IEEE Std 181-2003), pp. 1–71 (2011)
8. Jackson, M.: Software Requirements Specifications: A Lexicon of Practice, Principles and Prejudices. Addison-Wesley, New York (1995)
9. Jackson, M.: The operational principle and problem frames. Reflections on the Work of C. A. R. Hoare. Springer, London (2010)
10. Jin, Y., Parnas, D.L.: Defining the meaning of tabular mathematical expressions. Sci. Comput. Program. **75**(11), 980–1000 (2010)

11. Lawford, M., Froebel, P., Moum, G.: Application of tabular methods to the specification and verification of a nuclear reactor shutdown system. Formal Meth. Syst. Des. (2000). http://www.cas.mcmaster.ca/~lawford/papers/FMSD.html
12. Maamria, I., Butler, M.: Rewriting and well-definedness within a proof system. EPTCS **43**, 49–64 (2010)
13. Maibaum, T.S.E., Wassyng, A.: A product-focused approach to software certification. IEEE Comput. **41**(2), 91–93 (2008)
14. Meyer, B.: Object-Oriented Software Construction. Prentice Hall, New Jersey (1997)
15. Misra, J.: A Discipline of Multiprogramming: Programming Theory for Distributed Applications. Springer, New York (2001)
16. Ostroff, J.S., Paige, R.F.: The logic of software design. Proc. IEE - Softw. **147**(3), 72–80 (2000)
17. Ostroff, J.S., Wang, C.-W., Hudon, S.: Precise documentation of requirements and executable specifications. Technical Report CSE-2012-03, York University (2012)
18. Ostroff, J.S., Wang, C.-W., Hudon, S.: Precise documentation and validation of requirements. Technical Report CSE-2013-08, York University (2013)
19. Parnas, D.L.: Predicate logic for software engineering. IEEE Trans. Softw. Eng. **19**(9), 856–862 (1993)
20. Parnas, D.L., Madey, J.: Functional documentation for computer systems. Sci. Comput. Prog. **25**, 41–61 (1995)
21. Wassyng, A., Lawford, M.: Lessons learned from a successful implementation of formal methods in an industrial project. In: FME, pp. 133–153 (2003)
22. Wassyng, A., Lawford, M.: Software tools for safety-critical software development. STTT **8**(4–5), 337–354 (2006)
23. Wassyng, A., Lawford, M., Hu, X.: Timing tolerances in safety-critical software. In: Fitzgerald, J.S., Hayes, I.J., Tarlecki, A. (eds.) FM 2005. LNCS, vol. 3582, pp. 157–172. Springer, Heidelberg (2005)

Certainly Unsupervisable States

Simon Ware[1], Robi Malik[1]([✉]), Sahar Mohajerani[2], and Martin Fabian[2]

[1] Department of Computer Science, University of Waikato, Hamilton, New Zealand
{siw4,robi}@waikato.ac.nz
[2] Department of Signals and Systems, Chalmers University of Technology,
Gothenburg, Sweden
{mohajera,fabian}@chalmers.se

Abstract. This paper proposes an abstraction method for compositional synthesis. *Synthesis* is a method to automatically compute a *control program* or *supervisor* that restricts the behaviour of a given system to ensure safety and liveness. *Compositional synthesis* uses repeated abstraction and simplification to combat the state-space explosion problem for large systems. The abstraction method proposed in this paper finds and removes the so-called *certainly unsupervisable* states. By removing these states at an early stage, the final state space can be reduced substantially. The paper describes an algorithm with cubic time complexity to compute the largest possible set of removable states. A practical example demonstrates the feasibility of the method to solve real-world problems.

1 Introduction

Reactive systems are used extensively to control safety-critical applications, where a small error can result in huge financial or human losses. With their size and complexity continuously increasing, there is an increasing demand for formal modelling and analysis. *Model checking* [4] has been used successfully to automatically detect errors in reactive systems. In some cases, it is possible to go further and *synthesise*, i.e., automatically compute a controlling agent that removes certain kinds of errors from a system.

The controller synthesis problem has been studied by several researchers in computing and control. The synthesis of a stand-alone controller from a temporal logic specification is studied in [7,19]. Synthesis has been generalised to the extraction of an environment to interact with a given software *interface* [1], and to the construction controllers interacting with a given *environment* or *plant* [2,5]. *Supervisory control theory* [21] of discrete event systems provides a framework to synthesise a *supervisor* that restricts the behaviour of a given plant as little as possible while ensuring the safety and liveness properties of *controllability* and *nonblocking*.

Straightforward synthesis algorithms explore the complete *monolithic* state space of the system, and are therefore limited by the well-known *state-space*

C. Artho and P.C. Ölveczky (Eds.): FTSCS 2013, CCIS 419, pp. 280–296, 2014.
DOI: 10.1007/978-3-319-05416-2_18, © Springer International Publishing Switzerland 2014

explosion problem. The sheer size of the supervisor also makes it humanly incomprehensible, which hinders acceptance of the synthesis approach in industrial settings. These problems are addressed by *compositional* methods [3,8]. If a temporal logic specification is the conjunction of several requirements, it is possible to synthesise separate controller components for each requirement [5,7]. Compositional approaches in supervisory control [9,16] exploit the structure of the model of the plant to be controlled, which typically consists of several interacting components. These approaches avoid constructing the full state space by first simplifying individual components, then applying synchronous composition step by step, and simplifying the intermediate results again.

This kind of compositional synthesis requires specific abstraction methods to guarantee a least restrictive, controllable, and nonblocking final synthesis result. *Supervision equivalence* [9] and *synthesis abstraction* [16] have been proposed for this purpose, and several abstraction methods to simplify automata preserving these properties are known.

This paper proposes another abstraction method that can be used in compositional synthesis frameworks such as [9,16]. The proposed method finds all the states that will certainly be removed by any supervisor. Removing these so-called *certainly unsupervisable states* at an early stage reduces the state space substantially. Previously, *halfway synthesis* [9] was used for this purpose, which approximates the removable states. The set of certainly unsupervisable states is the largest possible set of removable states, and it can be computed in the same cubic complexity as halfway synthesis.

This paper is organised as follows. Section 2 introduces the terminology of supervisory control theory [21] and the framework of compositional synthesis [9,16]. Next, Sect. 3 explains the ideas of compositional synthesis with certainly unsupervisable states using the example of a manufacturing system. Section 4 presents the results of this paper: it defines the set of certainly unsupervisable states, gives an algorithm to compute it, performs complexity analysis, and compares certainly unsupervisable states to halfway synthesis. Finally, Sect. 5 adds some concluding remarks.

2 Preliminaries

2.1 Events and Languages

Discrete event systems [21] are modelled using events and languages. *Events* represent incidents that cause transitions from one state to another and are taken from a finite alphabet Σ. For the purpose of supervisory control, the alphabet is partitioned into two disjoint subsets, the set Σ_c of *controllable* events and the set Σ_u of *uncontrollable* events. Controllable events can be disabled by a supervising agent, while uncontrollable events occur spontaneously. In addition, the *silent controllable* event $\tau_c \in \Sigma_c$ and the *silent uncontrollable* event $\tau_u \in \Sigma_u$ denote transitions that are not taken by any component other than the one being considered. The set of all finite *traces* of events from Σ, including the

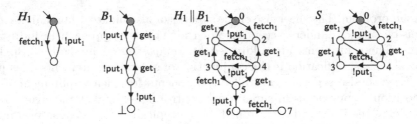

Fig. 1. Simple manufacturing system. Events fetch$_1$ and get$_1$ are controllable, while !put$_1$ is uncontrollable.

empty trace ε, is denoted by Σ^*. A subset $L \subseteq \Sigma^*$ is called a *language*. The *concatenation* of two traces $s, t \in \Sigma^*$ is written as st.

2.2 Nondeterministic Automata

System behaviours are typically modelled by deterministic automata, but nondeterministic automata may arise as intermediate results during abstraction.

Definition 1. A (nondeterministic) finite automaton is a tuple $G = \langle \Sigma, Q, \rightarrow, Q^\circ, Q^\omega \rangle$, where Σ is a finite set of events, Q is a finite set of *states*, $\rightarrow \subseteq Q \times (\Sigma \cup \{\tau_u, \tau_c\}) \times Q$ is the *state transition relation*, $Q^\circ \subseteq Q$ is the set of *initial states*, and $Q^\omega \subseteq Q$ is the set of *accepting states*.

The transition relation is written in infix notation $x \xrightarrow{\sigma} y$, and is extended to traces and languages in the standard way. For example, $x \xrightarrow{\tau_u^* \sigma} y$ means that there exists a possibly empty sequence of τ_u-transitions followed by a σ-transition that leads from state x to y. Furthermore, $x \xrightarrow{s}$ means $x \xrightarrow{s} y$ for some $y \in Q$, and $x \rightarrow y$ means $x \xrightarrow{s} y$ for some $s \in \Sigma^*$. These notations also apply to state sets and to automata: $X \xrightarrow{s} Y$ for $X, Y \subseteq Q$ means $x \xrightarrow{s} y$ for some $x \in X$ and $y \in Y$, and $G \xrightarrow{s} x$ means $Q^\circ \xrightarrow{s} x$.

Example 1. Figure 1 shows an automata model of a simple manufacturing system consisting of a handler H_1 and a buffer B_1. The handler fetches a workpiece (fetch$_1$) and then puts it into the buffer (!put$_1$). The event !put$_1$ also increases the number of workpieces in the buffer by 1. Afterwards the buffer can release the workpiece (get$_1$), reducing the number of workpieces in the buffer by 1. The buffer can store only two workpieces, adding more workpieces causes overflow as represented by the state $\bot$.

Definition 2. Let $G_1 = \langle \Sigma_1, Q_1, \rightarrow_1, Q_1^\circ, Q_1^\omega \rangle$ and $G_2 = \langle \Sigma_2, Q_2, \rightarrow_2, Q_2^\circ, Q_2^\omega \rangle$ be two automata. The *synchronous composition* of G_1 and G_2 is

$$G_1 \parallel G_2 = \langle \Sigma_1 \cup \Sigma_2, Q_1 \times Q_2, \rightarrow, Q_1^\circ \times Q_2^\circ, Q_1^\omega \times Q_2^\omega \rangle \tag{1}$$

where

$$(x_1, x_2) \xrightarrow{\sigma} (y_1, y_2), \quad \text{if } \sigma \in (\Sigma_1 \cap \Sigma_2) \setminus \{\tau_u, \tau_c\}, \ x_1 \xrightarrow{\sigma}_1 y_1, \text{ and } x_2 \xrightarrow{\sigma}_2 y_2 \ ; \tag{2}$$

$$(x_1, x_2) \xrightarrow{\sigma} (y_1, x_2), \quad \text{if } \sigma \in (\Sigma_1 \setminus \Sigma_2) \cup \{\tau_u, \tau_c\} \text{ and } x_1 \xrightarrow{\sigma}_1 y_1 \ ; \tag{3}$$

$$(x_1, x_2) \xrightarrow{\sigma} (x_1, y_2), \quad \text{if } \sigma \in (\Sigma_2 \setminus \Sigma_1) \cup \{\tau_u, \tau_c\} \text{ and } x_2 \xrightarrow{\sigma}_2 y_2 \ . \tag{4}$$

Automata are synchronised in lock-step synchronisation [11]. Shared events must be executed by all automata together, while events used by only one automaton (and the silent events τ_u and τ_c) are executed by only that automaton. Figure 1 shows the synchronous composition $H_1 \parallel B_1$ of the automata mentioned in Example 1.

Another common operation in compositional synthesis is *hiding*, which removes the identity of certain events and in general produces a nondeterministic automaton.

Definition 3. Let $G = \langle \Sigma, Q, \rightarrow, Q^\circ, Q^\omega \rangle$ be an automaton and $\Upsilon \subseteq \Sigma$. The result of *controllability preserving hiding* of Υ from G is $G \setminus_! \Upsilon = \langle \Sigma \setminus \Upsilon, Q, \rightarrow_!, Q^\circ, Q^\omega \rangle$, where $\rightarrow_!$ is obtained from $\rightarrow$ by replacing each transition $x \xrightarrow{\sigma} y$ such that $\sigma \in \Upsilon$ by $x \xrightarrow{\tau_c} y$ if $\sigma \in \Sigma_c$ or by $x \xrightarrow{\tau_u} y$ if $\sigma \in \Sigma_u$.

2.3 Supervisory Control Theory

Supervisory control theory [21] provides a means to automatically compute a so-called *supervisor* that controls a given system to perform some desired functionality. Given an automata model of the possible behaviour of a physical system, called the *plant*, a supervisor is sought to restrict the behaviour in such a way that only a certain subset of the state space is reachable. The supervisor is implemented as a *control function* [21]

$$\Phi \colon Q \to 2^{\Sigma \times Q} \tag{5}$$

that assigns to each state $x \in Q$ the set $\Phi(x)$ of transitions to be enabled in this state. That is, a transition $x \xrightarrow{\sigma} y$ with $\sigma \in \Sigma_c$ will only be possible under the control of supervisor Φ if $(\sigma, y) \in \Phi(x)$. Uncontrollable events cannot be disabled, so it is required that $\Sigma_u \times Q \subseteq \Phi(x)$ for all $x \in Q$. Controllable transitions can be disabled individually, i.e., if a nondeterministic system contains multiple outgoing controllable transitions from a state x, then the supervisor may disable some of them while leaving others enabled [9]. If the plant is modelled by a nondeterministic automaton, then such a supervisor can be represented as a *subautomaton*.

Definition 4. [9] Let $G = \langle \Sigma, Q_G, \rightarrow_G, Q_G^\circ, Q_G^\omega \rangle$ and $K = \langle \Sigma, Q_K, \rightarrow_K, Q_K^\circ, Q_K^\omega \rangle$ be two automata. K is a *subautomaton* of G, written $K \subseteq G$, if $Q_K \subseteq Q_G$, $\rightarrow_K \subseteq \rightarrow_G$, $Q_K^\circ \subseteq Q_G^\circ$, and $Q_K^\omega \subseteq Q_G^\omega$.

A subautomaton K of G contains a subset of the states and transitions of G. It represents a supervisor that enables only those transitions present in K, i.e., it implements the control function

$$\Phi_K(x) = (\Sigma_u \times Q) \cup \{ (\sigma, y) \in \Sigma_c \times Q \mid x \xrightarrow{\sigma}_K y \} . \tag{6}$$

As uncontrollable events cannot be disabled, the control function includes all possible uncontrollable transitions. Not every subautomaton of G can be implemented through control—the property of *controllability* [21] characterises those behaviours than can be implemented.

Definition 5. [9] Let $G = \langle \Sigma, Q_G, \rightarrow_G, Q_G^\circ, Q_G^\omega \rangle$ and $K = \langle \Sigma, Q_K, \rightarrow_K, Q_K^\circ, Q_K^\omega \rangle$ such that $K \subseteq G$. Then K is called *controllable* in G if, for all states $x \in Q_K$ and $y \in Q_G$ and for every uncontrollable event $v \in \Sigma_u$ such that $x \xrightarrow{v}_G y$, it also holds that $x \xrightarrow{v}_K y$.

If a subautomaton K is controllable in G, then every uncontrollable transition possible in G is also contained in K. In Fig. 1, automaton S is controllable in $H_1 \parallel B_1$. However, if state 5 was to be included in S, then because of the uncontrollable transition $5 \xrightarrow{!put_1} 6$, state 6 would also have to be included for S to be controllable. Controllability ensures that the control function (6) can be implemented without disabling any uncontrollable events.

In addition to controllability, the supervised behaviour is typically required to be *nonblocking*.

Definition 6. [15] Let $G = \langle \Sigma, Q, \rightarrow, Q^\circ, Q^\omega \rangle$ be an automaton. G is called *nonblocking* if for every state $x \in Q$ such that $Q^\circ \rightarrow x$ it holds that $x \rightarrow Q^\omega$.

In a nonblocking automaton, termination is possible from every reachable state. The nonblocking property, also referred to as *weak termination* [17], ensures the absence of livelocks and deadlocks. Combined with controllability, the requirement to be nonblocking can express arbitrary safety properties [9]. For example, the buffer model B_1 in Fig. 1 contains the $!put_1$-transition to the blocking state $\perp$ to specify a supervised behaviour that does not allow a third workpiece to be placed into the buffer when it already contains two workpieces, i.e., it requests a supervisor that prevents buffer overflow.

Given a plant automaton G, the objective of *supervisor synthesis* [21] is to compute a subautomaton $K \subseteq G$, which is controllable and nonblocking and restricts the behaviour of G as little as possible. The set of subautomata of G forms a lattice [6], and the upper bound of a set of controllable and nonblocking subautomata in this lattice is again controllable and nonblocking.

Theorem 1. [9] Let $G = \langle \Sigma, Q, \rightarrow, Q^\circ, Q^\omega \rangle$ be an automaton. There exists a unique subautomaton $\sup \mathscr{C}(G) \subseteq G$ such that $\sup \mathscr{C}(G)$ is nonblocking and controllable in G, and such that for every subautomaton $S \subseteq G$ that is also nonblocking and controllable in G, it holds that $S \subseteq \sup \mathscr{C}(G)$.

The subautomaton $\sup \mathscr{C}(G)$ is the unique *least restrictive* sub-behaviour of G that can be achieved by any possible supervisor. It can be computed using a fixpoint iteration [9], by iteratively removing blocking states and states leading to blocking states via uncontrollable events, until a fixpoint is reached.

Definition 7. [9] Let $G = \langle \Sigma, Q, \to, Q^\circ, Q^\omega \rangle$ be an automaton. The *restriction* of G to $X \subseteq Q$ is $G_{|X} = \langle \Sigma, X, \to_{|X}, Q^\circ \cap X, Q^\omega \cap X \rangle$, where $\to_{|X} = \{ (x, \sigma, y) \in \to \mid x, y \in X \}$.

Definition 8. [9] Let $G = \langle \Sigma, Q, \to, Q^\circ, Q^\omega \rangle$ be an automaton. The *synthesis step* operator $\Theta_G : 2^Q \to 2^Q$ for G is defined as $\Theta_G(X) = \Theta_G^{\text{cont}}(X) \cap \Theta_G^{\text{cont}}(X)$, where

$$\Theta_G^{\text{cont}}(X) = \{ x \in X \mid \text{for all transitions } x \xrightarrow{\upsilon} y \text{ with } \upsilon \in \Sigma_u \text{ it holds that } y \in X \} ; \tag{7}$$

$$\Theta_G^{\text{nonb}}(X) = \{ x \in X \mid x \to_{|X} Q^\omega \} . \tag{8}$$

Given a state set $X \subseteq Q$, the operator Θ_G^{cont} removes from X any states that have an uncontrollable successor not contained in X, and Θ_G^{nonb} removes any states from where it is not possible to reach an accepting state via transitions contained in X. Thus, Θ_G^{cont} captures controllability and Θ_G^{nonb} captures nonblocking. Both operators and their combination Θ_G are monotonic, and it follows by the Knaster-Tarski theorem [20] that they have greatest fixpoints. The least restrictive synthesis result $\sup \mathscr{C}(G)$ is obtained by restricting G to the greatest fixpoint of Θ_G.

Theorem 2. [9] Let $G = \langle \Sigma, Q, \to, Q^\circ, Q^\omega \rangle$. The synthesis step operator Θ_G has a greatest fixpoint $\text{gfp} \Theta_G = \hat{\Theta}_G \subseteq Q$, such that $G_{|\hat{\Theta}_G}$ is the greatest subautomaton of G that is both controllable in G and nonblocking, i.e.,

$$\sup \mathscr{C}(G) = G_{|\hat{\Theta}_G} . \tag{9}$$

Example 2. The automaton $H_1 \parallel B_1$ in Fig. 1 is blocking, because the trace $\text{fetch}_1!\text{put}_1\text{fetch}_1!\text{put}_1\text{fetch}_1!\text{put}_1$ leads to state 6, from where no accepting state is reachable. To prevent this blocking situation, event $!\text{put}_1$ needs to be disabled in state 5. However, $!\text{put}_1$ is an uncontrollable event that cannot be disabled by the supervisor, so the best feasible solution is to disable the controllable event fetch_1 in state 3. Figure 1 shows the least restrictive supervisor $S = \sup \mathscr{C}(H_1 \parallel B_1)$.

In the finite-state case, the state set of the least restrictive supervisor can be calculated as the limit of the sequence $X^0 = Q$, $X^{i+1} = \Theta_G(X^i)$. This iteration converges in at most $|Q|$ iterations, and the worst-case time complexity is $O(|Q||\to|) = O(|\Sigma||Q|^3)$, where $|\Sigma|$, $|Q|$, and $|\to|$ are the numbers of events, states, and transitions of the plant automaton G. However, often the behaviour of the system is specified by a large number of synchronised automata, and when measured by the number of components, the synthesis problem is NP-complete [10].

2.4   Compositional Synthesis

Many discrete event systems are *modular* in that they consist of a large number of interacting components. This modularity allows to simplify individual components before composing them, in many cases avoiding state-space explosion. This idea has been used successfully for verification [8] and synthesis [9,16] of large discrete event systems.

Given a system of concurrent plant automata

$$\mathcal{G} = G_1 \parallel G_2 \parallel \cdots \parallel G_n \,, \tag{10}$$

the objective of synthesis is to find a least restrictive supervisor, which ensures nonblocking without disabling uncontrollable events. The standard solution [21] to this problem is to calculate a finite-state representation of the synchronous composition (10) and use a synthesis iteration to calculate $\sup \mathscr{C}(\mathcal{G}) = \sup \mathscr{C}(G_1 \parallel \cdots \parallel G_n)$.

A compositional algorithm tries to find the same result without explicitly calculating the synchronous composition (10). It seeks to abstract individual automata G_i by removing some states or transitions, and replace them by abstracted versions $\tilde{G}_i$. If no more abstraction is possible, synchronous composition is computed step by step, abstracting the intermediate results again.

The individual automata G_i typically contain some events that do not appear in any other automata G_j. These events are called *local* events, denoted by the set Υ in the following. After hiding the local events, the automaton G_i is replaced by $G_i \setminus_! \Upsilon$, which increases the possibility of further abstraction.

Eventually, the procedure leads to a single automaton $\tilde{G}$, the abstract description of the system $\mathcal{G}$. After abstraction, the automaton of $\tilde{G}$ has less states and transitions compared to (10). Once $\tilde{G}$ is found, the final step is to use it instead of the original system, to obtain a synthesis result $\sup \mathscr{C}(\tilde{G}) = \sup \mathscr{C}(\mathcal{G})$.

The abstraction steps to simplify the individual automata G_i must satisfy certain conditions to guarantee that the synthesis result obtained from the final abstraction is a correct supervisor for the original system.

Definition 9. Let G and H be two automata with alphabet Σ. Then G is *synthesis equivalent* to H, written $G \simeq_{\text{synth}} H$ if, for every automaton T, it holds that $\sup \mathscr{C}(G \parallel T) = \sup \mathscr{C}(H \parallel T)$.

Definition 9 is a special case of synthesis abstraction [16]. Synthesis equivalence requires that the abstracted automaton H yields the same supervisor as the original automaton G, no matter what the remainder of the system T is.

3   Manufacturing System Example

This section demonstrates compositional synthesis using a modified version of a manufacturing system previously studied in [13]. The manufacturing system consists of two machines (M_1 and M_2) and four pairs of handlers (H_i) and

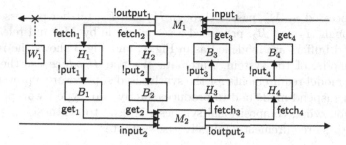

Fig. 2. Manufacturing system overview.

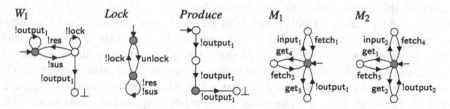

Fig. 3. Automata for manufacturing system model. Uncontrollable events are prefixed by !.

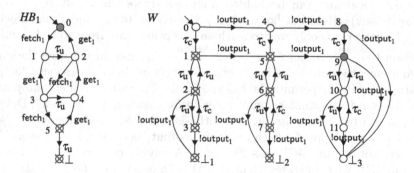

Fig. 4. Automata encountered during compositional synthesis of manufacturing system example.

buffers (B_i) for transferring workpieces between the machines. Figure 2 gives an overview of the system.

The manufacturing system can produce two types of workpieces. Type I workpieces are first processed by machine M_1 (input$_1$). Then they are fetched by handler H_1 (fetch$_1$) and placed into buffer B_1 (!put$_1$). Next, they are processed by M_2 (get$_1$), fetched by H_4 (fetch$_4$) and placed into B_4 (!put$_4$). Finally, they are processed by M_1 once more (get$_4$), and released (!output$_1$). Using a switch W_1, users can request to suspend (!sus) or resume (!res) production of M_1, provided that the switch has been unlocked (unlock) by the system. Type II workpieces are first processed by M_2, passed through H_3 and B_3, further processed by M_1, passed through H_2 and B_2, processed a second time by M_2, and released. The handlers and buffers are modelled as in Fig. 1, and Fig. 3 shows the rest of the automata model of the system. Automata W_1 and *Produce* use the blocking states $\perp$ to model requirements for the synthesised supervisor to prevent output from M_1 in suspend mode and to produce exactly two Type I workpieces.

In the following, compositional synthesis is used to synthesise a supervisor subject to these requirements. Initially, the system is

$$\mathcal{G} = M_1 \parallel M_2 \parallel W_1 \parallel Lock \parallel Produce \parallel H_1 \parallel B_1 \parallel \cdots \parallel H_4 \parallel B_4 . \quad (11)$$

In the first step, H_1 and B_1 are composed, so that event !put$_1$ becomes an uncontrollable local event and can be hidden. Thus, H_1 and B_1 are replaced by $HB_1 = (H_1 \parallel B_1) \setminus_! \{!\text{put}_1\}$ shown in Fig. 4, where for graphical simplicity the two blocking states from Fig. 1 are replaced by the state $\perp$. Clearly, such blocking states must be avoided, and since the silent uncontrollable transition $5 \xrightarrow{\tau_u} \perp$ cannot be disabled by the supervisor or by any plant, state 5 must also be avoided. States 5 and $\perp$ are *certainly unsupervisable states* and are crossed out in Fig. 4. Automaton HB_1 is replaced by the synthesis equivalent abstraction $\tilde{HB}_1$ with 5 states, which is obtained by deleting states 5 and $\perp$. The same abstraction is applied to the other buffers and handlers.

After composition of W_1, *Produce*, and *Lock*, events !sus, !res, !lock, and unlock are local and can be hidden. Figure 4 shows the result $W = (W_1 \parallel Produce \parallel Lock) \setminus_! \{!\text{sus}, !\text{res}, !\text{lock}, \text{unlock}\}$. Clearly, states $\perp_1$ and $\perp_2$ are blocking states. Moreover, the only way to reach an accepting state from state 1 is via the transition $1 \xrightarrow{!\text{output}_1} 5$. However, $1 \xrightarrow{\tau_u} 2 \xrightarrow{!\text{output}_1} \perp_1$, and since neither the supervisor nor any other plant can disable τ_u, a supervisor that enables event !output$_1$ in state 1, inevitably permits the blocking state $\perp_1$. State 1 is a certainly unsupervisable state, and similar arguments hold for states 2, 3, 5, 6, and 7. Deleting these states from W results in the synthesis equivalent automaton $\tilde{W}$. Next, M_1 and $\tilde{W}$ are composed, which results in !output$_1$ becoming a local event. The composed automaton, MW, has 28 states. Applying certain unsupervisability results in $\tilde{MW}$ with 20 states. Replacing W_1, *Produce*, and *Lock* by $\tilde{MW}$ gives the final abstracted system $\tilde{\mathcal{G}} = \tilde{MW} \parallel M_2 \parallel \tilde{HB}_1 \parallel \tilde{HB}_2 \parallel \tilde{HB}_3 \parallel \tilde{HB}_4$.

Finally, the components of $\tilde{\mathcal{G}}$ are composed to calculate a supervisor. This requires the exploration of the synchronous composition $\tilde{\mathcal{G}}$ with 48400 states, in contrast to the state space of the original system $\mathcal{G}$ with 1.3×10^6 states. The final supervisors calculated from $\mathcal{G}$ and $\tilde{\mathcal{G}}$ are identical and have 4374 states.

4   Certain Unsupervisability

4.1   Certainly Unsupervisable States and Transitions

The above example shows that some states of an automaton G must be avoided by synthesis in every possible context. That is, no matter what other automata are later composed with G, it is clear that these states are unsafe. Blocking states are examples of such states, but there are more states with this property.

Definition 10. Let $G = \langle \Sigma, Q, \rightarrow, Q^\circ, Q^\omega \rangle$ be an automaton. The *certainly unsupervisable state set* of G is

$$\hat{U}(G) = \{x \in Q \mid \text{for every automaton } T = \langle \Sigma, Q_T, \rightarrow_T, Q_T^\circ, Q_T^\omega \rangle \text{ and every}$$
$$\text{state } x^T \in Q_T \text{ it holds that } (x, x^T) \notin \hat{\Theta}_{G\|T}\}. \tag{12}$$

A state x of G is certainly unsupervisable, if there exists no other automaton T such that the state x is present in the least restrictive synthesis result $\hat{\Theta}_{G\|T}$. If a state is certainly unsupervisable, it is known that this state will be removed by every synthesis. If such states are encountered in an automaton during compositional synthesis, they can be removed before composing this automaton further.

Example 3. Consider again automaton HB_1 in Fig. 4. Clearly, the blocking state $\perp$ is certainly unsupervisable. In addition, state 5 is also certainly unsupervisable, because of the local uncontrollable transition $5 \xrightarrow{\tau_u} \perp$. As this transition is silent, no other component disables it, and as it is uncontrollable, the supervisor cannot disable it. Therefore, if the automaton ever enters state 5, blocking is unavoidable. It holds that $\hat{U}(HB_1) = \{5, \perp\}$.

In addition to states, it is worth considering transitions as certainly unsupervisable. If an uncontrollable event υ can take a state x to a certainly unsupervisable state, then all υ-transitions from x are certainly unsupervisable. Such transitions can be removed because it is clear that no supervisor will allow state x to be entered while υ is possible in the plant.

Definition 11. Let $G = \langle \Sigma, Q, \rightarrow, Q^\circ, Q^\omega \rangle$ be an automaton. A transition $x \xrightarrow{\upsilon} y$ with $\upsilon \in \Sigma_u$ is a *certainly unsupervisable transition* if $x \xrightarrow{\tau_u^* \upsilon} \hat{U}(G)$.

Example 4. Consider automaton W in Fig. 4. States $\perp_1$, $\perp_2$, and $\perp_3$ are blocking and therefore certainly unsupervisable. The transition $5 \xrightarrow{!\text{output}_1} 9$ is certainly unsupervisable, because $!\text{output}_1$ is uncontrollable and $5 \xrightarrow{\tau_u} 6 \xrightarrow{!\text{output}_1} \perp_2 \in \hat{U}(W)$. The uncontrollable event $!\text{output}_1$ cannot be allowed in state 5, because if it was possible, blocking in state $\perp_2$ would be unavoidable.

Further, as every path from state 5 to an accepting state must take the certainly unsupervisable transition, it follows that state 5 is certainly unsupervisable. By similar arguments, it is established that $\hat{U}(W) = \{1, 2, 3, 5, 6, 7, \perp_1, \perp_2, \perp_3\}$.

If the certainly unsupervisable states and transitions are known, they can be used to simplify an automaton to form a synthesis equivalent abstraction.

Definition 12. Let $G = \langle \Sigma, Q, \rightarrow, Q^\circ, Q^\omega \rangle$ be an automaton. The result of *unsupervisability removal* from G is the automaton

$$\text{unsup}\,\mathscr{C}(G) = \langle \Sigma, Q, \rightarrow_{\text{unsup}}, Q^\circ \setminus \hat{U}(G), Q^\omega \setminus \hat{U}(G) \rangle, \tag{13}$$

where

$$\rightarrow_{\text{unsup}} = \{ (x, \sigma, y) \in \rightarrow \mid \sigma \in \Sigma_c \text{ and } x, y \notin \hat{U}(G) \} \cup \tag{14}$$

$$\{ (x, \upsilon, y) \in \rightarrow \mid \upsilon \in \Sigma_u, \ x \notin \hat{U}(G), \text{ and } y \in \hat{U}(G) \} \cup \tag{15}$$

$$\{ (x, \upsilon, y) \in \rightarrow \mid \upsilon \in \Sigma_u, \ x \notin \hat{U}(G), \text{ and } x \xrightarrow{\tau_u^* \upsilon} \hat{U}(G) \text{ does not hold} \}. \tag{16}$$

The automaton resulting from unsupervisability removal has the same state set as the original automaton G, only the initial and accepting state sets are reduced by removing certainly unsupervisable states. All controllable transitions to certainly unsupervisable states are removed (14), as these transitions can always be disabled by the supervisor and therefore never appear in the final synthesis result. Uncontrollable transitions to certainly unsupervisable states, however, are retained (15), because they are needed to inform future synthesis steps. If another component disables these events, they may disappear in synchronous composition with that component, otherwise the source state may have to be removed in synthesis. Uncontrollable transitions to other states are deleted if they are certainly unsupervisable (16).

Example 5. When applied to automaton W in Fig. 4, unsupervisability removal deletes all transitions linked to the crossed out states. While state $\perp_3$ is certainly unsupervisable, the shared uncontrollable !output$_1$-transitions to this state are retained. They are needed in the following steps of compositional synthesis. If some other component disables !output$_1$ while in state 10 or 11, then these states may be retained, otherwise they will be removed at a later stage.

The following theorem confirms that unsupervisability removal results in a synthesis equivalent automaton. Therefore, the abstraction can be used to replace an automaton during compositional synthesis without affecting the final synthesis result.

Theorem 3. Let G be an automaton. Then $G \simeq_{\text{synth}} \text{unsup}\,\mathscr{C}(G)$.

Unsupervisability removal by definition only removes transitions and no states. Yet, states may become unreachable as a result of transition removal, and unreachable states can always be removed. Furthermore, it is possible to combine all remaining unsupervisable states, which have no outgoing transitions, into a single state [16].

4.2   Iterative Characterisation

The following definition provides an alternative characterisation of the certainly unsupervisable states through an iteration. It forms the basis for an algorithm to compute the set of certainly unsupervisable states.

Definition 13. Let $G = \langle \Sigma, Q, \rightarrow, Q^\circ, Q^\omega \rangle$ be an automaton. Define the set $U(G)$ inductively as follows.

$$U^0(G) = \emptyset \; ; \tag{17}$$

$$U^{k+1}(G) = \{ x \in Q \mid \text{for all paths } x = x_0 \xrightarrow{\sigma_1} \cdots \xrightarrow{\sigma_n} x_n \in Q^\omega$$
$$\text{there exists } i = 0, \ldots, n \text{ such that } x_i \xrightarrow{\tau_u^*} U^k(G) \text{ or } i > 0$$
$$\text{and } \sigma_i \in \Sigma_u \text{ and } x_{i-1} \xrightarrow{\tau_u^* \sigma_i \tau_u^*} U^k(G) \}; \tag{18}$$

$$U(G) = \bigcup_{k \geq 0} U^k(G) \; . \tag{19}$$

The set $U^k(G)$ contains unsupervisable states of *level k*. There are no unsupervisable states of level 0, and the unsupervisable states of level 1 are the blocking states, i.e., those states from where it is not possible to ever reach an accepting state. Unsupervisable states at a higher level are states from where every path to an accepting state is known to pass through an unsupervisable state or an unsupervisable transition of a lower level.

Example 6. Consider automaton W in Fig. 4. It holds that $U^0(W) = \emptyset$, and $U^1(W) = \{\perp_1, \perp_2, \perp_3\}$ contains the three blocking states. Next, it can be seen that $1 \in U^2(W)$, because every path from 1 to an accepting state includes the transition $1 \xrightarrow{!\text{output}_1} 5$ with $!\text{output}_1 \in \Sigma_u$ and $1 \xrightarrow{\tau_u} 2 \xrightarrow{!\text{output}_1} \perp_1 \in U^1(W)$. Likewise, it holds that $2, 3, 5, 6, 7 \in U^2(W)$. No further states are contained in $U^2(W)$ or in $U^k(W)$ for $k > 2$, so that $U(W) = U^2(W) = \{1, 2, 3, 5, 6, 7, \perp_1, \perp_2, \perp_3\} = \hat{U}(W)$.

The following Theorem 4 confirms that the iteration $U^k(G)$ reaches the set of certainly unsupervisable states.

Theorem 4. Let $G = \langle \Sigma, Q, \rightarrow, Q^\circ, Q^\omega \rangle$ be an automaton. Then $U(G) = \hat{U}(G)$.

To determine whether some state x is contained in the set $U^{k+1}(G)$ of unsupervisable states of a new level, the definition (18) considers all paths from state x to an accepting state. Such a condition is difficult to implement directly. It is more feasible to search backwards from the accepting states using the following secondary iteration.

Definition 14. Let $G = \langle \Sigma, Q, \rightarrow, Q^\circ, Q^\omega \rangle$ be an automaton. Define the sets of *supervisable states* $S^k(G)$ for $k \geq 1$ inductively as follows.

$$S_0^{k+1}(G) = \{ x \in Q^\omega \mid x \xrightarrow{\tau_u^*} U^k(G) \text{ does not hold} \}; \tag{20}$$

$$S_{j+1}^{k+1}(G) = \{ x \in Q \mid x \xrightarrow{\sigma} S_j^{k+1}(G), \text{ and } x \xrightarrow{\tau_u^*} U^k(G) \text{ does not hold},$$
$$\text{and if } \sigma \in \Sigma_u \text{ then } x \xrightarrow{\tau_u^* \sigma \tau_u^*} U^k(G) \text{ does not hold} \}; \tag{21}$$

$$S^{k+1}(G) = \bigcup_{j \geq 0} S_j^{k+1}(G) \; . \tag{22}$$

Given the set $U^k(G)$ of unsupervisable states at level k, the iteration $S_j^{k+1}(G)$ computes a set of supervisable states, i.e., states from where a supervisor can reach an accepting state while avoiding the unsupervisable states in $U^k(G)$. The process starts as a backwards search from those accepting states from where it is not possible to reach a known unsupervisable state using only τ_u-transitions (20). Then transitions leading to the states already found are explored backwards (21). However, source states x that can reach a known unsupervisable state using only τ_u-transitions ($x \xrightarrow{\tau_u^*} U^k(G)$), and known unsupervisable transitions ($x \xrightarrow{\tau_u^* \sigma \tau_u^*} U^k(G)$) are excluded.

Example 7. As shown in Example 6, the first iteration for unsupervisable states of automaton W in Fig. 4 gives the blocking states, $U^1(W) = \{\perp_1, \perp_2, \perp_3\}$. Then the first set of supervisable states for the next level contains the two accepting states, $S_0^2(W) = \{8,9\}$ according to (20). Then $4 \xrightarrow{!output_1} 8 \in S_0^2(W)$ and $8 \xrightarrow{\tau_u} 9 \in S_0^2(W)$ and $10 \xrightarrow{\tau_u} 9 \in S_0^2(W)$, and it does not hold that $4 \xrightarrow{\tau_u^*} U^1(W)$ or $4 \xrightarrow{\tau_u^* !output_1 \tau_u^*} U^1(W)$ or $8 \xrightarrow{\tau_u^*} U^1(W)$ or $10 \xrightarrow{\tau_u^*} U^1(W)$. Therefore, $S_1^2(W) = \{4,8,10\}$ according to (21). Note that $5 \notin S_1^2(W)$ because despite the transition $5 \xrightarrow{!output_1} 9$ it holds that $5 \xrightarrow{\tau_u} 6 \xrightarrow{!output_1} \perp_2 \in U^1(W)$. The next iteration gives $S_2^2(W) = \{0,4,9,11\}$, and following iterations do not add any further states. The result is $S^2(W) = \{0,4,8,9,10,11\} = Q \setminus U^2(W)$.

The following theorem confirms that the iteration $S_j^{k+1}(G)$ converges against the complement of the next level of unsupervisable states, $U^{k+1}(G)$.

Theorem 5. Let $G = \langle \Sigma, Q, \rightarrow, Q^\circ, Q^\omega \rangle$ be an automaton. For all $k \geq 1$ it holds that $S^k(G) = Q \setminus U^k(G)$.

4.3 Algorithm

Algorithm 1 is an implementation of the iterations in Definitions 13 and 14 to compute the set of certainly unsupervisable states for a given automaton G. First, the sets of certainly unsupervisable states U and certainly unsupervisable transitions UT are initialised in lines 2 and 3. Then the loop in lines 4–28 performs the iterations for $U^k(G)$.

The first step is to compute the supervisable states $S^{k+1}(G)$, which are stored in S. In line 5, this variable is initialised to the set $S_0^{k+1}(G)$ containing the accepting states that are not yet known to be unsupervisable. Then the loop in lines 7–15 uses a *stack* to perform a backwards search over the transition relation, avoiding known unsupervisable source states and known unsupervisable transitions. Upon termination, the variable S contains the set $S^{k+1}(G)$ of supervisable state for the next level.

Then the loop in lines 17–27 updates the sets U and UT. For every state that was not added to S, it explores the predecessor states reachable by sequences of τ_u-transitions, and adds any states found to U, if not yet included. By adding the τ_u-predecessors to the set U immediately, the reachability tests in (20) and (21)

Algorithm 1. Calculate $U(G)$

```
 1: input G = ⟨Σ, Q, →, Q°, Qω⟩
 2: U ← ∅
 3: UT ← ∅
 4: repeat
 5:     S ← { x ∈ Qω | x ∉ U }
 6:     stack.init(S)
 7:     while stack not empty do
 8:         x ← stack.pop()
 9:         for all w ⟶σ x do
10:             if w ∉ S and w ∉ U and (w, σ) ∉ UT then
11:                 S ← S ∪ {w}
12:                 stack.push(w)
13:             end if
14:         end for
15:     end while
16:     done ← true
17:     for all x ⟶τu* Q \ S do
18:         if x ∉ U then
19:             U ← U ∪ {x}
20:             done ← false
21:             for all v ∈ Σu \ {τu} do
22:                 for all w ⟶τu*v x do
23:                     UT ← UT ∪ {(w, v)}
24:                 end for
25:             end for
26:         end if
27:     end for
28: until done
29: return U
```

can be replaced by the direct membership tests in line 10. Next, for any new unsupervisable state x, the loop in lines 21–25, searches for possible uncontrollable transitions followed by sequences of τ_u and adds such combinations of source states and uncontrollable events to the set certainly unsupervisable transitions UT.

The algorithm terminates if no new unsupervisable states are found during execution of the loop in lines 17–27, in which case the flag *done* retains its true value. At this point, the set U contains all certainly unsupervisable states.

4.4   Complexity

This section gives an estimate for the time complexity of Algorithm 1. Each iteration of the main loop in lines 4–28, except the last, adds at least one state to U, which gives at most $|Q| + 1$ iterations. During each of these iterations, the loop in lines 7–15 visits each transition at most once, giving up to $|\rightarrow|$ iterations, and the loop in lines 17–27 visits up to $|Q|$ predecessors of each state, which gives another $|Q|^2$ iterations. Assuming that the transitive closure of τ_u-transitions is calculated in advance, these iterations can be executed without overhead. The inner loop in lines 21–25 has another $|Q|^2$ iterations, again assuming that the closure of τ_u-transitions is calculated in advance. However, the inner loop is not executed more than once per state during the entire algorithm. The complexity to compute the τ_u-closure in advance is $O(|Q|^3)$ [18].

Summing up these computation costs, the worst-case time complexity of Algorithm 1 is found to be:

$$O((|Q|+1) \cdot (|\rightarrow| + |Q|^2) + |Q| \cdot |Q|^2 + |Q|^3) \;=\; O(|\Sigma||Q|^3) \,. \tag{23}$$

Thus, the set of certainly unsupervisable states can be computed in polynomial time. This is surprising given the nondeterministic nature of similar problems, which require *subset construction* [12]. For example, the *set of certain conflicts* [14], which is the equivalent of the set of certainly unsupervisable states in nonblocking verification, can only be computed in exponential time. In synthesis, the assumption of a supervisor with the capability of full observation of the plant makes it possible to distinguish states and avoid subset construction.

4.5 Halfway Synthesis

This section introduces *halfway synthesis* [9], which has been used previously [9,16] to remove unsupervisable states in compositional synthesis, and compares it with the set of certainly unsupervisable states. It is shown that in general more states can be removed by taking certain unsupervisability into account.

Definition 15. Let $G = \langle \Sigma, Q, \rightarrow, Q^\circ, Q^\omega \rangle$, and let $\hat{\Theta}_{G,\tau_u}$ be the greatest fixpoint of the synthesis step operator according to Definition 8, but computed under the assumption that $\Sigma_u = \{\tau_u\}$. The *halfway synthesis result* for G is

$$\mathrm{hsup}\,\mathscr{C}(G) = \langle \Sigma, Q, \rightarrow_{\mathrm{hsup}}, Q^\circ \cap \hat{\Theta}_{G,\tau_u}, Q^\omega \cap \hat{\Theta}_{G,\tau_u} \rangle \,, \tag{24}$$

where

$$\rightarrow_{\mathrm{hsup}} = \{\, (x,\sigma,y) \in \rightarrow \mid x,y \in \hat{\Theta}_{G,\tau_u} \,\} \cup \tag{25}$$

$$\{\, (x,\upsilon,y) \in \rightarrow \mid x \in \hat{\Theta}_{G,\tau_u}, \; \upsilon \in \Sigma_u \setminus \{\tau_u\}, \text{ and } y \notin \hat{\Theta}_{G,\tau_u} \,\} \tag{26}$$

The idea of halfway synthesis is to use standard synthesis, but treating only the silent uncontrollable event τ_u as uncontrollable. All other events are assumed to be controllable, because other plant components may yet disable shared uncontrollable events, so it is not guaranteed that these events cause controllability problems [9]. After computing the synthesis fixpoint $\hat{\Theta}_{G,\tau_u}$, the abstraction is obtained by removing controllable transitions to states not contained in $\hat{\Theta}_{G,\tau_u}$, while uncontrollable transitions are retained for the same reasons as in Definition 12.

Theorem 6. Let G be an automaton. Then $\text{unsup}\,\mathscr{C}(G) \subseteq \text{hsup}\,\mathscr{C}(G)$.

Example 8. When applied to automaton HB_1 in Fig. 4, halfway synthesis removes the crossed out states and produces the same result as unsupervisability removal. However, it only considers states $\bot_1$, $\bot_2$, and $\bot_3$ of W in Fig. 4 as unsupervisable, because the shared uncontrollable event $!output_1$ is treated as a controllable event. This automaton is left unchanged by halfway synthesis.

Halfway synthesis only removes those unsupervisable states that can reach a blocking state via local uncontrollable τ_u-transitions, but it does not take into account certainly unsupervisable transitions. Theorem 6 confirms that unsupervisability removal achieves all the simplification achieved by halfway synthesis, and Example 8 shows that there are cases where unsupervisability removal can do more. On the other hand, the complexity of halfway synthesis is the same as for standard synthesis, $O(|\Sigma||Q|^3)$, which is the same as found above for certain unsupervisability (23).

5 Conclusions

The set of *certainly unsupervisable states* of an automaton comprises all the states that must be avoided during synthesis of a controllable and nonblocking supervisor, in every possible context. In compositional synthesis, the removal of certainly unsupervisable states gives rise to a better abstraction than the previously used halfway synthesis, while maintaining the same cubic complexity.

The results of this paper are not intended to be used in isolation. In future work, the authors will integrate the removal of certainly unsupervisable states with their compositional synthesis framework [16]. It will be investigated in what order to apply unsupervisability removal and other abstraction methods, and how to group automata together for best performance.

Certainly unsupervisable states are also of crucial importance to determine whether two states of an automaton can be treated as equivalent for synthesis purposes. The results of this paper can be extended to develop abstraction methods that identify and merge equivalent states in compositional synthesis.

References

1. de Alfaro, L., Henzinger, T.A.: Interface automata. In: Proceedings of the 9th ACM SIGSOFT International Symposium on Foundations of Software Engineering 2001, pp. 109–120, Vienna, Austria (2001)
2. Asarin, E., Maler, O., Pnueli, A.: Symbolic controller synthesis for discrete and timed systems. In: Antsaklis, P.J., Kohn, W., Nerode, A., Sastry, S.S. (eds.) HS 1994. LNCS, vol. 999, pp. 1–20. Springer, Heidelberg (1995)
3. Aziz, A., Singhal, V., Swamy, G.M., Brayton, R.K.: Minimizing interacting finite state machines: a compositional approach to language containment. In: Proceedings of the IEEE International Conference on Computer Design: VLSI in Computers and Processors, ICCD '94, pp. 255–261 (1994)

4. Baier, C., Katoen, J.P.: Principles of Model Checking. MIT Press, Cambridge (2008)
5. Baier, C., Klein, J., Klüppelholz, S.: A compositional framework for controller synthesis. In: Katoen, J.-P., König, B. (eds.) CONCUR 2011. LNCS, vol. 6901, pp. 512–527. Springer, Heidelberg (2011)
6. Fabian, M.: On object oriented nondeterministic supervisory control. Ph.D. thesis, Chalmers University of Technology, Göteborg, Sweden. https://publications.lib.chalmers.se/cpl/record/index.xsql?pubid=1126 (1995)
7. Filiot, E., Jin, N., Raskin, J.-F.: Compositional algorithms for LTL synthesis. In: Bouajjani, A., Chin, W.-N. (eds.) ATVA 2010. LNCS, vol. 6252, pp. 112–127. Springer, Heidelberg (2010)
8. Flordal, H., Malik, R.: Compositional verification in supervisory control. SIAM J. Control Opt. **48**(3), 1914–1938 (2009)
9. Flordal, H., Malik, R., Fabian, M., Åkesson, K.: Compositional synthesis of maximally permissive supervisors using supervision equivalence. Discrete Event Dyn. Syst. **17**(4), 475–504 (2007)
10. Gohari, P., Wonham, W.M.: On the complexity of supervisory control design in the RW framework. IEEE Trans. Syst. Man Cybern. **30**(5), 643–652 (2000)
11. Hoare, C.A.R.: Communicating Sequential Processes. Prentice-Hall, Upper Saddle River (1985)
12. Hopcroft, J.E., Motwani, R., Ullman, J.D.: Introduction to Automata Theory, Languages, and Computation. Addison-Wesley, Boston (2001)
13. Lin, F., Wonham, W.M.: Decentralized control and coordination of discrete-event systems with partial observation. IEEE Trans. Autom. Control **35**(12), 1330–1337 (1990)
14. Malik, R.: The language of certain conflicts of a nondeterministic process. Working Paper 05/2010, Dept. of Computer Science, University of Waikato, Hamilton, New Zealand. http://hdl.handle.net/10289/4108 (2010)
15. Malik, R., Streader, D., Reeves, S.: Conflicts and fair testing. Int. J. Found. Comput. Sci. **17**(4), 797–813 (2006)
16. Mohajerani, S., Malik, R., Fabian, M.: A framework for compositional synthesis of modular nonblocking supervisors. IEEE Trans. Autom. Control. **59**(1), 150–162 (2014)
17. Mooij, A.J., Stahl, C., Voorhoeve, M.: Relating fair testing and accordance for service replaceability. J. Logic Algebr. Program. **79**(3–5), 233–244 (2010)
18. Nuutila, E.: Efficient transitive closure computation in large digraphs. Acta Polytechnica Scandinavica, Mathematics and Computing in Engineering Series, vol. 74. Finnish Academy of Technology, Helsinki (1995)
19. Pnueli, A., Rosner, R.: On the synthesis of a reactive module. In: Proceedings of the 16th ACM Symposium on Principles of Programming Languages, pp. 179–190 (1989)
20. Tarski, A.: A lattice-theoretical fixpoint theorem and its applications. Pacific J. Math. **5**(2), 285–309 (1955)
21. Wonham, W.M.: On the control of discrete-event systems. In: Nijmeijer, H., Schumacher, J.M. (eds.) Three Decades of Mathematical System Theory. LNCIS, vol. 135, pp. 542–562. Springer, Heidelberg (1989)

Author Index